MYTH AND RELIGION IN MIRCEA ELIADE

THEORISTS OF MYTH
VOLUME 11
GARLAND REFERENCE LIBRARY OF THE HUMANITIES
VOLUME 1168

THEORISTS OF MYTH
ROBERT A. SEGAL, *Series Editor*

MYTH AND RELIGION IN MIRCEA ELIADE

DOUGLAS ALLEN

GARLAND PUBLISHING, INC.
A MEMBER OF THE TAYLOR & FRANCIS GROUP
NEW YORK AND LONDON
1998

Library of Congress Cataloging-in-Publication Data

Allen, Douglas, 1941–
    Myth and religion in Mircea Eliade / by Douglas Allen.
        p.   cm. — (Theorists of myth ; vol. 11) (Garland reference library
of the humanities ; vol. 1168)
    Includes bibliographical references and index.
    ISBN 0-8240-3720-0 (hardcover : alk. paper)
    1. Eliade, Mircea, 1907–   . 2. Myth—History—20th century.
3. Religion—Philosophy—History—20th century.   I. Title. II. Series.
III. Series: Garland reference library of the humanities ; vol. 1168.
BL43.E4A65   1998
200'.92—dc21   98-30209
                                                     CIP

Printed on acid-free, 250-year-life paper
Manufactured in the United States of America

Contents

Series Editor's Foreword

Theories of myth are always theories of something larger such as literature, society, and the mind. To theorize about myth is to apply to the case of myth this larger theory. Theories of myth hail from an array of disciplines throughout the humanities and the social sciences. Of the theories that come from the field of religious studies, by far the most influential has been that of Mircea Eliade. Indeed, his is the only contemporary theory from religious studies that has had much influence outside of religious studies.

Douglas Allen is widely admired as the foremost authority on Eliade generally, and in his present book he brings to bear his mastery of Eliade's corpus and of the considerable scholarship on Eliade. Allen's position is atypical and almost unique among writers on Eliade: he is neither a devotee nor an antagonist but instead an expositor. He seeks neither to endorse nor to condemn Eliade's theory but, more fundamentally, to reconstruct it. He strives to work out the fundamental tenets that underlie Eliade's theory of myth, and by no coincidence those tenets also underlie Eliade's theory of religion. Allen is hardly unique in linking Eliade's theory of myth to Eliade's theory of religion, but he is unique in the rigor with which he unravels the philosophical roots of that theory of myth. Allen rallies to the defense of Eliade not when Eliade's philosophy is challenged but when Eliade's theory is dismissed as less than a well-conceived philosophy, when it is dismissed as the mere expression of Eliade's personal religiosity. Again and again, Allen spurns not those who disagree with Eliade but those who disagree without recognizing what Eliade is "getting at," to use one of Allen's pet phrases. Allen himself by no means concurs in all of his subject's views.

Allen's previous books on Eliade present some of the same basic points of Eliade's philosophy as his present book, but only in *Myth and Religion in Mircea Eliade* does he hone in on the subject of myth. As much as Allen connects Eliade's theory of myth to Eliade's larger theory of religion, he also identifies the distinctively mythic element in religion for Eliade. As Allen says continually, all myth for Eliade is religious, but not all religion is mythic.

Allen shows that for Eliade myth is an indispensable element in achieving the kind of life that all humans crave. Eliade is therefore especially zealous to detect the scent of myth even among those who profess to be indifferent, if not hostile, to it. The presence of myth everywhere is taken as confirmation of its indispensability. While not all theorists of myth consider it a pre-modern, outdated phenomenon, Eliade is one of the most zealous to deem it a panhuman one. Among major theorists, only Joseph Campbell and perhaps C. G. Jung are as committed to the eternality of myth as he. At the same time the tie for Eliade between myth and religion remains: in claiming that even scrupulously rational, scientific moderns still cling to myths, Eliade is claiming that those same moderns also still cling to religion—a link rejected by both Campbell and Jung. Ever sensitive to the nuances of Eliade's views, Allen maintains that Eliade is not thereby effacing the difference between "primitives" and moderns, as he is often charged with doing. But once again, Allen's concern is less to defend Eliade's position than to present it accurately. On this point, as on so many other points, Allen's book provides an unsurpassed overview of Eliade as theorist of at once myth and much else.

Robert A. Segal

Preface

Mircea Eliade, who was born in Bucharest in 1906 and died in Chicago in 1986, was often described by scholars and in the popular press as the world's most influential historian of religion and the world's foremost interpreter of symbol and myth. For example, an article in *Time* magazine identified Eliade as "probably the world's foremost living interpreter of spiritual myths and symbolism," and an article in *People Weekly* claimed that "Eliade is the world's foremost living historian of religions and myths."[1] Not unusual was the claim by former Eliade student and leading historian of religions Lawrence Sullivan that "Eliade has been the single most important individual in introducing the world to what religion means."[2] An incredibly prolific writer, Eliade had what he described as a "dual vocation" as a scholar of religion and as a writer of literary works.[3] Romanian was his literary language. His major scholarly works—from *Traité d'histoire des religions* (English translation: *Patterns of Comparative Religion*) and *Le mythe de l'éternel retour (The Myth of the Eternal Return)* in 1949 through the third volume of *Histoire des croyances et des idées religeuses (A History of Religious Ideas)* in 1983—were written in French. He served as editor-in-chief of the sixteen-volume The *Encyclopedia of Religion* published in 1987.

As influential as Eliade was as a scholar of myth and religion, he has remained extremely controversial. Indeed, many scholars, especially those in the social sciences, have completely ignored or vigorously attacked Eliade's scholarship on myth and religion as methodologically uncritical, subjective, and unscientific. Critics charge that Eliade is guilty of uncritical universal generalizations; reads all sorts of "profound" mythic and religious meaning into his data; ignores rigorous scholarly procedures of verification; and interjects all sorts of unjustified, personal, metaphysical, and ontological assumptions and judgments into his scholarship.

Both Eliade's style and the contents of his scholarly studies add to the controversial nature of his scholarship. He never seems as bothered as critics think any serious scholar should be by his eclectic approach, by contradictions and inconsistencies in his writings, or by his mixing of particular scholarly studies with sweeping controversial personal assertions and highly normative judgments. Unlike the self-imposed limited approaches of specialists studying myth and religion, he views his subject matter as the entire spiritual history of humankind. He often does many different things simultaneously, resists simple classification of his scholarship, and describes himself as "an author *without a model.*"[4]

Adding to the controversial nature of his scholarship on myth and religion is the fact that Eliade, while not hesitating to criticize the approaches of other scholars, never seems to feel the need to defend his work against the attacks of critics. In the Foreword to my *Structure and Creativity in Religion,* Eliade wrote the following: "For myself, I plan someday to dedicate an entire work to discussing the objections put forth by some of my critics, those who are responsible and acting in all good faith (for the others do not deserve the bother of a reply.)"[5] But during the last year of his life, after noting that "methodological" criticisms brought against his conception of the history of religions had increased, Eliade wrote the following: "The fault is, in part, mine; I've never replied to such criticisms, although I ought to have done so. I told myself that someday, 'when I'm free from works in progress,' I'll write a short theoretical monograph and explain the 'confusions and errors' for which I am reproached. I'm afraid I'll never have time to write it."[6]

My original intention was to deal with some of this confusion and controversy about Eliade's scholarship by writing the first book focusing entirely on Eliade's theory of myth. I was motivated to undertake this project by at least three major considerations. First, it is remarkable that no one has written a book on Eliade's approach to myth, especially since there has been such an upsurge in general interest in myth and Eliade has often been regarded as the world's leading interpreter of myth.

Second, in terms of my own discipline of philosophy, it is equally remarkable that few philosophers have written books on myth since Ernst Cassirer's works published from 1925 through 1946. Anthologies on myth include writings by scholars in anthropology, sociology, literature, history, religious studies, and other disciplines but almost never include anything by a philosopher. Undeniably, traditional philosophy tended to classify and dismiss myth as prephilosophical and unphilosophical, but much of recent philosophy—as seen in the influential works of Richard Rorty and many scholars identified with postmodernism—has attempted to undermine traditional approaches to truth, objectivity, and rationality. Distinctions between philosophy and literature, for example, have become blurred, and there has been great interest in narrative discourse. And yet none of the most influential recent works on myth have been written by philosophers.

Third, one might assume incorrectly from my past scholarship on Eliade that I must have already focused on his theory of myth. However, because of the need to set some limits, I intentionally ignored or deemphasized my consideration of Eliade's theory of myth. In several writings, I explicitly noted this glaring omission. Therefore, the present work is an attempt to fill that obvious gap and provide a more comprehensive analysis and evaluation of Eliade's scholarship.[7]

It soon became clear that I could not restrict my focus to "myth," and this book was gradually expanded to include "myth and religion." Since for Eliade all myth is religious myth and myth has a religious structure and fulfills a religious function, it is impossible to comprehend his theory of myth without understanding his complex theory of religion. Therefore, I have included two chapters on the sacred, the dialectic of the sacred and the profane, cosmic religion, and other aspects of Eliade's general theory of religion.

In addition, it became clear that I had to expand the book's focus to emphasize Eliade's theory of symbolism. Since for Eliade myths are symbolic narratives and mythic language is necessarily symbolic, it is impossible to comprehend Eliade's theory of myth without understanding his theory of symbolism. One cannot identify and interpret the meaning of mythic structures without grasping Eliade's underlying hermeneutical framework consisting of interconnecting symbolic structures.

Finally, it became clear I had to expand my focus to include detailed analysis of Eliade's antireductionist approach. Central to Eliade's theory of myth are general assumptions and judgments about the irreducibility of the sacred, as well as specific claims about the irreducibility of the mythic. To comprehend Eliade's theory of myth, it therefore became necessary to consider the heated debates over reductionism, in terms of both Eliade's antireductionist claims and the attacks by reductionistic critics.

In my previous studies of Eliade—especially in *Structure and Creativity in Religion* and *Mircea Eliade et le phénomène religieux*—perhaps my major original contribution has been to submit that there is an impressive, underlying, implicit *system* at the foundation of Eliade's history and phenomenology of religion. Eliade is not simply a brilliant, unsystematic, intuitive genius, as extolled by some supporters, or a methodologically uncritical, unsystematic, hopelessly unscientific charlatan, as attacked by some critics. I formulated Eliade's foundational system primarily in terms of two key interacting concepts: the dialectic of the sacred and the profane, the universal structure in terms of which Eliade distinguishes religious phenomena, and religious symbolism, the coherent structural systems of religious symbols in terms of which Eliade interprets the meaning of religious phenomena. I maintain that it is the essential universal systems of symbolic structures, when integrated with the essential universal structure of the dialectic of the sacred, that primarily constitute Eliade's hermeneutical framework and serve as the foundation for his phenomenological approach.

Several other scholars have emphasized this key of an underlying system as essential to Eliade's approach.[8] Most significant, in this regard, is Bryan Rennie's recent book, *Reconstructing Eliade*. Rennie correctly maintains that most scholars have not recognized that there is a complex, coherent, implicit theoretical system at the foundation of Eliade's approach to religion. Eliade tends to resist clear definition, and he never attempts an overall systematization of his thought. But Rennie is correct in contending that "Eliade's thought *is* systematic, its internal elements referring to, supported by, and reciprocally supporting its other elements." Without attempting to reconstruct Eliade's implicit system, often functioning on the level of the prereflective, one cannot comprehend his approach to myth and religion.[9]

My emphasis on the specific systematic nature of Eliade's theory of myth and religion not only differs from most interpreters of Eliade's writings but also may produce some confusion on the part of many readers of this book. Following variations of the procedures outlined by René Descartes in his *Discourse on Method,* most scholars see the necessity of starting with simple component elements, as seen in providing clear definitions of basic terms, and then developing one's thesis (argument, analysis, presentation) through some structure of rational linear progression. When social scientists and other readers look for clear definitions and linear progressive development in Eliade's writings, they are usually frustrated.

For Eliade, ambiguities, enigmas, and contradictions are not necessarily problems to be removed through rational systematic analysis. Just the opposite: Eliade often embraces and sustains ambiguities, enigmas, and contradictions as essential to mythic and spiritual life. Many of Eliade's key terms are highly idiosyncratic and by their very nature resist clear definition and analysis. The sacred simultaneously reveals and conceals itself. Eliade often attacks other scholars who insist on clear definitions and linear development as employing rationalistic, scientific, positivistic, historicistic, naturalistic, or other reductionistic approaches that destroy the specific intentionality and nature of the mythic and religious world.

Eliade's systematic approach, as reflected in some of my mode of presentation, tends to be holistic, organic, and dialectical. The whole is more than the sum of its parts. No element can be understood in isolation but only in terms of its dynamic, mutually interacting relations with other key elements. New structures and meanings emerge through dynamic relations that cannot be found in any separate component part. The image of weaving, while limited, gets better at Eliade's approach than some analytic model of clear, linear progression. Therefore, even if it initially causes some confusion, I have resisted superimposing some non-Eliadean clear definition and analysis on key terms and positions. As new interrelated terms and analyses are introduced in subsequent chapters, earlier concepts and positions will gain greater clarity and depth of understanding.

The eleven chapters on myth and religion in Eliade's thought have been organized in terms of six general topics: principle of antireductionism; theory of religion; theory of symbolism; nature of myth; myth, religion, and history (or time and history); and myth, religion, and the contemporary world. The first two chapters focus on the key methodological issue of reductionism. Chapter 1 presents Eliade's antireductionist approach to myth and religion. Chapter 2 formulates a variety of reductionistic attacks on Eliade's scholarship as well as some suggestions as to why Eliade and his critics are often speaking at crosspurposes. The next two chapters focus on Eliade's general theory of religion. Chapter 3 presents Eliade's foundational concept of the sacred and his formulation of the dialectic of the sacred as the essential universal structure of sacralization. Chapter 4 develops this analysis of Eliade's approach to religion by presenting his emphasis on nature, cosmos, and cosmic religion and by considering whether his theory of religion reflects an archaic, Indian, or some other religious bias. Chapters 5 and 6 focus on Eliade's general theory of symbolism: first presenting his view of symbolism as the language of myth and religion and as disclosing the centrality of symbolic structures and then formulating the essential characteristics and functions of symbolism and clarifying the confusing concept of "archetypes."

Although the first six chapters are all essential to comprehending Eliade's theory of myth, it is only with chapter 7 that I formulate Eliade's analyses of the specific nature, structure, and function of myth, along with his claims about the primacy of the cosmogonic myth and myths of origins. The following two chapters consider Eliade's controversial interpretations of history (and time) in his theory of myth and religion. Chapter 8 examines Eliade's antihistorical attitudes, both in terms of his personal autobiographical reflections and his personal scholarly interpretations, as well as claims by other scholars that his scholarship tends to be antihistorical. Chapter 9 then examines in detail Eliade's scholarly interpretations of time and history. Eliade is seen to focus on the primacy of nonhistorical structures and the antihistorical atemporal essence of myth and religion, and he makes strong antihistorical judgments. But he also emphasizes the complex dialectical interaction between the historical and the nonhistorical.

Finally, we consider the relation of Eliade's theory of myth and religion to his analysis of the major existential crises and issues confronting modern human beings and the contemporary world. In our previous chapters, Eliade has usually directed his attention to phenomena that he considers traditionally and explicitly mythic and religious. He now reflects on phenomena of the modern world in which the mythic and religious is often explicitly rejected. Chapter 10 focuses on Eliade's frequent claim that the sacred rather than being completely absent is frequently camouflaged, and hence unrecognizable, in the modern profane. By failing to recognize the concealed sacred, Eliade charges that modern human beings suffer from a self-defeating and dangerous Western provincialism. Chapter 11 presents Eliade's more positive proposals for overcoming modern anxiety, meaninglessness, and provincialism through a radical cultural and spiritual renewal. Such renewal can be achieved through a creative hermeneutics involving the rediscovering of our own symbolic and mythic structures and the authentic encounter with the mythic and religious world of "the other."

My approach to Eliade's works on myth and religion tends to be both sympathetic and at the same time critical. In evaluating my past writings, some of Eliade's strongest critics have labeled me an Eliade supporter, while strong Eliade supporters have sometimes classified me as a critic, even if more sympathetic than most other critics. As can be seen throughout this book, I am impressed by Eliade's great contributions toward understanding much of traditional myth and religion, as well as toward uncovering mythic and religious structures still shaping much of contemporary secular life. At the same time, I recognize that Eliade's method and interpretations of myth and religion must often be amended, reformulated, and supplemented if we are to deal with the many relevant criticisms of his scholarship.

In formulating several of the chapters in this book, I have utilized material from some of my previous publications. Especially in my presentation of Eliade dialectic of the sacred and his theory of symbolism, I have included, usually in revised and expanded form, material from my *Structure and Creativity in Religion* and *Mircea Eliade et le phénomène religieux*. In formulating Eliade's approach to history, I have utilized material that appeared in my "Eliade and History."[10] In summarizing the views of several of Eliade's strongest supporters and in presenting some of the recent controversy over the political and the spiritual in Eliade's personal life and writings, I have used material from my "Recent Defenders of Eliade."[11]

I would especially like to thank Robert Segal, the editor of Garland's series on "Theorists of Myth," for his invaluable suggestions and support. Over the years, I have benefited greatly from the responses of Professor Segal and others scholars to my works and from their very different interpretations and evaluations of Eliade's history of religions. I am also appreciative of the patience and support shown to me by Phyllis Korper of Garland Publishing. Chuck Bartelt of Garland was of great assistance in working with me to overcome problems involved in preparing my first camera-ready book. I also appreciate the support of those at the Institute for Ecumenical and Cultural Research in Collegeville, Minnesota, where I began writing this book, and of the Office of Vice Provost at the University of Maine, which provided financial assistance for costs involved in the preparation of this book. Finally, as with my previous books I deeply appreciate the support, care, humor, invaluable feedback, and love of Ilze Petersons, who has had to live with the creative stress and abnormalities involved in scholarly projects.

NOTES

1. See "Scientist of Symbols," *Time* 87 (11 February 1966): 68; and Giovanna Breu, "Teacher: Shamans? Hippies? They're All Creative to the World's Leading Historian of Religions," *People Weekly* 9 (27 March 1978): 49.

2. Lawrence Sullivan is quoted by Delia O'Hara in the introduction to her interview with Mircea Eliade. See "Mircea Eliade" (interview of Eliade by Delia O'Hara), *Chicago* 35, no. 6 (1986): 147. In her introduction, O'Hara also identifies Eliade as "the world's foremost historian of religions."

3. For works by and about Eliade through 1978, see Douglas Allen and Dennis Doeing, *Mircea Eliade: An Annotated Bibliography* (New York: Garland, 1980).

4. See Mircea Eliade, *Journal IV, 1979-1985,* trans. Mac Linscott Ricketts (Chicago: University of Chicago Press, 1990), p. 41.

5. Mircea Eliade, "Foreword" to my *Structure and Creativity in Religion: Hermeneutics in Mircea Eliade's Phenomenology and New Directions* (The Hague: Mouton Publishers, 1978), p. vii.

6. *Journal IV, 1979-1985,* p. 143.

7. While providing a more comprehensive analysis by examining Eliade's theory of myth, I necessarily exclude from this book many important topics central to my previous writings on Eliade. For example, in *Structure and Creativity in Religion, Mircea Eliade et le phénomène religieux* (Paris: Payot, 1982), and other works, I attempt to provide detailed analysis of Eliade's phenomenological method: his hermeneutical framework and procedures for interpreting meaning, his specific sense of phenomenological induction, his attempts at overcoming traditional descriptive versus normative dichotomies, and the distinguishing of different levels of meaning in his phenomenological approach. In this book, I occasionally add a note referring to such analysis in earlier works, but I do not address these central concerns.

8. For example, Ioan Couliano entitles his introduction to Mircea Eliade and Ioan P. Couliano, *The Eliade Guide to World Religions* (San Francisco: HarperCollins Publishers, 1991) "Religion as a System" and attributes to Eliade the view that "religion is an *autonomous system*" (p. 1).

9. See Bryan S. Rennie, *Reconstructing Eliade: Making Sense of Religion* (Albany: State University of New York Press, 1996), pp. 1-6. I did not read Rennie's important book until after I had completed all eleven chapters. I have added relevant analysis from Rennie to different sections of my book, but a number of his significant claims—such as his contention that Eliade has a significant idiosyncratic sense of "history"—would have received greater consideration if Rennie's book had been published earlier.

10. Douglas Allen, "Eliade and History," *Journal of Religion* 68 (1988): 545-65.

11. Douglas Allen, "Recent Defenders of Eliade: A Critical Evaluation," *Religion* 24 (1994): 333-51.

MYTH AND RELIGION
IN MIRCEA ELIADE

CHAPTER 1

Eliade's Antireductionism

One cannot read Mircea Eliade's writings on myth, in particular, and religion, in general, without soon encountering his concern, often bordering on an obsession, with the evils of modern forms of "reductionism." It is such reductionism, as evidenced in modern scholarly approaches and in much of contemporary life, that prevents us from appreciating, or even recognizing, the nature, function, significance, and meaning of myth and religion. Eliade sees much of his task, as defined by the proper and urgently needed "creative hermeneutics" of the history of religions, as reclaiming the mythic and renewing modern scholarship and contemporary life by an "antireductionist" orientation toward the "irreducibility of the sacred," including the irreducibly sacred world of myth.

Already introduced is Eliade's frequent use of the term "antireductionism." Defenders of the methodological assumption of the irreducibility of the religious, as well as critics such as Robert Segal, often use the term "nonreductionism" and present the basic distinction as reductionism versus nonreductionism. As used within the history of religions and religious studies, "nonreductionism" refers to approaches that analyze religious data only in religious terms; "reductionism" refers to the analysis of religious data in secular terms. Eliade, in this regard, claims to adopt a nonreductionist method and interpretation of religious myth.

The stronger, more assertive sense of "antireductionism" gets better at Eliade's position: his vigorous critique and condemnation of dominant, inadequate, and oppressive reductionist accounts; his claim not only for a more adequate interpretation of the irreducibly mythic but also for the irreplaceable significance of his threatened, autonomous discipline of history of religions; and even his vision of the mythic spiritual renewal of modern, desacralized, impoverished, reductionist, Western culture.

With regard to Eliade's general approach to reductionism and myth, we may distinguish two related claims: the irreducibility of the religious, or of the "sacred," and the irreducibility of the mythic. First, for Eliade myth is religious myth; therefore, the most common way to violate the irreducibly mythic dimension of the data is to reduce its irreducibly religious structure and function to some nonreligious plane of reference and explanation. This focus on the irreducibility of the religious will be the main concern of chapters 1 and 2. Chapter 3 will examine Eliade's claims about the universal structure of the dialectic of the sacred that defines the irreducibly religious nature of his mythic data.[1] Second, there are claims about the irreducibility of the mythic that go beyond claims about its irreducibly religious nature. All mythic data are religious, but not all religious data are mythic. In chapter 7 it will be seen that there are unique, irreducible mythic structures, functions, and modes of being in the world that distinguish myth not only from nonreligious but also from other religious phenomena.

Eliade's frequent concern with "reductionism" raises many complex issues. Reductionism has been and continues to be a central methodological and theoretical focus in many scholarly disciplines. It will be important to situate Eliade's antireductionist analysis within some of these larger theoretical debates on reductionism. First, we shall uncover some of the motives and concerns that contributed to Eliade's primary focus on the evils of reductionism and his insistence on an irreducibly religious approach to myth. Emphasized in chapter 1 will be Eliade's formulation of the irreducibility of the sacred. Chapter 2 will then consider some of the criticisms of Eliade's antireductionism that have arisen within the field of history of religions or *Religionswissenschaft* and social scientific approaches to religion.

THE NEED FOR A NEW PROCEDURE

In his so-called antireductionist approach to myth and other religious phenomena, Mircea Eliade has been criticized and praised as a "romantic" scholar who privileges the mythic world of the "primitive" and the "archaic." [2] As we shall see, he is very critical of major characteristics of the Western Enlightenment that have defined much of "modernity." Therefore, it is not surprising that scholars such as Ivan Strenski should characterize Eliade's approach to myth as extolling an irrationalist traditionalism and a "Volkish," neo-romantic primitivism, one largely devoid of any modern, rigorous, scholarly methodology. [3]

Nevertheless, Eliade, while appreciating and even defending much of the traditional mythic world view, intends his antireductionist approach to myth to be more advanced than that of earlier scholarly interpretations with which he is often compared. He claims to be avoiding methodological pitfalls of past theories and to be offering new, more adequate interpretations of the meaning of myth, as well as a creative future-oriented response for dealing with personal and even global crises confronting humanity. In his approach to myth, Eliade recognizes profound differences in the modern hermeneutical situation from that of earlier interpreters. In studying myth as part of the scholarly discipline of *Religionswissenschaft,* he distinguishes what he is doing from the earlier, highly subjective and normative theories of Tylor, Frazer, and other scholars, as well as from the normative approaches defining such disciplines as theology and the philosophy of religion. [4]

As a scholarly historian of religions, Eliade repeatedly claims to use an "empirical" approach to myth and other religious phenomena. The "historian of religions uses an empirical method of approach. He is concerned with religio-historical facts which he seeks to understand and to make intelligible to others." [5] The modern scholar begins by collecting mythic and other religious documents, empirical facts that need to be interpreted. [6] She or he studies myths as factual, empirical phenomena. In siding with R. J. Zwi Werblowsky and others signing the so-called Marburg platform at the Tenth International Congress for the History of Religions in 1960, Eliade agreed that "the common ground on which students of religion *qua* students of religion meet is the realization that the awareness of the numinous or the experience of transcendence (where these happen to exist in religion) are—whatever else they may be—undoubtedly empirical facts of human experience and history, to be studied like all human facts, by the appropriate methods. Thus also the value systems of the various religions, forming an essential part of the factual, empirical phenomenon, are legitimate objects of our studies."[7]

A profound difference in the modern hermeneutical situation is seen in the attempt by most contemporary scholars to differentiate their approaches from earlier interpretations that ignored the irreducibly historical nature of the mythic data. "Almost without noticing it, the historian of religions found himself in a cultural milieu quite different from that of Max Müller and Tylor, or even that of Frazer and Marrett [*sic*]. It was a new environment nourished by Nietzsche and Marx, Dilthey, Croce, and Ortega; an environment in which the fashionable cliché was not *Nature* but *History*."[8] Modern scholars realize that in studying myth they work exclusively with historical documents. As Eliade affirms in many places, his point of departure is historical data that express mythic and other religious experiences of humankind. Through his phenomenological approach, he attempts to decipher the empirical, historical, mythic data, to describe the phenomena that constitute the mythic world of *homo religiosus* and to interpret their religious meaning.

Although Eliade upholds the empirical and historical nature of his approach to myth and occasionally goes out of his way to distinguish what he is doing from the theological, metaphysical, subjective, non-empirical, nonhistorical, and "unscientific" nature of earlier approaches, many critics claim that his own approach is nonempirical and nonhistorical, even antihistorical.[9] Indeed, some critics compare his approach with that of various uncritical, nineteenth-century generalists whom he claims to reject. They claim that "Eliade, like Frazer, lumps religious beliefs and practices together in a comparative way which ignores the differences and the cultural and historical situations" and that "every methodological error of which Sir James Frazer and his contemporaries have ever been accused is here exhibited in its purest form."[10]

Eliade not only wants to distinguish his approach to myth from that of earlier nonempirical and nonhistorical theorists but also from that of twentieth-century, "scientific" empiricists, historicists, and other specialists. He keeps insisting that we need a new theoretical approach, a new hermeneutics more adequate to interpret the meaning of myth and other religious phenomena:

The correct analyses of myths and of mythical thought, of symbols and primordial images, especially the religious creations that emerge from Oriental and "primitive" cultures, are, in my opinion, the only way to open the Western mind and to introduce a new, planetary humanism. These spiritual documents—myths, symbols, divine figures, contemplative techniques, and so on—had previously been studied, if at all, with the detachment and indifference with which nineteenth-century naturalists studied insects. But it has now begun to be realized that these documents express existential situations, and that consequently they form part of the history of the human spirit. Thus, the proper procedure for grasping their meaning is not the naturalist's "objectivity," but the intelligent sympathy of the hermeneut. *It was the procedure itself that had to be changed.* For even the strangest or the most aberrant form of behavior must be regarded as a human phenomenon; it cannot be interpreted as a zoological phenomenon or an instance of teratology. This conviction guided my research on the meaning and function of myths, the structure of religious symbols, and in general, of the dialectics of the sacred and the profane.[11]

This important formulation is typical of claims found throughout Eliade's writings. Usually when he makes these points about the need for a new hermeneutical procedure, qualitatively different from earlier approaches insisting on scholarly "detachment" and "nonhuman" models of "objectivity," he presents them as part of a critique of "reductionism" and as promoting "the irreducibility of the sacred."

In an essay on how to understand polarities, oppositions, and antagonisms in archaic and traditional societies, Eliade tells us that we need a hermeneutical effort, not another secular demystification: "Our documents—be they myths or theologies, systems of space divisions or rituals enacted by two antagonistic groups, divine dualities or religious dualism, etc.—constitute, each according to its specific mode of being, so many creations of the human mind." "We do not have the right to reduce them to something other than what they are, namely spiritual creations. Consequently, it is their meaning and significance that must be grasped."[12] In short, Eliade frequently attacks earlier and many contemporary interpreters as reductionists, who ignore the irreducibly sacred dimension of their mythic data.

In this introductory section, it has simply been asserted that Mircea Eliade claims to be using an empirical approach to myth, to recognize the historical nature of the mythic data, and to collect mythic religious documents expressing phenomena that need to be described and interpreted. But how does he know which documents to collect, which phenomena to describe and interpret? To answer these and similar questions, we need to introduce several methodological principles in terms of which Eliade can distinguish religious phenomena. The most important principles allowing Eliade to distinguish religious phenomena are the irreducibility of the religious and the dialectic of the sacred and the profane. This chapter considers his criticism of reductionistic approaches to myth and other religious phenomena and his methodological alternative in terms of the irreducibility of the sacred. Chapter 3 will focus on a formulation of Eliade's universal structural criteria for distinguishing religious from nonreligious phenomena.

THE IRREDUCIBILITY OF THE SACRED

This presentation of Eliade's position has referred to his critique of "reductionism" and his insistence on "the irreducibility of the sacred." Such language reflects Eliade's own formulations. At times, other expressions such as Eliade's "methodological assumption of the irreducibility of the sacred" and his "so-called antireductionist principle" will be used, since my position is that all approaches, including Eliade's, are in certain broad respects necessarily reductionistic.[13] But not all reductionistic approaches are necessary or justifiable on scholarly grounds. The key question is whether Eliade's kind of reductionism, as reflected in the assumption of the irreducibility of the religious and the irreducibility of the mythic, is justified in providing a more adequate interpretation of the function, structure, meaning, and significance of myth than alternative reductionistic approaches.

In what is his best-known, antireductionist formulation, cited by both defenders and critics of his position, Mircea Eliade claims that "a religious phenomenon will only be recognized as such if it is grasped at its own level, that is to say, if it is studied *as* something religious. To try to grasp the essence of such a [religious] phenomenon by means of physiology, psychology, sociology, economics, linguistics, art or any other study is false; it misses the one unique and irreducible element in it—the element of the sacred."[14] Here we have the twentieth-century, antireductionist claim made not only by Eliade but also by Rudolf Otto, Gerardus van der Leeuw, Joachim Wach, and many others: investigators of mythic and other religious phenomena must respect the irreducibly religious nature of religious phenomena.[15]

Romanian Roots
Mac Linscott Ricketts, focusing on the Romanian roots of Eliade's life and thought, has contended that by age twenty Eliade had formulated the main lines of his scholarly method and that most of his fundamental methodological principles had been worked out in his "Spiritual Itinerary" series and other youthful Romanian writings before he left for India.[16] Ricketts believes that the most basic of these youthful principles that continued to guide Eliade's thinking throughout his life was the principle of separate "planes of reality": the antireductionist principle that religion be approached as an autonomous, irreducible reality. This principle was taught by Nae Ionescu, the person who had the greatest influence on Eliade's personal philosophy and who is mentioned more than any other person in Eliade's *Autobiography*.[17]

Ionescu assumed the existence of three irreducible planes of reality, each requiring its own, unique method of cognition. "There exist in the order of cognition a scientific plane, a philosophical plane, and a religious plane of reality: each independent, with methods of its own, mutually irreducible." For each of these "planes of existence" or "realms" ("orders," "worlds"), "we *must* have special means of investigation." "The greatest 'sin' for Ionescu was to confuse the planes: to try to approach one level of reality with methods appropriate to another."[18]

Starting with articles in Ionescu's newspaper *Cuvântul* in 1926 and 1927, Eliade wrote often of this principle of separate "planes of reality" and of the need to approach the religious plane as an autonomous world or reality, known by its own method, and not reduced or "explained" by the criteria of other planes with their distinct instruments of cognition.

The practical effect of accepting this principle was to remove religion from criticisms arising from other "planes"—above all, from positivistic science. It led Eliade also to reject what he called "Gourmontine method," the fallacy of judging a complex cultural phenomenon (such as religion) by its "origins" (such as fear of the dead). Here, then, is the philosophical basis of his life long insistence that religion be studied *as such,* and not "demystified" by being "reduced" to something else. Furthermore, this principle permitted him to look behind the religious phenomenon to the *essence* of the reality as it exists on its *own plane,* apart from its expression in "history," and to make comparisons of phenomena drawn from many times and places on the basis of their common essence.[19]

In some of his early, often highly personal, Romanian newspaper and other articles, Eliade gives this so-called antireductionist principle a formulation that is at the heart of many contemporary scholarly debates. In studying religious or other phenomena on their own "plane," must the scholar "believe" in the reality of that plane? And if so, what does it mean to be such a believer? Some phenomenologists and other scholars of myth will grant that the interpreter must believe in the mythic phenomena in the sense of taking them seriously, acknowledging that for mythic people the myths are real, and trying, at least as part of one's scholarship, to empathize with and describe just what myths and their reality claims mean for mythic people.

Eliade accepts such a scholarly position. In his later scholarly works, his usual position is that the scholar's role is to approach mythic or other religious phenomena on their own plane, to interpret what is real for *homo religiosus,* and not to impose the scholar's own views of what is real or unreal. The scholar, for example, must assume that the sacred is irreducible and ultimately real for mythic persons, and this must guide interpretations of the meaning and significance of mythic phenomena regardless of what the individual scholar may personally disbelieve about the sacred reality. Otherwise, the secular scholar will reduce myth to some nonreligious, nonmythic meaning and significance and will fail to grasp the irreducibly religious, mythic essence.

However, in some youthful Romanian writings on the "confusion of planes," in some later, often personal, antireductionist reflections on the history of religions and the modern world, and interspersed throughout his scholarly writings, Eliade presents stronger claims about the scholar as believer. Not only must mythic and other religious phenomena be understood in irreducibly religious terms of believers, but only scholars who are themselves believers are capable of providing adequate interpretations of such phenomena. Citing such passages, many critics and some supporters have maintained that Eliade-the-scholar has ulterior motives, a hidden agenda, a highly personal normative position on myth and religion that shapes not only his autobiographical and literary writings but also his scholarly works.

In some early Romanian writings, Eliade maintains that for someone to understand and evaluate mythic or other religious phenomena on their own plane, the person must have personal experiential knowledge of the mythic and the religious. Eliade agrees with Rudolf Otto's controversial, often attacked claim early in *The Idea of the Holy* that if the reader has not already had a numinous experience, then she or he will be incapable of grasping Otto's description of the religious essence and is "requested to read no farther."[20] Eliade tells us that to judge religious or metaphysical phenomena, "one must *believe in the existence* of the religious and metaphysical planes." Just as "laymen" are unqualified to judge literature and art on moral grounds, since this involves a "confusion of planes," nonbelievers are laypersons unqualified to say anything about mythic and other religious beliefs: "You cannot judge a spiritual reality without knowing it, and you do not know it without contemplating it on its own plane of existence." Only by "loving supra-sensible realities (i.e., *believing* in their existence and autonomy) can you judge and accept or reject a metaphysics, a dogma, or a mystical experience."[21]

One can understand how such formulations, including similar personal interjections in later scholarly works, have led many critics to charge that Mircea Eliade is not only interpreting and describing the believer's mythic view but in fact endorsing it; that he is maintaining that scholars themselves must be believers in the religious origin, function, meaning, truth, and reality of myth and the sacred.[22]

Antireductionist Claims

The methodological assumption of the irreducibility of the sacred can be seen as arising from Eliade's frequent criticisms of past reductionist positions. According to Eliade, earlier scholars, utilizing certain assumed norms (rationalist, positivist, etc.), usually forced their data into unilinear, evolutionary schemes. He grants that twentieth-century anthropologists, sociologists, psychologists, and historians opened up new dimensions of the sacred, but he criticizes them for reducing the meaning of the religious to its anthropological, sociological, psychological, or historical analysis.

The upshot of Eliade's criticism may be expressed by the following antireductionist claim: the scholar must attempt to grasp religious phenomena "on their own plane of reference," as something religious. To reduce an interpretation of myths to some nonreligious plane of reference (sociological, psychological, economic, etc.) is to neglect their full intentionality and to fail to grasp their unique and irreducible "element": the sacred.

Although historians and phenomenologists of religion, in opposing psychological, sociological, and other reductionisms, often maintain that myths reveal "an irreducible reality, the experience of the sacred," they "do not agree among themselves even apropos of the nature of this experience." "For some of them, the 'sacred' as such is a historical phenomenon, i.e., it is the result of specific human experiences in specific historical situations. Others, on the contrary, leave open the question of 'origins'; for them the experience of the sacred is *irreducible,* in the sense that, through such an experience, man becomes aware of his specific mode of being in the world and consequently assumes responsibilities which cannot be explained in psychological or socio-economic terms."[23]

Eliade uses his antireductionist claim—that religious phenomena must be grasped as irreducibly religious, that one must make "an effort to understand them *on their own plane of reference*"[24] —to define the autonomous nature of his discipline. In contrast to most anthropologists, sociologists, psychologists, and other past investigators, historians of religions attempt to define their own unique perspective *qua* historians of religions. If there are certain irreducible modes by which mythic and other religious experiences and their expressions are given, then our "method of understanding must be commensurate with the givenness of the mode."[25]

Such formulations do not exhaust all of the aspects of Eliade's analysis of the irreducibility of the sacred. As was seen in the above passage from *Patterns* (p. xiii) and in numerous other writings, Eliade primarily attacks reductionist accounts for being "false." On phenomenological grounds, he claims that reductionist explanations fail to grasp the unique, irreducibly religious structure and meaning expressed through the mythic data. Sometimes his attacks on such misconceived and inappropriate approaches, with their misplaced and false explanations, will be seen to go beyond phenomenological grounds and involve personal, ontological, normative concerns.

In the above quotation from *No Souvenirs* (p. xii), as in many of his other writings, Eliade also criticizes reductionist approaches for not doing justice to the "human" dimension of religious mythic phenomena, for reducing "living" data to impersonal "dead" data and for providing us with inappropriate models of "objectivity." An interpreter must do justice to, not explain away, the essential personal dimension of mythic data with a central focus on intentionality, human agency, and a specific human mode of existence and specific human constitution of a sacred, meaningful, mythic world.

Eliade's works contain many criticisms of reductionistic interpretations and explanations that do not do justice to the "complexity," "totality," "ambiguity," and "unrecognizability" of the sacred, but instead reduce the mythic to some partial, oversimplified, one-sided, or otherwise incomplete perspective. For example, Eliade will be seen to maintain that myths and other expressions of the sacred are symbolic in nature. He criticizes Freud and some other reductionists for focusing on only one, limited valorization of a complex, multivalent, inexhaustible religious symbolism and then claiming that their very narrow interpretation or explanation is sufficient. Many of his antireductionist formulations will be seen as arising from his criticisms of approaches that do not do justice to the complexity and ambiguity, paradoxical and contradictory aspects, and camouflage and concealment of the mythic sacred and to the multivalence and other functions and structures of religious symbolism, the language of myth.

Eliade repeatedly expresses his antireductionist claim in terms of the following principle: "the scale creates the phenomenon." He quotes the following ironical query of Henri Poincaré: "Would a naturalist who had never studied the elephant except through the microscope consider that he had an adequate knowledge of the creature?" Eliade continues: "The microscope reveals the structure and mechanism of cells, which structure and mechanism are exactly the same in all multi-cellular organisms. The elephant is certainly a multicellular organism, but is that all that it is? On the microscopic scale, we might hesitate to answer. On the scale of human vision, which at least has the advantage of presenting the elephant as a zoological phenomenon, there can be no doubt about the reply."[26]

The methodological assumption of the irreducibility of the sacred can be seen as arising from Eliade's view of the role of the historian of religions. His justification for such an assumption seems to be that the task of the phenomenologist, at least in the beginning, is to follow and attempt to understand an experience as it is for the person who has had that experience. What his mythic data reveal is that certain people have had experiences which they have considered religious. Thus the phenomenologist must first of all respect the original intentionality expressed by the mythic data; he or she must attempt to understand such myths as something religious. One's approach must be commensurate with the nature of the subject matter. *Homo religiosus* experiences the sacred as something *sui generis*. If Eliade is to participate in and sympathetically understand the mythic phenomena of others, his scale must be commensurate with the scale of the mythic other. Consequently, he insists on an irreducibly religious scale of understanding in order to have the most adequate knowledge possible of mythic and other irreducibly religious phenomena.

To gain some sense of the extreme significance of this hermeneutical principle for Eliade, we shall provide four of his illustrations: the lofty status of Australian medicine men; the strange shamanic imitation of animal sounds; expressions of "madness" by religious specialists; and the extraordinary value that human beings place on gold.

How are we to understand the enormous prestige and the various functions and duties of the Australian medicine man? Eliade's data, such as the mythic models and initiation rituals for becoming a medicine man, reveal that the Australians have placed these experiences within a religious context. Eliade, using a "religious scale," attempts to understand these phenomena "on their own plane of reference." He finds that "only the medicine man succeeds in surpassing his human condition, and consequently he is able to behave like the spiritual beings, or, in other words, to partake of the modality of a spiritual being." It is because of his "transmutation," his "singular existential condition," that the medicine man can cure the sick, be a rainmaker, and defend his tribe against magical aggression. In short, his "social prestige, his cultural role, and his political supremacy derive ultimately from his magico-religious 'power.'"[27]

How are we to understand the shaman's strange imitation of animal cries? Many have interpreted this phenomenon as manifesting a pathological "possession," clear evidence of the shaman's mental aberration. However, suppose we suspend our normative judgments and first attempt to understand the religious meaning which such shamanic experience has had for the religious other. Understood in terms of such a religious scale, Eliade finds that the shaman's friendship with animals and knowledge of their language reveal a mythic "paradisal syndrome." As part of one of his favorite religious scenarios, Eliade interprets communication and friendship with animals as a means of partially recovering the paradisal situation of primordial human beings. This blessedness and spontaneity existed in *illo tempore,* before the "fall," and is inaccessible to our ordinary nonsacred state. From this religious perspective, Eliade begins to understand that the "strange behavior" is "actually part of a coherent ideology, possessing great nobility." In terms of this ideology, this "yearning for Paradise," Eliade is able to interpret the meaning of particular variations of the shaman's central ecstatic experience and other related phenomena of shamanism.[28]

A third illustration, again involving Eliade's use of a religious scale to interpret phenomena that may otherwise be dismissed as simply expressing a psychopathological condition, is seen in many contexts of the "madness" of the religious specialist. "Certain prophets were even accused of 'madness' (like Hosea: 'the prophet is mad, this inspired fellow is raving' [Hos. 9:7]), but we cannot speak of a true psychopathological disease. Rather there are emotional shocks, brought on by the terrifying presence of God and the gravity of the mission the prophet has just assumed. The phenomenon is well known from the 'initiatory maladies' of shamans to the 'madnesses' of the great mystics of all religions." "What distinguishes Dionysus and his cult [from other cases of *mania* brought on by the Greek gods] is not these psychopathic crises *but the fact that they were valorized as religious experience,* whether as a punishment or as a favor from the god."[29]

One might grant the usefulness, if not the necessity, of assuming the irreducibility of the sacred when attempting to interpret the meaning of the myths of Australian medicine men, initiations of Siberian shamans, Dionysiac orgiastic ecstasies, or the "ravings" of Biblical prophets. But some of Eliade's most interesting interpretations involve the utilization of a religious scale to interpret phenomena usually considered non-religious.[30]

For example, Eliade uses a religious scale in his inquiry as to why human beings, from prehistory to the present, have been so obsessed with the desperate search for gold and have placed such an extraordinary value on this particular metal. At least in one respect Eliade would agree with the analysis in the first volume of *Capital* in which Karl Marx shows that gold (or any other fetishized commodity), when "demystified," has no inherent exchange value; its value—what it is worth quantitatively—expresses a dynamic social relation. Of course, Eliade does not agree that this value relation is primarily determined by the amount of socially necessary labor time embodied in the production of the commodity gold and by other economic factors. Rather he submits that this value relation is primarily a mythic, sacred relation constituted by *homo religiosus.*

When interpreting the extraordinary value placed on gold, Eliade notes that there are impressive mythologies of *homo faber* concerned with the first decisive conquests of the natural world: "But gold does not belong to the mythology of *homo faber.* Gold is a creation of *homo religiosus:* this metal was valorized for exclusively symbolic and religious reasons. Gold was the first metal utilized by man, although it could be employed neither as tool nor as weapon. In the history of technological innovations—that is to say, the passage from stone technology to bronze industry, then to iron and finally to steel—gold played no role whatsoever. Furthermore, its exploitation is the most difficult of any metal."[31]

Using a religious scale of interpretation, Eliade submits that the mythology of *homo religiosus* that allows us to comprehend the exaltation of gold involves the belief that all ores "grow" in the belly of the earth; that given sufficient time there is a natural transmutation of metals into gold, since gold or perfection is the final goal of Nature. "The primordial symbolic value of this metal could not be abolished, in spite of the progressive desacralization of Nature and of human existence." This primordial symbolic value involves the idea that "gold is immortality." Therefore, alchemists, using the Elixir or the Philosopher's Stone to complete the work of Nature, not only "heal" base metals by accelerating their "maturation," transmuting them finally into gold. The "alchemists went even further: their elixir was reputed to heal and to rejuvenate men as well, indefinitely prolonging their lives and making them into immortal beings."[32]

Only brief mention will be made of Eliade's few, explicit references to "the transconscious" as a unique, irreducible state of religious consciousness, since this positing of a "higher" religious consciousness is sometimes presented by Eliade as part of his general, antireductionist orientation.[33] It is not entirely clear what Eliade intends by "transconsciousness." Most of his references focus on essential symbols and images. Several passages mention C. G. Jung's insights, although Eliade also indicates that by "transconscious" he intends something more than the psychological. Ricketts analyzes the concept of the transconscious as Eliade's attempt to render more adequately Otto's *a priori* category of the Holy. Ricketts claims that "Eliade wishes to designate a mental structure or capacity set apart from all others, one which comes into play only in religious experience."[34]

For Eliade, the transconscious—whether analyzed as some essential, religious, mental state, capacity, faculty, category, or structure—has a universal, transcultural, nonhistorical status. In some passages, Eliade seems to employ the concept of the transconscious as a necessary criterion for all religious experience: for distinguishing mythic and other religious phenomena from nonreligious phenomena. In this sense, the intentionality of the sacred and the unique universal structure of the dialectic of the sacred require a "higher," or at least unique, irreducibly religious structure of consciousness. In other passages, Eliade seems to maintain that the transconscious "zone" or state of consciousness functions only in Yoga, shamanism, mysticism, and other examples of the "highest," "most elevated" mythical and other religious states of spiritual realization. As I have tried to show elsewhere, much of this Eliadean positing of a unique, irreducibly religious transconscious as a way of establishing the irreducibly religious nature of mythic and other religious phenomena rests upon assumed ontological moves and normative judgments that go far beyond a descriptive history and phenomenology of religion.[35]

No Purely Religious Phenomena

Eliade's hermeneutic principle of the irreducibility of the sacred may be seen as consistent with twentieth-century scholarly approaches that reacted against what was perceived as the threat of scientific and other forms of reductionism. Such approaches often attempted to carve out and insulate their own unique subject matter, requiring their own, specialized interpretations and explanations. Eliade certainly fears that reductionist approaches will not only explain inadequately but also explain away the irreducibly religious subject matter. But unlike some other scholars within religious studies who also attempt to interpret religious phenomena religiously, Eliade is not interested in a narrow, highly specialized, religiously insulated, scholarly method and discipline.[36] This can be seen in his frequent assertions that there are no "purely" religious phenomena and in his emphasis on integration and synthesis as part of his antireductionism.

The methodological principle of the irreducibility of the sacred does not mean that the scholar can focus on purely religious phenomena. "Obviously there are no *purely* religious phenomena; no phenomenon can be solely and exclusively religious. Because religion is human it must for that very reason be something social, something linguistic, something economic—you cannot think of man apart from language and society. But it would be hopeless to try and explain religion in terms of any one of those basic functions which are really no more than another way of saying what man is. It would be as futile as thinking you could explain *Madame Bovary* by a list of social, economic and political facts; however true, they do not affect it as a work of literature." Eliade goes on to assert that he does "not mean to deny the usefulness of approaching the religious phenomenon from various different angles," although some of his formulations certainly minimize or deny such usefulness.[37] Typically, Eliade then concludes that the religious phenomenon "must be looked at first of all in itself, in that which belongs to it alone and can be explained in no other terms."[38]

Sometimes such general formulations, conceding that there are no purely religious phenomena and then arguing for the legitimacy and primacy of interpretations focusing on the irreducibility of the religious, are expressed in terms of Eliade's acceptance of the view that all data are "historical":

> This does not mean, of course, that a religious phenomenon can be understood outside of its "history," that is, outside of its cultural and socioeconomic contexts. There is no such thing as a "pure" religious datum, outside of history, for there is no such thing as a human datum that is not at the same time a historical datum. Every religious experience is expressed and transmitted in a particular historical context. But admitting the historicity of religious experiences does not imply that they are reducible to nonreligious forms of behavior. Stating that a religious datum is always a historical datum does not mean that it is reducible to a nonreligious history—for example, to an economic, social, or political history. We must never lose sight of one of the fundamental principles of modern science: *the scale creates the phenomenon.*[39]

Since there are no purely religious phenomena, Eliade is dependent for his data and for some of his interpretations and explanations on the contributions of anthropologists, psychologists, sociologists, historians, and other scholars who usually do not assume the irreducibility of the sacred. The "autonomous" history of religions, with its assumption of the irreducibility of the religious, cannot insulate itself and claim to be self-sufficient. It not only provides irreducibly religious interpretations of specific mythic and other religious data but also has the special role of integrating and synthesizing the contributions of other specialized approaches within its broad, coherent, meaningful, irreducibly religious framework.

As part of his emphasis on comparative research and the need for generalizations, Eliade criticizes his colleagues—even those accepting the irreducibility of the religious—for their self-imposed specialized inhibitions, and he frequently argues for the indispensable function and urgency of bold, creative, imaginative syntheses.[40] Both Eliade's reflections on hermeneutics and his interpretation of the intentionality and meaning of the religious data contain such synthesizing terms as integration, unification, harmonious whole, revalorization, homologization, and cosmicization. For example, religious symbolism will be seen to have a function of unification in which diverse, fragmented, multivalent, often contradictory aspects of experience are synthesized within coherent, meaningful, spiritual wholes. And much of Eliade's critique of modern, desacralized culture will be seen as arising from his claim that it lacks this creative power of synthesis. The essays in Eliade's *The Quest* maintain that the irreducibly religious history of religions must aim to become a "total discipline," with a method of "creative hermeneutics," grounded in the creative power of synthetic interpretation. This disciplinary approach will be essential for bringing about a "new humanism" and a "cultural renewal" arising from a creative, global, synthetic confrontation and integration.

But once again, this dependence on the contributions of other approaches that then are subjected to a hermeneutical process of creative synthesis in no way lessens Eliade's insistence on the need for irreducibly religious interpretations. The history of religions' "mission is to integrate the results of ethnology, psychology, and sociology. Yet in doing so, it will not renounce its own method of investigation or the viewpoint that specifically defines it. . . . In the last analysis, it is for the historian of religions to synthesize all the studies of particular aspects of shamanism and to present a comprehensive view which shall be at once a morphology and a history of this complex religious phenomenon."[41]

NOTES

1. Throughout this chapter on reductionism, we shall use Eliade's term: "the sacred." Only in chap. 3 will there be a precise formulation of Eliade's interpretation of the nature and structure of the sacred.

2. See, for example, Robert D. Baird, *Category Formation and the History of Religions* (The Hague: Mouton, 1971), esp. pp. 86-87, 152-53; Thomas J. J. Altizer, *Mircea Eliade and the Dialectic of the Sacred* (Philadelphia:

Westminster Press, 1963), esp. pp. 17, 30, 36, 41, 84. Summaries of many of the critiques of Eliade may be found in R. F. Brown, "Eliade on Archaic Religions: Some Old and New Criticisms," *Sciences Religieuses* 10 (1981): 429-49; Seymour Cain, "Mircea Eliade," *International Encyclopaedia of the Social Sciences Biographical Supplement,* vol. 18 (New York: Macmillan, Free Press, 1979), pp. 166-72; Guilford Dudley III, *Religion on Trial: Mircea Eliade and His Critics* (Philadelphia: Temple University Press, 1977); John A. Saliba, *"Homo Religiosus" in Mircea Eliade: An Anthropological Evaluation* (Leiden: Brill, 1976); Douglas Allen, *Mircea Eliade et le phénomène religieux* (Paris: Payot, 1982); and Bryan S. Rennie, *Reconstructing Eliade: Making Sense of Religion* (Albany: State University of New York Press, 1996).

3. Ivan Strenski, *Four Theories of Myth in Twentieth-Century History: Cassirer, Eliade, Lévi-Strauss and Malinowski* (Iowa City: University of Iowa Press, 1987), pp. 95, 126, and passim.

4. See, for example, Mircea Eliade, *Images and Symbols: Studies in Religious Symbolism,* trans. Philip Mairet (New York: Sheed and Ward, 1961), pp. 175-76.

5. Mircea Eliade, "Methodological Remarks on the Study of Religious Symbolism" in Mircea Eliade and Joseph M. Kitagawa, eds., *The History of Religions: Essays in Methodology* (Chicago: University of Chicago Press, 1959), p. 88. This essay appears as chap. 5 "Observations on Religious Symbolism," in Mircea Eliade, *Mephistopheles and the Androgyne: Studies in Religious Myth and Symbol* (New York: Sheed and Ward, 1965). This book was also published under the title *The Two and the One.*

6. For example, see Mircea Eliade, *The Myth of the Eternal Return,* trans. Willard R. Trask (New York: Pantheon Books, 1954), pp. 5-6 (hereafter cited as *Eternal Return).*

7. Annamarie Schimmel, "Summary of the Discussion," *Numen* 7 (1960): 234-35, 236-37.

8. Mircea Eliade, "The Quest for the 'Origins' of Religion," *History of Religions* 4 (1964): 166, which appears as chap. 3 in Mircea Eliade, *The Quest: History and Meaning in Religion* (Chicago: University of Chicago Press, 1969), p. 50 (hereafter cited as *Quest).*

9. In chaps. 3 and 4, it will be seen that Eliade's analysis of the universal structure of religion seems to emphasize "nature" and deemphasize "history." In chapters 8 and 9, we shall see that there is something essentially anti-historical in Eliade's analysis of myth and history.

10. Saliba, *"Homo Religiosus" in Mircea Eliade,* p. 111, and Edmund Leach, "Sermons by a Man on a Ladder," *New York Review of Books* 7 (October 20, 1966): 28. For similar comparisons and critiques of Eliade, see the reviews by W. A. Lessa, *American Anthropologist* 61 (1959): 122-23, and Lord Raglan, *Man* 59 (March 1959): 53-54. See also Northrop Frye, "World Enough

Without Time," *The Hudson Review* 12 (1959): 426-27, and Altizer, *Mircea Eliade and the Dialectic of the Sacred,* pp. 41, 42.

11. Mircea Eliade, *No Souvenirs: Journal, 1957-1969,* trans. Fred H. Johnson, Jr. (New York: Harper & Row, 1977), p. xii (hereafter cited as *No Souvenirs).* Republished as Mircea Eliade, *Journal II, 1957-1969* (Chicago: University of Chicago Press, 1989).

12. Mircea Eliade, "Prolegomenon to Religious Dualism: Dyads and Polarities," in *Quest,* pp. 132-33.

13. I am using "reductionistic" in a broad sense and not in its more narrow, highly technical uses in the philosophy of science and the natural sciences.

14. Mircea Eliade, *Patterns in Comparative Religion,* trans. Rosemary Sheed (New York: World Publishing Co., Meridian Books, 1963), p. xiii (hereafter cited as *Patterns).* In interpreting how Eliade may have understood this relationship between his antireductionism and the reductionistic approaches he attacked as "false," Elzey provides four different interpretations of the word "false" in this passage from *Patterns.* See Wayne Elzey, "Mircea Eliade and the Battle Against Reductionism," in *Religion and Reductionism: Essays on Eliade, Segal, and the Challenge of the Social Sciences for the Study of Religion,* ed. Thomas A. Idinopulos and Edward A. Yonan (Leiden: E. J. Brill, 1994), pp. 82-87.

15. For one of the best-known and most influential of such antireductionist positions, see the claim for the *sui generis* numinous essence of religious experience based on an *a priori,* irreducibly religious, category of mind or mental capacity, in Rudolf Otto, *The Idea of the Holy,* trans. John W. Harvey (New York: Oxford University Press, A Galaxy Book, 1958), pp. 3-4, 132, 175, and passim.

16. Mac Linscott Ricketts, *Mircea Eliade: The Romanian Roots, 1907-1945* (Boulder: East European Monographs, No. 248, 1988), vol. 1, pp. 188, 520; vol. 2, p. 1205 (hereafter cited as *Eliade: Romanian Roots,* 1, and *Eliade: Romanian Roots,* 2). "Itinerariu spiritual" (Spiritual Itinerary) appeared as a series of twelve articles in the newspaper *Cuvântul* from September to November 1927. In my review of *Eliade: Romanian Roots* in the *Journal of the American Academy of Religion* 60 (1992): 174-77 and at greater length in my "Recent Defenders of Eliade: A Critical Evaluation," *Religion* 24 (1994): 333-51, I maintain that Ricketts greatly exaggerates the originality of the scholarly principles in Eliade's youthful writings, which often reflect the position of Eliade's teacher Nae Ionescu and were shared by many others at the time. In addition, if Eliade's scholarly method of his mature scholarly works was already basically formulated in these youthful, often highly personal and immature writings, then Ricketts has unintentionally left Eliade even more vulnerable to attacks on his scholarship. These points are developed in chap. 4 in the section on "Cosmic Christianity" and especially in the section on "Eliade's Personal Faith and His Scholarship."

17. Ricketts, *Eliade: Romanian Roots,* 1, pp. 91-126.

18. Nae Ionescu, *Roza vânturilor* (Bucharest: Ed. Cultura Nationala, 1937), pp. 12, 60; Ricketts, *Eliade: Romanian Roots,* 1, pp. 98-99. Eliade edited and wrote an afterword for *Roza vânturilor,* an anthology of Ionescu's newspaper articles. We shall not present Ionescu's specific analysis of the three irreducible planes of reality, his attack on reductionism as a "confusion of planes," his Eastern Orthodox view of metaphysics and religion, or his reactionary, anti-Semitic, and fascistic political views.

19. Ricketts, *Eliade: Romanian Roots,* 2, pp. 1205-6.

20. Otto, *The Idea of the Holy,* p. 8.

21. Mircea Eliade, "Religia în viaţa spiritulu," *Est-Vest* 1, no. 1 (January 1927): 28; Mircea Eliade, "Profanii," *Vremea,* December 11, 1936, reprinted in Mircea Eliade, *Fragmentarium* (Bucharest: Vremea, 1939), pp. 86-89; Ricketts, *Eliade: Romanian Roots,* 2, pp. 866-67.

22. See, for example, Robert A. Segal, "In Defense of Reductionism," *Journal of the American Academy of Religion* 51 (1983): 97-124, reprinted in revised form in Segal, *Religion and the Social Sciences: Essays on the Confrontation* (Atlanta: Scholars Press, 1989), pp. 5-36; Segal, "Are Historians of Religions Necessarily Believers?" republished in *Religion and the Social Sciences,* pp. 37-41.

23. Mircea Eliade, "Historical Events and Structural Meaning in Tension," *Criterion* 6, no. 1 (1967): 30.

24. Eliade, "A New Humanism," in *Quest,* p. 4, which first appeared as "History of Religions and a New Humanism," *History of Religions* 1 (1961): 1-8; Mircea Eliade, *Myths, Dreams and Mysteries,* trans. Philip Mairet (New York: Harper & Row, Torchbooks, 1967), pp. 13-14.

25. Charles H. Long, "The Meaning of Religion in the Contemporary Study of Religions," *Criterion* 2 (1963): 25. See also Joachim Wach, *The Comparative Study of Religions,* ed. Joseph M. Kitagawa (New York: Columbia University Press, 1961), p. 15.

26. Mircea Eliade, "Comparative Religion: Its Past and Future," in *Knowledge and the Future of Man,* ed. Walter J. Ong, S.J. (New York: Holt, Rinehart and Winston, 1968), p. 251. See also *Patterns,* p. xiii, and *Myths, Dreams and Mysteries,* p. 131.

27. Mircea Eliade, "The Medicine Men and Their Supernatural Models," in *Australian Religions: An Introduction* (Ithaca: Cornell University Press, 1973), pp. 128-64, esp. 129, 157, 158.

28. Mircea Eliade, *Shamanism: Archaic Techniques of Ecstasy,* trans. Willard R. Trask (New York: Pantheon Books, 1964), pp. 96-99 (hereafter cited as *Shamanism);* and Mircea Eliade, "The Yearning for Paradise in Primitive Tradition," *Daedalus* 88 (1959): 258, 261-66, reprinted as chap. 3, "Nostalgia for Paradise in the Primitive Traditions," in *Myths, Dreams and Mysteries.* For a concise formulation of Eliade's interpretation of this key

ecstatic experience of the shaman, see Mircea Eliade, *Journal I, 1945-1955,*
trans. Mac Linscott Ricketts (Chicago: University of Chicago Press, 1990), pp.
180-81 (hereafter cited as *Journal 1).*

29. Mircea Eliade, *A History of Religious Ideas.* Vol. 1: *From the Stone
Age to the Eleusinian Mysteries,* trans. Willard R. Trask (Chicago: University
of Chicago Press, 1978), pp. 343, 366 (hereafter cited as *History 1).* On p. 366
n. 15, Eliade adds: "What separates a shaman from a psychopath is that he
succeeds in curing himself [through his shamanic initiation and other religious
experiences] and ends by possessing a stronger and more creative personality
than the rest of the community." See also *Shamanism,* pp. 14, 23-32, and
Eliade, "Recent Works on Shamanism: A Review Article," *History of Religions*
1 (1961): 155.

30. Chapter 10 will provide illustrations of Eliade's religious mythical
interpretation of modern, Western, "secular" phenomena.

31. Mircea Eliade, "The Myth of Alchemy," *Parabola* 3 (1978): 12.

32. Ibid., pp. 12-14. See Mircea Eliade, *The Forge and the Crucible,* trans.
Stephen Corrin (New York: Harper & Brothers, 1962), pp. 50-52, 114-15, and
passim.

33. See *Patterns,* pp. 450, 454; *Images and Symbols,* pp. 17, 37, 119-20;
The Forge and the Crucible, p. 201; Mircea Eliade, *Yoga: Immortality and
Freedom,* trans. Willard R. Trask (New York: Pantheon Books, 1958), pp. 99,
226 (hereafter cited as *Yoga).*

34. Mac Linscott Ricketts, "The Nature and Extent of Eliade's 'Jungianism'," *Union Seminary Quarterly Review* 25 (Winter 1970): 229.

35. See Douglas Allen, *Structure and Creativity in Religion: Hermeneutics
in Mircea Eliade's Phenomenology and New Directions* (The Hague: Mouton,
1978), pp. 218-22 and passim.

36. As will become apparent, Eliade is open to the opposite criticism. In
his insistence on the irreducibility of the religious and his broad, ambitious,
universalistic goals, Eliade often goes far beyond a defense of the irreducibly
religious descriptions, interpretations, and explanations of his discipline. He
often attacks the very legitimacy, not simply the disciplinary boundaries and
perspectival limitations, of secular reductionist explanations of religious
phenomena.

37. Although Eliade often writes that he is not denying the value of other
perspectives, he also claims that interpretations and explanations not respecting
the irreducibility of the sacred are illegitimate or false. As will be seen, in
making these negative judgments about reductionist approaches, Eliade sometimes goes beyond the perspectival limitations of the history and phenomenology of religion and offers highly personal, as well as metaphysical and
theological, views.

38. *Patterns,* p. xiii.

39. *Quest,* p. 7. See also Eliade, "Comparative Religion: Its Past and Future," pp. 250-51.

40. In *Eliade: Romanian Roots,* 2, Ricketts entitles his concluding chapter "Experiences for a Synthesis" (pp. 1204-16). He claims that "from one point of view, this aim of promoting personal and cultural *syntheses* on the basis of spiritual experiences could be seen as the unifying principle in all Eliade's work" (p. 1209).

41. *Shamanism,* p. xiii.

CHAPTER 2

Reductionistic Critics and Eliade

Eliade's writings, from youthful newspaper columns and autobiographical reflections through his later scholarly works, are full of attacks on "reductionism" and claims for the antireductionist defense of the "irreducibility of the sacred." We shall now consider some of the criticisms of Eliade's antireductionism that have arisen within the field of history of religions or *Religionswissenschaft* and social scientific approaches to religion. A more general, nontechnical criticism will be followed by some of the more technical theoretical analysis of reductionism that has arisen within the philosophy of science, physics, and other disciplines and which some scholars of myth and religion have applied to Eliade and to their own discipline. It will be important to clarify in which ways such analysis helps explain what Eliade is doing, undermines his antireductionist approach to myth and religion as uncritical and unscientific, or is largely irrelevant to his central antireductionist sources and concerns.

ALL APPROACHES ARE REDUCTIONIST

Debates over "reductionism" in twentieth-century philosophy of science and many debates in the study of religion during recent decades have focused on technical analyses of theory and explanation. To take the best-known model, various reductionists have argued that one can arrange data in a hierarchical manner so that phenomena from one theoretical domain—say, biology—can be translated into and explained by another theoretical domain, say, physics.

There is another, broad, nontechnical defense of reductionist approaches that attacks claims to the irreducibility of the religious.

Although one can relate this attack on antireductionism to the more technical analyses, it is possible to accept or reject this defense of reductionism without knowing the specialized literature. John Fenton will be used to illustrate this general approach since Eliade and his followers are clearly a target of his criticism.

In attacking this antireductionist claim for the irreducibility of the sacred, Fenton uses the term "theologism" to describe "a concept properly and primarily developed and used in a theological context that has been transferred with some residue as a non-theological concept to another domain such as that of the secular scholarly study of religions." Fenton then attacks one of these central theologisms: "The conception of religion as *sui generis,* i.e., as a primary datum which can be understood only in its own terms, has generally been accompanied in theological circles by its natural corollary: reductionistic explanations of religion are entirely incorrect." "The secular study of religions should no longer be restricted by the need to defend the faith, or to defend its theologistic residue, the anti-reductionistic *sui generis* character of the so-called 'discipline of religion.'"[1]

"[E]very systematic attempt to understand phenomena reduces the phenomena." In the study of mythic, religious, or any other phenomena, "systematic interpretation necessarily translates the phenomena into disciplinary terms, simplifies, and narrows the perspective." With scholars like Eliade obviously in mind, Fenton contends that there is "nothing wrong with reductionism in the study of religions, unless the investigator does not self-consciously realize that he is reductionistic, unless the reductionistic scholar thinks that his discipline alone allows him to isolate the essence of religious phenomena from their accidents, unless he overextends his method beyond its legitimate scope."[2] Reduction is a legitimate and necessary form of explanation of mythic and other phenomena as long as the reductionistic scholar recognizes that one's approach does not provide a complete explanation and so allows for other accounts of the phenomena.

Fenton is correct in his basic critique of this kind of antireductionism.[3] In a very fundamental way, all methodological approaches are perspectival, limiting, and necessarily reductionistic. Eliade's assumption of the irreducibility of the sacred limits what phenomena will be investigated as properly mythic, what aspects of those mythic phenomena will be described, and what mythic meanings will be interpreted.[4] Fenton's focus on "theologisms" and theological defenses of the faith can be broadened. All approaches that assume and insist on the irreducibility of the religious are reductionistic in that they privilege various religious perspectives and devalue or exclude other perspectives and other aspects of the data. In his hermeneutical strivings for synthesis and integration within an irreducibly religious framework of interpretation, Eliade cannot do justice to anthropological, sociological, psychological, economic, and other approaches that do not assume the irreducibility of the sacred. He translates the contributions of other approaches into his own irreducibly religious framework, simplifying and excluding aspects of other scales of interpretation and explanation that do not privilege the Eliadean perspective.

When scholars, including critics, identify Eliade's position as "nonreductionistic," this is really, in the broad sense raised by Fenton, a certain *kind of reductionism.* In Eliade's "nonreductionist" reductionism, he assumes the irreducibility of the religious and privileges a specific religious perspective. He refuses to reduce the phenomena he interprets as religious to nonreligious scales of interpretation and explanation. In doing this, he necessarily reduces the complexity of phenomena to his religious plane of reference.

One can grant this broad sense in which all approaches are reductionist and then argue on phenomenological grounds for a certain methodological primacy of the irreducibility of the religious.[5] Such an orientation, assuming the irreducibility of the sacred but avoiding some of the more objectionable features of the so-called antireductionism, appeals to the need for some kind of phenomenological *epoché.* Other human beings claim to have had religious mythic experiences, to believe in religious myths, and to engage in religious practices based on those myths. If the scholar is attempting to describe and interpret the meaning of their data, then it makes sense, at least in the early stages of one's methodological procedure, to suspend one's own value judgments about the reality or unreality, religious or nonreligious nature, deeper explanatory causes, etc., of that data. Scholars giving nonreligious explanations often seem to have *a priori* reductionist explanations and hence have little or no interest in listening to what believers have to say about their mythic experiences. On a basic descriptive, phenomenological level, their reductive accounts do not do justice to the intentionality and givenness of the phenomena as experienced by religious mythic persons. Therefore, if mythic people have assumed the irreducibility of the religious and understood their own data on a religious plane of reference, then it makes sense for the scholar to assume a religious scale of description and interpretation to do justice to the mythic data of the other.

This phenomenological justification for a kind of religious nonreduction in no way allows Eliade and other so-called antireductionists to claim that all nonreligious reductionist accounts are *a priori* "false." A need for more adequate phenomenological descriptions and interpretations from the perspective of a religious plane of reference of the mythic other does not allow us to prejudge the weaknesses and strengths of specific reductive accounts. After describing the nature, meaning, function, and significance of the mythic data from the perspective of *homo religiosus,* scholars may formulate all sorts of interpretations and explanations, religious and nonreligious. In some cases, a nonreligious reductive account, uncovering economic and material conditions of class domination, oppression, poverty, and suffering or psychological conditions of fear, guilt, and repression, may have greater explanatory power than an antireductionist insistence on the irreducibility of the sacred.

This methodological privileging of the irreducibility of the sacred in no way negates the previous claim that all approaches are necessarily reductionist. We have just stated that it makes sense, at least in the early stages of one's scholarly procedure, to suspend one's own value judgments about the reality or unreality and the religious or nonreligious nature of the data. But in assuming the irreducibility of the sacred and the fundamental primacy of the category of *homo religiosus* as the subject of one's investigation of mythic data, Eliade has not completely suspended all value judgments. He has determined *a priori* that all kinds of nonreligious causes, conditions, and explanations are secondary or completely irrelevant for describing and interpreting the constitution and basic nature of his data. And, as will become clear, Eliade also makes all sorts of assumptions and value judgments about the reality of the sacred and its world of myth.

The phenomenological *epoché* is not something that one simply prescribes or invokes psychologically or mysteriously, as if Eliade were some intuitively empathetic genius and one must leave it at that. If the phenomenological "bracketing" is to be of scholarly value, it requires a self-critical attitude, a methodological procedure and hermeneutical framework, intersubjective checks, and a method of verification. In assuming the irreducibility of the sacred, a universal process of sacralization through the dialectic of the sacred and the profane, and a universal hermeneutical framework of structural systems of religious symbols, Eliade is not only privileging the religious in his investigation of myth; he is privileging a specific interpretation of the religious. Therefore, built into his assumption of the irreducibility of the sacred, as possibly justified on phenomenological grounds, is a devaluing or outright dismissal not only of nonreligious aspects of myth but also of other religious accounts that do not fit in with his methodological framework.

It might seem that our methodological privileging on phenomenological grounds of the assumption of the irreducibility of the sacred, at least in the early stage of one's investigation of myth and other religious phenomena, is completely noncontroversial. After all, as we shall see in the next section, Robert Segal, the most forceful and persistent critic of Eliade's antireductionism, grants that even the strongest reductionist does not deny the need to accept the irreducibility of the religious as a starting point. Such a religious perspective is required in order to describe and understand the religious views of religious believers on the "manifest" level of interpretation.

Nevertheless, even this limited, initial privileging of the irreducibility of the religious may be challenged. Rosalind Shaw argues that "the concept of the *sui generis* nature of religion also entails the decontextualization of religion. In mainstream history of religions, understandings of 'the uniquely religious' are usually constituted by excluding or peripheralizing social and political content in defining what really counts as 'religion.'"[6] Antireductionists, claiming that this desocialized, irreducibly religious must be interpreted "on its own terms," typically deflect questions of power and inequality and dismiss social and political analysis as reductionist. By making the concept of the *sui generis* nature of religion "central to their discourse, scholars in the history of religions are effectively insulated from uncomfortable questions about standpoint and privilege—questions upon which feminist scholarship is based."[7]

Shaw's analysis clearly applies to the deeper levels of analysis when scholars attempt to interpret and explain the irreducibly religious point of view of believers. But it also applies to the initial, manifest level in which one attempts to understand myth and other religious phenomena as understood by the believers. The complex, diversified, often contradictory manifest level of religious beliefs and practices is not constituted exclusively through some essentialized assumption of the irreducibility of the sacred. The religious phenomena of religious people are also constituted through assumptions about relations of class, caste, gender, race, privilege, and so forth. If the scholar assumes a certain irreducibly religious view of the *sui generis* nature of religion that excludes or marginalizes the importance of such relations of inequality and power, then the very data selected, described, and interpreted on the first level of analysis will express such a bias. Not only nonreligious but also significant religious aspects of the data will be devalued or excluded from one's description of religious phenomena. Many religious voices will be excluded or completely silenced, and others will be distorted since the scholar's assumptions and interpretive framework cannot do justice to their experiences and religious points of view.

At this stage of presentation, the raising of these serious questions is not meant to be a fatal criticism of Eliade's kind of reductionism. What must be determined is whether his particular kind of reductionism, as seen in his religiously "nonreductionistic" assumption of the irreducibility of the sacred, has explanatory power in making sense of the nature, meaning, and significance of myth.

NONREDUCTIONISM BEGS THE QUESTION

During the past two decades, a group of scholars from religious studies and the social sciences has engaged in a vigorous, ongoing debate on reductionism in such journals as the *Journal of the American Academy of Religion, Religion, Journal of Religion, Religious Traditions, Religious Studies, Journal for the Scientific Study of Religion, Zygon, Scottish Journal of Religious Studies,* and *Method and Theory in the Study of Religion.* Typically, one scholar writes an article, a second scholar publishes a rejoinder, the first scholar then formulates a rejoinder to the rejoinder, and so forth, until we have a thriving religion-and-reductionism industry. Although Mircea Eliade has been the major target of such publications, his strongest supporters or "religionists"—with the notable exception of Daniel Pals and a few other nonreductionists—have simply ignored the debate and the attacks on their approaches. The consequence of this has been that the debate on reductionism and religion has been dominated by reductionists who have often debated the differences in their reductionistic approaches.[8]

The most prolific of these scholars on reductionism and religion has been Robert Segal.[9] He has repeatedly attacked nonreductionists in general, and Mircea Eliade in particular, while defending the viability and necessity for social scientific reductive approaches to religion. Since Segal has written so extensively on reductionism and since our focus is on Eliade's position, I shall not present his overall position. Instead I shall be selective, focusing on one of his major attacks on Eliade and religionists and then delineating a few of his claims challenging Eliade's position.

A brief summary and perhaps oversimplification of Segal's argument is that Eliade and other religionists, in assuming the irreducibility of the religious, simply assume what needs to be explained. In dogmatically proclaiming the *sui generis,* irreducibly religious nature of religious phenomena, they beg the basic questions about the nature, origin, function, meaning, object, and truth of religion.

According to Segal, even the strongest reductionists do not deny that religious believers believe in the reality of the sacred, the object or referent of their mythic and other religious beliefs. No one denies that religious data also reveal that believers accept the religious basis for the origin, function, and meaning of their religious phenomena. But the acceptance of the irreducibility of the religious for the religious believer is on the manifest level of description and interpretation. This is a legitimate and even necessary starting point for scholars, including reductionists, but it is not the end point of analysis.[10]

What remains for the reductionistic scholar is the need for a latent or deeper level of analysis and explanation. The fact that religious or nonreligious people believe something to be true does not automatically make it true. Eliade is correct that *homo religiosus* has a strong desire and nostalgia for the sacred. On a deeper level of analysis, reduction- istic scholars have the right to try to explain psychologically and in other ways the causes and conditions of such desires that have been expressed in religious terms. Eliade is certainly correct that *homo religiosus* accepts the sacred as a transcendent, ultimate reality. On a deeper level of analysis, reductionist scholars have the right to try to explain sociologically and in other ways the basis and consequences of such beliefs in a sacred reality. Reductionistic scholars also have the right to reflect critically on religious attempts to justify such beliefs. In simply assuming that the irreducibility of the sacred on the manifest level of the believers must also be respected as the irreducibility of the sacred on the deepest levels of interpretation and explanation, Eliade and other religionists have arbitrarily and dogmatically insulated themselves in a self-serving manner, cut off and declared as illegitimate serious scholarly concerns, and begged many of the questions that are in need of scholarly analysis.

According to Segal, the adequacy of reductive analyses of religion "is an open rather than closed question, an empirical rather than *a priori* one." Eliade simply keeps asserting "that reductive interpretations of religion are either irrelevant or secondary because they skirt the believer's own view of the irreducibly religious meaning of religion. But he thereby begs, not answers, the key question: whether the believer's own view of the meaning of religion *is* the true meaning of religion both for the believer and in itself."[11] "[T]o assert *a priori* that the social sciences study the mind, culture, or society *rather than* religion is conspicuously to beg the question: what is the nature of religion?"[12]

Many other reductionists, in attacking Eliade's antireductionist dismissal of reductionist approaches, offer the same kind of argument: that Eliade is simply begging serious, legitimate questions. For example, Ivan Strenski cites some of Eliade's antireductionist formulation previously quoted (*The Quest,* pp. 132-33)[13] in which he asserts that scholars do not have the right to reduce their mythic and other religious documents "to something other than what they are, namely spiritual creations." Strenski says that "Eliade of course blatantly begs the question here, since it is the very *identity* of so-called religious phenomena which is in question. If I am right about the intellectual history of the notion of religion, it has shifted several times in the last hundred years already. . . . But . . . Eliade slams the door shut on possible competitors to his own 'spiritualist' position. Instead, he just insists on the identity of religious phenomena by appeal to 'what they are . . . .' But 'what they are' is or should be an open question: Eliade's antireductionist (by replacement) stance rejects alternatives out of hand."[14]

In developing his analysis of how Eliade's nonreductionism begs serious questions facing scholars of religion, Segal offers many criticisms of Eliade's approach. Two of Segal's claims are that Eliade's nonreductionism interprets religion from the (conscious) point of view of the religious believer and that the basic dichotomy is between believer=nonreductionist and sceptic/nonbeliever=reductionist. By clarifying and challenging these claims, it is possible to gain a greater understanding not only of Eliade's antireductionism but also of his general approach to myth and religion.

In his "In Defense of Reductionism" and numerous other works, Segal characterizes Eliade's nonreductionism as the insistence that the scholar must interpret mythic and other religious phenomena in "the terms of the believers themselves," from "the believer's point of view." While briefly demonstrating that Eliade sometimes goes beyond the conscious understanding of believers, Segal then typically asserts that he will assume that by nonreductionism Eliade means the conscious point of view of the religious believer.[15] Segal then directs many criticisms at this antireductionist position that insists on the irreducibly religious point of view of religious believers. In terms of his strongest attacks on how Eliade begs the question, Segal repeatedly argues that

Eliade not only assumes and presents religion in terms of believers but in fact endorses the believer's point of view.[16]

Although Eliade often claims that one must do justice to the irreducibly religious plane of reference of the religious believer, his approach is not restricted to—or often even interested in—the specific religious terms of believers themselves, whether expressed consciously or unconsciously. Eliade does not endorse the extreme descriptive phenomenology of W. Brede Kristensen, for whom the sole "religious reality" is "the faith of the believer" and for whom the value of religious phenomena "is the value that they have had for the believers themselves."[17] Nor does Eliade endorse methodological recommendations by Wilfred Cantwell Smith, such as the claim "that no statement about a religion is valid unless it can be acknowledged by that religion's believers."[18]

Eliade is not primarily concerned with interpreting the meaning of religious phenomena for believers. He does not interview believers through any kind of fieldwork. He selectively refers to the fieldwork of particular anthropologists when believers' testimony seems to provide empirical evidence for his irreducibly religious interpretations. His main sources for his empirical data are myths and other religious texts themselves. Indeed, he is often attacked by anthropologists and other scholars for attributing religious meaning to others that he has personally "read into" his data and that goes far beyond the understanding of actual believers. In many respects, such criticisms are justified, although they often miss what Eliade is actually doing. He often provides interpretations that go beyond, and even contradict, the point of view of the believer. As we shall see, Eliade claims that symbolic and mythic structures and meanings "are there," even when non-believers and believers themselves do not recognize them.

For now, we shall simply delineate several major reasons for rejecting the claim that Eliade's nonreductionism interprets religion from the (conscious) point of view of the religious believer. First, far from focusing on the conscious views of believers, Eliade greatly emphasizes the unconscious in his interpretations. Profoundly influenced by depth psychology, certain literary and artistic creativity, Eastern spiritual practices, and other approaches for exploring the unconscious, he attacked nineteenth-century and more recent reduction-ists for either ignoring or oversimplifying the unconscious in their approaches to religion. He affirms that *homo religiosus* is "the total person," including the unconscious, and he claims that the sacred survives in contemporary secular life on the level of the unconscious.

Second, as a particularly important aspect of our first observation, Eliade claims that symbols and myths communicate their meanings even when religious persons are unaware of them. What is important is that mythic structures and meanings are there whether or not they are understood. This claim will be seen as especially significant for Eliade's approach to myth and religion: without it, his hermeneutical framework for interpreting mythic structures and meanings collapses. It will also be seen that Eliade sees as a most urgent and significant task for the history and phenomenology of religion the formulation of a bold creative hermeneutics: the scholar should uncover and interpret deep, hidden, camouflaged, symbolic and mythic sacred structures and meanings that function on the unconscious level in the contemporary, Western, consciously profane mode of being in the world.

This may present a challenge to Eliade's antireductionist insistence that the scholar avoid "a confusion of planes" and respect the irreducibility of the sacred in the experiences of religious persons. As has just been seen, Eliade claims that modern secular persons, who consciously affirm that they are nonreligious, in some deeper sense, really are religious. Or at least he claims that he can uncover hidden, camouflaged, imaginary, and unconscious sacred structures and meanings that help him to interpret and explain much of overt secular existence. But Eliade is unwilling to grant what seems to be a parallel approach by Freud, Marx, and other reductionists, who grant that religious people consciously affirm that they are religious, but then attempt to uncover hidden psychological, economic, and other structures and meanings that help them to interpret and explain much of overt religious existence. Eliade, as has been seen, simply dismisses such approaches as reductionistic and "false."

Third, even if one grants that Eliade is concerned with the point of view of religious believers, it is still necessary to ask: which believers? In Eliade's antireductionist approach to myth, not all believers count.

Built into his principles of selectivity and his most basic levels of description are all sorts of evaluative judgments as to which believers and what religious phenomena count.[19] Mystics, shamans, and other kinds of "religious specialists," for example, may count a lot. Their data express profound, multivalent, universal, essential, mythic structures and realizations. Conversely, many religious believers have beliefs that Eliade evaluates as "infantile," "immature," "inauthentic," or "false," and he is not very interested in such data that do not reveal the essential mythic structures and meanings.

Fourth, Eliade often asserts that he is interested in interpreting the believer as *homo religiosus,* but it is not clear what this term means. It would be false to identify *homo religiosus* with historically particular, flesh-and blood, individual, religious believers. *Homo religiosus* may be the subject of religious experiences of the irreducibly sacred, but it is a type, a category, an essence, a view of human nature. In his formulations of *homo religiosus,* as with his formulations of essential symbolic and mythic structures, Eliade is involved in a complex process of imaginary idealization at a very high level of abstraction. He presents and argues for this idealized, essentialized subject of mythic experience. Critics charge that this idealized abstraction of essential sacred structures and meanings exists primarily in Eliade's head and is largely detached from the empirical, historical data of actual religious persons. Jonathan Z. Smith charges that this conception of the human being as *homo religiosus* is based on Eliade's inadequate *a priori* ontology.[20] To meet such challenges, Eliade must show that his interpretations of this essentialized *homo religiosus* and of the irreducibly religious, mythic, and symbolic structures have explanatory value in helping to make sense of the religious life of real religious believers.

Fifth and most important, Mircea Eliade is primarily concerned with formulating a general theory of myth and religion and not with presenting religion in the terms of the believer. In doing this, he assumes an antireductionist perspective and formulates his own, general, theoretical terms and principles: the universal sacred as the transcendent referent of mythic and religious experience; the universal dialectic of the sacred as the general structure of sacralization; the language of myth as expressed through universal, coherent, structured systems of religious symbols; a general theory of the nature, function, and structure of myth; the primacy of the cosmogonic myth in disclosing the overall structure and meaning of myth; and so forth. These terms are Eliade's, not those of the religious believers.[21]

That is why Eliade frequently asserts that it does not really matter whether religious persons use the sacred and other Eliadean terminology or whether believers recognize the profound mythic structures and meanings underlying their points of view. Of course, in moving beyond and often ignoring or even contradicting the terms and views of actual believers, Eliade faces the frequent charges that his interpretations are arbitrary, dogmatic, and subjective.[22] If his antireductionist approach has serious scholarly merit, he must show that his general theory of myth and religion is adequate, or more adequate than alternative approaches, in allowing him to interpret and explain the nature, structure, meanings, and significance of mythic and other religious phenomena.

Segal's second claim is that the basic dichotomy is between believer=nonreductionist and sceptic/nonbeliever=reductionist. In simply insisting that scholars must adopt an irreducibly religious scale of interpretation, Eliade has supposedly begged the basic question of how this is possible. Segal counters that this is impossible for the nonbeliever. While reductionistic interpretations may be impossible for believers, such as Eliade, reductionistic accounts of religion are the only ones possible for nonbelieving scholars.

In many of his writings, Segal adopts a clear-cut scholarly dichotomy formulated by numerous scholars. On the one side, we have scholars of religion primarily from the humanities, attempting to be descriptive, providing interpretations, interpreting meaning and significance, and restricting their interpretations to what believers believe. On the other side, we have scholars of religion primarily from the social sciences, attempting to analyze the data, providing explanations, explaining causes and functions, explaining why believers believe, and evaluating whether such beliefs are true.[23]

In this regard, Eliade is primarily concerned with interpreting the meaning of myth and religion. In many of his antireductionist formulations, he insists on a claim made by philosophical phenomenologists and proponents of *Verstehen:* that uncovering and analyzing historical and temporal conditions or providing psychological, economic, scientific, and other causal explanations of phenomena is not tantamount to interpreting the meaning and significance of those phenomena. Eliade repeatedly tells us that after reductionistic, causal accounts of religious phenomena have been completed, the major task for the historian and phenomenologist of religion still remains: to provide antireductionist interpretations of the religious meaning and significance of mythic and other data.

Why does Segal claim that nonbelieving scholars must be reductionists? To focus only on the most important point in his argument against Eliade and other religionists, he claims, on logical grounds, that reductionistic nonbelievers cannot follow Eliade's nonreductionism primarily because they cannot "accept" the meaning, truth, and reality of the religious object. Otherwise they would be believers. "The issue is not whether nonbelievers can accept the reality of the sacred as the *conscious* meaning of religion for the believer. The issue is whether nonbelievers can accept the reality of the sacred as the *true* meaning of religion for the believer. The issue is not whether nonbelievers can *describe* the believer's view of the meaning—or origin or function—of religion. The issue is whether nonbelievers can *accept* that view as the *true* meaning, origin, or function of religion for the believer." "How can nonbelievers accept the reality of the sacred for even the believer when they themselves refuse to accept the reality of it?"[24] In their reductionistic analyses and explanations nonbelievers necessarily assume that the religious beliefs of the believers are false: that the sacred is not irreducibly religious, transcendent, and ultimately real as claimed by believers.

It seems to me that this argument by Segal against Eliade is not convincing: it is often misleading in its clear-cut believer-nonbeliever oppositions, sometimes even concedes too much in accepting an antireductionist agenda (while then often arguing against it), and unnecessarily involves psychological, metaphysical, and theological issues. Obviously, if the believer believes in the reality of a sacred that is irreducibly religious, supernatural, and transcends rational analysis, and if the reductionistic sceptic claims to provide a rational or scientific analysis that is sufficient for understanding the true nature of the sacred, then there is a clear contradiction between these two positions. But in analyzing basic methodological issues involving Eliade's assumption of the irreducibility of the sacred, there need not be such a primary scholarly concern with whether the sacred is ultimately real and whether the religious claims of the believer are ultimately true.

Remarkably, Segal's argument seems to place him in agreement with much of Eliade's most controversial claims about the scholar-as-religious believer previously formulated: that only the scholar-as-believer can understand and interpret the irreducibly religious meaning of myth and other religious phenomena. Where Segal disagrees, of course, is in his defense of reductionistic approaches by nonbelievers who cannot accept the irreducibility of the sacred.

On methodological grounds, it is a serious mistake to make of such paramount scholarly concern the believer-nonbeliever distinction with its focus on the truth or falsity of the sacred. For most scholarly investigations of religious phenomena, whether the scholar is person-ally a believer or a nonbeliever should be secondary or completely irrelevant. For example, we previously formulated a phenomenological argument for assuming an initial methodological primacy of the irreducibility of the religious in providing more adequate accounts of what myth and other religious phenomena mean for religious persons. Past studies clearly demonstrate that not only certain believers, but also many nonbelieving scholars, have been quite good at describing the nature of the origin, function, meaning, and significance of myth and other phenomena for the religious other. Past studies also clearly demonstrate that not only various sceptics, but also many believing scholars, have been incapable—for psychological, metaphysical, theological, and other reasons—of providing accounts that do justice to the experiences and beliefs of the religious other.

On the one hand, many religious believers have distorted and rejected the irreducibly religious phenomena of others. A well-known example is that of the Neo-Calvinist scholar Hendrik Kraemer, who contends that the study of religion must be grounded in theology; that no one can "know" the divine except through the absolute revelation of

"Biblical realism"; and that Biblical Christianity provides an absolute standard against which to judge negatively all religions, including historical Christianity.[25] Such a narrow methodological approach, assuming the irreducibility of the religious, produces narrow normative interpretations that distort an understanding of "the other." Similarly, many Christian and Islamic fundamentalist scholars not only attack secular reductionism but also the irreducibly religious claims of other religions and the beliefs of others within Christianity and Islam who do not agree with their specific faith commitments. Not only do they make no pretense of doing justice to the irreducibly religious claims of the other, but they find much of Eliade's antireductionist approach—such as his formulation of the universal dialectic of the sacred in terms of an essential structure of revelation that is always limited, relative, partial, and camouflaged—personally offensive and false on theological grounds.[26]

On the other hand, there is no reason to assume *a priori* that nonbelievers are incapable of grasping and "accepting" in certain methodological senses the irreducibly religious claims of believers. What is invaluable for the investigator, whether personally a believer or nonbeliever, is a self-critical attitude, a genuine intellectual curiosity, a desire and capacity to empathize with phenomena of the other, a capacity to free one's imagination from rigid assumptions and constraints of one's personal stance, and a satisfaction derived from grasping the meaning and significance of phenomena for the other. This attitude, of course, is not sufficient to provide adequate descriptions and interpretations of the irreducibility of the sacred. The scholar, whether personally a believer or nonbeliever, must also be concerned with methodological procedure, intersubjective checks, and means of verifying one's irreducibly religious interpretations.

Therefore the nonbeliever can assume the irreducibility of the sacred when trying to describe and interpret the meaning and significance of mythic and other religious phenomena for the believer or when trying to interpret the religious meaning of mythic and symbolic structures even if they are not understood consciously or unconsciously by the believer. The nonbeliever may be satisfied with such a scholarly achievement. Perplexed by certain mythic phenomena, scholars may satisfy their intellectual curiosity by imaginatively recreating and interpreting the religious meaning of the mythic world. Indeed, Eliade himself is personally sceptical of the truth claims of some of his mythic and religious data, but he nevertheless has a tremendous curiosity and desire to uncover mythic structures and interpret mythic meaning in order to make some sense of what mythic people believe and why myths have such power over people's lives.

None of these rejoinders are meant to deny the fact that most nonbelievers will probably be personally and intellectually dissatisfied with religious accounts and will want to go beyond the perspectives of believers and beyond any irreducibly religious interpretation of myth. When they do, Eliade and other religionists have no right to assert *a priori* that reductionistic interpretations and explanations in the social and natural sciences, philosophy, and other disciplines are false.

TECHNICAL ANALYSIS OF REDUCTIONISM AND ELIADE'S THEORY

At the same time that Eliade formulated his attacks on reductionism, there emerged a complex and sophisticated theoretical literature in the philosophy of science in terms of which "reduction" and "reductionism" were given their technical definitions and analyses. It is tempting, as some critics have done, to apply such philosophical analysis to Eliade's antireductionist "theory" to determine if his critique of reduction can be justified on scientific grounds.

Although it may disappoint many of the critics, it seems to me that discussing some of the technical debates on reductionism within philosophy of science and relating the various theoretical models and analyses to Eliade's formulations on reductionism is largely a waste of time if our focus is on making sense of Eliade's approach to myth. If we apply such technical theoretical analysis to Eliade's formulations, the result is usually predictable: Eliade's antireductionism is vague, confused, uncritical, unscientific, and indefensible.

Typical is the outright dismissal by Thomas Ryba, who after listing fundamental questions central to investigating the foundations of the possibility of reduction, simply asserts the following: "In asking these questions, it seems to me that the antireductionist approach of Eliade is besides the point, because Eliade's own approach has little to do with science as it is practiced by natural or social scientists. It would better be termed—to indulge in a neologism—religiosophy. . . . The way I framed my preceding comments about Eliade is a clue to my general position about the rigor of most theories proposed by religionists—which, if not already transparent, is that they are, for the most part, muddleheaded."[27] Similar is the typical assertion of Donald Wiebe that only reductionistic approaches meet scientific criteria and are "appropriate for the *scientific* study of religion." Therefore, regardless of how one assesses the truth or falsity of Eliade's antireductionistic account on nonscientific grounds, his approach has nothing to do with a "scientific" investigation of myth and religion.[28]

As one attempts to apply the scientific analysis on reductionism to Eliade's approach, there emerges a definite feeling that something is wrong: that Eliade and the scholars of scientific reductionism are talking at cross-purposes. Even more to the point: although their respective vocabularies emphasize the terms "reduce," "reduction," and "reductionism," they seem to be speaking different languages. There is no evidence that Eliade was aware of the technical debates on reductionism within philosophy of science. For example, one cannot even imagine him debating whether the formal or logical conditions of scientific reduction as a methodological procedure within philosophy of science are appropriate for the study of myth. Indeed, Eliade seemed completely uninterested in such scientific debates on reductionism and had little concern as to whether he would be considered "unscientific" in terms of such scientific models and criteria.[29]

Therefore, in this concluding section on Eliade's antireductionist approach to myth and religion, we will not formulate the technical scientific models and analyses but will instead focus on three topics. First, the most general and widespread definition of reductionism in terms of reducing complexity to simplicity will be used to shed light on Eliade's approach. Second, an important claim on the relation of theory to phenomena or data made in some of the theoretical literature will be examined and related to Eliade's approach. Finally, it will be shown that although Eliade was not interested in the scientific debates on reductionism from the philosophy of science, a very different literature on reductionism did fascinate him.

Reduction as Simplifying the Complexity

The most general and widely held meaning of "reductionism" is that of "a procedure or theory that reduces complex data or phenomena to simpler terms."[30] As Daniel Pals notes, "In its basic sense a 'reduction' is a form of explanation; it arises from the essential (and laudable) desire of all science for simplicity in the face of complexity, its search for singularity in the presence of multiplicity.... At this specifically defined level, reduction might well be called the cardinal principle of all science; its purpose is to explain, to simplify by connecting."[31]

In this basic sense, Eliade's antireductionistic assumption of the irreducibility of the sacred, as seen in Fenton's critique, involves reducing by simplifying the complexity of mythic and other religious phenomena. Eliade recognizes that there are countless, extremely diverse mythic expressions referring to supernatural or transcendent beings and realities. In terms of his theory of myth and religion and his phenomenological approach to the data, he connects mythic phenomena through the universal category or structure of the sacred, thus simplifying the complexity of the mythic data. Indeed, reductionistic critics have often accused Eliade of gross oversimplification by an extreme reduction of the complexity of his data to a few, simple, theoretical principles and terms.

Too much emphasis on reducing the complexity of mythic and other religious phenomena through a procedure of simplification runs the risk of obscuring an opposite tendency in Eliade's approach. As was seen, he often attacks Freud and other reductionists for providing simple, narrow explanations of complex mythic and other religious data. Even more to the point, while Eliade wants to present more adequate, coherent, meaningful interpretations of the mythic data, he delights in paradox, contradiction, enigma, mystery, and complexity that resists reductive simplification. He usually has little use for Ockham's razor in choosing between competing interpretations. While he shows little interest in the criteria of scientific reductionism, simplification, and theory translatability, he shows great interest in literary, aesthetic,

mystical, and other approaches that place highest priority on the
irreducible complexity of cultural creativity. Eliade sometimes uses the
term "science of religion," but for him this is a creative scholarly
approach to religion that should not imitate dominant, Western,
scientific models of reductive simplification. And as was emphasized
throughout chapter 1, Eliade's antireductionism is directed much more
at the reduction of religious to nonreligious phenomena than at the
reduction of complexity to simplicity.

Theory and Religious Phenomena or Data

One of the most frequent themes in the writings of scholars of religion
who use models of scientific reductionism involves a clear-cut distinction between reductive theory and the actual religious phenomena,
facts, or data. Scientific reductionism, it is claimed, operates on a
theoretical level. It involves theories about theories, about how theories
may be reduced to other theories, and theoretical explanations accounting for conceptual changes in scientific knowledge. Theories may be
reduced, not phenomena or data.

This argument has been stated most forcefully and persistently by
Hans Penner. Along with Edward Yonan, he contends that "reduction is
an operation concerned with theories or systems of statements, not with
phenomena, data, or the properties of phenomena." Scientific scholars
of reductionism do not maintain "that reduction wipes out, levels, or
demeans the phenomena or data being explained. On the contrary,
reduction in the sciences implies an *explanation* of one *theory* by the
use of another in the same discipline (or, different disciplines). The sole
purpose of reduction is to offer adequate theoretical explanations and to
provide for the continued progress of scientific knowledge." The
confused "popular conception" of Eliade on this methodological issue
of reductionism "is simply false."[32] Eliade and other religionists
completely misunderstand reductionism when they fear that it will in
any way undermine, diminish, or explain away religion and the mythic
and religious data. If in falsely resisting reductionism, Eliade insists
that the sacred is some irreducibly religious, transcendent source and
essence of religion and "is not a theoretical object," so that the proper
study of religion is "exempted from intertheoretical reduction," then

such an approach has nothing in common with serious, scholarly, scientific approaches to religion.[33] As noted, Eliade's antireductionism can then be dismissed as hopelessly confused, uncritical, and unscientific.

This attack on Eliade's antireductionism for misunderstanding and fearing that reduction threatens the existence of religion itself is usually misdirected. As an aside, in many passages Eliade shows extreme hostility toward the dominant forms of Western religion and claims that they are already demeaned, ossified, and "dead." As a matter of fact, the central concern in most of Eliade's antireductionist formulations is more the fear that reductionistic explanations threaten his anti-reductionist theory, method, and discipline which are necessary to do justice to the irreducibly religious, mythic phenomena.

Without presenting similar formulations and attacks on Eliade by other reductionists, let me simply observe that the situation may be far more complex and open to honest debate than some reductionists rather arrogantly and dogmatically assume. Some reductionists seem to operate within a framework of classical empiricism, as seen in the influential works of David Hume and continuing through the writings of many twentieth-century philosophers, in which a clear-cut dichotomy is made between foundational sense impressions (objective data) and ideas, concepts, theories (based on the sense data, but often subjective and unverifiable). Much of contemporary philosophy has critiqued and rejected such a naive empirical view of objective data, facts, or givens. Similarly, much of the technical literature on scientific reductionism, as seen in the best-known account—the Derivational Model of Intertheoretic Reduction by Ernest Nagel—assumes a dominant neo-positivist philosophical framework that no longer is widely accepted by philosophers.

In short, the nature and status of "phenomena," "data," "facts," and "theory" and the relationship between theory and religious phenomena or data may be very complex and not a closed matter. Without minimizing the serious criticisms of Eliade for being "unscientific," some reductionists should be more modest in their claims that, say, anyone who does not recognize that theoretical reduction has nothing to do with phenomena or "things" is absolutely wrong. It is not my intention to explore the many analyses challenging such traditional clear-cut dichotomies as descriptive-normative, objective-subjective, and fact-theory that are central to analyzing the relation of theory to phenomena or data. Only two general observations relevant to Eliade's antireductionist approach will be presented.

First, it is not obvious that reductionistic theories always have absolutely no effect on the religious phenomena they attempt to explain. Granted, there is a basic sense, consistent with the initial methodological primacy we granted the irreducibility of the religious, in which a scholar respects on a largely descriptive manifest level the religious nature of the religious data. The scholar may then formulate a reductionistic, nonreligious explanation of the data. The scholar's theory may displace other theories, but the basic religious phenomena or data, experienced as irreducibly religious by religious people, remain unaffected by the scholar's theoretical explanation.

Nevertheless, Pals is correct when granting that reduction certainly applies to theories, but that "theories, after all, are about things." "Penner and Yonan seem to be saying that because there is such a thing as theoretical reduction, there is no such thing as ontological reduction. The current literature of explanation offers little support for such a notion. It recognizes a *distinction* between ontological and theoretical, but then goes on to assume there is a connection, though there is no clear agreement on its precise nature."[34]

When we examine what actually occurs when religious people, such as some of our students, study reductionistic accounts of religion, the matter of the relation of theory to things becomes very complicated. Consider very briefly a little of the reductionistic accounts of Eliade's most targeted reductionists, Freud and Marx, who are often Segal's favorites. In reading Freud's *The Future of an Illusion,* the religious student is exposed to what is often a very disturbing explanation. Religion is analyzed as an immature, neurotic condition. Unable to cope with threatening forces of nature, the believer, dogmatically and with little concern for reason or evidence, believes in illusions created as the result of imaginary wish-fulfillment. Such illusions can be explained in terms of the religious person's regression to a childlike wish-fulfillment experience of dependence on one's father. The clear implication of this Freudian account is that a rational, psychologically mature adult would have no need for religion.[35]

In reading Marx's "Contribution to the Critique of Hegel's *Philosophy of Right:* Introduction," the student is exposed to an analysis of religion as a symptom of a more basic negative condition of human powerlessness and alienation. Religion, as an "inverted world consciousness," is an imaginary projection arising from and reflecting a real world of alienation, suffering, and oppression. Rather than dealing with the real causes of alienation, religious people create religious illusions by projecting all that is positive and lacking in this alienated world onto some imaginary, unreal, supernatural world. Once again, the clear message is that rational, unalienated human beings will free themselves from religious illusion and address the real causes of the exploitation and injustice that afflict humankind.[36]

Now there is certainly no necessary relation between studying such reductionistic explanations and the diminishment or complete removal of religious phenomena from the religious student's life. Most religious students reject Freudian and Marxian explanations. Many others find the explanations theoretically convincing but still manage to live in two, often contradictory worlds, since religion continues to fulfill deep needs. But there are students who find the theoretical explanations convincing and then experience confusion, anxiety, crisis, and a sense of personal loss. In some cases, their religious phenomena may even be "explained away." They may no longer be able to take seriously what had been meaningful religious myths or to participate with sincere faith in what had been meaningful religious rituals.[37]

Similarly, Eliade is not completely confused and absolutely without cause to feel that his discipline of history of religions *(Religionswissenschaft)* is threatened by reductionistic approaches. He may be wrong, but he has reason to worry that Freudian, Marxian, and various historical and scientific reductionisms may "explain away" the irreducibly religious phenomena that have given rise to the need for his "autonomous" discipline with its irreducibly religious orientation.

None of these cautions are meant to insulate Eliade's anti-reductionism or accept the claim that all reductionistic accounts are *a priori* false. As a matter of fact, Freud and Marx present powerful explanatory theories for making sense of much of religion. A student who does not take seriously their reductionistic accounts is not a serious student of religion. The point is simply that the theory-data or theory-phenomena relation is more complicated than has sometimes been presented.

Second, and much more fundamental, it is not clear that there are such basic religious "data" or "phenomena" so free from theoretical interpretation and explanation. Not only does this pertain to the level of interpretation and explanation of phenomena by religious mythic people and to the latent level of interpretation and explanation by scholars of myth and religion. Even on the manifest level of "immediate" perceptions and sensations, we may hesitate to embrace traditional classifications of phenomena as completely uninterpreted and unexplained, value-free, theory-free, bare data. Even what may appear to be simple phenomena, data or "facts" may in varying degrees be surprisingly complex and, at least to some extent, the result of constituting, synthesizing subjects.

Consider briefly what certainly seem to be the least controversial kinds of examples often offered by reductionists: a simple sensation, such as experiencing pain, or a simple perception, such as perceiving the changes in the lunar cycle. It would seem that Hempel, Nagel, and others are correct: one's scientific theory attempting to account for these phenomena in no way denies, explains away, or affects the basic experience of the pain or of the changing lunar cycle.

It was not without reason that classical philosophers, recognizing the subjective aspects of pain and similar experiences, refused to classify them as primary qualities of things. What strikes one about asceticism and other phenomena in the history of religions is not only how variously "pain" has been interpreted, explained, endured, and justified but also how it has been experienced in such radically different ways. In some cases, data of "simple pain" are not even experienced as pain. In short, what seems simple may be very complex. Mythic beliefs, theoretical interpretations and explanations, religious assumptions, and a complex process of cultural socialization may be integral constitutive aspects of what at first seems to be a simple, given sensation.

The case of "simple perception" is even more revealing and relevant to many of Eliade's claims about the dialectic of the sacred and the profane and the functioning of symbolic and mythic structures. Modern persons look at the moon and do not "see" what mythic persons observe. This is not simply a case of religious and nonreligious persons observing the same lunar cycle, starting with the same perceptual datum, and then *homo religiosus* interpreting the religious mythic meaning of this phenomenon as revealing endless cycles of birth, death, and rebirth, of inexhaustible life repeating itself rhythmically. One cannot so clearly dichotomize observational and theoretical languages and then specify the qualities of observational statements free of all theoretical content, as Hempel, Nagel, and others propose. Because of mythic beliefs and other theoretical content, specific religious and other linguistic acquisition, specific religious and other motives, religious and other assumptions, and other aspects of cultural socialization, the mythic and religious person actually intuits and perceives—often on a prereflective unconscious level—different phenomena, structures, and meanings when observing the moon.

These considerations are true not only of the mythic religious person on the experiential level, but also of the scholar of religion attempting to account for the mythic and other religious phenomena. Even before formulating explicit scholarly interpretations and explanations, what the investigator focuses on and selects as legitimate religious data in need of interpretation and how the scholar describes the basic uninterpreted phenomena cannot be understood as phenomena unaffected by theory. On the basis of largely unacknowledged assumptions, tacit normative judgments, and theoretical views about myth and religion, Eliade claims to "see" all sorts of religious phenomena, structures, and meanings unrecognized or denied by other scholars, and vice versa.

For example, using an extension of some of the analysis of "vocabularies of motive" from C. Wright Mills, Eliade as scholar, as well as mythic persons themselves, imputes and doesn't simply describe certain religious motives.[38] In terms of a dominant religious vocabulary of motives, he attempts to make sense of the mythic and religious world of human relations and interactions. As a specific kind of antireductionistic scholar, he has been socialized in such a way that his descriptions and interpretations are guided by a specific vocabulary of motive in terms of the sacred. Assuming and privileging such a dominant vocabulary of religious motive, Eliade is able to describe his basic data or phenomena in certain ways, while necessarily devaluing, dismissing, or not recognizing alternative vocabularies of motive integral to the complex, constituted, descriptive phenomena of other scholarly approaches.

Mircea Eliade often presents his antireductionism and phenomenological approach in ways that seem exceedingly naive with regard to this complex theory-phenomena relation. He frequently asserts that he simply collects empirical, religious facts or data that need to be interpreted. Indeed, there is a pervasive sense in which Eliade's view of mythic and other religious experiences incorporates this unacceptable clear-cut dichotomy. As will become evident, Eliade usually asserts that the sacred manifests itself, the essential symbolic and mythic structures reveal certain meanings, and so forth. Phenomenologically and ontologically not unlike the expressions found in most traditional, religious accounts, Eliade often conveys a specific sense of essence preceding existence. The essential, metaphysical, sacred reality is taken as an ontological given, and real, existing human beings discover, find, and experience that given that is already there. Thus Eliade often conveys the sense that *homo religiosus* is rather passive, simply experiencing the religious phenomena revealed to him or her, and is not a dynamic, constituting subject whose language, assumptions, and beliefs play a vital role in how and what phenomena are constituted.

With some very notable exceptions, most Western philosophy since Immanuel Kant has emphasized the indispensable role of the self as dynamic, synthesizing subject in constituting experience, phenomena, and meaning.[39] Rejected as naive and inadequate have been empirical, positivistic, and other traditional approaches that assume the existence of value-free, uninterpreted, objective, given data, facts, or phenomena free from the influences of assumptions, beliefs, and theories.

In *Structure and Creativity in Religion,* I tried to reconstruct and at times reformulate Eliade's phenomenological approach to deal with some of these methodological difficulties. For example, I made considerable use of the concept of a *"constituted given."*[40] Phenomenologically, religious and nonreligious persons encounter a world of phenomena already given, already constituted, not of their own making. This sense of givenness includes a specific mode of production and system of economic relations, forms of linguistic acquisition, political and legal institutions, social structures including class and gender and other relations of domination, dominant cultural and ideological forms, military and other coercive forces, systems of ethics and views of human nature, religious myths and rituals and institutions, and so forth. This sense of givenness is necessary but not sufficient for understanding the real experiential world of religious and secular phenomena. This real sense of givenness is both limiting but also enabling. The real world of mythic phenomena involves how perceiving, willing, feeling, imagining, conceptualizing, synthesizing, constituting subjects relate to the givenness: what they accept or reject, consciously or unconsciously; what symbolic possibilities are appropriated and how they are revalorized; and how the mythic phenomena are reconstituted as mythic or nonmythic phenomena. In other words, as constituted givens, mythic, religious, and other phenomena are very complex and cannot be understood in terms of a sharp dichotomy between theory and phenomenon.

Scientific Reductionism and Eliade's Different Interests

As one reads some of the technical literature on reductionism, especially in the philosophy of science, it is not always evident what proponents, much less opponents, of reductionism in the study of religion mean by the term. A number of the contributors to *Religion and Reductionism,* including staunch supporters of Robert Segal's defense of reductionism, have indicated that it is not even clear precisely what Segal means by "reductionism."

What one finds are many radically different, competing theories of reductionism. Thomas Ryba, for example, presents Daniel Bonevac's classification of six major varieties of reduction in the natural sciences and mathematics. Best known is Nagel's Derivational Model of Intertheoretic Reduction with its two necessary conditions of connectability and derivability and its assumption that reduction is a variety of logical entailment.[41] Edward Yonan presents Arthur Peacocke's classification of three kinds of reductionism: methodological, ontological, and epistemological. He then presents a similar, more developed classification of three models of reduction from Sahotra Sarkar: theory reduction (similar to methodological reductionism and including the Nagel-Schaffner type), explanatory reduction (is epistemological reductionism), and constitutive reduction (is ontological reductionism), with each of these models exemplified by several types of reductionism.[42]

To cite only one other classification, Ivan Strenski presents the "primary classes" of reduction according to "kinds," "directions," and "interpretations" of reductions. Most interesting is his use of Paul Feyerabend to illustrate the class of "interpretations" of reduction "by replacement." Unlike Nagel's "interpretation" of reduction "by deduction"—which, according to Strenski, has no relevance for the present state of scholarship in religious studies—this interpretation emphasizes discontinuity in the growth of knowledge, theoretical change or reduction in terms of new paradigms or models of things, and the wholesale dismissal of one theory and its replacement by another. According to Strenski, it is this reduction by replacement that Eliade really fears (while practicing his own extreme reduction by replacement): the total replacement of his irreducibly religious "picture" by some nonreligious model.[43]

While the application of theoretical clarifications and debates on reductionism from philosophy of science to the study of religion may be of some value, it seems largely to miss the point if one is trying to make sense of Eliade's critique of reductionism. For example, the youthful Eliade was a voracious reader and professed a strong interest in science, especially in etymology. But there is no evidence in his many antireductionistic writings that the youthful Eliade was aware of, much less threatened by, a technical Russellian reduction that might translate all statements about religious objects into scientific statements. Similarly, Eliade's writings of the 1930s and 1940s repeatedly express his concerns about the dangers of reductionism. But there is no evidence that Eliade was aware of, much less threatened by, a technical Carnapian reduction that might construct a logical system in terms of which one could not only translate but also show the meaninglessness of Eliadean religious formulations. Eliade, of course, frequently lashed out at positivism, materialism, and historicism—often rather uncritically lumping them together in his attacks on reductionism—but he showed no interest in the technical formulations on reductionism in the philosophy of science.

Similarly, in the decades after World War II, Eliade showed no interest in, or even awareness of, the derivational models of intertheoretic reduction or the later counterfactual models of reduction in the natural sciences. One could attempt to apply such theoretical clarifications, analyses, and debates to Eliade's formulations. For example, a scholar could submit that Eliade was most threatened by derivational models of reduction in which one theory (say, of religion) reduces to and is explained by another reducing theory (say, of one of the social sciences). Or a scholar could submit that Eliade did in fact agree with counterfactual models that there is a fundamental logical incompatibility of two theories (say, religious and secular), while then opposing the addition of special provisions allowing for reduction. A scholar could also submit that Eliade was most threatened by "reduction by replacement," but one can make this same kind of obvious point without the technical theories of Paul Feyerabend, Rom Harré, and other philosophers of science.

In short, while such technical debates on methodological, epistemological, and ontological reductionism can be used to argue that Eliade was hopelessly unscientific, such efforts have limited explanatory value when trying to grasp Eliade's antireductionist approach to myth and religion. What such efforts with their focus on technical scientific theories neglect is that there were strong, very different influences on Eliade's views of reductionism that may be more instructive for understanding his position.[44]

Without providing documentation or enumerating the great number and variety of influences, suffice it to indicate that Eliade was always drawn, through his readings and personal relations, to scholars and literary and other figures who opposed what they evaluated as negative, post-Enlightenment, reductionistic influences in modern Western life:

excessive rationalistic forms of reductionism that ignored or devalued the imagination and nonrational phenomena; glorification of scientific and technological reductionism that ignored or devalued other modes of experience and of cognition; and narrow secular forms of reductionism that ignored or devalued spiritual, mythic, aesthetic, and other phenomena.

The dominant early antireductionist influence on Eliade emerged through the writings and personal example of Nae Ionescu. Although he may have been Professor of Logic and Metaphysics at the University of Bucharest, in his so-called religious antireductionism Ionescu emphasized an "irrationalist" approach to "lived experience"; a highly personal, engaged, existential philosophy of "authenticity"; and a mystical, spiritual orientation incorporating an Eastern Orthodox Christian metaphysics with love as an essential instrument of cognition.

Eliade's autobiography, journal, and other writings are full of appreciation for the contributions of scholars outside of and critical of dominant, modern, reductionistic, Western traditions of philosophy, culture, and science. He often believed that their metaphysical, synthesizing, spiritual orientations represented the higher consciousness and superior knowledge, the new science, philosophy, and humanism of the future. One could enumerate a long list of such significant, influential figures, many of whom are primarily identified with romanticism, mysticism, alchemy, and the occult. A small sample includes Goethe, B. P. Hasdeu, Balzac, G. Papini, V. Macchioro, E. Buonaiuti, E. M. Cioran, E. Ionescu, L. Blaga, G. Tucci, Henry Corbin, A. Coomaraswamy, R. Steiner, R. Guénon, J. Evola, P. Mus, and scholars associated with the Eranos Conference at Ascona.[45]

Significant, although rarely acknowledged by Eliade, was the great influence of philosophical phenomenology on his attempts to formulate an antireductionist phenomenological method and antireductionist morphological classification of mythic structures and meanings.[46] As a student of philosophy in the 1920s and as a teacher of philosophy in the 1930s, Eliade could not have been unaware of the vigorous attacks on "psychologism," "scientism," and other forms of modern reductions by Edmund Husserl and later phenomenologists. Not much influenced by Husserl's "transcendental phenomenology," Eliade's antireductionist approach has more in common with the "existential phenomenology" of French and other European writers and especially with the "hermeneutic phenomenology" of such philosophers as Martin Heidegger and Paul Ricoeur. In different ways, major characteristics from philosophical phenomenology—aiming for a radically descriptive science or approach that does justice to the phenomena themselves, claiming to adopt an antireductionist approach that opposes all forms of reductionism, focusing on intentionality or the intentional structure of phenomena, emphasizing the need for the phenomenological epoché or "bracketing" on the part of the investigator, and adopting a method that attempts to achieve the eidetic vision or insight into essential structures and meanings—all find a prominent place in how Eliade conceives of his antireductionist interpretation of myth and religion.

In short, there have been many traditions using antireductionist language that have influenced Eliade and have existed largely or totally independent of the debates on reductionism within twentieth-century philosophy of science. This is not to deny that Eliade was often uncritical in his antireductionistic formulations and that his extreme attacks on other approaches open him to counterattacks. But to appreciate his attempt to provide an antireductionist interpretation of myth and religion, it is necessary to incorporate influences and concerns not captured by the technical debates in the philosophy of science.

NOTES

1. John Y. Fenton, "Reductionism in the Study of Religions," *Soundings* 53 (1970): 62.

2. Ibid., pp. 63, 64. Fenton goes on to argue for the value of various reductive studies of religions (pp. 64-67) and to challenge the view that religions must be studied as something religious (pp. 67-71).

3. See Allen, *Structure and Creativity in Religion,* pp. 98-101.

4. See Douglas Allen, "Phenomenology of Religion," in *The Encyclopedia of Religion,* vol. 11 (New York: Macmillan, 1987), p. 283.

5. Willard G. Oxtoby, *"Religionswissenschaft* Revisited," in *Religions in Antiquity: Essays in Memory of Erwin Ramsdell Goodenough,* ed. Jacob Neusner (Leiden: E. J. Brill, 1968), pp. 560-608, argues that phenomenology within *Religionswissenschaft* has endorsed the faith of religious persons and has itself become something religious rather than scientific. While granting that

various scholars identified with phenomenology of religion within *Religions-wissenschaft* have assumed such a religious orientation, I would submit that a methodological approach more consistent with philosophical phenomenology can avoid such a theologistic defending the faith.

6. Rosalind Shaw, "Feminist Anthropology and the Gendering of Religious Studies," in *Religion and Gender,* ed. Ursula King (Oxford: Black-well, 1995), p. 68. For other feminist approaches to Eliade, see Valerie Saiving, "Androcentism in Religious Studies," *Journal of Religion* 56 (1976): 177-97, and Carol Christ, "Mircea Eliade and the Feminist Paradigm Shift," *Journal of Feminist Studies* 7 (1991): 75-94

7. Shaw, "Feminist Anthropology and the Gendering of Religious Studies," pp. 69, 70. While agreeing with Shaw that the dominant history and phenomenology of religion have functioned this way, I am not convinced that all versions of the phenomenological *epoché* necessarily entail this insulation from questions of standpoint, power, and privilege. A phenomenological approach, integrated with other approaches, might be invaluable in opening up Shaw's "view from below"; in recovering and doing justice to the specific intentionalities and subjectivities of the experiences and silenced voices of oppressed and exploited peoples.

8. Similarly, it is at first surprising and perhaps revealing that Eliade, although obsessed with the need to attack "reductionists" and to insist on the irreducibility of the sacred, never felt the need to engage his reductionistic opponents in debate. For the most part, he simply asserted his antireductionism and ignored criticisms of his approach. In the next section, I shall suggest some reasons that Eliade may have not been very interested in the technical methodological debates over reductionism.

9. See Robert A. Segal, "In Defense of Reductionism" (cited p. 23, n. 22), reprinted in revised form with an addendum in his *Religion and the Social Sciences.* We shall use the revised "In Defense of Reductionism" in *Religion and the Social Sciences* rather than the original journal version. This book is a collection of thirteen of Segal's articles and reviews, many of which have a focus on reductionism. A second collection of ten of his articles was published as Robert A. Segal, *Explaining and Interpreting Religion: Essays on the Issue* (New York: Peter Lang, 1992). Segal's writings on reductionism, especially his "In Defense of Reductionism" and his attacks on Eliade's approach, served as the focus for Thomas A. Idinopulos and Edward A. Yonan, eds., *Religion and Reductionism: Essays on Eliade, Segal, and the Challenge of the Social Sciences for the Study of Religion.*

10. See Segal, "In Defense of Reductionism," p. 28, and Robert A. Segal and Donald Wiebe, "Axioms and Dogmas in the Study of Religion," republished in Segal, *Explaining and Interpreting Religion,* pp. 45-47.

11. Segal, "In Defense of Reductionism," pp. 12-13, 24.

12. Segal, "Reductionism in the Study of Religion," in *Religion and Reductionism,* ed. Idinopulos and Yonan, p. 5.

13. See *Quest,* pp. 132-33.

14. Ivan Strenski, "Reduction without Tears," in *Religion and Reductionism,* ed. Idinopulos and Yonan, p. 101. See Shaw, "Feminist Anthropology and the Gendering of Religious Studies," pp. 69-70. For a reductionist approach generally in agreement with Segal but critical of some of this question-begging argument, see Donald Wiebe, "Beyond the Sceptic and the Devotee: Reductionism in the Scientific Study of Religion," in *Religion and Reductionism,* ed. Idinopulos and Yonan, pp. 111-12.

15. See, for example, Segal, "In Defense of Reductionism," pp. 6-13. In this revised version of "In Defense of Reductionism," Segal has retained his formulations of "the believer's point of view" and has equated this point of view with the believer's "conscious" view, but he has added notes indicating that he has now "come to realize that Eliade is *not* identifying the irreducibility of religion with its irreducibility for believers, in whom Eliade is in fact interested only secondarily. Eliade is primarily interested in the irreducibility of religion in and of itself" (p. 6 n. 2).

16. See, for example, Segal, "Are Historians of Religions Necessarily Believers?" pp. 37-41, and Segal, "In Defense of Reductionism," pp. 8-12. After completing this and later chapters, I came across Segal's essay "How Historical Is the History of Religions?" reproduced as chap. 9 in his *Explaining and Interpreting Religion.* Segal says that after reading Quinton Skinner he realized that he had been wrong in thinking that Eliade's intention was primarily to present his interpretations of religious phenomena "from the believer's point of view." Segal now realizes that "Eliade is really appealing not to the meaning of religion for believers but to the meaning—better, significance—of religion itself" (p. 143). In *Structure and Creativity in Religion,* I make many of these same claims, as seen in my section distinguishing "meaning for *homo religiosus* versus meaning for Eliade (pp. 208-12) and sections on Eliade's interpretations and normative judgments that go far beyond, and often contradict, the understanding of religious believers.

17. W. Brede Kristensen, *The Meaning of Religion,* trans. John B. Carman (The Hague: Martinus Nijhoff, 1960), pp. 2, 6, 14.

18. Wilfred Cantwell Smith, "Comparative Religion: Whither—and Why?" in *The History of Religions: Essays in Methodology,* ed. Mircea Eliade and Joseph M. Kitagawa (Chicago: University of Chicago Press, 1959), p. 42. Smith's position on the need to respect the believer's point of view is developed in his *The Meaning and End of Religion* (New York: Macmillan, 1963), *The Faith of Other Men* (New York: Mentor Books, 1963), and *Faith and Belief* (Princeton: Princeton University Press, 1979).

19. In *Structure and Creativity in Religion,* I attempt to elucidate and analyze many levels of "descriptive evaluations" in Eliade's approach.

20. See Jonathan Z. Smith, *Map Is Not Territory* (Leiden: E. J. Brill, 1978).

21. See Thomas A. Idinopulos, "Must Professors of Religion be Religious? Comments on Eliade's Method of Inquiry and Segal's Defense of Reductionism," in *Religion and Reductionism,* ed. Idinopulos and Yonan, pp. 75-77.

22. In *Structure and Creativity in Religion,* esp. chap. 7 "Descriptive Evaluations and Levels of Meaning," I analyze many of these issues. For example, in the section entitled "meaning for *homo religiosus* versus meaning for Eliade" (pp. 208-12), I attempt to reformulate this dichotomy as "conscious meaning for *homo religiosus*" versus "total meaning for *homo religiosus.*" Although such a reformulation has merit in allowing us to understand many of Eliade's interpretations that seem to go far beyond the views of believers, I also show that Eliade sometimes makes ontological assumptions, presents normative judgments, and offers interpretations that go beyond any perspective of *homo religiosus.*

23. In several writings, Segal correctly maintains that this clear-cut interpretation versus explanation dichotomy can mean many different things and often imposes an oversimplified and false state of affairs. For example, while Eliade certainly places his highest priority on interpreting the meaning and significance of the sacred, he often attempts to explain the nature, source, and function of mythic and other religious phenomena in religious terms. On the other side, reductionistic social scientists often attempt to interpret the meaning, as well as provide explanations, of their data. See, for example, Segal, "Reductionism in the Study of Religion," pp. 6-10; Segal, "Fending Off the Social Sciences," in Segal, *Explaining and Interpreting Religion,* pp. 29-31; and Segal, "Misconceptions of the Social Sciences," in *Explaining and Interpreting Religion,* pp. 11-13. See also J. Samuel Preus, *Explaining Religion* (New Haven: Yale University Press, 1987), p. ix.

24. Segal, "In Defense of Reductionism," p. 21. See, esp. pp. 20-25. In his "Addendum" (pp. 27-28), Segal provides a list of brief responses to the criticisms of his position formulated by Donald Wiebe, "Beyond the Sceptic and the Devotee: Reductionism in the Scientific Study of Religion," *Journal of the American Academy of Religion* 52 (1984): 157-65, and Daniel Pals, "Reductionism and Belief: An Appraisal of Recent Attacks on the Doctrine of Irreducible Religion," *Journal of Religion* 66 (1986): 18-36. Some of Segal's responses in this "Addendum" seem to weaken, confuse, or even contradict some of his forceful, earlier claims. He does reaffirm that "the decisive issue is whether [the nonbeliever] can appreciate [i.e., accept] the *reality* of [the object of] religion for the believer."

25. See, for example, Hendrik Kraemer, *Religion and the Christian Faith* (Philadelphia: Westminster Press, 1956), pp. 50-53, and Hendrik Kraemer, *The Christian Message in a Non-Christian World* (London: James Clarke, 1956), pp. 61ff.

26. These examples also illustrate our previous point: that Eliade is not primarily concerned with interpreting religion in the terms of the believer. He knows that such fundamentalists, as well as most other Christians and Muslims, express their religious beliefs in terms of exclusivistic, absolute truth claims. And yet he interprets these same religious expressions as limited, relative, partial valorizations of complex, multivalent, universal systems of symbols.

27. Thomas Ryba, "Are Religious Theories Susceptible to Reduction?" in *Religion and Reductionism,* ed. Idinopulos and Yonan, pp. 17-18.

28. Donald Wiebe, "Postscript: On Method, Metaphysics, and Reductionism," in *Religion and Reductionism,* ed. Idinopulos and Yonan, pp. 120-21.

29. Although he frequently attacked reductionistic approaches to myth and religion, Eliade felt little need to respond to reductionists and other critics of his history or religions. Even at age 70, he wrote "For myself, I plan someday to dedicate an entire work to discussing the objections put forth by some of my critics, those who are responsible and acting in all good faith (for the others do not deserve the bother of a reply)." See Mircea Eliade, "Foreword," to my *Structure and Creativity in Religion,* p. vii. It would seem that he felt that almost all of his reductionistic critics did not deserve the bother of a reply, and Eliade never got around to responding to his responsible critics who were acting in good faith.

30. *Webster's Ninth New Collegiate Dictionary* (Springfield, Mass.: Merriam-Webster, 1987), p. 988, or *Webster's Third New International Dictionary of the English Language* (Springfield, Mass.: Merriam-Webster, 1959), p. 1905. See Ryba, "Are Religious Theories Susceptible to Reduction?" p. 19 and p. 19 n. 12; and Arvind Sharma, "What Is Reductionism?" in *Religion and Reductionism,* ed. Idinopulos and Yonan, p. 128. Ryba notes that this general definition, unlike many others, is the most "value neutral." Sharma notes that this definition from *Webster's* includes reference to *"oversimplification,"* thus pointing to the purpose of simplifying phenomena but also the danger of oversimplifying them.

31. Daniel L. Pals, "Is Religion a *Sui Generis* Phenomenon?" *Journal of the American Academy of Religion* 55, (1987): 261-62. Pals continues: "It is not until explanation moves beyond the relating of data in a single, clearly defined realm of experience to the more ambitious goal of explaining one entire realm of data as in fact belonging to another that reduction acquires its classic and more controversial meaning."

32. Hans H. Penner and Edward A. Yonan, "Is a Science of Religion Possible?" *Journal of Religion* 52 (1972): 130-31.

33. Hans H. Penner, *Impasse and Resolution* (New York: Peter Lang, 1989), pp. 23, 25. See William E. Paden, "Before 'The Sacred' Became Theological: Rereading the Durkheimian Legacy," in *Religion and Reductionism,* ed. Idinopulos and Yonan, pp. 198-200.

34. Daniel Pals, "Reductionism and Belief: An Appraisal of Recent Attacks on the Doctrine of Irreducible Religion," *Journal of Religion* 66 (1986): 23-25.

35. Sigmund Freud, *The Future of an Illusion,* trans. W. D. Robson-Scott (New York: Liveright, 1961), chap. 8.

36. Karl Marx, "Contribution to the Critique of Hegel's *Philosophy of Right:* Introduction," in *The Marx-Engels Reader,* ed. Robert C. Tucker (New York: W. W. Norton, 1972), pp. 11-12.

37. For a discussion of how reductionism involves redescription and how under certain conditions those redescribed may experience real loss, but with the conclusion that "reductionist agendas do not jeopardize truth" and "redescription does not entail displacement," see Tony Edwards, "Religion, Explanation, and the Askesis of Inquiry," in *Religion and Reductionism,* ed. Idinopulos and Yonan, pp. 174, 180.

38. C. Wright Mills, "Situated Actions and Vocabularies of Motive," *American Sociologist Review* 5 (1940): 904-13. For an excellent treatment of "vocabularies of motive and religion," see Lorne Dawson, "Human Reflexivity and the Nonreductive Explanation of Religious Action," in *Religion and Reductionism,* ed. Idinopulos and Yonan, pp. 158-60.

39. In the first of his "Theses on Feuerbach," I interpret Marx as maintaining that philosophical idealists, who really know nothing about objective reality, had focused on the active, thinking, imagining, constituting, experiencing subject or subjective self. On the other side, materialists such as Feuerbach and philosophers identifying with naturalistic scientific models had neglected the role of the subject engaged in sensuous practical activity. Instead they had presented an account of an impersonal, detached, passive subject contemplating and uncovering the given, objective facts and laws of nature. Both philosophical approaches are one-sided and inadequate. What is required is a dialectical integration of the subjective and the objective which does justice to the dynamic, complex, interactional relations between a real, objective, given world—a world that is not an essentialized given, but whose nature and meaning are continually constituted—and real, embodied, creative, human subjects or agents whose practical, critical activity is necessary for understanding how a meaningful world of facts and phenomena is constituted. See Karl Marx, "Theses on Feuerbach," in *The Marx-Engels Reader,* ed. Tucker, p. 107.

40. See, for example, Allen, *Structure and Creativity in Religion,* pp. 181-90.

41. Daniel Bonevac, *Reduction in the Abstract Sciences* (Cambridge: Hackett, 1982), pp. 7-59; Ryba, "Are Religious Theories Susceptible to Reduction?" pp. 19-30; Ernest Nagel, *The Structure of Science* (New York: Harcourt, Brace and World, 1961), chap. 11. See also Carl Hempel, *Philosophy of Natural Science* (Englewood Cliffs, N.J.: Prentice-Hall, 1966).

42. Arthur Peacocke, ed., *Reductionism in Academic Disciplines* (Worcester, England: Billing & Sons Ltd., 1985), pp. 3-4 and 7-16; Sahotra Sarkar, "Models of Reduction and Categories of Reductionism," *Synthese* 91 (1992): 167-94; Edward A. Yonan, "Clarifying the Strengths and Limits of Reductionism in the Discipline of Religion," in *Religion and Reductionism,* ed. Idinopulos and Yonan, pp. 45-47.

43. Paul Feyerabend, "Explanation, Reduction, and Empiricism," *Minnesota Studies in the Philosophy of Science,* vol. 3, ed. Herbert Feigl and Grover Maxwell (Minneapolis: University of Minnesota Press, 1962), pp. 28-97; Strenski, "Reduction without Tears," pp. 98-103. See also Lorne Dawson's discussion of kinds of reduction in his *Reason, Freedom and Religion: Closing the Gap Between the Humanistic and the Scientific Study of Religion* (New York: Peter Lang, 1988), pp. 161-79.

44. A clue to Eliade's very different antireductionist influences and concerns can be seen in the very tone of many of his formulations. Rather than the dispassionate, objective analysis one might expect from technical, scientific formulations of reductionism, Eliade's passages are often highly emotional and passionate, with personal attacks on the dangers and evils of reductionistic approaches.

45. Eliade was attracted to some of these and other writers not only because of his reaction against the reductionisms of modernity but also because of his reaction against a modern tendency toward narrow specialization. Eliade was always attracted to bold, synthesizing polygraphs; to "universal" authors who create polymorphous works. Such writers often attempted to integrate and synthesize the mythical and spiritual with the historical and scientific. Eliade was also attracted to various scholars, such as Raffaele Pettazzoni, who did not share his commitment to the irreducibility of the sacred.

46. See Allen, "Phenomenology of Religion," pp. 272-85; Allen, *Structure and Creativity in Religion,* esp. pp. 107-13, 190-200, 201-203, 231-32, 240-43.

CHAPTER 3

The Dialectic of the Sacred

For Mircea Eliade, myth is religious myth. Whenever Eliade points to mythic behavior, he is directing us to certain kinds of religious behavior. In chapter 7, myth will be seen to have an irreducibly religious structure and function. In chapters 8 and 9, mythic time will be viewed as sacred time and mythic history as sacred history. Not all religious phenomena, of course, may be subsumed under the category of "myth." Eliade also investigates nonmythic religious data. Eliade has a particular interest in religious symbolism and its symbolic expression in religious myths. In chapters 5 and 6, all religious expressions will be seen to be necessarily symbolic, but myth will be interpreted as a specific type of religious symbolic expression.

On the one hand, Mircea Eliade maintains that myth often provides the foundation for understanding the meaning and significance of other religious data. For example, he may first examine some folk belief about the magical value of certain medicinal herbs, such as "popular" peasant beliefs in the curative virtues of ritually applying these herbs. Often these magico-religious beliefs and practices will strike most "modern" readers as infantile, backwards, and superstitious. But, then, Eliade will show how the deeper structures and meanings of such beliefs and practices are disclosed only after they are situated within their larger, often hidden, mythic contexts: how such peasant phenomena are related to myths about the origins of medicinal herbs; how such origin myths are related to their cosmogonic myth; and how the mythic structure of sacred time and history orients these peasants so that they must abolish degenerate, worn-out, exhausted forms (integral to the illness) and return mythically to the fullness of mythic origins in order to regenerate sacred time and history as essential for the cure.[1]

On the other hand, Eliade maintains that religion provides the foundation for understanding myth. For Eliade, all myths are religious myths, and he has a specific conception of religion based on his structural analysis of the foundational experience of the sacred. Myths both make possible and give expression to central experiences of the sacred. It is the universal process of sacralization, as formulated in Eliade's dialectic of the sacred and the profane, that allows him to comprehend the structure in terms of which the sacred, through myths and other religious phenomena, manifests itself in the experiences of religious persons.

THE SACRED AND TRANSCENDENCE

Consistent with his antireductionist assumption of the irreducibility of the religious, Mircea Eliade writes that "in the title of the 'history of religions' the accent ought not to be upon the word *history,* but upon the word *religions.* For although there are numerous ways of practising *history*—from the history of technics to that of human thought—there is only one way of approaching *religion*—namely, to deal with the religious facts. Before making the *history* of anything, one must have a proper understanding of what it *is,* in and for itself."[2]

Following Roger Caillois's analysis in *Man and the Sacred,* Eliade begins by asserting that "all the definitions given up till now of the religious phenomenon have one thing in common: each has its own way of showing that the sacred and the religious life are the opposite of the profane and the secular life." Caillois admits that this sacred-profane distinction is not always sufficient to define the phenomenon of religion, but that this opposition is still involved in every definition of religion. As Eliade writes, "the dichotomy of sacred and profane is the invariable par excellence in the religious life of man."[3]

Not all scholars agree with Eliade's insistence on the centrality of the sacred-profane dichotomy. John Saliba, for example, argues that the sacred-profane dichotomy cannot be assumed to be universal and that Eliade's "definition of religion is just too narrow." Ninian Smart submits that Eliade's "key polarity" may be "an instance of a more inclusive one": whether or not something has "positive emotional charge." He suggests that "it may be that we do not need to begin with the sacred-profane polarity as an ultimate but see it in a wider theory of emotional charges and their ritual accompaniments."[4] As will be seen, many scholars charge that Eliade's clear-cut oppositional conception of religion, even when useful for helping us to grasp the meaning of "archaic" religious phenomena, is inadequate for understanding the innovations of the so-called "historical religions" (Judaism, Christianity, and Islam) and of "modern" religious phenomena.

Eliade's interpretation of the sacred emphasizes the experiential basis of religion: religion is understood as arising from existential crises and as expressing a human mode of existence in the world. "The greatest claim to merit of the history of religions is precisely its effort to decipher in a 'fact', conditioned as it is by the historical moment and the cultural style of the epoch, the existential situation that made it possible."[5] According to Eliade, religion "does not necessarily imply belief in God, gods, or ghosts, but refers to the experience of the sacred, and, consequently, is related to the ideas of *being, meaning,* and *truth.*" The sacred is that which is experienced as meaningful, real, and true. It is "an element in the structure of consciousness, not a stage in the history of consciousness." The sacred and the profane constitute "two modes of being in the world, two existential situations assumed by man in the course of history."[6]

In a summary of the orientation of archaic religion, but in terms identical with descriptions of religion in general found throughout his writings, Eliade writes that

> religion maintains the "opening" toward a superhuman world, the world of axiological values. . . . Myths are the most general and effective means of awakening and maintaining consciousness of another world, a beyond, whether it be the divine world or the world of the Ancestors. This "other world" represents a superhuman, "transcendent" plane, the plane of *absolute realities.* It is the experience of the sacred—that is, an encounter with a transhuman reality—which gives birth to the idea that something *really exists,* that hence there are absolute values capable of guiding man and giving a

meaning to human existence. It is, then, through the experience of the sacred that the ideas of *reality, truth,* and *significance* first dawn, to be later elaborated and systematized by metaphysical speculations.[7]

Thus, the meaningful, significant, real world "is the result of a dialectical process which may be called the manifestation of the sacred." Eliade claims that human beings cannot live in "chaos," or that living in "chaos," such as that defining much of the modern world, results in a fragmented, meaningless, dehumanized existence. "Human life becomes meaningful by imitating the paradigmatic models revealed by supernatural beings. The imitation of transhuman models constitutes one of the primary characteristics of 'religious' life, a structural characteristic which is indifferent to culture and epoch."[8] Those "paradigmatic," "transhuman models" are primarily revealed through myths that allow human beings to orient themselves in a centered, coherently structured, meaningful universe.

What is most characteristic of religion is its preoccupation with the sacred, which it distinguishes from the profane. Several illustrations will help us to begin to understand this sacred-profane relation. The mystical experience of "inner light," according to Eliade, "expresses always an Epiphany of the Spirit. Such experiences project the subject into another universe from that of everyday existence, radically altering his ontological status, opening him to the values of the Spirit." These experiences are religious because "they bring a man out of his worldly Universe or historical situation, and project him into a Universe different in quality, an entirely different world, transcendent and holy."[9] The religious meaning of masks is "always bound up with the idea of time": the "wearer transcends earthly time" and "personal temporal identity," thus becoming something "other" ("even when the mask is his own portrait").[10] "The frantic and ecstatic cult of Dionysus," especially the "Dionysiac orgiasm" as portrayed in the *Bacchae* of Euripides, discloses the religious meaning of "the mystery" as consisting "in the participation of the bacchantes in the total epiphany of Dionysus." "The Dionysiac ecstasy means, above all, surpassing the human condition, the discovery of total deliverance, obtaining freedom and spontaneity inaccessible to human beings."[11]

If one considers the tremendous number of descriptions of the sacred in Eliade's writings, there emerges this constant: religion always entails some aspect of *transcendence*. This is a phenomenological "invariant," an essential, universal structure of the sacred. Indeed, Eliade writes in *No Souvenirs* that the "goal" of the history of religions is *"to identify the presence of the transcendent in human experience."* This passage is especially fascinating since Eliade does not provide his almost automatic condemnation of Marx and his usual condemnation of Freud as "modern" reductionists but instead compares an essential feature of their revolutionary approaches with what he is trying to do in investigating religion and the sacred: "For several years, another thought has been haunting me as well: if it is true that Marx has analyzed and unmasked the social unconscious, and that Freud did likewise for the personal unconscious—if it is then true that psychoanalysis and Marxism teach us how to pierce through 'superstructures' to arrive at the true causes and motives, then the history of religions, as I understand it, would have the same goal: *to identify the presence of the transcendent in human experience:* to isolate—in the enormous mass of the 'unconscious'—that which is *transconscious."* Eliade adds that he has never explained "the analytical function of the history of religions, the way in which it helps us to unmask the presence of the transcendent and the suprahistorical in everyday life."[12]

This emphasis on the transcendent structure of the experience of the sacred is evident in a dramatic passage from *The Sacred and the Profane* in which Eliade contrasts the modern nonreligious mode of being in the world to the traditional religious orientation:

> The nonreligious man refuses transcendence, accepts the relativity of "reality," and may even come to doubt the meaning of existence. . . . Modern nonreligious man assumes a new existential situation; he regards himself solely as the subject and agent of history, and he refuses all appeal to transcendence. In other words, he accepts no model for humanity outside the human condition as it can be seen in the various historical situations. Man *makes himself,* and he only makes himself completely in proportion as he desacralizes himself and the world. The sacred is the prime obstacle to his freedom. He

will become himself only when he is totally demysticized. He will not
be truly free until he has killed the last god.[13]

The transcendent sacred has been described by religious persons
and by Eliade himself in such terms as "God," "divine," "supernatural,"
"absolute reality," "ultimate reality," "being," "eternal,"
"transhistorical," "infinite," "source of life," "power," and "bliss." But
Eliade intends this sense of transcendence to be viewed as a *universal*
structure of religion: to restrict it to any specific mythic or other
religious description or content—as so many missionaries, theologians,
anthropologists, and others have done—is to particularize and limit it.
All expressions are too specific. For Eliade, religion involves a radical
break with all of the profane modalities. It invariably points us
"beyond" the relative, historical, "natural" world of "ordinary"
experience. Indeed, Eliade goes as far as to assert that "the principal
function of religion" and of myth is to render human existence "open"
to a "superhuman" world of "transcendent" values.[14]

At this point, Eliade is not committed to some metaphysical or
ontological position endorsing the ultimate reality of the transcendent
sacred. In the overwhelming majority of his descriptions and interpretations of the sacred, he is pointing to an intentional structure revealed
in the religious experience. Religion involves a human mode of being
in the world in which there is a unique, irreducible, intentional relation
to the sacred experienced as transcendent. Eliade equates the sacred
with the real as the intentional object of belief. As Bryan Rennie states,
"Eliade is not discussing an ontological substratum, like Aristotle's *hyle*
or Kant's noumenal, but the psycho-phenomenological real—that
which is *apprehended* as real by the consciousness of the aware,
experiencing subject."[15] Eliade does not "assume an ontological
category existing *independently* of human involvement," a
metaphysical referent corresponding to "the sacred." "Eliade's sacred is
a systematic rather than an ontological proposition." By "the sacred,"
he is simply indicating what religious persons have perceived and
considered "the real" in the history of religions.[16]

Rennie's interpretation is valuable in countering the tendency of
scholars to attribute to Eliade a metaphysical and ontological position

whenever he uses the category of "the sacred." This tendency leads to a misinterpretation of Eliade's approach to myth and religion and his specific descriptions and interpretations of his data. However, Rennie goes too far in his reconstruction and defense of Eliade to the extent that he claims that there is only one point in the entire structure of Eliade's thought in which Eliade makes a real ontological assumption.[17] As was seen and will become increasingly clear, Eliade does not always restrict his scholarship, including many references to ontology, to the actual perceptions and awareness of religious people. He makes ontological assumptions and judgments in his formulations of universal structures of the dialectic of the sacred, symbolism, and myth; in his claims about sacred structures as being constitutive of the human condition as such; in his judgments about the primacy of nonhistorical structures; and in his critique of the modern mode of being as inhuman and incapable of solving existential crises.

In claiming that Eliade does not make ontological assumptions and judgments, Rennie defines "ontology" as restricted to a view of reality as existing completely independent of human perception, consciousness, awareness, and involvement.[18] Part of my disagreement is that I do not restrict "ontology," the investigation of being, to such narrow terms. The two best-known works on ontology in twentieth-century European philosophy are probably Martin Heidegger's *Being and Time* and Jean-Paul Sartre's *Being and Nothingness: An Essay in Phenomenological Ontology.*[19] Sartre develops Heidegger's ontological hermeneutical analysis of the meaning of "being" from the perspective of existing human beings ("being-in-the-world"). In recent years, there has been great attention devoted to Emmanuel Levinas's analysis of ontology—with ethics as "first philosophy" and ethics preceding ontology— as seen in such works as *Otherwise Than Being or Beyond Essence* and *Totality and Infinity.*[20] In all of these existential and hermeneutical phenomenological works, one cannot ignore the role of the constituting subject, and ontology is not conceived as completely independent of human consciousness and human involvement.[21]

Mircea Eliade presents a conception of religion based on the experience of the sacred, a structure of consciousness and mode of being in the world that always reveals a sense of transcendence. But we have not yet examined his methodological principles and hermeneutical framework for perceiving sacred manifestations. Eliade must recreate imaginatively the conditions for the manifestations of the sacred. In so doing, he seems to adopt a phenomenological approach by focusing on the intentionality of his data. In the "authentically phenomenological attitude the world no longer appears to us as a whole of objective data, but as an 'intentional configuration' *[Sinngebilde]* which is born and becomes meaningful in the course of an existential movement of orientation."[22] When Eliade examines his religious data, they do reveal a certain sacred intentionality. He attempts to recreate imaginatively the "intentional configuration" which expresses the specific existential orientation of *homo religiosus.*

As was seen, Eliade's theory of myth and religion involves a conception of the human being as *homo religiosus:* the human being who experiences the irreducibly sacred dimension of existence as ultimate reality; whose consciousness reveals a sacred structure of transcendence; and whose existential orientation reveals an essential relation to the foundational sacred that defines an irreducibly religious mode of being in the world. Although the conception *homo religiosus* is an essential part of Eliade's theory of religion, it is not always clear precisely what he means by this term. As was seen in chapter 2, by *homo religiosus* Eliade is not referring to historically particular, individual believers. *Homo religiosus* as the idealized, essentialized subject of the experience of the sacred functions as an abstract generic term. It designates a specific religious type, category, or essence involved in a unique religious way of constituting what it is to be an authentic human being related to a transcendent ultimate reality.

Gregory Alles distinguishes three general meanings of *homo religiosus.* After discussing a more particular meaning of *homo religiosus* as a "religious leader," Alles presents two generic senses: "*homo* referring not to an individual but, as with Linnaeus, to humanity. In one usage, the term is a general designation for all human beings, referring specifically to religion as one constitutive aspect of humanity distinct from others. This usage assumes a fundamental unity of all humankind that is more than biological, and its proponents speak more of the human condition than they do of concrete religious phenomena."[23]

Although Eliade sometimes adopts this usage of *homo religiosus* as "religious humanity" and as referring to all human beings, Alles is justified in identifying Eliade as the main proponent of the other general meaning in which *homo religiosus* is distinguished from *homo modernus*.

"In a third meaning, as in the second, *homo religiosus* is a generic term, but here it does not extend to the entire species. Instead it characterizes the mode of human existence prior to the advent of a modern, secular consciousness."

> [Eliade] contrasts two distinct modes of existing in and experiencing the world. His *homo religiosus* is driven by a desire for being; modern man lives under the dominion of becoming. *Homo religiosus* thirsts for being in the guise of the sacred. He attempts to live at the center of the world, close to the gods and in the eternal present of the paradigmatic mythic event that makes profane duration possible. His experience of time and space is characterized by a discontinuity between the sacred and the profane. Modern man, however, experiences no such discontinuity. For him, neither time nor space is capable of distinctive valorization. He is determined indiscriminately by all the events of history and by the concomitant threat of nothingness, which produces his profound anxiety.[24]

As will be seen in the last two chapters, Eliade rejects a complete break between *homo religiosus* and *homo modernus*. Moderns are still influenced by their premodern spiritual mythic history and by the *homo religiosus* and the mythic symbolic structures buried within the modern unconscious. Nevertheless, for Eliade "there is a profound difference between archaic reality and modern relic. For *homo religiosus,* recognized structures determine a whole world and a whole person. For modern man, these unrecognized structures are particular and private, repressed or relegated to peripheral activities."[25]

Religious experiences have a specific, universal, religious structure. In terms of the unique structure of sacralization, one may distinguish mythic and other religious phenomena from nonreligious phenomena. To recreate the essential conditions for the intentional mode of religious manifestations, we must now explicate the structure of the dialectic of the sacred.[26]

THE DIALECTIC OF THE SACRED
The Sacred-Profane Dichotomy and Hierophanic Object

If Eliade emphasizes the oppositional sacred-profane dichotomy and the disclosure of structures of the sacred that transcend the profane, he is also preoccupied with the manifestations of the sacred in the profane. He uses the term "hierophany" (from Greek *hiero-,* "sacred," and *phainein,* "to show") to designate the manifestation of the sacred.[27]

> Man becomes aware of the sacred because it manifests itself, shows itself, as something wholly different from the profane. To designate the *act of manifestation* of the sacred, we have proposed the term *hierophany.* It is a fitting term, because it does not imply anything further; it expresses no more than is implicit in its etymological content, i.e., that *something sacred shows itself to us.* It could be said that the history of religions—from the most primitive to the most highly developed—is constituted by a great number of hierophanies, by manifestations of sacred realities. From the most elementary hierophany—e.g., manifestation of the sacred in some ordinary object, a stone or a tree—to the supreme hierophany (which, for a Christian, is the incarnation of God in Jesus Christ) there is no solution of continuity. In each case we are confronted by the same mysterious act—the manifestation of something of a wholly different order, a reality that does not belong to our world, in objects that are an integral part of our natural "profane" world.[28]

Eliade writes of hierophanies, in particular, and the process of sacralization, in general, in such terms as "the sacred shows (manifests, reveals) itself to us." Rennie contends that such formulations, based on misleading translations, have led to serious misinterpretations. He cites the above formulation from *The Sacred and the Profane:* "man becomes aware of the sacred because it manifests itself, shows itself, as something wholly different from the profane" (p. 11). Rennie continues: "It must be pointed out here that Willard Trask, the translator of *The Sacred and the Profane* from French into English, seems to have been rather insensitive to the common French (and Romanian) usage of the reflexive to avoid the passive which Eliade would have learned in the formal French of the twenties. An acceptable alternative translation of the original "le sacré se manifeste," is *'the sacred is manifested,'* rather than 'the sacred manifests itself.' The former permits an implication of the sacred as the object of the phrase, rather than as the active subject."[29] On the one hand, "the sacred is manifested" allows Rennie to emphasize an active constructivist attitude on the part of religious persons. In his theory of religion, Eliade emphasizes the *awareness* of sacrality and the *perception* of the sacred. On the other hand, the misleading "the sacred manifests itself" can give a false sense of passivity on the part of *homo religiosus,* and it has contributed to the many false interpretations that attribute to Eliade some ontology of the sacred. According to Rennie, Eliade is presenting a psychological-phenomenological account free from normative judgments and ontological commitments.

Rennie's original interpretation has the advantage of guarding against many approaches that transform *homo religiosus* into some passive receptor and that focus exclusively on objective structures of the sacred. As I have maintained in previous works and as I develop throughout this book, there is no mythic or religious experience without the active participation of *homo religiosus* as perceiving, imagining, constituting subject. However, I have two main reservations regarding Rennie's thesis.[30] First, Eliade was fluent in English, and it would be incredible if he had allowed thousands of such false or misleading formulations to appear in his works. And this was not simply a case of insensitive translators. Even late in his life, Eliade himself continued to use such formulations as "the sacred manifests itself."

Second, the more passive construction does in fact get at a key phenomenological point. Many existential phenomenologists present an analysis of experience as revealing an initial sense of passive givenness. As Heidegger maintains in *Being and Time,* a phenomenon is not something that is a product of consciousness but rather something that exhibits itself, shows itself, to human consciousness. In Merleau-Ponty, Ricoeur, and others, there is a sense of a "constituted given," an "in itself for us." We experience a world of given structures and meanings revealed to us, but a world that is always unfinished and given to us in ways that require our participation as active constituting subjects. What emerges is a radical intentionality of human consciousness: universal structures are given but are always experienced as given for the perceiving consciousness.[31] As will be seen, this gets at Eliade's emphasis on essence precedes existence; on the sacred that shows itself to us; on atemporal, ahistorical, essential, mythic and symbolic structures and meanings that are given to us, but in such ways as to be actively revalorized and reconstituted by us.

What interests *homo religiosus* are hierophanies. These manifestations of the sacred are never unmediated: the sacred is always revealed through something natural, historical, ordinarily profane, such as the sky, the earth, water, a person, a sound, or a story. The profane has significance for *homo religiosus* only insofar as it reveals the sacred. As Eliade says, "Neither the objects of the external world nor human acts, properly speaking, have any autonomous intrinsic value. Objects or acts acquire a value, and in so doing become real, because they participate, after one fashion or another, in a reality that transcends them."[32]

The process of sacralization involves the "radical ontological separation" of the thing which reveals the sacred, the hierophanic object, from everything else. A certain stone has been singularized because of its size or shape or heavenly origin; because it protects the dead or is the site of a covenant; because it represents a theophany, commemorates a mythical act, or is an image of the "center." A medicine man has been singularized because of his selection by gods or spirits, because of his heredity, because of various physical defects (such as a nervous disorder), or because of an unusual accident or event (lightning, apparition, dream).[33]

According to Eliade, such religious phenomena are not separated from other phenomena simply because of unusual natural and historical characteristics. What is important is that there is always something else, something other: That which is singularized is "chosen" because it manifests the sacred. Unlike the way religion has often been viewed, for Eliade religious persons do not worship stones or trees as stones or trees. If a large rock is singled out, it is not simply because of its impressive natural dimensions but rather because its imposing appearance reveals something transcendent: a permanence, a power, an absolute mode of being that is different from the precariousness of human existence. If the medicine man is singled out from other persons, it is because his distinctive quality is a "sign" of something transcendent. He has the capacity to transcend the human and profane and to make contact with and manipulate the sacred.

Eliade stresses how difficult it is for us to recognize hierophanies. Modern human beings tend to see natural objects where our ancestors saw hierophanies. Eliade has observed that "to the primitive, nature is never purely 'natural.'"[34] Yet the difficulty of recognizing hierophanies is not for Eliade an exclusively modern phenomenon, one arising from the existential and historical situation of Western persons not consciously aware of the sacred dimension of existence. The difficulty is simply more extreme for modern, secular persons. But it would be a mistake to think that "traditional" societies have no difficulty recognizing hierophanies. As we shall observe, their myths reveal that even they are "fallen" beings who have lost easy access to the sacred. In addition, as we shall see, even for traditional religious societies, the dialectic of revelation is always at the same time the dialectic of "concealment and camouflage."

According to Eliade, all phenomena are potentially hierophanic: "We must get used to the idea of recognizing hierophanies everywhere, in every area of psychological, economic, spiritual and social life. Indeed, we cannot be sure that there is *anything*—object, movement, psychological function, being or even game—that has not at some time in human history been somewhere transformed into a hierophany. It is a very different matter to find out *why* that particular thing should have become a hierophany, or should have stopped being one at any given moment. But it is quite certain that anything man has ever handled, felt, come in contact with or loved *can* become a hierophany."[35]

In several contexts, Eliade asserts that Judaism and Christianity have contributed greatly to the process by which secular, Western, scientific moderns tend to see natural objects where "archaic" and other traditional religious persons saw hierophanies. For traditional *homo religiosus,* nature "was full of signs and hierophanies." "Modern science would not have been possible without the Judeo-Christian tradition, which emptied the cosmos of the sacred, and thus neutralized and banalized it. Science would not have been possible without a nature that was desacralized and emptied of gods."[36] This analysis will be seen as relevant to Eliade's approach to nature and the cosmos, "cosmic religion," history and nature, and modern human beings and the contemporary world.

At this point, we may note that Eliade's view of hierophanies challenges many past and present naturalistic interpretations of religious phenomena. Because we moderns tend to see natural objects where religious persons saw hierophanies, there is the tendency to interpret the dialectic of the sacred as a "natural" mode of manifestation. But to do so would be to fail to grasp the true intentionality of the sacred manifestation.

We must now examine the relationship between the sacred and the profane disclosed by the dialectic of hierophanies. This dialectical relationship has been the source of much confusion and misinterpretation.

The Paradoxical Relationship

Thomas J. J. Altizer seizes upon the point "that the sacred is the opposite of the profane" as Eliade's "cardinal principle" and the key to interpreting his phenomenological method. He takes this opposition to mean that the sacred and the profane are mutually exclusive and logically contradictory. From this "cardinal principle," Altizer sees the key to Eliade's approach in terms of a "negative dialectic": "a single moment cannot be sacred and profane at once." An understanding of myth, for example, is possible "only through the negation of the language of the profane." The "meaning of the sacred is reached by inverting the reality created by modern man's profane choice." In short, to grasp the sacred one must totally negate the profane and vice versa.[37]

Unfortunately, this interpretation destroys the dialectical complexity of the religious mode of manifestation and leads to an oversimplification and distortion of Eliade's phenomenological method.[38] Eliade criticizes this interpretation: "Altizer's most serious criticism concerns my understanding of the dialectic of the sacred as a hierophany. He interprets this as meaning that the *sacred* abolishes the *profane object* in which it manifests itself. But I have repeatedly pointed out that, for example, a *sacred* stone does not cease to be a *stone;* in other words, it preserves its place and function in the cosmic environment. In fact, hierophanies could not abolish the profane world, *for it is the very manifestation of the sacred that establishes the world,* i. e., transforms a formless unintelligible and terrifying chaos into a cosmos."[39]

Rather than being incompatible, the sacred and the profane for Eliade *coexist in a paradoxical relationship.* This process is the intention of the hierophany that constitutes the structure and lies at the foundation of the sacred manifestation. "One must remember the dialectic of the sacred: any object whatever may paradoxically become a hierophany, a receptacle of the sacred, while still participating in its own cosmic environment (a *sacred* stone, e.g., remains nevertheless a *stone* along with other stones)." "One need only recall the dialectic of hierophany: an object becomes *sacred* while remaining just the same as it is." The dialectic of the sacred consists of the fact that "the sacred expresses itself through some thing other than itself; it appears in things, myths, or symbols, but never wholly or directly." "In every case the sacred manifests itself limited and incarnate." It is "this paradox of incarnation which makes hierophanies possible at all."[40]

> In fact, this paradoxical coming-together of sacred and profane, being and non-being, absolute and relative, the eternal and the becoming, is what every hierophany, even the most elementary, reveals. . . . [E]very hierophany shows, makes manifest, the coexistence of contradictory essences: sacred and profane, spirit and matter, eternal and non-eternal, and so on. That the dialectic of hierophanies, of the manifestation of the sacred in material things, should be an object for even such complex theology as that of the Middle Ages seems to prove that it remains *the* cardinal problem of any religion. . . . In fact, what is paradoxical, what is beyond our understanding, is not that the sacred can be manifested in stones or in trees, but that it can be manifested at all, that it can thus become limited and relative.[41]

Thus we observe the paradoxical coexistence revealed by the dialectic of the sacred and the profane in all religious myths. What is paradoxical and incomprehensible to the rational, logical mind is that an ordinary, finite, historical thing, such as a tree or river or person, while remaining a natural thing, can at the same time manifest something that is infinite, transhistorical, and supernatural. Conversely, what is paradoxical is that something transcendent, supernatural, infinite, and transhistorical limits itself by manifesting itself in stones, animals, or other relative, finite, natural, historical things.[42]

The Dialectical Movement

To summarize up to this point, in all myths and other religious phenomena, the dialectic of the sacred discloses a distinction between sacred and profane, an ontological separation of a hierophanic object, and a paradoxical relationship that brings together the sacred and the profane. This paradoxical coexistence of the sacred and the profane is not some static relation: It expresses itself *as a dialectical tension and movement.* We must now examine the dynamic structure of the passage of the sacred to the concrete, the process by which the sacred "historicizes" and "limits" itself, which is at the same time that process by which a historical, temporal, natural, and limited thing embodies and reveals that which is transhistorical, eternal, supernatural, and absolute.

The process of sacralization reveals the dynamic tension and movement of two contrary but interacting processes. On the one hand, there is the movement from the sacred—essential, nonhistorical structure, atemporal model—to the particular, historical, conditioned manifestation. The sacred is not expressed in some unmediated "perfect form." "The great mystery consists *in the very fact that the sacred is made manifest:* for . . . in making itself manifest the sacred *limits* and 'historicizes' itself."[43] In every hierophany, the sacred undergoes this process of radical conditioning. The sacred is fragmented and particularized; it is embodied in new objects and takes new forms.

If this incarnational movement totally dominates its dialectical correlate, the sacred structure may collapse, the transhistorical may be overwhelmed by the historical object, and one may lose all awareness of the sacred or transcendent meaning. Eliade seems to evaluate those hierophanies that are most conditioned, limited, and relativized as "lower" or less spiritual phenomena.[44]

On the other hand, "the movement from the sacred to an incarnate form—that is, the movement from an archetype to a particular manifestation—is a movement that has its dialectical correlate in the tendency of the incarnate form, the new object, to realize its archetypal, universal meaning."[45] Eliade formulates this "reverse" incarnational movement in many passages. For example, "When once it is 'realized'—'historicized'—the religious form tends to disengage itself from its conditions in time and space and to become universal, to return to the archetype."[46]

> There is no religious form that does not try to get as close as possible to its true archetype, in other words, to rid itself of "historical" accretions and deposits. Every goddess tends to become a Great Goddess, taking to herself all the attributes and functions that belong to the archetypal Great Goddess. So much so that we can identify a double process in the history of things religious: on the one hand, the continual brief appearance of hierophanies with the result that the manifestation of the sacred in the Universe becomes ever more fragmentary; on the other, the unification of those hierophanies because of their innate tendency to embody their archetypes as perfectly as they can and thus wholly fulfil their own nature.[47]

This "second" dialectical movement toward the transhistorical, the universal, the "perfect form" is essential not only for Eliade's general conception of religion but especially for his formulation of the nature of myth. Religious people tend "periodically toward archetypes, toward 'pure' states; hence the tendency to return to the first moment, to the repetition of that which was *at the beginning*. So long as the 'simplifying', 'archetypizing' function of *returns, repetitions,* and *rebeginnings* is not understood, we will not understand how religious experience and the continuity of divine forms are possible—in a word, how it is possible to have *history* and *form* in 'religion.'"[48] The centrality of origins, returns, and repetitions will be seen as key to Eliade's understanding of myth.

If this second dialectical movement totally dominates its dialectical correlate, the transhistorical sacred structure or exemplary form may become disengaged or freed from the particular historical and existential situation within which it is incarnated. If the sacred becomes so "distant," so transcendent, that it no longer is experienced as historically imminent, then the hierophany will cease to be experienced as relevant to the specific existential crises of religious persons.

An excellent illustration of this incarnational tension and movement is seen in Eliade's studies of the oral literature and folklore of archaic and other traditional societies. The dialectical process of these collective creations moves in two contrary directions: On the one hand, there is the localization, ethnicization, historicization, and "degradation" of nonhistorical, universal, mythical structures into more specific, conditioned, historical, and personal events. On the other hand, there is the remythicization or assimilation of the particular historical and personal events into their transhistorical exemplary forms or universal models.[49]

In his journal of February 6, 1960, Eliade discusses his momentous discovery of this dynamic incarnational process of sacralization in which foundational experiences of the sacred, disclosing essential religious structures, are always expressed through specific myths and other religious forms that are necessarily inadequate for expressing the full meaning and significance of the experience of the sacred:

> I came to understand that the "historico-religious forms" are only the infinitely varied expressions of some fundamental religious experiences. When he discovers the sacredness of heaven or of the earth, religious man expresses his discovery by forms (divine figures, symbols, myths, etc.) which never succeed in translating exactly or totally what is signified by the sacred, be it celestial or telluric. That is indeed why other expressions replace them, just as incomplete and approximate and, in a sense, different from those whose places they are taking. If one analyzes all these expressions, one begins to see the *structures* of the religious universe: one finds out the archetypes, the models of these divine figures, which try to be entirely realized and communicated and manage, nevertheless, only a new "expression." For everything that is realized, that is concretely expressed, is

inevitably conditioned by history. Every religious expression is therefore only a mutilation of plenary experience.[50]

Since the researcher, according to Eliade, must start from the empirical data, which are expressions of historical manifestations of the sacred, it would seem that one's methodological approach must proceed in accordance with one of the two directions of the hierophanic process: from the particular historical manifestations taken as evidence of essential mythic and other religious structures. Yet this approach is an oversimplification and misinterpretation of Eliade's hermeneutical methodology. Since the dialectic of the sacred and the profane requires a tension and movement of two contrary but necessarily interacting processes, Eliade's phenomenological method emphasizes the dynamic interaction of facts and essences, of particular historical manifestations and their exemplary mythic structures.

Crisis, Evaluation, and Choice

Religious data do not simply reveal a distinction between sacred and profane, as seen in the paradoxical coexistence and in the dialectical tension and movement inherent in all myth and religion. The dialectic of hierophanies shows that *homo religiosus* is involved in an "existential crisis." Confronted by a hierophany, the religious person must evaluate two orders of being and make a choice. In evaluating and choosing the sacred as that which is superior, meaningful, and exemplary, Eliade does not mean that religious persons reject the profane by completely denying the reality of its existence. The sacred can only be manifested through the profane, and all religious phenomena reveal the paradoxical coexistence of the sacred and the profane.

Such terms as "evaluation" and "choice" are not used as exclusively intellectual or rational terms. *Homo religiosus* encompasses the total person, involving emotional and volitional as well as rational planes, unconscious as well as conscious behavior. The arising of crises and the subsequent judgments and choices are part of a total existential orientation, a total mode of being in the world. In many religious experiences, the dimension of rational deliberation and choice seems completely nonexistent.

Charles Long describes this sense of evaluation in the following manner: "The world of man exists as a limitation or qualification of his environment, and this qualification or limitation is at the same time a criticism. Man's world is an ordered world of meaning, but the organizing principle is interpreted as a revelation which comes from a source outside of his ordinary life. It is this source which is given (revealed) and (it) defines any future possibility of man's existence."[51]

In experiencing the dialectic of hierophany, *homo religiosus* faces an "existential crisis." Indeed, one's very existence may be called into question. Because of the dichotomy of sacred and profane, as revealed in their paradoxical coexistence, distinction, value, and even meaning are all introduced into one's existence.[52] "The awareness of a real and meaningful world is intimately related to the discovery of the sacred. Through the experience of the sacred, the human mind grasped the difference between that which reveals itself as real, powerful, rich, and meaningful, and that which does not—i.e., the chaotic and dangerous flux of things, their fortuitous, meaningless appearances and disappearances."[53] In short, one dimension of being is seen as more significant, as wholly other and powerful and ultimate, as containing a surplus of meaning, as paradigmatic and normative in judging one's existence.

Eliade usually describes the religious person's choice and evaluation "negatively." The dialectic of hierophanies throws the realm of natural ordinary existence into sharp relief. After the "rupture" of the sacred and the profane, the person evaluates ordinary natural existence as a "fall." One feels separated from what is now viewed as ultimate and real. One longs to transcend the natural, historical, profane mode of being and to live permanently in the sacred.

This essential structure of the dialectic of the sacred is extremely important for Eliade's hermeneutics. Eliade states that his objective in writing *A History of Religious Ideas* is "to elucidate the major contributions to the history of religious ideas and beliefs." In identifying these great contributions, he emphasizes "the crises in depth and, above all, the creative moments of the different traditions."[54] Indeed, without this structure of crisis and evaluation—this rupture of the sacred and the profane, negative evaluation of one's natural existence as a "fall," and longing for the transcendent—there would be no religious experience and, consequently, no religion: "Religion is indeed the result of the 'fall', 'the forgetting', the loss of the state of primordial perfection. In paradise, Adam knew nothing of religious experience, nor of theology, that is, the doctrine of God. Before 'sin', *there was no religion.*"[55] Indeed, as we shall see in chapter 6, it was the initial recognition by archaic human beings of their place in the cosmos, as separated from some state of primordial unity and perfection, that was constitutive of religion and myth as responses to their human condition in the world.

To summarize: through the dialectic of hierophanies, the profane is set off in sharp relief and the religious person "chooses" the sacred and evaluates the "ordinary" mode of existence negatively. At the same time, through this evaluation and choice, human beings are given possibilities for meaningful judgments and creative action and expression. The positive religious value of the negative evaluation of the profane is expressed in the intentionality toward meaningful communication with the sacred and toward religious action that now appears as a structure in the consciousness of *homo religiosus.*

This structure of crisis, evaluation, and choice emphasizes the fact that religious experience is practical and soteriological, producing a transformation of human beings. In the dialectic of the sacred—unlike much of the history of Western philosophy since Aristotle—knowledge does not exist for the sake of knowledge. The epistemological cannot be separated from the ontological: in coming to know the sacred, one is transformed in one's very being.

Eliade's interpretation of religion as viewing human existence as a fallen condition, as a loss of primordial perfection, raises a frequent misinterpretation of Eliade's phenomenology of religion and especially of his analysis of myth. Many interpreters, primarily critics, have seized upon Eliade's "personal doctrine" of a "fall" as being a pivotal notion in his history of religions. Supposedly, it is only because of Eliade's "theological assumptions" that he considers modern secularization to be a "fall."[56] Eliade is supposedly a "romantic" who believes that history is a "fall" and who "insists upon the reality of man's prefallen state."[57] More recently, Mac Linscott Ricketts has devoted hundreds of pages to Eliade's youthful unpublished notebooks, journals, newspaper columns, and other Romanian documents in order to uncover his subject's personal views about religion and other matters. Ricketts repeatedly maintains that such youthful attitudes and commitments are essential for understanding Eliade's "mature" scholarly works.[58]

The problem with these and numerous other interpretations is that such scholars often do not take Eliade seriously enough on his own grounds. Some are theologians who criticize Eliade's theological position of a "fall." Some are supporters who are sympathetic toward Eliade's theological and other normative judgments. I in no way want to maintain that Eliade, or any other scholar, provides "value-free" interpretations. Eliade's own crises, evaluations, and choices are not irrelevant to his formulations of the universal structure of crisis, evaluation, and choice in the dialectic of the sacred. It will be shown that there are basic assumptions, normative judgments, and ontological moves, often unacknowledged by Eliade, that structure his methodology and his interpretations of myth and other religious and nonreligious phenomena.

But Mircea Eliade, throughout his scholarly writings, at least purports to be a historian and phenomenologist of religion. His scholarly claim is not that he is committed to some personal view or theological doctrine of a "fall" but that myths themselves reveal that mythic persons have had such a religious orientation. For example, Eliade finds that "the paradisiac myths" speak of an epoch in which primordial beings enjoyed freedom, immortality, and easy communication with the gods. Unfortunately, they lost all of this because of "the fall"—the primordial event that caused the "rupture" of the sacred and the profane. These myths help religious persons understand their present "fallen" existence and express a "nostalgia" for that "prefallen" paradise.[59] If history is a "fall" for *homo religiosus,* it is because historical existence is seen as separated from and inferior to the "transhistorical" (absolute, eternal, transcendent) sacred.

Therefore, one must, first of all, take seriously Eliade's scholarly claims: that he is a historian and phenomenologist of religion who is attempting to provide descriptions and interpretations of the meaning of myths and other phenomena of religious (and nonreligious) persons. We shall also show that Eliade's personal assumptions and judgments are not irrelevant to his interpretations of religious data and that he is

sometimes concerned with issues that go far beyond scholarly interpretations of the documents of *homo religiosus.*

Concealment and Camouflage

The dialectic of the sacred and the profane in structuring myth is even
more subtle and complex than the preceding analysis suggests. It has
been seen that the sacred would not be able to manifest itself other than
through the profane, which enables it to historicize, concretize, and
limit itself. It has also been seen that the sacred must become an object
of evaluation and choice on the part of religious persons. It must now
be added that such religious disclosures and responses do not proceed
in a way that could be analyzed in simple, clear, and mechanical terms.
In its very act of showing itself, the sacred "conceals and camouflages
itself."[60]

In his *Autobiography,* Eliade records that in 1940 in England, after
he had left Romania and before he had assumed his position with the
Romanian legation in Portugal, he had "the fundamental idea" for
Patterns in Comparative Religion: "hierophanies, i.e., the manifestation
of the sacred in cosmic realities (objects or processes belonging to the
profane world), have a paradoxical structure because they *show* and at
the same time *camouflage* sacrality."[61] In manifesting itself through
new objects and in taking other forms, the sacred at the same time
"conceals" or "hides" itself. "When something sacred manifests itself
(hierophany), at the same time something 'occults' itself, becomes
cryptic. Therein is the true dialectic of the sacred: by the mere fact of
showing itself, the sacred *hides itself.*"[62]

Eliade writes that his scholarly and literary works lead to the same
problem: "the unrecognizability of the transcendent" or transhistorical
sacred that "camouflages itself in history." "My conception of the
fantastic in literature . . . has its roots in my theory of 'the incognizabil-
ity of miracles'—or in my theory that, after the Incarnation, the transcendent is camouflaged in the world or in history and thus becomes
'incognizable.'" "Ultimately, the real problem is this: How to recognize
the real camouflaged in appearances."[63]

In his preface to *The Forbidden Forest,* Eliade mentions the "hidden
meanings" of many episodes that appeared to him only after he had

finished writing this novel. He refers to symbolic meanings that had "not been camouflaged consciously and deliberately in a narrative of the 'historical fresco' type of novel. They were imposed upon me by the process of literary imagination itself." He adds: "Actually, in even the most commonplace narrative, *any* event (a meeting, a reading, the recollection of an ordinary dialog, etc.) can camouflage a meaning or a message which the protagonists and the readers—at least those of a certain type—do not discern. There is no more perfect camouflage of 'transcendent' meanings than the gray banality of everyday realism."[64] Similarly, in his *Autobiography,* Eliade writes:

> Unconsciously and unintentionally, I succeeded in "showing" in *Şarpele* something I was to develop later in my works of philosophy and history of religions: namely, that the "sacred" *apparently* is not different from the "profane," that the "fantastic" is camouflaged in the "real," that the world is what it shows itself to be, and is at the same time a cipher. That same dialectic ... also sustains *The Forbidden Forest* ... with the difference that at this time no longer was it a question of the profound meaning of the Cosmos, but of the "cipher" of historical events. The theme of the "fantastic" camouflaged in everyday occurrences is found again in several of my novellas written still more recently, for example: *La Ţigănci* (With the Gypsy Girls, written in 1959) and *Podul* (The Bridge, written in 1964). In a certain sense, one could say that this theme constitutes the key to all the writings of my maturity.[65]

Perhaps more than any other commentator on Eliade's works, Matei Calinescu has emphasized the importance of the structures of camouflage and with them the central theme of the "unrecognizability of miracle." More specifically, Calinescu insists on "the opposition between unknowable and unrecognizable": "The agnostic thesis that ultimate reality is unknowable is replaced here by the hypothesis of unrecognizability—a variant of the Platonic doctrine of *anamnesis.* At first sight, the difference between the two approaches may seem slight, indeed irrelevant. Let me stress therefore that in the case of agnosticism the main concern is that of epistemological validity (implying a relativistic theory of knowledge) while in the second case true knowledge is in principle accessible to everyone who can recognize it (or who can remember it, according to Plato). The latter way of thinking is structurally symbolic, and its main concern is to discover the actual *meaning* of the innumerable signs which constitute our consciousness."[66]

One finds throughout Eliade's works many examples of these concealments and camouflages. We must not restrict our investigation of the sacred only to those myths that strike us as the most impressive or spectacular. All natural phenomena are potentially hierophanic. Consequently, the sacred can appear and be hidden in any form. Many of Eliade's most creative interpretations are of myths and other religious phenomena generally considered unworthy of our attention or even as nonreligious by both believers and nonbelievers.

For example, the sacred can be found hidden in sexuality, not only in those expressions of sublime love steeped in spirituality but also in the kinds of love judged the most carnal, frivolous, lustful, and even abominable: "There is here a *religious* justification of sexuality; for, incited by Aphrodite, even sexual excesses and outrages must be recognized as of divine origin." "It is physical love, fleshly union, that she inspires, praises, and defends." This "irrational and irreducible sexuality" was then "exploited by writers and plastic artists." "We are almost tempted to see, in this artistic flowering under the sign of Aphrodite, the radical desacralization of physical love. But in fact it is a camouflage, inimitable and rich in meanings, such as is found in so many other creations of the Greek genius. Under the appearance of a frivolous divinity is hidden one of the most profound sources of religious experience: the revelation of sexuality as transcendence and mystery."[67]

Another classical example, very significant with regard to modes of being in the contemporary world, is the propensity of ancient Greeks to consider destiny and the human condition in a tragic and pessimistic way and to live with an awareness of the precariousness and limits of human existence. Death resolves nothing, there is only the present life, and it is useless to look beyond. Such an outlook, emphasizing the need to live fully and nobly in the present, seems to exclude all feelings about transcendence. This is certainly the case in the deliberate rejection of appeals to religious transcendence by Albert Camus and many other secular existentialists. But for Eliade, "far from inhibiting the creative forces of the Greek religious genius, this tragic vision led to a paradoxical revalorization of the human condition." This revalorization, embracing the realization that the gods had forced mortals not to go beyond their human limits, ended with the human realization of "the *perfection* and, consequently, the *sacrality of the human condition.*" Thus "it is above all the religious valorization of the present that requires emphasizing. The simple fact of *existing,* of *living in time,* can comprise a religious dimension. This dimension is not always obvious, since sacrality is in a sense camouflaged in the immediate, in the 'natural' and the everyday. The joy of life discovered by the Greeks is not a profane type of enjoyment: it reveals the bliss of existing, of sharing—even fugitively—in the spontaneity of life and the majesty of the world. Like so many others before and after them, the Greeks learned that the surest way to escape from time is to exploit the wealth, at first sight impossible to suspect, of the lived instant."[68]

According to Eliade, many seemingly secular phenomena of Western civilization reveal this structure of the sacred in concealed and camouflaged forms.[69] In the foreword to *Images and Symbols,* Eliade maintains that symbols and myths, although they may become disguised, mutilated, or degraded, do not disappear from the psyche. In *Myth and Reality, Myths, Dreams and Mysteries,* and other studies, Eliade recognizes the survival of certain camouflaged myths at the heart of contemporary society.

Eliade affirms, for example, that the sacred has not completely disappeared in modern art. "But it has become *unrecognizable;* it is camouflaged in forms, purposes, and meanings which are apparently 'profane.'" We are not able to recognize this concealment that is at the same time a potential revelation. "Modern man has 'forgotten' religion, but the sacred survives, buried in his unconscious." After examining specific characteristics of modern art, Eliade concludes: "From a structural point of view, the attitude of the artist in regard to the cosmos and to life recalls to a certain extent the ideology implicit in 'cosmic religion.'"[70]

According to Calinescu, this structure of concealment and camouflage that makes the sacred "unrecognizable" "leads to a theory of interpretation or hermeneutics, interested in the disguises, variations, and analogical ramifications of meaning." "Meaning shrinks, as it were, disappears behind meaningless appearances. Its signs, which no one can read any longer, are hidden *among* and not beneath the trivia of day-to-day life. From this standpoint, hermeneutics, whose task is to recover lost worlds of meaning, may be defined simply as the *science of recognition.* "[71]

We may better comprehend Eliade's approach to the dialectic of revelation as a power that simultaneously is a dialectic of occultation by contrasting his emphasis to the most widespread forms of recent religious growth in the modern West and throughout the world. Various denominations or sects within Christianity, Islam, and other religions have gained millions of converts by claiming to provide access to God or to some other sacred reality in an explicit and unequivocal manner. In the United States of the 1970s, 1980s, and 1990s, the churches gaining the most followers have been those reclaiming a very conservative "fundamentalism," often based on literalist interpretations of the Bible. In a period marked by ambiguity, anxiety, alienation, and insecurity, the success of these churches may be attributed in large part to the dogmatic, clear-cut, even mechanical answers they provide. This appeal of religions offering unconcealed and uncamouflaged access to the sacred may be seen to confirm Eliade's emphasis on the difficulty of recognizing the sacred in the modern world.

In contrast to this tendency, Eliade is attracted to that which is enigmatic and paradoxical, to the complexity, ambiguity, open-ended richness, organic interrelatedness, and unlimited creativity of religious experience. The religious symbolic and mythic structures which Eliade favors, such as those expressing the *coincidentia oppositorum,* are those that express extremely complex existential situations while preserving a profound sense of mystery. Eliade rejects all interpretations tending to reduce the complexity of religious phenomena to some simple and univocal explanation. Similarly, those phenomena evaluated by Eliade as the most "elevated" or most spiritual are those mystical and other religious experiences that best allow *homo religiosus* to "live the universal" in exploring the multiple possibilities of the sacred in all of its complexity.

Eliade's interpretation of the dialectic of the sacred has disclosed the extreme complexity of religious phenomena: anything is potentially hierophanic; the sacred paradoxically coexists with the profane in every religious manifestation; the sacred continually historicizes and limits itself in new objects and assumes new forms while at the same time attempting to disengage itself and realize its essential structure; and the sacred, in revealing itself, conceals and hides itself.

Awareness of this complexity of the dialectic of the sacred and the profane, as seen in its structure of concealment and camouflage, leads Eliade to assume an attitude toward myths and other religious phenomena in clear contrast to the typical approach of religious fundamentalists and others who propose rather literal readings of sacred texts. For Eliade, an insistence on simple, clear, definitive revelations of the religious reality provides evidence of a rather impoverished imagination and rudimentary perspective on the dialectic of the sacred. We are no longer able to see how the sacred is able to manifest itself in its complexity, ambiguity, and profundity. It is only in light of the dialectic of concealment that it becomes possible to gain some appreciation of the immensity of that which is hidden behind any disclosure and of its hidden potential as an inexhaustible source of creativity and meaning. In short, it is this hiddenness of the sacred, a structure constitutive of its very revelation, which confers on the religious experience its depth and vitality.

RELIGION AS AN "OPENING"

We have seen that Eliade believes that the principal function of religion and of myth is to maintain an "opening" toward a superhuman or transcendent world. "On the one hand, the sacred is, supremely, the *other* than man—the transpersonal, the transcendent—and, on the other hand, the sacred is the exemplary in the sense that it establishes patterns to be followed: by being transcendent and exemplary it compels the religious man to come out of personal situations, to surpass the contingent and the particular and to comply with general values, with the universal."[72] Myths disclose the sacred as transcendent "other" and are the primary source establishing the exemplary foundational patterns to be followed.

Now we may understand how the dialectic of hierophanies helps to maintain this "opening." By means of this process of sacralization, the "closed" profane world is "burst open." A natural object, such as a tree, while remaining a tree, reveals something "other." "No tree or plant is ever sacred simply as a tree or plant; they become so because they *share* in a transcendent reality, they become so because they *signify* that transcendent reality. By being consecrated, the individual, 'profane' plant species is transubstantiated; in the dialectic of the sacred a part (a tree, a plant) has the value of the whole (the cosmos, life), a profane thing becomes a hierophany."[73] For example, a ritual in shamanism is that of climbing a tree in which a certain number of notches have been cut. It is only because mythical themes reveal that the "natural" tree has the value of "World Tree," the notches signifying the various heavens, that we can interpret the climbing of a particular natural tree as the celestial ascent of the shaman, an ecstatic journey beyond the heavens.[74] Without this sense of religious "opening," the meaning of the shaman's experience of the sacred remains unintelligible.

If the process of sacralization evident in myths and other religious phenomena depended on the "direct" consecration by hierophanies, the scope of Eliade's investigation would be severely restricted. From the above illustration of celestial ascent, one may already detect the importance of symbolism in the process of sacralization. In chapter 5, the primary role of symbolism, the language of myth, will be seen as carrying further the dialectic of the sacred. Through symbolism the profane is "burst open" so that it reveals something "other."

NOTES

1. For example, Eliade shows how the effectiveness of certain medicinal herbs was based on the Christian mythic belief that they "grew for the first time (i.e., *ab origine*) on the sacred hill of Calvary at the 'center' of the Earth" and that "their prototypes were discovered at a decisive cosmic moment *(in illo tempore)* on Mount Calvary." Similarly, in India and elsewhere, "herbs owed their curative virtues to the fact that they were first discovered by gods." See *Eternal Return,* pp. 30-31.

2. *Images and Symbols,* p. 29. Eliade's approach to "history" will be examined in detail in chapters 8 and 9.

3. *Patterns,* p. 1; *Sacred and Profane,* p. 10; Mircea Eliade, "Structures and Changes in the History of Religions," trans. Kathryn K. Atwater, in *City Invincible,* ed. Carl H. Kraeling and Robert M. Adams (Chicago: University of Chicago Press, 1960), p. 353; Roger Caillois, *Man and the Sacred,* trans. Meyer Barash (Glencoe, Ill.: Free Press, 1959), pp. 13, 19.

4. Saliba, *"Homo Religiosus" in Mircea Eliade,* pp. 150-55; Ninian Smart, "Beyond Eliade: The Future of Theory in Religion," *Numen* 25 (1978): 174-76. As will become clear, Eliade would reverse Smart's criticism, claiming that such "emotional charges" are particular aspects of a more inclusive sacred-profane framework.

5. Eliade, "Methodological Remarks," p. 89.

6. Mircea Eliade, "Preface," *Quest,* p. v; *History 1,* p. xiii; *Sacred and Profane,* p. 14. In *No Souvenirs,* Eliade writes: "First argument: 'The sacred' is an element of the *structure* of consciousness, and not a moment in the *history* of consciousness. Next: The experience of the sacred is indissolubly linked to the effort made by man to construct a meaningful world" (p. 313). See also Ira Progoff, "Culture and Being: Mircea Eliade's Studies in Religion," *International Journal of Parapsychology* 2 (1960): 53.

7. *Myth and Reality,* p. 139. See also Mircea Eliade, "Preface," to Thomas N. Munson, *Reflective Theology: Philosophical Orientations in Religion* (New Haven: Yale University Press, 1968), pp. viii-ix.

8. *Quest,* p. vi.

9. Mircea Eliade, *Autobiography, Volume II: 1937-1960, Exile's Odyssey,* trans. Mac Linscott Ricketts (Chicago: University of Chicago Press, 1988), pp. 188-89 (hereafter cited as *Autobiography 2); Mephistopheles and the Androgyne,* p. 76. See also Eliade, "Experiences of the Mystic Light," in *Mephistopheles and the Androgyne,* pp. 19-77, and Eliade, "Spirit, Light, and Seed," in *Occultism, Witchcraft, and Cultural Fashions: Essays in Comparative Religions* (Chicago: University of Chicago Press, 1976), pp. 93-119.

10. Mircea Eliade, "Masks: Mythical and Ritual Origins," in *Encyclopedia of World Art,* vol. 9, col. 524 (London and New York: McGraw-Hill, 1964). This essay is reprinted in Mircea Eliade, *Symbolism, the Sacred, and the Arts,* ed. Diane Apostolos-Cappadona (New York: Crossroad, 1986), pp. 64-71.

11. *History 1,* pp. 363-68.

12. *No Souvenirs,* p. 83. Although this fascinating journal entry of December 5, 1959, dramatically and accurately emphasizes Eliade's focus on the transcendent nature of the sacred, it is very atypical in its "generous" interpretation of Marx and Freud. Eliade maintains that both Marx and Freud failed to arrive at "the true causes and motives" not only of religious experience but even of so-called "modern," "secular," "historical" phenomena. In addition,

Eliade's references to "causes" and "explains" confirms a point made in chap. 2: a clear-cut dichotomy of interpretation (Eliade) and explanation (reductionists) often oversimplifies and distorts what Eliade and other scholars are actually doing.

13. *Sacred and Profane*, pp. 202-3. See also *Myths, Dreams and Mysteries*, p. 236.

14. "Structure and Changes in the History of Religion," p. 366. See also *Sacred and Profane*, p. 28. We noted a similar formulation in *Myth and Reality*, p. 139.

15. Bryan S. Rennie, *Reconstructing Eliade: Making Sense of Religion* (Albany: State University of New York Press, 1996), p. 20.

16. Ibid., pp. 21-24 and passim. See also Paden, "Before 'The Sacred' Became Theological," p. 208.

17. See, for example, Rennie, *Reconstructing Eliade*, p. 40.

18. Even in this narrow view of "ontology," Rennie has to ignore or reconstruct in a non-Eliadean way hundreds of passages in Eliade's works.

19. Martin Heidegger, *Being and Time*, trans. John Macquarrie and Edward Robinson (New York: Harper, 1962); and Jean-Paul Sartre, *Being and Nothingness: An Essay in Phenomenological Ontology*, trans. Hazel E. Barnes (New York: Philosophical Library, 1956).

20. Emmanuel Levinas, *Otherwise Than Being or Beyond Essence*, trans. Alphonso Lingis (The Hague: Martinus Nijhoff, 1981); and Levinas, *Totality and Infinity*, trans. Alphonso Lingis (Pittsburgh: Duquesne University Press, 1969).

21. This point is not meant to deny the critique of such existential and hermeneutic phenomenology of the absolute or extreme emphasis on the autonomous constituting ego or self found in Descartes and much of modern philosophy. Even before his later rejection of humanism, Heidegger's emphasis in *Being and Time* on ontology rather than epistemology counters the overemphasis on the perceiving, thinking, knowing, constituting subject found in post-Cartesian philosophy and in Husserl's transcendental ego. Levinas's emphasis on "alterity," on the primacy of the other, is a radical challenge to the modern philosophical emphasis on the self as autonomous subject.

22. Stephen Strasser, *The Soul in Metaphysical and Empirical Psychology* (Pittsburgh: Duquesne University Press, 1962), p. 3.

23. Gregory D. Alles, *"Homo Religiosus,"* in *The Encyclopedia of Religion*, vol. 6 (New York: Macmillan, 1987), p. 443. Alles identifies this generic usage of *homo religiosus* as "religious humanity" with Gerardus van der Leeuw and Wilhelm Dupré.

24. Ibid., p. 444.

25. Ibid.

26. I use "the dialectic of the sacred," "the dialectic of the sacred and the profane," and "the dialectic of hierophanies" interchangeably.

27. See Mircea Eliade and Lawrence E. Sullivan, "Hierophany," in *The Encyclopedia of Religion,* vol. 6 (New York: Macmillan, 1987), pp. 313-17.

28. *Sacred and Profane,* p. 11. Eliade first used the term "hierophany" in *Traité d'histoire des religions* (Paris: Payot, 1949; trans. *Patterns in Comparative Religion).* See *Patterns,* p. 7 and chap. 1; *Myths, Dreams and Mysteries,* p. 124.

29. Rennie, *Reconstructing Eliade,* p. 19. See also pp. 13-15, 69, 194, and passim.

30. In addition, as was just seen and will become increasingly clear, while I also maintain that most of Eliade's formulations of the sacred should be taken as phenomenological descriptions and interpretations, I do not agree that he is so free from normative judgments and ontological assumptions and claims.

31. See Allen, *Structure and Creativity in Religion,* pp. 188-89.

32. *Eternal Return,* pp. 3-4. Eliade is speaking of the orientation of the archaic, but his description applies to his analysis of *homo religiosus* in general.

33. See *Patterns,* pp. 216-38; *Eternal Return,* p. 4; *Shamanism,* esp. pp. 31-32.

34. *Patterns,* p. 38.

35. Ibid., p. 11.

36. *No Souvenirs,* p. 71. See also Mircea Eliade, "The Sacred and the Modern Artist," *Criterion* 4 (1965): 23.

37. Altizer, *Mircea Eliade and the Dialectic of the Sacred,* esp. pp. 34, 39, 45, 65.

38. See Mac Linscott Ricketts, "Mircea Eliade and the Death of God," *Religion in Life* (Spring 1967): 40-52; Rennie, *Reconstructing Eliade,* pp. 27-31.

39. Eliade, "Notes for a Dialogue," in *The Theology of Altizer: Critique and Response,* ed. J. B. Cobb (Philadelphia: Westminster Press, 1970), p. 238.

40. *Images and Symbols,* pp. 84-85, 178; *Patterns,* p. 26.

41. *Patterns,* pp. 29-30. See also *Myths, Dreams and Mysteries:* "there remains always this paradoxical—that is, incomprehensible—fact that it is the *sacred* that is manifesting, and thereby *limiting* itself and ceasing to be *absolute"* (p. 125).

42. In addition to this structure of paradoxical coexistence, Eliade emphasizes the paradoxical nature of myth and religion in many other related ways. All aspects of the dialectic of the sacred and the profane are described as paradoxical in different contexts. For example, in the universal structure of sacralization, the sacred conceals and camouflages itself at the same time that it shows and reveals itself. Under the characteristics and functions of religious symbolism, Eliade's emphasis on the symbolic expression of paradoxical and

contradictory aspects of reality will become clear. Through the symbolic function of unification, based on the logic of symbols and the homologization of multivalent symbols, *homo religiosus* is able to integrate paradoxical and contradictory aspects of reality into structurally coherent wholes. In addition, Eliade is particularly drawn to the specific paradoxical nature of certain mythic and symbolic structures such as the *coincidentia oppositorum*, in which there is a unity-totality of what are ordinarily symbolic polar opposites: the feminine and masculine, the lunar and solar, and so forth.

43. *Myths, Dreams and Mysteries*, p. 125.

44. See Allen, *Structure and Creativity in Religion*, pp. 212-16.

45. Dudley, *Religion on Trial*, p. 54. See also pp. 55-57, 81.

46. *Images and Symbols*, p. 121.

47. *Patterns*, p. 462. This "second" dialectical movement is crucial for Eliade's methodology. In *Images and Symbols*, he maintains: "It is this same tendency towards the archetype, towards the restoration of the *perfect form* —of which any myth or rite or divinity is only a variant, and often rather a pale one—that makes the history of religions possible. Without this, magico-religious experience would be continually creating transitory or evanescent forms of gods, myths, dogmas, etc.; and the student would be faced by a proliferation of ever new types impossible to set in order" (p. 121). See also Eliade, *Shamanism*, p. xvii. These nonhistorical essential structures or "perfect forms" are at the foundation of Eliade's phenomenological method.

48. *Journal 1*, p. 20.

49. See Eliade, "Les livres populaires dans la littérature roumaine," *Zalmoxis* 2 (1939): 63-78; "Littérature orale," in *Histoire des littératures*. Vol. 1: *Littératures anciennes orientales et orales*, ed. R. Queneau (Paris: Gallimard, 1956), pp. 3-26. See also Mircea Eliade, *Zalmoxis, The Vanishing God: Comparative Studies in the Religions and Folklore of Dacia and Eastern Europe*, trans. Willard R. Trask (Chicago: University of Chicago Press, 1972); Eliade, "History of Religions and 'Popular' Cultures," *History of Religions* 20 (1980): 1-26; Douglas Allen and Dennis Doeing, *Mircea Eliade: An Annotated Bibliography* (New York: Garland, 1980), sec. B.

50. *No Souvenirs*, p. 91.

51. Charles H. Long, *Alpha: The Myths of Creation* (New York: George Braziller, 1963), pp. 10-11. In *Religion on Trial*, Dudley writes: "For Eliade, man's finitude is the limitation nonbeing places on being. The goal of *homo religiosus* is infinite transcendence of the conditions imposed on him in his finite state" (p. 88).

52. See *Myth and Reality*, p. 139, and G. Richard Welbon, "Some Remarks on the Work of Mircea Eliade," *Acta Philosophica et Theologica* 2 (1964): 479.

53. *Quest*, p. v.

54. *History 1*, p. xiv.

55. *No Souvenirs*, p. 67.

56. See Kenneth Hamilton, "*Homo Religiosus* and Historical Faith," *Journal of Bible and Religion* 33 (1965): 214-16. The following discussion also applies to Eliade's frequent claim that "from the Christian [or religious] point of view" it could be said that modern nonreligion is equivalent to a new or second "fall," that the "unconscious" of modern human beings alone is still religious. See, for example, *Sacred and Profane*, p. 213; "Archaic Myth and Historical Man," *McCormick Quarterly* 18 (1965): 35-36; *No Souvenirs*, p. 156.

57. Altizer, *Mircea Eliade and the Dialectic of the Sacred*, pp. 84, 86, 88, 161; Altizer, "Mircea Eliade and the Recovery of the Sacred," *The Christian Scholar* 45 (1962): 282-83. See also Eliade, *Images and Symbols*, p. 173; *Eternal Return*, p. 162.

58. For a summary, see Ricketts, *Eliade: Romanian Roots*, 2, pp. 1205-11.

59. Such mythic interpretations are found throughout Eliade's writings. See, for example, *Myths, Dreams and Mysteries*, pp. 59-72.

60. This structure of "concealment and camouflage" is most evident in Eliade's journals and literary works and in several of his studies of myth, such as "Survivals and Camouflages of Myths," *Diogenes* 41 (1963): 1-25 (reprinted as chap. 9 in *Myth and Reality*). Those interpreters most aware of this structure have been Calinescu, Ierunca, and other Romanians familiar with Eliade's literary production as well as Ricketts and several other Westerners who have focused in recent years on Eliade's Romanian and translated literary works. See, for example, Matei Calinescu, "Imagination and Meaning: Aesthetic Attitudes and Ideas in Mircea Eliade's Thought," *Journal of Religion* 57 (1977): 1-15; and Matei Calinescu, "Introduction: The Fantastic and Its Interpretation in Mircea Eliade's Later Novellas," in Mircea Eliade, *Youth Without Youth and Other Novellas*, ed. Matei Calinescu, trans. Mac Linscott Ricketts (Columbus: Ohio State University Press, 1988), pp. xiii-xxxix.

61. *Autobiography 2*, p. 84.

62. *No Souvenirs*, p. 268. Eliade continues: "We can never claim that we definitively understand a religious phenomenon: something—perhaps even the essential—will be understood by us later, or by others immediately."

63. *No Souvenirs*, pp. 31, 191, and passim; "Bucureşti, 1937," in *Fiinţa Românească* 5 (1967), p. 64; "Fragment autobiographic," in *Caete de Dor* 7 (1953).

64. Mircea Eliade, "Preface," *The Forbidden Forest*, trans. Mac Linscott Ricketts and Mary Park Stevenson (Notre Dame: University of Notre Dame Press, 1978), p. ix.

65. Mircea Eliade, *Autobiography, Volume I: 1907-1937, Journey East, Journey West*, trans. Mac Linscott Ricketts (San Francisco: Harper & Row, 1981), p. 322 (hereafter cited as *Autobiography 1*); Mircea Eliade, *Şarpele (The*

Snake; Bucharest: Naţională Ciornei, 1937). See Virgil Ierunca, "The Literary Work of Mircea Eliade," in *Myths and Symbols: Studies in Honor of Mircea Eliade,* ed. Joseph M. Kitagawa and Charles H. Long (Chicago: University of Chicago Press, 1969), p. 347.

66. Matei Calinescu, "Imagination and Meaning," p. 4.

67. *History 1*, p. 283. See also *Mephistopheles and the Androgyne,* pp. 98-100 and passim for a fascinating study of the modern desacralization of the myth of the hermaphrodite. The theme of the hiddenness of the sacred in sexuality is particularly characteristic of Eliade's works on Yoga, with his emphasis on Tantric Yoga, and in a number of his novels.

68. *History 1*, pp. 259-63. This analysis is not only extremely relevant to the condition of modern Western persons but also relates to Mircea Eliade's own efforts at finding meaning in a seemingly desacralized world. Eliade concludes with the observation that this "sacralization of human finitude and of the banality of an ordinary existence is a comparatively frequent phenomenon in the history of religions. But it is especially in China and Japan of the first millennium of our era that the sacralization of 'limits' and 'circumstances'—of whatever nature—achieved excellence and profoundly influenced the respective cultures" (p. 263).

69. In the preface to *History 1*, p. xvi, Eliade writes that in the last chapter of the third volume of *A History of Religious Ideas,* he will examine "the sole, but important, religious creation of the modern Western world. I refer to the ultimate stage of desacralization. The process is of considerable interest to the historian of religions, for it illustrates the complete camouflage of the 'sacred'—more precisely, its identification with the 'profane'." Because of ill health, Eliade never completed this task.

70. "The Sacred and the Modern Artist," pp. 22-24.

71. Calinescu, "Imagination and Meaning," pp. 4-5.

72. *Myths, Dreams and Mysteries,* p. 18. See also *Quest,* p. ii.

73. *Patterns,* p. 324.

74. *Shamanism,* esp. pp. 117-27.

CHAPTER 4

Nature, Cosmos, and Religious Bias

In the last chapter, Eliade was seen to have a specific conception of religion based on his structural analysis of the foundational experience of the sacred. Myths reveal experiences of the sacred and express the universal structure of the dialectic of the sacred and the profane. It is the universal structure of the sacralization, as formulated in Eliade's dialectic of the sacred, that allows Eliade to differentiate myths and other religious phenomena from nonreligious phenomena.

In this chapter, Eliade's analysis will be developed by exploring some of his uses of "nature" and "cosmos," since they appear so prominently in his conception and analysis of religion, hierophanies, the dialectic of the sacred, symbolism, and the structure and function of myth. Then, taking up the contention of many critics and some supporters, we shall explore whether Eliade's conception of religion and the dialectic of the sacred reveals a particular religious bias that is then reflected in his interpretations of myth and other religious phenomena. Does he privilege archaic religion or some Eastern European, peasant, "cosmic Christianity"? In making sense of Eliade's scholarly interpretations, is it necessary to include, as an essential part of his scholarship, his personal faith assumptions, beliefs, and commitments?

NATURE AND COSMOS

Throughout *Patterns in Comparative Religion* as well as other major works, Eliade places an extreme emphasis on "nature" and "cosmos" in his interpretation of hierophanies, archaic religion, cosmic religion,

religion in general, religious symbolism, and religious myth. Religion and myth are interpreted as intended by religious persons to enable them to unify and harmonize themselves with natural phenomena and the rhythms of nature, to allow them to integrate themselves as parts of an ordered, meaningful cosmos.

Since "nature" and "cosmos" are so central to Eliade's history and phenomenology of myth and religion, it is important to note a pervasive ambiguity and possible confusion in his use of these terms. Much of this ambiguity arises from their general, at times contradictory meanings. To distinguish only a few of its meanings, "nature" is most often used by scholars and others to refer to the physical or "natural" world existing independently of human beings and their activities, such as mythmaking. This sense of "nature," encompassing trees, mountains, rivers, animals, and other "natural" existing things, is often extended to include the totality of the "universe" and all of its known or supposed phenomena. Second, sometimes "nature," as encompassing all "natural" existing phenomena, is viewed as including human beings. We are part of nature. Third, "nature" is also used to refer to inherent or essential characteristics or distinguishing qualities, as in references to the "nature of myth" or to "human nature." In this sense, human nature may be analyzed as an integral part of the natural world or as uniquely and essentially separated from natural phenomena.

In pointing to a major source of ambiguity, confusion, and irrationality in the political uses and abuses of "nature" and "natural," John Stuart Mill notes that these terms "are sometimes used to mean the way things would be without human intervention and sometimes to mean the way things ought to be, as though the two are somehow synonymous." This specific confusion has become "one of the most copious sources of false taste, false philosophy, false morality, and even bad law."[1] Eliade sometimes conflates these two distinct meanings and unintentionally introduces possible confusion. Often he uses these terms in a more descriptive manner, as when referring to lunar rhythms and seasonal cycles of nature. But in other contexts, he introduces a normative dimension, as when he asserts that human beings, when ignoring or violating the "messages" of such natural rhythms and cycles, are alienated from their true nature, from how they ought to live to realize a meaningful human existence. In this sense, human beings are mythic beings, and myths allow us to realize our nature as integral parts of a coherent, meaningful, significant natural world and cosmos.

"Cosmos," although sometimes used by scholars simply to refer to the universe of all known or supposed objects and phenomena, most often refers more specifically to the world or universe regarded as an orderly, harmonious whole or system. "Cosmos" here is distinguished from "chaos." The dialectic of the sacred, symbolism, and myths "cosmicize," or make something into a cosmos, in the sense of transforming fragmented, unstructured, meaningless phenomena into a coherent, structured, meaningful whole. Eliade's theory of myth and religion is not unrelated to his phenomenological method in which he interprets the meaning of a specific myth, ritual, or other religious phenomenon by situating it within a total hermeneutical framework of coherent (lunar, solar, aquatic, vegetative, etc.) systems of symbolic associations. What was unintelligible becomes meaningful and significant as part of a structured whole. In this sense, Eliade's method and theory both express a process of cosmicization.

Sometimes "nature" and "cosmos," "natural" and "cosmic" are used interchangeably by Eliade, since it is most often the hierophanization of natural phenomena, the extension of the dialectic of the sacred through the symbolization of nature, and the mythic transformation through which human beings realize a harmonious relation with nature that allows for the transformation of chaos into cosmos.

In a significant formulation, full of ontological and metaphysical assumptions and judgments, Eliade responds to a question about the future of religion in the following manner:

> One can't predict anything. But I believe that certain primordial revelations can never disappear. . . . As long as we still have night and day, summer and winter, I don't think man can be changed. Whether we will or no, we are part of that cosmic rhythm. One can change values. The religious values of agricultural community— summer, night, seed—are no longer ours; yet that rhythm still remains: light and dark, night and day. Even the most areligious person alive still exists within that cosmic rhythm. . . . Of course, we

are conditioned by our economic and social structures, and the expressions of our religious experience are always conditioned by our language, by society, by our interests. But, nevertheless, we still assume that human condition here—here in this cosmos, whose rhythms and cycles are ineluctably given. So we assume our human condition on the basis of that fundamental existential condition. And that "basic" human being—it is permissible to call him "religious," whatever appearances may seem to say, because we are talking about the meaning of life.[2]

Having delineated several widespread meanings of "nature" and "cosmos" and related these to a few specific features of Eliade's approach to religion and myth, we may now distinguish general uses of "nature" and "natural" in Eliade's writings. As with the most common usage just cited, Eliade often refers to nature as that which exists independent of human intervention, outside of human time, history, and culture. He describes nature as having its own rhythms, patterns, and even "mode of being." Independently existing nature "speaks" to human beings, often revealing to us truths about our own mode of being in the world, such as lunar rhythms disclosing truths about our human destiny. "The World 'speaks' to man, and to understand its language he needs only to know the myths and decipher the symbols. Through the myths and symbols of the Moon man grasps the mysterious solidarity among temporality, birth, death and resurrection, sexuality, fertility, rain, vegetation, and so on. The World is no longer an opaque mass of objects arbitrarily thrown together, it is a living Cosmos, articulated and meaningful. In the last analysis, *the World reveals itself as language.* It speaks to man through its own mode of being, through its structures and its rhythms."[3]

Sometimes this "speaking" or revelation of nature is so intimately connected with our human mode of being in the world that Eliade deemphasizes the sense of nature existing independent and separate from humans and presents more of a sense of the "homologization" of human beings with nature. Human beings are nature, are an essential part of nature. When we intuit and decipher fundamental truths of nature, we at the same time understand essential truths of human nature and the nature of our mode of being in the world. In this sense, Eliade contends that modern humans, in being alienated from external nature, are at the same time alienated from their own nature.

In a more interactionist sense, Eliade frequently begins by recognizing a clear separation between human beings and nature, expressed as our "fallen" human mode of being in the world, our "profane" condition in time and history. Our spiritual mythic project then involves a creative dynamic interaction with a nature with which we are not completely homologous. Independently existing nature interacts with, modifies, restructures, and adds significance and meanings to human existence; at the same time, human beings interact with, modify, restructure, and add significance and meanings to nature. Key to this nature-human interaction is the role of symbols as a kind of "linguistic bridge." Often there is the Eliadean sense of celestial, telluric, aquatic, and other symbols of nature as "givens," as "ciphers" "speaking" to human beings, as inexhaustible sources for the disclosure of meaning. But there is also the sense that such symbols are human language, reveal basic structures of human consciousness and ways humans situate themselves in the world, and are essential means for the human constitution of cosmos out of chaos. This sense of human-nature interaction may be described as a "constituted given."

Finally, there is a common use of "natural" not to be found in Eliade. In Hobbes, Freud, and many other "modern" thinkers, "the state of nature" and "human nature" are violent, threaten human survival, and must be subdued and controlled. This "negative" use of nature has clear theological precedents in Augustine and many other theologians who often distinguish fallen and sinful nature from divine grace. In some contexts, Eliade has a rather "romantic" and exalted view of nature; in other writings, he describes nature in a more "neutral" manner. But the common theological and modern usage of nature as "evil" and that which needs to be controlled and dominated are foreign both to his scholarly uses and to his own attitude, values, and personality.

PARTICULAR RELIGIOUS BIAS?

In chapter 3, we formulated Eliade's universal structure of sacralization, his universal criteria for distinguishing religious phenomena. Since Eliade claims that all myths are religious, the sacred-profane dichotomy and the dialectic of the sacred must be present in all myths. For example, all myths are constituted by and disclose the paradoxical coexistence of the supernatural and the natural, the eternal and the temporal, the transhistorical and the historical. Mythic narratives incarnate, condition, and limit gods and other sacred realities, while the sacred at the same time moves to disengage itself from its embodied mythic forms and realize its exemplary, perfect, paradigmatic structures. And sacred histories in mythic form reveal and at the same time camouflage and conceal inexhaustible sacred meanings and significations.

We shall assume that recent critiques of deconstructionists, postmodernists, pragmatists, and relativists directed at all efforts at totalization and universalization do not necessarily doom all such efforts to failure and that attempts at formulating universal criteria for distinguishing myths and other religious phenomena are worth considering. In other words, while acknowledging that Eliade's attempt at formulating a universal structure of the dialectic of the sacred and the profane necessarily involves a high level of abstraction, which does not do justice to class, gender, race, ethnic, and other specific variables defining the cultural and historical boundaries of particular myths and other religious phenomena, one may consider whether such formulations still have explanatory value in shedding light on the meaning and significance of religious data.

Does Eliade's attempt at formulating a universal dialectic of hierophanies betray a particular religious bias?[4] Does he go far beyond a level of abstraction, necessary for any universalization, to favor certain kinds of religion? Does the dialectic of the sacred privilege certain kinds of myths while devaluing, ignoring, or distorting others? Critics and some supporters have contended that Eliade favors "archaic religion," assumes an "archaic ontology," and accepts the archaic as his model of what it is to be religious. Others, fewer in number, have criticized or occasionally supported Eliade for adopting a Christian, normative, theological position. Many have either attacked or praised Eliade for favoring antihistorical religions and for adopting an approach not commensurate with the unique characteristics of the historical religions of Judaism and Christianity. In *Structure and Creativity in Religion,* I argued for an interpretation in which Eliade does make assumptions and normative judgments that favor archaic religions, privileges religious phenomena more characteristic of Eastern rather than Western religions, and evaluates as the "highest" or most "elevated" spiritual phenomena those mystical expressions most clearly found in certain forms of Hindu spirituality.

These concerns will be considered in later chapters when we examine the nature and function of myth, especially where Eliade typically uses "archaic myth" to formulate the characteristics of myth in general, and when we consider mythic history as sacred history, especially where Eliade seems to endorse a radically antihistorical model as part of his universal formulation. For now we may begin to formulate some of Eliade's analysis of archaic religion, cosmic religion, Indian religion, and Christianity, including cosmic and Eastern Orthodox Christianity. Throughout this study, it will be important to note whether Eliade's theory of myth and religion privileges these kinds of religions and religious phenomena.

Archaic Religion and India

The overwhelming majority of examples cited by Eliade in his scholarly works are taken from archaic religions. Eliade admits that he has devoted most of his attention to archaic religious phenomena. He provides several fascinating personal explanations for his focus. For example, in a number of writings, he discusses his early dissatisfaction with Romanian and even Western "provincialism" and his quest for "the universal." His research in Italy in 1928 for his "master's thesis" (licentiate thesis) on Italian Renaissance philosophy, especially that of Pico della Mirandola, Giordano Bruno, and T. Campanella, was an opening out to a larger world of mythic and spiritual meaning. Most decisive were the three years he then spent in India. It was in India that he discovered the meaning of religious symbolism, the language of myth, and a kind of religiosity observed in Indian peasant religion and folklore, which then allowed him to appreciate myths, rituals, and other religious phenomena in Romanian and other peasant "cosmic religions." For ten years, he held open the hope that Indian spirituality would allow him to grasp the universal, but he finally realized that even that spiritual horizon was too narrow. He then broadened his investigation of religious phenomena to focus on peasant archaic religion and folklore, the major focus of his scholarly studies of myth.[5]

Eliade's clearest formulation of the decisive influences of his experiences in India appears in the section entitled "India's Three Lessons" in his *Ordeal by Labyrinth*.[6] First, Eliade claims that he discovered an Indian philosophy or an Indian spiritual dimension that had pre-Aryan roots and that had been neglected by other scholars. In various writings, he describes this as India's "tendency toward the concrete" and claims this as his "original insight," the original thesis of his doctoral research in India from 1929 to 1931 and of his dissertation, which was completed in 1935 and published in 1936 as *Yoga: Essai sur les origines de la mystique indienne.* Unlike most Westerners investigating Indian philosophy, Eliade was not drawn to the Upanishads—the Vedic scriptural source of India's classical, Orthodox, Hindu philosophies—or to the influential monistic philosophy of Vedānta. He was not attracted to an abstract, otherworldly, life-renouncing India. Nor was he drawn to a second, popular tradition of *bhakti,* or religious devotion. Instead, he discovered a third approach, expressed in some forms of Sāmkhya and Yoga, in which "man, the world, and life are not illusory. Life is real, the world is real. And one can master the world, gain control of life." What is more, he "discovered that India had a knowledge of certain psychophysiological techniques that enable man to enjoy life and at the same time gain control of it. Life can be transfigured by a sacramental experience." Such techniques and methods, expressing this tendency toward the concrete in which human life is transfigured, allow for the resanctification of life and nature.[7]

At first, it may seem that this "discovery," in contrast to the more general second and third "lessons," is restricted to Eliade's specialized research on Indian spirituality. This theme certainly appears in *Yoga: Immortality and Freedom* and his other books on Yoga and in his numerous articles and literary works focusing on India.[8] This point, with detailed illustrations from Tantrism, alchemy, and folklore, distinguishes Eliade's interpretation from most Western approaches emphasizing classical Yoga. Nevertheless, it seems to me that this more restricted discovery extends to Eliade's entire scholarship on myth and religion. The focus on concrete psychophysiological techniques allowing for the transfiguration of life, the concrete integration of theory with transforming ritual and practice, and the concrete sanctification and homologization of nature and cosmos are key to Eliade's major interpretations of myth and religion. For example, it is evident in his many studies of shamanism, as seen in *Shamanism: Archaic Techniques of Ecstasy,* and in his many studies of alchemy, as seen in *The Forge and the Crucible.* Indeed, in this discovery of a dynamic process of concrete sacralization, it is possible to see one of the roots of Eliade's later key idea of hierophanies and the structure of the dialectic of the sacred and the profane.

Eliade's "second discovery" in India was that of "the meaning of symbols." Eliade recounts that in Romania he "hadn't been particularly attracted to religion; to my eyes, all those icons in the churches seemed merely to clutter them up." It was while living in a Bengali village that Eliade observed how women and girls related to the symbol of the Śiva *liṇgam.* "So this possibility of being religiously moved by the image and the symbol—*that* opened up a whole world of spiritual values to me." "This discovery of the importance of religious symbolism in traditional cultures—well, you can imagine its importance in my training as a historian of religions."[9] No "discovery" was more important for Eliade's methodology and his interpretation of myth and religion. Religious language is symbolic; symbolism is the language of myth; and symbolism expresses and itself extends the process of sacralization. Eliade's interpretive framework consists for the most part of structural systems of religious symbols. Chapters 5 and 6 will be devoted to Eliade's theory of symbolism.

Eliade's "third discovery" in India was the key to his interpretation of a universal, archaic, peasant religiosity. He tells us that this could be called "the discovery of Neolithic man." Shortly before returning to Romania, he spent several weeks with the Santal tribal aborigines in

Central India. There he discovered the roots of a pre-Aryan culture—a Neolithic civilization based on agriculture with its religious and mythic vision of cycles of nature constituting a model for spiritual life. He then recognized the importance of Romanian and Balkan peasant folk culture and a universal archaic mythic religion, an underlying spiritual unity, based on the cycles and mystery of agriculture. "In India I discovered what I later came to refer to as 'cosmic religious feeling.'" Eliade observes that many scholars did not treat such archaic, peasant religion with much respect. But having lived in India among those for whom the phenomena of "cosmic religion" were still a living thing, that "gave me a starting point, so that I was then able to grasp their importance for the general history of religions. In short, it was a question of revealing the importance and the spiritual value of what is called 'paganism.'"[10]

This discovery of a Neolithic, agriculturally-based, cosmic religion in aboriginal India later helped Eliade to understand "the structure of Romanian culture" as expressed in *Zalmoxis: The Vanishing God* and other major works. In addition, it led to his later claims of a common, symbolically structured, organic unity of a universal, archaic, cyclical, mythic spirituality. This peasant-based, archaic religion became the major focus of his scholarly work.[11]

In various writings, Eliade maintains that his personal decision to focus on archaic religion had nothing to do with favoring such a religious orientation. His decision was based on an assessment of the state of research in the history of religions: other investigators had ignored, devalued, or distorted the profound structures and meanings of archaic myth and religion. Therefore, he undertook as his primary hermeneutical task the goal of interpreting and rendering intelligible to modern Western societies the religious life-world of the archaic. Eliade also frequently asserts that he in no way proposes to establish the archaic as a model for modern societies or to suggest that modern persons should "return" to some archaic mode of being.

Essential features of archaic religion have already been delineated under the universal structure of sacralization. In *The Myth of the Eternal Return* and other works, Eliade presents the major aspects of an underlying "archaic ontology." Through the imitation and repetition of exemplary mythic models, an object or act becomes real, and profane time and history are abolished. Everything which lacks such exemplary mythic models is meaningless and unreal. This archetypal and antihistorical ontology reveals the desire of archaic *homo religiosus* to escape, abolish, or transcend historical time and thus experience the exemplary, mythic, sacred dimension as meaningful and real.[12]

Eliade does not intend to restrict this archaic religion with its specific ontology to "primitive" or pre-literate societies. Central to his interpretations are the phenomena of Eastern religions. There is little doubt that he believes that the archaic ontology, at the foundation of pre-literate religions, received its most developed expressions in Eastern, and most typically Hindu, religious experience.[13] In attempting to abolish profane time and history, Indian mystics realized that the "unification" and "cosmicization" of the world, as based on the revelations of the rhythms of nature and other cosmic phenomena, constituted an imperfect or "intermediate phase." One must go beyond such earlier archaic experiences in order *"to transcend the cosmic condition as such."* Such an acosmic religion expresses a transcendence of all that is limited, finite, "normal," "secular," "social," and "human"; a consciousness ("superconsciousness," "transconsciousness") of an unconditioned freedom that "exists nowhere in the cosmos."[14]

The question remains whether Eliade assumes a model from archaic religion, which he observes in pre-literate societies and which reaches its exemplary form in Indian spirituality and various other antihistorical mysticisms, and generalizes from it as his universal norm. Is such a formulation of myth and religion sufficient for interpreting Western "historical religion" or "modern" mythic phenomena? Does his universal model favor an antihistorical "cosmic Christianity" and other forms of "cosmic religion" found in peasant societies and in various forms of mysticism in the West and throughout the world? Because Eliade undoubtedly emphasizes archaic phenomena and what he calls the archaic ontology, one possible conclusion is that he does privilege an archaic orientation and generalizes from archaic religion to religion in general.

Another possible conclusion, for which there is also considerable evidence in Eliade's writings, is that he assumes, privileges, and essentializes a certain conception of what it is to be human and to live an authentic, meaningful existence. Such an essentialized conception is expressed in terms of his universal formulations and claims about the human as *homo religiosus, homo symbolicus,* and mythic being. For example, in the section on "archetypes" in chapter 6, we shall note several, significant, controversial ontological and metaphysical claims by Eliade about foundational "archetypal intuitions": about when human beings first became conscious of their position in the cosmos, which was when *homo religiosus* first experienced the structure of the sacred as revealing the true human place in the cosmos. Eliade seems to be claiming that such archetypal intuitions have a permanent, universal, transcultural and transhistorical status, that they reveal something essential about the human condition as such.

Therefore, in this second interpretation, some of Eliade's claims about archaic mythic structures and an archaic ontology do apply to nonarchaic phenomena, but not because of some generalization from an assumed archaic orientation to religion in general. Rather, one should conclude that what Eliade says about the archaic often applies to other mythic and religious phenomena because the archaic illustrates, without exclusively defining, his universal, essentialized theory of myth, religion, and human nature.

Cosmic Christianity
Eliade's formulation of religion, especially the universal process of sacralization revealed by the dialectic of the sacred and the profane, emphasizes the central importance of "nature" and "cosmos" in the world of archaic religion and of religion in general. Modern nonreligious human beings, by contrast, are alienated from nature and exist in "noncosmicized," fragmented, incoherent "chaos." Archaic religion usually emphasizes circular, cyclical, and nature-oriented "cosmic religion." "Specifically characteristic of agriculturists, cosmic religiosity continued the most elementary dialectic of the sacred, especially the belief that the divine is incarnated, or manifests itself, in cosmic objects and rhythms."[15] The Christianity that most interests Eliade is the agricultural-based, nature-oriented, antihistorical "cosmic Christianity" of eastern European peasants.

In many writings, Eliade shows how the "popular living religions" of European peasants, especially of South and Southeast Europe, resisted Christianity for many centuries and finally became Christianized, but only as new religious creations in which Christianity was understood as a cosmic liturgy and in which eschatology and soteriology were given cosmic dimensions.[16]

> The peasants, because of their own mode of existing in the Cosmos, were not attracted by a "historical" and moral Christianity. . . . The Christological mystery also involved the destiny of the Cosmos. "All Nature sighs, awaiting the Resurrection" is a central motif not only in the Easter liturgy but also in the religious folklore of Eastern Christianity. . . . "Nature" is not the World of sin but the work of God. After the Incarnation, the World had been re-established in its original glory; this is why Christ and the Church had been imbued with so many cosmic symbols. . . . Even more significantly, Christ, while remaining the Pantocrator, comes to Earth and visits the peasants just as, in the myths of archaic peoples, the Supreme Being was wont to do before he became a *deus otiosus;* this Christ is not "historical," since popular thought is interested neither in chronology nor in the accuracy of events and the authenticity of historical figures.[17]

Continuing with a claim that will strike many readers as quite contrived, but that clearly reflects Eliade's interpretation of myth and religion and his personal preferences, he tells us that "there is no contradiction between the Christ image of the Gospels and the Church and the Christ image of religious folklore." This popular, folkloric, "cosmic Christianity of the rural populations is dominated by nostalgia for a Nature sanctified by the presence of Jesus." Eliade is then able to relate this cosmic Christianity to two of his favorite archaic and universal mythic themes: the "nostalgia for Paradise" and a transfigured Nature representing a rebellion and protection against the "terror of History."[18]

In considering Mircea Eliade's attitude toward and interpretation of history and of contemporary Western society, it will become much more evident that his approach toward this cosmic religion, in general, and cosmic Christianity, in particular, is often in sharp contrast to his approach to Western, "historical" Christianity. Usually ignored or deemphasized in Eliade's scholarly studies are the rationalistic, theological, ethical, and historical dimensions of Christianity and other Western religions. Emphasized are nature-oriented, cosmic, and antihistorical Christian phenomena usually neglected by other scholars. For example, in *A History of Religious Ideas,* Eliade devotes less than two pages to St. Thomas Aquinas and his well-known and influential Thomistic theology, while he presents eastern European, peasant, ritual songs of Christmas and "cathartic dances" (revealing pre-Christian survivals) in considerable detail and with interpretations of mythic and religious meaning and significance.

Eliade's journals and other personal writings are full of sentiments reflecting "how far I feel, sometimes, from the spirit of Western Christianity," with its dogmatism and obsession with sin and evil, and his conviction that the Western historical religions of Judaism, Christianity, and Islam express forms of mythic and other religious experiences that are "fossilized" and "outmoded." By contrast, he approves of, even identifies with, the "optimism" of the cosmic religion of the Romanian Christian peasant who "believes that the world is good, that it returned to that state after the incarnation, death, and resurrection of the Savior." This is a cosmic Christianity "in which the historical element is ignored, and in which the dogmatic element is scarcely manifest." Indeed, "Christianity in general, and 'Christian philosophy' in particular, are capable of renovation if they develop the cosmic Christianity."[19] Does this unusual emphasis and preference distort Eliade's claim to a descriptive universal formulation of myth and religion?

A number of scholars have concluded that Eliade's history and phenomenology of religion have little do with the dominant forms of Christianity. Thomas Altizer, for example, maintains that Eliade's approach favors a return to an archaic mode of being and is therefore inconsistent with his "Christian ground"; Kenneth Hamilton assumes that Eliade's approach is theological and argues that his *homo religiosus* is inadequate for understanding a dominant, faith-oriented, "religionless" Christian theology; and Guilford Dudley contends that Eliade rejects historical Christianity and believes the essence of "true" Christianity to be an anti-historical archaic ontology.

At the same time, a minority of scholars have claimed that Eliade does not ignore Christianity in favor of archaic religion, even if the archaic includes a peasant-based cosmic Christianity with many pre-Christian attitudes and structures. Rather, they claim that he even favors Christianity in his general interpretation of religion. John Saliba, for example, asserts that Eliade "affirms that man is by nature a Christian"; and Stephen Reno, in the clearest argument for the Christian basis of Eliade's approach, maintains that his dialectic of the sacred discloses a "progressive vision" of hierophanies that is based on essentially Christian theological grounds.

Some of the confusion and debate on this issue of whether Eliade assumes a normative Christian position arises from the ambiguity in Eliade's writings. There are several passages which, if viewed in isolation and not related to Eliade's total presentation of myth and religion, might suggest an evaluation of Christianity as the superior religion.[20] In most of these passages, Eliade is emphasizing the continuity of all hierophanies from the simplest and most elementary to the "supreme hierophany" of the incarnation of God in Jesus Christ. That is, he is claiming that the structure of the process of sacralization is universal. In *The Sacred and the Profane,* Eliade clearly qualifies his assertion by stating that "for a Christian" this is "the supreme hierophany."[21] In several other works, it is clear that he is presenting such an evaluation from a particular religious point of view or within a specific religious context. Nevertheless, there are several passages in which Eliade simply asserts that the Christian incarnation is the supreme hierophany or theophany.

Stephen Reno argues that Eliade interprets religion in terms of sacred manifestations arranged in a hierarchical manner from the most elementary to the supreme Incarnation of Jesus Christ; that such a "progressive" vision of hierophanies is based on a Christian theological position; and that Eliade attempts (unsuccessfully) to resolve the mystery of the paradox of incarnation by appealing to Christian theology.[22] Reno bases almost his entire case on one passage from

Patterns in Comparative Religion: "One might even say that all hierophanies are simply prefigurations of the miracle of the Incarnation, that every hierophany is an abortive attempt to reveal the mystery of the coming together of God and man."[23] Eliade continues: "It does not, therefore, seem absurd in the least to study the nature of primitive hierophanies in the light of Christian theology: God is free to manifest himself under any form—even that of stone or wood." "One could attempt to vindicate the hierophanies which preceded the miracle of the Incarnation in the light of Christian teaching, by showing their importance as a series of prefigurations of that Incarnation. Consequently, far from thinking of pagan religious ways (fetishes, idols and such) as false and degenerate stages in the religious feeling of mankind fallen in sin, one may see them as desperate attempts to prefigure the mystery of the Incarnation. The whole religious life of mankind—expressed in the dialectic of hierophanies—would, from this standpoint, be simply waiting for Christ."[24]

Several scholars have maintained that the Christianity favored by Eliade and which most shaped his universal formulations of myth and religion was the Eastern Orthodoxy of his native Romania. Probably the strongest case has been made by Mac Linscott Ricketts in *Mircea Eliade: The Romanian Roots, 1907-1945.*[25] On the one hand, Eastern Orthodox interpretations of icons, the "deification" of human beings, and the emphasis on nature certainly fit in nicely with Eliade's views of hierophanies and the dialectic of the sacred. Scattered passages in Eliade's *Autobiography* and *Journal* express his attraction to Eastern Orthodoxy, often contrasted to his hostility toward Western religions, including Western Christianity. For example, he occasionally reveals that he has never been very interested in the theological "problem of evil," "never experienced an inferiority complex" often arising from a Western Christian sense of pessimism and sin, and never had to defend himself against the church.[26] "In Rumania, the children and youths of my generation were unburdened with these shackles. Religion was one of the components of the culture to which I belonged, and I couldn't have accepted it more naturally. Christianity in its Oriental form, Orthodoxy, was intimately linked to the very history of the Rumanian people." Eliade continues that in this Romanian context of Eastern

Orthodoxy, he was free to make his own criticisms, judgments, and refusals without risk: "It is to this full and total freedom that I owe the objectivity I've been able to have, and the sympathy I've shown toward the religious phenomenon. It is to that freedom that I owe having become a historian of religions without prejudice of any sort."[27]

On the other hand, there are many revealing passages in Eliade's *Autobiography, Journal,* and other personal writings in which, while emphasizing his youthful insistence on the "primacy of the spiritual" and his often remarkable and disturbing personal obsession with spiritual experiments, he concedes "how ignorant I was regarding Eastern Christianity and Romanian religious traditions, to say nothing of the 'Orthodox experience', which I did not have at all." "Personally, although I felt attracted to this [Romanian] tradition, I did not *live* it." Indeed, his own spiritual experiments, with his emphasis on the disciplined and determined will and without any notion of grace, were more like "magic" and other religious phenomena than Eastern Orthodox religious experience.[28] Thus, while the youthful Eliade was often preoccupied with "the spiritual," he was not religious in any traditional way, and he was often quite ignorant of the specific mythic and religious characteristics of Eastern Orthodoxy that were at odds with his personal orientation.

It was later, in India, that Eliade claims that he discovered the nature and meaning of the religious language of symbolism and a kind of peasant "cosmic religion" that helped him to understand the folklore and cosmic religiosity of Romanian, Eastern Orthodox peasants. Later in the 1930s, when Eliade focused on the need for "Romanianism," for a Romanian spiritual and cultural renewal, he envisioned the dual revolutionary forces as a new intellectual and cultural elite, of which he played a leading role, and traditional religious peasants.

The extent to which Eliade's upbringing within an Eastern Orthodox society, even if he did not practice or greatly understand the institutional and peasant religion, disposed him to his interpretations in India of symbolism, myth, Yoga, Tantra, a Hinduism of concrete sacralization, and a peasant cosmic religiosity is open to speculation. What seems clear is that his experiences of mythic and religious phenomena in India were significant in influencing his many writings in Romania, especially in the late 1930s, on Romanian spirituality and, more generally, on myths and symbols of archaic and traditional cosmic spirituality.

One may conclude that Eliade's formulation of religion, in terms of the universal dialectic of the sacred and the profane, does not reflect a normative bias toward Christianity. The religious phenomena toward which he is most sympathetic in Christian and other Western traditions are religious creations most similar structurally to archaic cosmic religions and antihistorical mysticisms most dominant in Hinduism and other Eastern religions. The serious question is not, then, whether Eliade's universal characterization of religion favors Christianity but whether it can do justice to the specific, sometimes unique, characteristics of traditional Western Christianity, as well as Judaism and Islam. The question is whether Eliade universalizes—as his essential model for all religion—an archaic ontology and certain kinds of Eastern spirituality that devalue the temporal and the historical. Does Eliade provide an interpretation of Christianity that favors archaic, cosmic, Hindu and other Eastern, nonhistorical religious roots, influences, and structures?

ELIADE'S PERSONAL FAITH AND HIS SCHOLARSHIP

In chapter 1, some very controversial claims from Eliade's early Romanian writings indicated a view that the scholarly interpreter of myth and religion must have had personal religious experience and be a religious believer. Many of Eliade's severest critics have always suspected and sometimes charged that he has a hidden, personal, religious agenda that informs and distorts his scholarly interpretations. Some evidence of such charges was presented in chapter 2, which discussed how reductionistic critics typically accuse him of having his own, personal, subjective, theological agenda, of an unscientific scholarship that amounts to an apologetic defending of the faith, of a dogmatic dismissal of scholarly approaches that challenge his religious commitment, and of reading all kinds of personal religious meanings and significance into his data.

What is intriguing is that a number of Eliade's supporters seem to have turned what was previously seen as a scholarly liability by many critics, and at times even by Eliade himself, into a virtue. Several of his defenders have written books maintaining that Eliade's personal life and literary and scholarly contributions are all of one piece; that one cannot understand his scholarship without understanding his personal religious and other beliefs and commitments. Mac Linscott Ricketts maintains that the essence of Eliade's scholarship can be found in his early Romanian religious and other experiences and writings; Carl Olson views Eliade's scholarship as essentially theological and philosophical; and David Cave interprets Eliade's scholarship as essentially based on his spiritual vision of a new humanism. Here we shall focus only on their claims that Eliade's Christianity is an essential part of his scholarship.[29]

As has been seen, Ricketts contends that Eliade's early Romanian views are the key to interpreting his later scholarly works. By using not only literary publications and scholarly studies of Eliade's youth but also notebooks and unpublished writings, hundreds of newspaper columns, radio talks, and other Romanian material not readily available, Ricketts is determined to reconstruct Eliade's evolving personal faith with his religious and philosophical beliefs. For example, using a youthful autobiographical work and a number of newspaper articles, Ricketts reconstructs Eliade's personal views of Eastern Orthodox Christianity. We find an Eliade obsessed with a philosophy of "virility" and heroism, which he, at least in a few places, identifies as a Christian philosophy of life. Christ is the great Christian hero. Eliade "believes in Christ, but not in God or in grace." Christianity becomes for him the only alternative to a tragic human life. His view of Orthodox Christianity is of a "Christ-mysticism," an imitation of Christ through love and through the determined human will.[30]

Several years later, after Nae Ionescu and others criticize Eliade's view of Orthodox Christianity (especially his extreme will to power and his denial of the necessity of grace for religious experience of the absolute) and after Eliade returns from India, Ricketts claims that Eliade's revised "personal religion" and "personal philosophy" are now of a piece. Now attracted to the "cosmic Christianity" of Romanian peasants, Eliade affirms a faith of the joyous celebration of life (not the former tragic heroism), the harmonious sacralization of nature, and a personal detachment from history.[31]

There is much that is revealing but also questionable about this kind of approach to Eliade. For example, Ricketts reconstructs Eliade's "personal religion" and philosophy from merely two newspaper pieces from the productive 1932-1933 period, when Eliade wrote several hundred articles indicating no interest in expressing his own personal faith. In addition, from his later writings and from my contact with him, it is not the case that Eliade, either in his personal life or in his scholarship, clearly renounced his early attitudes and commitments described as antithetical to his Christian Orthodox faith. For example, some of us marveled and were at times saddened by Eliade's obsession to write and publish right until his death. This determination allowed him to remain incredibly productive, even while suffering for years from extremely painful and debilitating arthritis and fading vision. Such an attitude kept him alive: he would not die because his scholarly work remained unfinished. His accounts of the last years of his life, especially as described in *Journal IV, 1979-1985,* make for a disturbing, painful, and sad reading.[32] Eliade is filled with melancholy, self-pity, self-criticism, and persistent dissatisfaction. Even at ages 77 and 78, this world-famous scholar is incapable of letting go and affirming his so-called "personal religion" and philosophy of life. There is little sense of the simple, faith-oriented, peasant affirmation of the joyousness of life; of the need to renounce a human will struggling heroically to achieve amidst a tragic sense of human existence; or of any acceptance of God's will and grace in determining his life. These religious and philosophical views do appear prominently through the characters in many of Eliade's literary works, including a number of late novellas of the 1970s, but they are less present in his general attitude toward his own life and especially toward his scholarship.

Most important for our purposes, such an approach attempting to reconstruct Eliade's personal faith may at times be insightful, but it is also extremely risky when interpreting Eliade's methodology and scholarly interpretations of religion and myth. We shall return to this danger of collapsing distinctions between the personal and the scholarly after commenting on Olson's and Cave's interpretations of Eliade's Christianity.

For now, it is important simply to note that it does not seem accidental that Eliade was completely silent, evasive, or extremely hesitant in expressing many of his earlier Romanian views, including his personal religious and philosophical beliefs, in his later "mature" scholarly works. Many personal views are expressed in later publications of his journals, autobiography, and interviews, but even there he is often silent or evasive. When prodded by Claude-Henri Rocquet in *Ordeal by Labyrinth* to disclose some of his personal religious and philosophical beliefs, Eliade typically answers as follows: "I made the decision long ago to maintain a kind of discreet silence as to what I personally believe or don't believe. But I have striven all my life to understand those who do believe in particular things: the shaman, the yogin, and the Australian aborigine as well as the great saints—a Meister Eckhart or a Saint Francis of Assisi. So I shall answer your question as a historian of religions."[33]

Responding to Rocquet's question about a passage in his journal describing a friend's spiritual experience, Eliade states that "there are certain transhuman experiences that we are forced to accept as fact. But what means do we have of knowing their nature?" When then asked whether he has had similar things happen to him, Eliade's total response is "I hesitate to answer that."[34] Later Rocquet notes that he has put off asking Eliade about the divine, sensing his reticence in advance. Eliade, at this point already in his 70s, responds: "It is true that certain questions are of such importance for my very existence, and for any reader who is deeply concerned with them, that it would not be fitting to broach them in conversation. The question of divinity, central as it is, is one I would not wish to let myself speak of lightly. But I do hope to tackle it one day, in a completely personal and coherent way, in writing."[35]

Were there good reasons that Eliade might have been so reticent to express the personal religious beliefs now at the foundation of some recent interpretations of his scholarship? Why did he sometimes deny, in print and in conversation, religious and other youthful views that Ricketts cites and at times claims as essential to his later scholarly development? Is it not likely that Eliade realized that some of what might appear in youthful, personal newspaper columns or in autobiographical works about his sexual desires or his will to gain revenge against his teachers and to overthrow the older generation would be inappropriate, even embarrassing, if included in rigorous scholarly studies? Is it not likely that the Eliade of forty or fifty might have been uncomfortable with some of his youthful expressions of age twenty? And is it not likely that many of his earlier cultural and political views about Romanian nationalism, fascism, the Iron Guard, and dictatorship, which he sometimes presented as part of his personal spiritual position, would prove scandalous if disclosed in the context of the United States and the West and would also prove devastating if scholars concluded they were essential to interpreting his scholarly works on myth and religion? In short, there are many reasons to be cautious in speculating and making strong connections between Eliade's personal life and religious faith, as revealed both in his early Romanian writings and in his mature scholarship on religion and myth in his history and phenomenology of religion.

In *The Theology and Philosophy of Eliade: A Search for the Centre,* Carl Olson analyzes Eliade's "call for the abolition of time as a nostalgic wish for a return to what he calls cosmic Christianity." According to Olson, cosmic Christianity expresses not only Eliade's formulation of the religion of Romanian and other eastern European peasants but also Eliade's own personal religious quest. Olson proposes that "the paradigmatic model and centre of existence for contemporary beings that Eliade advocates is cosmic Christianity."[36]

In a few places, Olson criticizes this view of cosmic Christianity as the paradigmatic model and "solution" for contemporary humankind: "Due to his cosmopolitan background, his criticism of cultural provincialism and his existential relativism, Eliade's theological reflections and nostalgia for the cosmic Christianity of Rumanian peasants is open to suspicion and suggests a possible camouflaging of his own theological position. Eliade's mind and body are in the twentieth century, but his heart is in the *illud tempus* of archaic religion."[37] By advocating this cosmic Christianity with its "abolition of time by an eternal recurrence to a primordial history embodied in myth," Eliade's "solution to the terror of history" is criticized by Olson for not accounting for progress and meaning. For Olson, a "better alternative for modern human beings" would be to place a more positive value on historical progress and "to strive to integrate history and nature."[38]

In focusing on certain passages and ignoring others, Olson overdoes Eliade's identification with the cosmic Christianity of eastern European peasants. In addition, Eliade was not so narrow, naive, and romantic as to propose that a premodern, mythic, peasant, cosmic Christianity could provide a simple religious model and solution for the existential crises of contemporary humanity. Eliade was an eclectic, synthethizing, universalizing thinker whose religious orientation was influenced by a combination of nonWestern archaic phenomena, Hindu and other forms of Asian spirituality, cosmic Christianity and other forms of "cosmic religion," and other expressions of the sacred. His relationship to Romanian cosmic Christianity, both in his own life and in his scholarship, expressed deep appreciation, but was often complex, ambiguous, and contradictory.

In *Mircea Eliade's Vision for a New Humanism,* David Cave also argues that Eliade favors Christianity—not the ahistorical cosmic Christianity emphasized by Olson, Ricketts, and others, but the superiority of Christianity as the most historical religion! Because the problem of history is the central theme in his works, Eliade "is led by necessity to value most Jesus Christ as a hierophany over all other hierophanies." His new humanism has "a decidedly Christian slant. For it is Christianity that most completely historicizes the sacred." "Eliade's theory of history and of hierophanies remains, in the end, provincial to Christianity."[39] On the basis of this interpretation, Cave, who is one of Eliade's strongest supporters, criticizes his new humanism as too limited: "Eliade's attention to the problem of history and his valorization of hierophanies limits his morphology to a Christian orientation, since Christianity boasts the most historically involved incarnation of the 'sacred.'"[40]

The danger with such approaches to Eliade, as found in the works of Ricketts, Olson, Cave, and other supporters, as well as in the attacks by critics, is that they tend to blur and collapse legitimate, albeit flexible, distinctions: the scholarly and the personal, the objective and the subjective, and the descriptive and the normative.[41] They often push Eliade where he, as a scholar, understandably refused to go. In emphasizing how Eliade's scholarship is essentially linked to his personal religious faith, they tend to collapse legitimate distinctions. One must distinguish different levels of interpretations: some relatively more descriptive; others clearly normative, theological, and metaphysical. Interpretations require different criteria of verification and provide different degrees of certainty. These supporters unintentionally render Eliade's scholarship even more open to scholarly criticism.

None of this is intended to endorse a clear-cut separation of the personal from the scholarly; of Eliade, the person with feelings, beliefs, and commitments, from Eliade, the scholar who interprets myth and religion. Eliade's scholarly approach and interpretations of myth and religion cannot be understood without uncovering and analyzing his assumptions, beliefs, and priorities. This is true not only of his privileging the religious, in general, and his specific theory of the sacred, in particular. In addition, there are all kinds of assumptions, normative judgments, and ontological moves—some that go beyond the perspectival limitations of the disciplines of the history and the phenomenology of religion—that are essential to his interpretations of myth, religion, and secular life. But to see the key to Eliade's scholarship in some largely hidden, personal faith, such as a personal endorsement of cosmic Christianity or Romanian Eastern Orthodox Christianity, both oversimplifies and misrepresents Eliade's personal life and, more importantly, his scholarly interpretations of religion.

NOTES

1. John Stuart Mill, "Nature," from *Three Essays on Religion,* in *The Philosophy of John Stuart Mill,* ed. Marshall Cohen (New York: Random House, 1961), pp. 445, 487; John Stuart Mill, "The Subjection of Women," in *Collected Works of John Stuart Mill,* ed. J. M. Robson, vol. 21 (Toronto: University of Toronto Press, 1984), pp. 269-70, 276-82; Susan Moller Okin, *Justice, Gender, and the Family* (New York: Basic Books, 1989), pp. 37-38.

2. Mircea Eliade, *Ordeal by Labyrinth: Conversations with Claude-Henri Rocquet,* trans. Derek Coltman (Chicago: University of Chicago Press, 1982), pp. 116-17.

3. *Myth and Reality,* p. 141.

4. By "a particular religious bias," I mean a religious bias in favor of particular religions or particular kinds of religious experience. There is no

doubt that Eliade has a general bias in favor of religious interpretations of religion and, as we shall see, religious interpretations of modern nonreligion.

5. See, for example, *Autobiography 1*, p. 204; *No Souvenirs*, pp. 17-18.

6. *Ordeal by Labyrinth*, pp. 54-60. Arriving in India before he was twenty-two, Eliade says that "the next three years were essential ones in my life. India was my education. Today, if I try to formulate what the decisive lesson was that I learned there, I see that it was threefold" (p. 54).

7. Ibid., pp. 54-55.

8. A significant article is Eliade's first publication in English, "Cosmical Homology and Yoga," *Journal of the Indian Society of Oriental Art* 5 (1937): 188-203. Published in Calcutta, this article not only affirms Eliade's interpretation of the tendency toward the concrete in Indian spirituality, but also introduces his specific uses of sacred and profane and develops his analysis of cosmic symbolism and of techniques for homologizing, unifying, and cosmicizing all levels of reality.

9. *Ordeal by Labyrinth*, p. 55.

10. Ibid., pp. 55-57.

11. Ibid., pp. 57-60; *Autobiography 1*, p. 204-6. In *Autobiography 1*, Eliade writes: "It was precisely the peasant roots of a good part of our Romanian culture that compelled us to transcend nationalism and cultural provincialism and to aim for 'universalism'. The common elements of Indian, Balkan, and Mediterranean folk culture proved to me that it is *here* that organic universalism exists, that it is the result of a common history (the history of peasant cultures) and not an abstract construct" (p. 204). With such common, archaic, peasant roots, Eastern Europeans could serve as a bridge between the West and Asia. Eliade indicates that a "good part of his activity in Romania between 1932 and 1940 found its point of departure in these intuitions and observations made in the spring and summer of 1931" in India.

12. For example, see *Eternal Return*, pp. 34-35.

13. In response to a question as to which tradition had most deeply influenced him, Eliade replied, "I consider myself deeply influenced, I can almost say 'formed' or 'shaped,' by the Indian tradition." See "Sacred Tradition and Modern Man: A Conversation with Mircea Eliade," *Parabola: Myth and the Quest for Meaning* 1 (1976): 80.

14. *Yoga*, pp. 95-100; *Images and Symbols*, pp. 85-91.

15. *History 1*, p. 354.

16. *Myth and Reality*, pp. 159-60, 170-74.

17. Ibid., pp. 171-73.

18. Ibid., pp. 173-74.

19. *No Souvenirs*, pp. 110, 189, 261; *Ordeal by Labyrinth*, pp. 116-17.

20. For example, see *Patterns*, pp. 26, 29, 30 n.1; *Sacred and Profane*, p. 11; *Images and Symbols*, pp. 169-70; *Myths, Dreams and Mysteries*, pp. 153-

54; *Eternal Return,* pp. 160-62; Mircea Eliade, *A History of Religious Ideas.* Vol. 2: *From Gautama Buddha to the Triumph of Christianity,* trans. Willard R. Trask (Chicago: University of Chicago Press, 1982), pp. 408-9 (hereafter cited as *History 2).*

21. *Sacred and Profane,* p. 11.

22. Stephen J. Reno, "Eliade's Progressional View of Hierophanies," *Religious Studies* 8 (1972): 153-60.

23. *Patterns,* p. 29.

24. Ibid., pp. 29, 30 n.1. Eliade has made clear, even in this controversial passage, that his interpretation is from a normative Christian perspective and is not intended as a general theory of religion. During my first meeting with Eliade, I cited this passage from *Patterns* and asked Eliade how he could justify such judgments about the supremacy of the Christian Incarnation, especially where he had not qualified his judgments from "the Christian point of view." He replied that such statements were not intended as theological or normative judgments. In some contexts, he simply meant by "supreme hierophany" a recognition of the fact that the Christian hierophany had attempted "to include more" by also sacralizing the historical event rather than rejecting history as meaningless and unreal. Cf. *Images and Symbols,* pp. 169-71.

25. As was seen in chap. 1, Ricketts claims that Eliade's basic assumptions and principles about religion were already formed in his adolescent and undergraduate student years. As was stated on p. 22 n. 16, I disagree with Ricketts on this point. He greatly exaggerates the originality of these youthful views on religion, which often reflected the position of Eliade's teacher Nae Ionescu and were shared by many others at the time. What distinguished Eliade as a remarkable historian and phenomenologist of religion—his interpretations of the nature and meaning of religious symbolism and myth, of hierophanies and the dialectic of the sacred, of the deeper structures and meanings of Yoga, shamanism, alchemy, and so forth—were "discovered" by him during his three years in India, his research in Romania in the 1930s, and his scholarly writings in Paris in the decade after World War II.

26. For example, in *Autobiography 1,* in discussing his novel *Isabek şi Apele Diavolului,* Eliade claims that "I had never believed in the Devil nor ever suffered an obsession with sin, and I was indifferent to the 'problem of evil,' . . " (pp. 167-18).

27. Mircea Eliade, *Journal III, 1970-1978,* trans. Teresa Lavender Fagan (Chicago: University of Chicago Press, 1989), p. 159 (hereafter cited as *Journal 3).* Those familiar with the history of Romania's Eastern Orthodoxy, including its national chauvinism, its anti-Semitism, and its anti-democratic values, may question some of the "objectivity" of Eliade's formulation.

28. *Autobiography 1,* pp. 132-33. It is revealing that in his *Autobiography,* at the point he is leaving Romania for India, Eliade has hardly said anything about his youthful Orthodox identification.

29. Most of what follows presents parts of my "Recent Defenders of Eliade: A Critical Evaluation," pp. 333-51.

30. See Ricketts, *Eliade: Romanian Roots,* 1, pp. 227-29, 261-94.

31. Ibid., "Personal Religion," pp. 602-4.

32. See Mircea Eliade, *Journal IV, 1979-1985,* trans. Mac Linscott Ricketts (Chicago: University of Chicago Press, 1990), (hereafter cited as *Journal 4).*

33. *Ordeal by Labyrinth,* p. 132.

34. Ibid., p. 147.

35. Ibid., p. 188. See also *Journal 3,* p. 275.

36. Carl Olson, *The Theology and Philosophy of Eliade: A Search for the Centre* (New York: St. Martin's Press, 1992), pp. 55-59, 153, 167-70.

37. Ibid., p. 59.

38. Ibid., p. 156.

39. David Cave, *Mircea Eliade's Vision for a New Humanism* (New York: Oxford University Press, 1993), pp. 40 and 53. In chapters 8 and 9, I show why those few interpretations claiming that Eliade places such a primary priority on history and favors a historical Christianity are unjustified. See also my "Eliade and History," *Journal of Religion* 68 (1988): 545-65.

40. Cave, *Mircea Eliade's Vision for a New Humanism,* p. 195. Cave also criticizes Eliade's new humanism for an elitist, top-heavy, and strongly masculine orientation (p. 139).

41. See Allen, "Recent Defenders of Eliade," pp. 346-48.

CHAPTER 5

Symbolic Language and Structure

An understanding of Mircea Eliade's theory of symbolism is essential for understanding his theory of myth. Symbolism is of the greatest importance in analyzing Eliade's approach for at least three major reasons. First, for Eliade, religious language is necessarily symbolic. Since myth is religious myth, mythic language is necessarily symbolic. Therefore, in understanding myth, one must interpret the religious meaning of its symbolic expression. Second, as will be seen in chapter 7, myths are specific kinds of religious phenomena in which symbols are put together in narrative form to present a "true" story or history disclosing sacred realities. It is necessary to understand symbolism in order to grasp the irreducibly religious nature and the irreducibly mythic nature of phenomena at the heart of Eliade's history and phenomenology of religion. Third, the most important key to understanding Eliade's entire scholarly approach, the methodological foundation of his history and phenomenology of religion, is his hermeneutical framework consisting of religious symbolisms. He most often interprets the meaning of specific mythic and other religious expressions by situating or "reintegrating" them within their coherent structural systems of symbolic associations or relevant symbolisms.[1]

Chapters 5 and 6 focus on symbolism and myth. We begin with a presentation of some of Eliade's basic analysis of symbolism as the language of myth: his fascination with religious symbols; his view of human beings as both *homo religiosus* and *homo symbolicus;* and reasons that religious symbolism is essential for his theory of myth. Next we examine the central role of "structure," especially the structural systems of religious symbols, in Eliade's approach to myth and other religious phenomena. Then in chapter 6, we formulate Eliade's analysis of the major characteristics and functions of symbolism, since this is key to his interpretation of the meaning of myths. This is followed by an attempt to clarify Eliade's ambiguous and often misunderstood uses of "archetype" and "archetypal" in his analysis of symbolism and myths. Finally, an illustration—the universal symbolism of the "centre"—is used to convey some sense of the hermeneutical framework of systems of religious symbols underlying Eliade's interpretation of myth.

SYMBOLISM: THE LANGUAGE OF MYTH AND RELIGION

Eliade has often been described as one of the world's leading interpreters of religious symbolism. For example, an article entitled "Scientist of Symbols" describes Eliade as "probably the world's foremost living interpreter of spiritual myths and symbolism."[2] Eliade was always fascinated by religious symbols. This is clearly reflected in his scholarly studies, his literary creativity, and his personal writings. In his notebook of a summer vacation of 1937, reproduced in his *Autobiography*, Eliade admits how "mediocre a memory" he has "for shapes and masses. But maybe it's because none of these interests me as a reality of the first order." Placing himself within a European cultural context, while differentiating his approach from much of the cultural creativity of his contemporaries, Eliade adds: "Like all European nationalists, I don't believe that form, line, and proportion are the only categories of culture. Beyond these worlds of forms—which fascinate a Paul Valéry, a Eugenio d'Ors—there exists a 'purer' world of a more stark spirituality, *the world of symbol.* My eye, which cannot retain for long the *design,* quickly seeks and discovers back of the forms and lines—the *symbol.*"[3]

This fascination with "seeing" endless symbols and profound symbolic meanings almost everywhere has been the source of much criticism. Critics frequently claim that when *they* look at the data, they don't see the "hidden" symbols, the symbolic "revalorizations," and the "profound" symbolic meanings. Eliade has "forced" symbols that pre-exist in his head onto the data and "read" all kinds of symbolic meanings into the mythic and other religious expressions.

In such discussions as those on the "concealment and camouflage" of the sacred and on the need for a "creative hermeneutics," as well as in his personal writings, Eliade admits that he often "sees" all sorts of symbols overlooked by others. For example, in his *Journal* of November 1945, he tells us that Ştefan "Lupaşcu marvels that I am so taken with a picture in which, he says, I 'see' things—symbols not seen by others. I reply that I see such symbols because they *are there.* If another doesn't see them, it doesn't mean they *don't exist* but simply that he can't see them."4

One could easily conclude that Eliade is an epistemological and a metaphysical idealist. He certainly is a metaphysical idealist, as is evident from his frequent attacks on "materialism." But from this journal entry and many other writings, it is clear that he does not endorse a kind of epistemological idealism that analyzes symbolism, myth, and other phenomena as totally accounted for by the operations of constituting human minds. In many respects, Eliade endorses an epistemological realism. Just as Plato claims that his nonmaterial Forms have an objective ontological status independent of individual intuiting minds, Eliade claims that he "sees" religious symbols and mythic and cosmic structures and meanings, not because he has invented or created them through his imagination, but rather because they have an "objective" reality. They are "really there."

At the same time, one should not interpret Eliade as maintaining that religious persons are passive in detecting and contemplating religious symbolic structures that are "really there." Far more than Plato, Eliade emphasizes the dynamic role of the perceiving, imagining, creative subject and the necessary interaction between constituting subject and essential symbolic structure. *Homo religiosus* experiences a real world of essential objective structures and meanings, but this is always an unfinished world of inexhaustible possibilities; a world whose particular meaning and significance must be actively constituted.

We have seen Eliade's attempt to define the human being as *homo religiosus.* In chapter 3, we analyzed the dialectic of the sacred in which natural, limited mythic and other religious expressions are used by *homo religiosus* to express paradoxically what is experienced as supernatural and unlimited. Such religious language is necessarily symbolic. Therefore, it is not surprising that *homo religiosus,* in particular, and the essential human being, in general, are often defined by Eliade in terms of *homo symbolicus:* "Since man is a *homo symbolicus,* and all his activities involve symbolism, it follows that all religious facts have a symbolic character. This is certainly true if we realize that every religious act and every cult aims at a meta-empirical reality. When a tree becomes a cult object, it is not as a *tree* that it is venerated, but as a *hierophany,* that is, a manifestation of the sacred. And every religious act, by the simple fact that it is *religious,* is endowed with a meaning which, in the last instance, is 'symbolic', since it refers to supernatural values or beings."[5]

No conception gets better at Eliade's view not only of mythic beings but also of his general approach to the essence of what it is to be a human being situated in the world than *homo symbolicus.* He tells us in 1950 that he'd like to write a book entitled *"L'Homme comme symbole* [Man as Symbol]." He "would show the need of man to live in conformity with symbol, with the archetype. I'd insist on the function that the imagination has of spiritual technique, of fulfillment, equilibrium, and fecundation."[6] Eliade frequently presents the image of the human being as *homo symbolicus,* as "a living symbol" who unifies phenomena on different levels of experience, establishes a structured meaningful orientation in the world, and creatively renews herself or himself by "bursting open" the limitations of temporal and historical conditionings and by "opening out" to the transcendent.

As part of this view of the human being as *homo symbolicus,* Eliade submits that it is religious symbolism that created or constituted what we recognize as distinctively human. In a passage full of claims central to his understanding of myth and humankind, Eliade, as historian of religions, criticizes a "doubly erroneous" reflection by Teilhard de Chardin that God still appears to us as a "Neolithic proprietor."

> First of all, the image of this "Neolithic proprietor" is relatively recent, going back only twelve or fifteen thousand years. It was preceded by other images, even more archaic: That of God "master of the sky," or those divinities of prehistoric hunters, the "lords of the beasts." Even more serious: for humanity, it is not with such images

that the history of religions began, but with the experience of the sacred, with the multiple hierophanies that structure the world and infuse it with meanings. In the end, it is religious symbolism that created man—that is, that differentiated him from the other primates. To realize this, it suffices to compare the behavior of primates in their "familiar space" with the *orientatio,* that rite that establishes the world of men.[7]

Symbolic myths reveal the essential ways by which *homo symbolicus* has constituted the essence of what it is to be a human being, and they provide the paradigmatic models in terms of which humans have oriented themselves in a meaningful, coherent, human world.

We began this chapter by outlining three general reasons that Eliade's theory of symbolism is key to understanding his approach to myth: religious language, and therefore mythic language, is necessarily symbolic; myths are a particular kind of symbolic narrative expression; and Eliade's methodological approach to myth is grounded in his hermeneutical framework of religious symbolisms. We now add three reasons that religious symbolism is crucial for Eliade's specific theory of religious myth. First, the sacred referent in mythic expression and the human need to establish some relation with that "meta-empirical reality" necessitate the use of religious symbolism. Second, mythic experience and expression are not restricted by the limits of conscious awareness but involve *homo religiosus* as the "total person," including the prereflective, the unconscious, and the "transconscious."[8] Third, as seen in the dialectic of the sacred, symbolism is an essential part of the extension of mythicization and other aspects of sacralization.

In chapter 3, we considered Eliade's claim that religion is always concerned with the sacred and that mythic religious expressions always refer to transcendent, supernatural values and beings. Typical of writers on symbolism, Paul Tillich states that "first and most fundamental is the character of all symbols to point beyond themselves." The symbol has a "figurative quality"; it is an indirect means of communicating that which is not the "usual," "ordinary," "literal" meaning. Paul Ricoeur analyzes this symbolic quality of "pointing beyond" in terms of a "double intentionality": a "first, literal, obvious meaning itself points analogically to a second meaning which is not given otherwise than in it." Ricoeur attempts to "understand the analogical bond between the literal meaning and the symbolic meaning."[9] Eliade frequently emphasizes that because of the nature of the sacred, and thereby of all mythic phenomena, *homo religiosus* must use symbolic expressions that "point beyond" themselves and communicate meanings that are not direct, literal, or ordinary.

Although Eliade usually emphasizes this need for symbolism as arising from the fact that the referent of religious expression is experienced as something transcendent, the sacred referent is never unmediated. In the paradoxical relationship and the dynamic dialectical movement between sacred and profane, the transcendent, supernatural "other" must be made humanly accessible and meaningful for there to be mythic and other religious experience. How is it possible for finite, conditioned human beings, situated within limited spatial, temporal, natural, cultural worlds, to relate to something infinite, unconditioned, supernatural, and transcendent?

Here Eliade and other theorists of symbolism emphasize the specificity of the religious symbol, which enables it to serve as a kind of bridge: the symbol uses specific, concrete, "natural" phenomena in its expression and enables *homo religiosus* to relate that which is "other" to her or his particular existential situation. Symbols "render the reality of the other accessible and open to participation and communion." "The religious symbol because of its specificity takes into itself those realities which are a part of the religious man's local environment, but in the symbolic ordering the local ingredients take on meanings which are more than natural."[10]

Symbolism is also central to Eliade's theory of myth because of his emphasis on the prereflective, unconscious, and transconscious dimensions of religious experience. We may better situate Eliade's approach by commenting briefly on the value placed on rationality in Western philosophy and in more recent orientations in philosophy, culture, religion, and history of religions.

Most Western philosophers since the classical Greek philosophies of Plato and Aristotle have tended to assume versions of the conception of the human being as essentially a "rational animal." It is our capacity for rationality that distinguishes us from, and "elevates" us over, other animals. Human beings often act in other than rational ways, but these reflect our "animal instincts" and "lower" or less fully developed levels of human behavior. Plato's "Divided Line" in *The Republic* illustrates this traditional, philosophical, hierarchical orientation.[11]

There have always been philosophers and other scholars who have rejected this conception of human nature. Mircea Eliade is certainly closer to German, Romanian, and other Romanticism, as well as Eastern and other mysticism, than to rationalistic influences of the Enlightenment that primarily defined the birth of the modern scientific study of religion *(Religionswissenschaft)* in the nineteenth century. Almost all religious orientations have recognized a level of spiritual realization transcending the limits of rationality. But even the most influential Christian theologians, St. Augustine and St. Thomas Aquinas, while leaving room for a faith that transcends rational comprehension, place a tremendous value on the human capacity for rationality. This is undoubtedly one of many reasons Eliade expresses such alienation from the history of mainstream Western Christian philosophy and theology.

In the twentieth century, there have been widespread attacks on the view of human beings as rational animals. Confidence in rationality has often been shaken by devastating wars of mass destruction and by the "irrational" behavior of so-called rational scientists and scholars in contributing to and justifying the attempted genocide of Jews and others in the Holocaust; the development of nuclear and other weapons threatening the survival of humankind; and the production of various technologies that destroy the environment and seem to produce even greater oppression, exploitation, poverty, domination, and suffering.

Depth psychology, a major influence on Eliade, has focused on prereflective levels of repression and preconceptual, unconscious, instinctive needs and desires. Existentialism and phenomenology have rejected the orientation of traditional philosophy by focusing on the intentionality of the prereflective, the emotions, and the imagination. Feminism, deconstructionism, and postmodernism have presented powerful critiques of modernity in which the theoretical privileging of rationality has been analyzed as excluding gender, race, class, and other "voices" and producing ideological justifications for dominant relations of power. Many twentieth-century cultural innovations in music, art, and theater defy rational and conceptual analysis and extol the absurd, nihilism, disharmony, and discontinuity.

Within religion, there has been a dramatic backlash in which neo-Orthodox or conservative theologies reject a liberal theological confidence in human rationality and progress. Recent decades have witnessed a dramatic, often militant, resurgence of charismatic and fundamentalistic groups with highly emotional, nonrational, or even antirational faith orientations. *Homo religiosus* is not viewed as essentially a rational animal. Quite the contrary: an assertion of human rationality is often seen as an expression of human arrogance and sinfulness.

Historians of religion and phenomenologists of religion have also tended to reject earlier conceptions of humans as rational animals. Nineteenth-century innovators in the modern scientific study of religion tended to assume hierarchical rational norms; rationally-defined evaluative influences were built into their descriptions of myths and other religious phenomena. On the basis of their narrowly rationalistic interpretations, Tylor, Müller, Frazer, and other scholars interpreted religion and myth as reflecting a prerational, prephilosophical, prescientific stage of human evolution. By contrast, Eliade agrees with his predecessor in the history of religions at the University of Chicago, Joachim Wach, who submitted that "the statement that experience must be conceived of as a total response of the total being to Ultimate Reality means that it is the integral person which is involved, not just the mind, the emotion, or the will." Wach contends that many previous theologians and philosophers failed to realize that religion is concerned with the total integral person and have argued about the "seat" of religion: "From Schleiermacher to James, Whitehead, and Otto it was sought in feeling; from Hegel and Martineau to Brightman, in the intellect; and from Fichte to Reinhold Niebuhr, in the will."[12]

Although Eliade's approach to myth is very critical of a number of the above mentioned twentieth-century developments, he strongly agrees that any attempt to conceive of the human being as in essence a rational animal is too narrow, too reductionistic, and too "provincial." It is *homo religiosus* as *homo symbolicus* that best gets at the prereflective, unconscious, and transconscious dimensions of mythic and other religious experience.

In comparing Hegel's conception of the *List der Vernunft* (Cunning of Reason) with his conception of the symbol and its function in psychical life, Eliade asserts that "symbols bring into the reality of experience transpersonal values and events that the individual was not capable of apprehending consciously and voluntarily." Only by emphasizing that thanks to symbols one's "psychic life is infinitely more interesting than the individual's conscious mind" can Eliade appreciate "the importance of myth (or of what is left of it) for the modern world."[13] "Real man is a *total* man, and the unconscious has its role and its importance; the unconscious represents *life* and *nature* in man. Symbols, images, and longings arise from the dramas and the revelations of the unconscious—and it is through these dramas and these revelations that man is in living communication with nature, the cosmic totality."[14] Eliade emphasizes that "hierophanies and religious symbols constitute a prereflective language. As it is a case of a special language, *sui generis,* it necessitates a proper hermeneutics."[15]

Therefore, rational analysis is often of very limited use in getting at many dimensions of mythic disclosure. Simply dismissing mythic phenomena as prerational or irrational, as so many scholars have done, is not very helpful if our objective is to understand the nature, function, and meaning of myth. It is religious symbols that arise from and reveal structures and meanings of the unconscious foundations of myth, and they provide the framework for that "proper hermeneutics" necessary to interpret prereflective mythic meanings.

Finally, as was suggested in the formulation of Eliade's view of the dialectic of the sacred, the extent of the process of mythicization and of sacralization would be severely limited if it depended only on "direct" hierophanies. Religious symbolism extends this process of sacralization by "bursting open" the profane so that it reveals something other. Eliade claims that symbolism has played an important part "in the magico-religious experience of mankind . . . primarily because it [the symbol] is able to carry on the process of hierophanization and particularly because, on occasions, it is *itself* a hierophany—it itself reveals a sacred or cosmological reality which no other manifestation is capable of revealing." He then states that "the authentic nature and function of symbols can best be grasped by a closer study of symbols as a prolongation of hierophanies and an autonomous form of revelation."[16] Symbolism "carries further the dialectic of hierophanies by transforming things into *something other* than what they appear to profane experience to be."[17]

Eliade provides illustrations of this function of religious symbolism in his studies of alchemy, beginning with articles in the 1920s, then leading to three books and monographs in the 1930s, and culminating in *The Forge and the Crucible* in 1956.[18] According to Eliade, alchemy was not a rudimentary uncritical science, a prechemistry, but a traditional spiritual technique with cosmology, initiation, and soteriology. Although there were physical operations, attempting to transmute nature, the goal arose from the hierophanization of matter and included not some scientific conquest of nature but rather the transmutation and salvation of the alchemist.

In interpreting the meaning of the myths and rituals of alchemy, Eliade focuses on the "passion," "death," and "marriage" of substances in transmuting matter and life and on the goals of the Philosopher's Stone and the Elixir Vitae. In such interpretations, the role of symbolism is evident in carrying further the dialectic of the sacred which arises from particular magico-religious experiences of relations with matter. Eliade focuses on the ambivalent alchemical symbolism of death—the alchemical operation referring either to the alchemist or to the mineral substance—as permeating the whole *opus alchymicum.* He notes texts with "the reduction of substances to the *materia prima,* to the *massa confusa,* the fluid, shapeless mass corresponding—on the cosmological plane—to chaos. Death represents regression to the amorphous, the reintegration of chaos." This is why aquatic religious symbolism is so prominent in alchemical procedures. "The alchemical regression to the fluid state of matter corresponds, in the cosmologies, to the primordial chaotic state, and in the initiation rituals, to the 'death' of the initiate." Eliade then shows that this alchemical reduction to the *prima materia* can also be interpreted symbolically as disclosing "a regression to the pre-natal state, a *regressus ad uterum,* " "a spiritual experience corresponding to any other 'projection' outside Time—in other words, to the reintegration of a primal situation":

> The dissolution and reintegration of chaos is an operation which, whatever the contexts, presents at least two interdependent significations: cosmological and initiatory. Every "death" is at once a reintegration of cosmic night and pre-cosmological chaos. . . . Initiatory death and mystic darkness thus also possess a cosmological significance: they signify the reintegration of the "first state," the germinal state of matter, and the "resurrection" corresponds to the cosmic creation. . . . In this respect the alchemist was not an innovator. While seeking the *materia prima* he pursued the reduction of substances to their pre-cosmogonic state. He knew that he could not achieve transmutation if he used as his starting point "forms" already worn by time. In the initiatory context, "dissolution" meant that the initiate "was dying" as far as his profane, worn, fallen existence was concerned. That cosmic night was compared to death (darkness) as well as to the regression *ad uterum* is something which emerges both from the history of religions and from the alchemical texts.[19]

It should be evident from these limited references to Eliade's interpretation of the mythico-ritual meaning of alchemy that the dialectic of the sacred, arising from the direct hierophanization of matter, has been extended in complex and multivalent ways through cosmological, initiatory, aquatic, sexual, and other symbolisms.

SYMBOLISM AND STRUCTURALISM
Mircea Eliade often writes of the primary importance that he places on religious "structures"; of how structures are at the foundation of his methodology and provide the framework for his interpretation of religion and myth. By "structure" we simply mean that when examining the endless and often confusing variety of variables appearing in myths and other religious phenomena, Eliade detects "invariables," intentional configurations and relations, or at least

patterns with some sense of permanency. He interprets meaning through structure.

For some of these mythic and religious structures, Eliade claims a universal, transcultural, and transhistorical status. Illustrations of such fundamental structures are seen in Eliade's analysis of the dialectic of the sacred and the profane, the "symbolism of the center," and the "symbolism of ascension." Other mythic structures are much more dependent on specific, local, cultural, and historical variables, such as a particular mode of production and socioeconomic organization or the conquest of or defeat by others. When these particular variables are radically altered, as in the destruction of traditional economic and cultural relations or the apparent futility of invoking the example of the mythic hero in staving off military defeat, the corresponding mythic structures often lose their existential value and explanatory power for these mythic peoples. By contrast, more universal structures, such as fundamental lunar structures of endless rhythmic cycles of life, death, and periodic regeneration, allow for new and creative symbolic revalorizations so that mythic peoples can cope with or at least tolerate tragic and contradictory historical and cultural developments.

Eliade's notebooks, etymological and other "scientific" studies, and other youthful writings show a fascination with structure. Revealing, for example, is his account of an oral logic examination taken under Nae Ionescu, not only his favorite, revered professor but also, as has been noted, the major influence on shaping his early approach toward myth and religion. Ionescu asked about Newton's discovery of the universal law of gravitation. "What sort of logical operation took place in his mind that allowed him to understand that an apple—that is, a particular object—illustrated a universal law?" After pausing, Eliade responded that he had recently read a book by Lucian Blaga and had been impressed that "certain minds see elements of unity in nature or culture, they see what is essential and fundamental, and this allows them to discover structures." The examination ended as Ionescu interrupted with "that's the answer!" "It's a matter of *structure*. The logical operation effected in Newton's mind did this: it apprehended the structure of the phenomenon of universal gravitation."[20]

Eliade's approach to religion, with his sense of a phenomenological *epoché,* is directed against all forms of reductionism. By suspending his interpretations about what is "real," this phenomenologist attempts sympathetically to reenact the experiences of religious beings and to describe the meaning of their religious mythic phenomena.

Such a "bracketing" by itself does not suffice to provide Eliade with insight into the fundamental structures and meanings of mythic experience. Earlier this century, Franz Boas and many other anthropologists insisted on cultural relativity and pluralism and were reluctant to acknowledge "common structures." More recently, Derridian deconstructionists with their insistence on "difference" and all kinds of anti-essentialist relativists and pragmatists have insisted on cultural pluralism and diversity. Claims for common structures are often critiqued as ideological attempts at justifying ethnocentric, Eurocentric, classist, racist, sexist, and other relations disclosing hegemonic projects of domination. Therefore a claim by Eliade and other theorists of myth and religion that they intend to respect the irreducibility of their mythic data and to attempt to reenact the experiences of other mythic beings might very well lead to an unlimited plurality of diverse mythic and religious life-worlds, each disclosing highly individualized structures and irreducible differences that vary according to specific time, place, and culture.

In order to understand how Eliade might respond to these typical objections to his approach, often formulated as attacks on him as an uncritical generalist and universalist, we must examine how he attempts to gain insight into essential structures and meanings of mythic experience. This requires an elucidation of the structuralistic nature of his phenomenological approach.

David Rasmussen correctly notes that Eliade "suggests that phenomena of a given type or structure will tend toward system." The "initial structure tends toward a larger context of structural associations."[21] Morphological analysis is Eliade's "hermeneutic alternative" to replace the "historical-evolutionary hypothesis" that one finds in the works of Tylor and other anthropologists and historians of religion. Through morphological analysis and classification, Eliade attempts "to separate those phenomena which have structural similarities from those which do not." Rasmussen turns to structural linguistics and cites the diachronic-synchronic distinction found in Ferdinand de Saussure's *Course in General Linguistics* as providing the "analogy which clarifies best a hermeneutic grounded in structuralism." He submits that "Eliade has asked the structural question regarding the place of a religious phenomenon within a total synchronic system. This leads to the basic judgment that religious phenomena tend toward system. This tendency is the intentional mode of every particular sacred manifestation. On this assumption morphological analysis is held to be necessary; its consequence is the transition from appearance to under-standing." Therefore, Eliade has a distinctive "phenomenological procedure" grounded in structuralism: "Understanding does not occur by the reconstruction of a particular phenomenon, but rather by the reintegration of that phenomenon within its system of associations through the use of morphology and structuralism."[22]

This phenomenological procedure has considerable support because of the nature of religious symbolism. Such a procedure is not arbitrarily superimposed on the mythic religious data but is largely derived from the nature of structural systems of religious symbols. In examining various modalities of the sacred, Eliade looks at different human existential situations, at different ways that human beings have been situated in the world. In analyzing myths and other cultural creations, he finds that they are not isolated and arbitrary expressions but must be viewed as aspects of different structural systems. The key to under-standing these structural systems is Eliade's interpretation of symbol-ism. What he finds are lunar, aquatic, and other structural systems of religious symbols, and these symbolisms provide the theoretical framework within which he interprets the meaning of particular mythic expressions.

If Eliade finds a tendency toward system, this is primarily because of "the function of symbols" of "unification" of different zones and levels of experience, of enabling isolated fragments to become part of a whole system. His morphological analysis reveals that "the various meanings of a symbol are linked together, interconnected in a system, as it were," and Eliade reserves the term "symbolism" for such a "structurally coherent ensemble."[23] What Eliade finds is that "we are faced with, respectively, a sky symbolism, or a symbolism of earth, of vegetation, of sun, of space, of time, and so on. We have good cause to look upon these various symbolisms as autonomous 'systems' in that they manifest more clearly, more fully, and with greater coherence what the hierophanies manifest in an individual, local and successive fashion. And I have tried, whenever the evidence in question allowed of it, to interpret a given hierophany in the light of its proper symbolism so as to discover its deepest significance."[24] If understanding of myth occurs when the phenomenon is "reintegrated" into "its systems of associations," this is possible because Eliade's hermeneutics is grounded in "autonomous," "coherent," "universal" systems of symbolic associations.

Eliade's emphasis is on the structural relations among symbols that constitute coherent systems of religious symbolism. Edmund Leach and other critics have attacked him for emphasizing the individual symbol, and Eliade is inconsistent on this matter.[25] However, if one examines all of his writings, it becomes clear that what is most important for his phenomenological approach is not the particular symbol but the structure of the whole symbolism. A phenomenologist cannot grasp the meaning of the specific symbol's expression in myth unless she or he sees the particular as one of many possible symbolic "valorizations" of the structural system. This emphasis is seen in such claims as the following: "But it is not by 'placing' a symbol in its own history that we can resolve the essential problem—namely, to know what is revealed to us, not by any 'particular version' of a symbol but by the *whole* of a symbolism." Eliade goes on to claim that the contradictions between particular versions of a symbol are usually "resolved as soon as we consider the symbolism as a whole and discern its structure."[26]

This key claim is then illustrated through a series of examples: the new valorization of the Cross with the mythic structure of the Cosmic Tree at the "center" of the world; the mythic theme of the descent into Hell (by shamans, Orpheus, Jesus, etc.) for the sake of the salvation of another's soul; mystical celestial ascension (by shamans, the Buddha, Muhammed, Christ, etc.); and mythic portrayals of the mystical life as a return to a paradisiac state (shamanism, Judaeo-Christianity, etc.). Eliade cautions that in formulating symbolic structural "homologies," he does not mean simply to equate the endless valorizations of the symbolic and mythic structures; they express specific historical and cultural contents with their irreducible differences. Nevertheless, Eliade's major emphasis and hermeneutical contribution is to show that individual mythic symbols and their seemingly confusing and even contradictory versions reveal their most profound religious meanings when they are interpreted as valorizations of coherent universal symbolisms; as variations of essential symbolic and mythic structures.[27]

Eliade's emphasis throughout his phenomenological approach and hermeneutics is on systems of structural relations. In discussing the "opaqueness" of prehistoric documents, Eliade speculates on the mythical-religious values surrounding the tools, implements, and especially weapons of the Paleanthropians. "We need only think of the mythologies built up around lances that pierce the vault of the sky and thus make an ascent to heaven possible, of arrows that fly through clouds, transfix demons, or form a chain reaching to heaven, and so on." Such rich mythologies convey some sense of "all that the worked stones of the Paleanthropians *can no longer communicate to us.* The semantic opaqueness of these prehistoric documents is not peculiar to them. Every document, even of our own time, is spiritually opaque as long as it has not been successfully deciphered by being integrated into a system of meanings."[28] The previous formulation of the structure of the dialectic of the sacred made clear that Eliade cannot even distinguish a particular myth as some individual, isolated, religious phenomenon. The particular mythic manifestation can only be perceived structurally as expressing a unique religious system of structural relations.

In *Structure and Creativity in Religion,* I provide an extended illustration showing that Eliade can interpret the meaning of a particular (snake) symbol only as part of a structural (lunar) system of symbolic associations. Later I use this illustration to elucidate Eliade's phenomenological method in general.[29] The particular symbol *qua* particular symbol proves unintelligible. Here we shall simply provide one brief illustration to show the methodological primacy of the structure of the total symbolism in Eliade's hermeneutics.

In his discussion of the symbolism of the arrow, Eliade examines a number of myths in which gods, culture heroes, shamans, and magicians ascend to heaven by means of a chain of arrows. One cannot interpret the meaning of any of these myths by isolating a particular arrow symbol. Unlike many other examples of ascension symbolism, this particular symbolism of chains of arrows emphasizes not mystical or magical flight but instead "the communication obtained through a 'paradox': the transformation of an eminently fragile and flying object—the arrow—into a solid chain." The meaning of such a paradox becomes clear when the chain-arrow is understood as part of the symbolism of *coincidentia oppositorum* (symplegades, razor bridges, passing through mountains, and so forth). Eliade continues his interpretation of these myths by submitting that "through the paradoxical transformation of flying arrows into a stable and solid chain, a new means of communication between Earth and Heaven has been obtained, comparable to the Cosmic Tree, the Mountain, the Ladder, and so on." Therefore, one must interpret the symbolism of the chain of arrows as part of Eliade's frequent interpretation of the symbolism of the *Axis Mundi*.[30]

In this chapter, we have focused on Eliade's emphasis on *homo symbolicus* and religious symbolism, on how religious symbolism is essential for his interpretation of myth, and on how his phenomenological approach to myth and religion grants primacy to structure, especially the structural systems of religious symbols. The next chapter will develop this analysis by presenting Eliade's formulation of the major characteristics and functions of symbolism. This will provide a better sense of the symbolic, hermeneutical framework at the foundation of Eliade's interpretation of myth and religion.

NOTES

1. This was a major claim developed at great length in my earlier studies *Structure and Creativity in Religion* and *Mircea Eliade et le phénomène religieux*. For a history of the study of symbolism, see James W. Heisig, "Symbolism," in *The Encyclopedia of Religion,* vol. 14 (New York: Macmillan, 1987), pp. 198-208.

2. *Time* (February 11, 1966): 68, 70.

3. *Autobiography 2*, pp. 36-37.

4. *Journal 1*, p. 8.

5. "Methodological Remarks," p. 95. See also *Mephistopheles and the Androgyne,* p. 199.

6. *Journal 1,* pp. 107-8.

7. *Journal 3,* p. 186.

8. For references to Eliade's use of the "transconscious," see p. 24 nn. 33, 34, 35.

9. Paul Tillich, "The Meaning and Justification of Religious Symbols," in *Religious Experience and Truth,* ed. Sidney Hook (New York: New York University Press, 1961), p. 4; Tillich, "The Religious Symbol," in *Religious Experience and Truth,* ed. Sidney Hook, p. 301; Paul Ricoeur, *The Symbolism of Evil,* trans. Emerson Buchanan (New York: Harper & Row, 1967), pp. 10-18.

10. Long, *Alpha,* pp. 8, 10. See also John E. Smith, *Reason and God* (New Haven: Yale University Press, 1967), p. 229.

11. The hierarchical Divided Line, with its four stages of cognition, appears in *The Republic,* Book VI 509-511. A less abstract, nonmathematical presentation of this hierarchical orientation toward knowledge and reality appears in the famous Allegory of the Cave—sometimes called the Myth of the Cave—in *The Republic,* Book VII 514-521. The Divided Line and Cave Allegory appear in numerous translations of *The Republic,* collections of the dialogues of Plato, and other edited anthologies. See, for example, Plato, *The Republic of Plato,* trans. Francis MacDonald Cornford (New York and London: Oxford University Press, 1945) or Plato, *The Collected Dialogues of Plato,* ed. Edith Hamilton and Huntington Cairns (New York: Pantheon Books, Bollingen Series LXXI, 1963).

12. Joachim Wach, *The Comparative Study of Religion* (New York: Columbia University Press, 1961), pp. 32, 33.

13. *No Souvenirs,* p. 87.

14. Ibid., p. 286.

15. Ibid., p. 313. In this journal entry from June 1968, Eliade continues: "I have tried to elaborate this hermeneutics; but I have illustrated it in a practical way on the basis of documents. It now remains for me or for another to systematize this hermeneutics." In *Structure and Creativity in Religion* and *Mircea Eliade et le phénomène religieux,* I try to systematize Eliade's hermeneutics, especially in terms of the dialectic of the sacred and the profane and the hermeneutical framework of structural systems of religious symbols.

16. *Patterns,* pp. 446-47, 448.

17. Ibid., p. 452. Eliade describes the symbol's "function" as follows: "it is to transform a thing or an action into *something other* than that thing or action appears to be in the eyes of profane experience" (p. 445).

18. Eliade felt that his original, controversial interpretations of alchemy were later universally accepted: see *Autobiography 1,* pp. 56, 294.

19. *The Forge and the Crucible,* pp. 8-11, 152-57.

20. *Autobiography 1,* p. 112. A major concern of mine in *Structure and Creativity in Religion* is to analyze the primary status of universal, symbolic, religious structures in Eliade's methodology and hermeneutical framework. See, for example, pp. 175-77, 195-99, 210-12.

21. David Rasmussen, "Mircea Eliade: Structural Hermeneutics and Philosophy," *Philosophy Today* 12 (1968): pp. 141-42.

22. Ibid., p. 143. See the section entitled "Synchronicity" in Mircea Eliade, "The Sacred in the Secular World," *Cultural Hermeneutics* 1 (1973): 104-6.

23. *Patterns,* pp. 451-53; *Images and Symbols,* p. 163; "Methodological Remarks," p. 96.

24. *Patterns,* pp. 449-50.

25. See, for example, Leach, "Sermons by a Man on a Ladder," pp. 30-31.

26. *Images and Symbols,* pp. 163-64.

27. See *Images and Symbols,* pp. 164-69. Each of these examples is developed in great detail in *Shamanism, Myths, Dreams and Mysteries, Quest,* and other works.

28. *History 1,* pp. 5-8. Since the prehistoric documents are so "opaque," Eliade cautions against a common interpretation which focuses exclusively on the tools and weapons and avoids speculation on the myths and rituals of prehistoric hunting peoples. "*Homo faber* was at the same time *Homo ludens, sapiens,* and *religiosus.* Since we cannot reconstruct his religious beliefs and practices, we must at least point out certain analogies [with structural systems of meaning of other hunting peoples] that can illuminate them, if only indirectly."

29. See Allen, *Structure and Creativity in Religion,* pp. 148-57, 190-200.

30. Mircea Eliade, "Notes on the Symbolism of the Arrow," in *Religion in Antiquity: Essays in Memory of Erwin Ramsdell Goodenough,* ed. Jacob Neusner (Leiden: E. J. Brill, 1968), pp. 471-72. One could show the importance of several other symbolisms for Eliade's interpretation of these myths. Our limited formulation should suffice to show that even in this rather specific illustration of the symbolism of the arrow, Eliade's emphasis is not on the individual symbol but on the structural systems of symbolic associations.

CHAPTER 6

Characteristics and Functions of Symbolism

According to Eliade, the symbol arises as a "creation of the psyche," is constituted "as the result of existential tensions," and must be regarded as an "autonomous mode of cognition." "The phenomena of nature are freely transformed by the psyche in 'an autonomous act of creation' into symbols of the power and holiness they reveal to the beholder."[1] Eliade's primary concern in interpreting the meaning of myths and other religious phenomena is with determining how religious symbols function and what they reveal. In this regard he makes the following crucial assertions: that symbolic, and hence mythic, thought is an autonomous mode of cognition that has its own structure; that symbols have their own "logic" and fit together to make up coherent structural systems; that every coherent symbolism is universal; that the symbolic system, and the myths that incorporate such symbolism, will preserve its structure regardless of whether it is understood by the person who uses it.[2]

CHARACTERISTICS AND FUNCTIONS OF SYMBOLISM

In commenting on "the imagination of matter" from Gaston Bachelard's *Water and Dreams,* Eliade summarizes several of his major claims about religious symbolism.

> [T]he imagination constitutes an instrument of cognition, because it reveals to us, in an intelligent and coherent form, the modes of the real. . . . once constituted, the symbol is invested with a double

function: "existential" and "cognitive." On the one hand, a symbol unifies various sectors of reality (aquatic symbolism, for example, reveals structural solidarity among Water, Moon, becoming, vegetation, femininity, germs, birth, death, rebirth, etc.). On the other hand, the symbol is always *open,* in the sense that it is capable of revealing "transcendent" meanings which are not "given" (not *evident)* in immediate experience. For example, the rites of baptism reveal a plane of the real other than the biocosmic (birth-death-rebirth): they reveal the "spiritual birth," rebirth to a transcendent mode of being ("salvation," etc.). The aquatic symbol is . . . a means of intuiting the real in its totality, because it reveals the fundamental unity of the Cosmos. A symbol becomes autonomous at the moment when it is constituted as such, and its polyvalence helps us to discover homologies among different modes of our being—homologies which the simple "imagination of matter" could not make possible.[3]

In the following formulations of the general characteristics and functions of religious symbolism, Eliade's structural analysis usually refers to all symbolism, both religious and nonreligious. For example, it is only because there is a "logic of symbols" operating on the levels of dreams, fantasies, aesthetic imagination, nationalistic and other political ideologies, "psychopathic" creativity, among others, that Eliade can "homologize" symbolic structures of religious mythic phenomena with phenomena on other planes of manifestation. As will be seen in chapter 10, this is a major reason that Eliade is able to claim that his insight into the functions and structures of religious symbolism help him to uncover hidden symbolic and mythic meanings in contemporary, consciously secular phenomena. The following structural features refer, for the most part, to symbolism in general but emerge as features of religious symbolism when related to the structure of the dialectic of the sacred. Symbols are religious symbols when they function within religious contexts. All symbols "point beyond" themselves, but religious symbols, while using specific, ordinary, finite, natural phenomena in their expressions, point beyond themselves to "something" transcendent, supernatural, transhistorical, transhuman. They point to sacred meanings.

The mythic sacred "speaks" or "reveals" itself through symbols. This symbolic revelation cannot be translated into a "utilitarian and objective language." In enumerating "the different aspects of depths of this [symbolic] revelation," Eliade describes the nature and function of religious symbolism in general: religious symbols can reveal structures of the world not evident on the level of immediate experience; religious symbolism is multivalent; because of this polyvalence, religious symbols can integrate diverse meanings into a whole or a system; because of this capacity for unification or systematization, religious symbols can express paradoxical situations or other structures otherwise inexpressible; finally, religious symbolism always has an "existential value."[4]

Stephen Reno notes "the absence of any systematic statement by Eliade himself on the uses of the religious symbol. Apart from his essay, 'Methodological Remarks on the Study of Religious Symbolism', which presents a brief statement regarding the structure of symbols and the morphology of the sacred, there is no explicit statement of the ways in which Eliade himself interprets religious symbols."[5] In the following discussion of these characteristics and functions of religious symbolism, Eliade's treatment in "Methodological Remarks on the Study of Religious Symbolism" from *The History of Religions: Essays in Methodology*—also reproduced as the final chapter in his *Mephistopheles and the Androgyne*—will be supplemented with relevant observations from his other works and from our earlier discussions of religious symbolism. One could mention several other essays,[6] but Reno's point is well taken. Of course, most of Eliade's works are statements on religious symbolism. It is our task to provide a more systematic formulation. We begin with "the logic of symbols" because this is the key methodological concept in Eliade's interpretation of religious symbolism.

The "Logic of Symbols"

Symbols for Eliade are not arbitrary creations of the psyche but function according to their own "logical" principles. Various symbols can combine or "fit together" to form coherent symbolic "systems." Symbolism enables religious persons to bring heterogeneous phenomena into structurally interlocking relationships. In terms of the logic of symbols, Eliade submits that "symbols of every kind, and at whatever level, are always consistent and systematic." "Certain groups of symbols, at least, prove to be coherent, logically connected with one another; in a word, they can be systematically formulated, translated into rational terms."[7]

Paul Ricoeur, citing Eliade as his major example of such "purely comparative phenomenology," describes this concept as functioning on the "first level" of analysis. This level of descriptive phenomenology "limits itself to understanding symbols through symbols." This analysis is on the "horizontal" and "panoramic" plane in which the phenomenologist of religion attempts to describe the internal coherence of the world of symbols and to place symbols in a whole "which forms a system on the plane of the symbols themselves."[8]

Eliade's "logic of symbols" does function on this horizontal plane of internal coherence, but it is also manifest on ever higher levels of reality. It is in terms of the "highest" or most "elevated" symbolic expressions that the logic is best revealed and the "center" of the symbolic system or web is understood. The logic of symbols enables Eliade not only to differentiate planes of manifestation but also to evaluate certain levels as "higher," "deeper," "mature," and "elevated." Therefore, Eliade's concept of the logic of symbols not only functions on the horizontal plane, where one appeals to some criterion of internal coherence, but also involves a "vertical" appeal to some criterion of adequacy. It is this vertical type of appeal which many critics of Eliade find so objectionable. Some of these critics may be willing to grant the existence of internally coherent, symbolically structured ensembles or systems, but they argue that vertical evaluations of different symbolic levels of reality take Eliade far beyond the descriptive and involve him in highly normative judgments based on an assumed ontological position.[9]

Almost every other significant feature of Eliade's analysis of religious symbolism rests on this concept of "the logic of symbols." Only because of the logic of symbols can Eliade speak of the symbol's autonomous mode of cognition. Largely on the basis of such a logic of symbols, he can maintain that symbols preserve their structure and reveal a sense of continuity and universality, regardless of particular historical and temporal conditionings and of whether their meaning is consciously understood. Only on the basis of such a concept can Eliade analyze symbolism as being multivalent and comprehend the unification of structurally coherent meanings into symbolic wholes or systems. Without such a logic of symbols, it would be impossible for him to distinguish different levels of religious manifestations and to evaluate certain levels as "higher," "elevated," or at the "center" of symbolic systems. In short, without such a logic of symbols, Eliade's primary basis for interpreting the meaning of myth and religion, his hermeneutical foundation consisting of autonomous, coherent, structural systems of symbolic associations, would collapse. It might then be seen as at best a highly imaginative and creative formulation, but one devoid of the methodological rigor and sense of objectivity demanded of any scholarly approach.

The Multivalence

"Religious symbols are capable of revealing a modality of the real or a structure of the world that is not evident on the level of immediate experience."[10] This view is illustrated by the many myths in which Eliade interprets snakes as lunar symbols. On the level of immediate experience and in terms of intuitive appeals to rationality, it is certainly not obvious that one ought to interpret the meaning of particular snake or serpent symbols as possible valorizations of lunar symbolism. Such snake symbols reveal the world as a living totality, as inexhaustible life repeating itself rhythmically.[11] Such a revelation is a matter not of purely rational or reflective knowledge but of an immediate intuition of a "cipher" of the world. The world "speaks" through the religious symbol. By such "graspings" the mythic religious world is constituted.

What most allows such a revelation of meaning is the symbolism's "multivalence": "its capacity to express simultaneously a number of meanings whose continuity is not evident on the plane of immediate experience." In his analysis of lunar symbolism, Eliade shows that this religious symbolism is able "to reveal a multitude of structurally coherent meanings": the lunar rhythms, "the law of universal becoming," death and rebirth or regeneration, rain and waters, vegetation and plant life, fertility, "the female principle," human destiny, weaving, and so forth. "In the final analysis, the symbolism of the moon reveals a correspondence of mystical order between the various levels of cosmic reality and certain modalities of human existence. Let us note that this correspondence becomes evident neither spontaneously in immediate experience nor through critical reflection. It is the result of a certain mode of 'being present' in the world."[12]

This emphasis on the multivalence of religious symbolism reaffirms one of Eliade's foremost phenomenological concerns: the criticism of all forms of modern reductionism. The meaning of lunar symbolism cannot be reduced to some "rational" interpretation, even though certain of its aspects, such as the relationship between the lunar cycle and menstruation, may seem to us to have developed by some method of logical or rational analysis. The meaning of lunar symbolism cannot be reduced to one of its many frames of reference, such as the erotic or sexual, even though the erotic is indeed one of its many valorizations and in various myths and rituals may constitute its own "center" and structural system of erotic symbols. Eliade criticizes interpreters for consistently producing "unilateral and therefore aberrant interpretations of symbols." According to Eliade, such a reduction is necessarily "false," because it is a "partial" and "incomplete" interpretation of a religious symbolism and of a symbolic myth. Such reductionism annihilates symbolism as "an autonomous mode of cognition." It is the religious symbolism as multivalent, as a totality of structurally coherent meanings, that is "true."[13]

Eliade illustrates this important methodological point by arguing that Freud, in his interpretation of sexuality and the Oedipus Complex, fails to comprehend the polyvalent function of sexuality symbolism, as seen in the multivalent "Image of the Mother." What is most revealing is not the infant's attraction toward "this or that mother *hic et nunc,* as Freud gives one to understand," but rather "the Image of the Mother which reveals—and which *alone can reveal*—her reality and her functions, at once cosmological, anthropological and psychological." "We need only remember that the attraction to the mother, if we interpret it on the plane of the immediate and 'concrete'—like the desire to possess one's own mother—can *never tell us anything more than what it says;* whereas, if we take account of the fact that what is in question is the Image of the Mother, this desire means many things at once, for it is the desire to re-enter into the bliss of living Matter that is still 'unformed', with all its possible lines of development, cosmological, anthropological, etc.[14] For . . . Images by their very structure are *multivalent.*"[15]

This "unilateral" reduction of religious symbolism is seen in Eliade's interpretation of the symbolic meaning of various mythico-ritual motifs involving caves: "Now the cave represents the otherworld, but also the entire Universe. It is not the immediate, 'natural' valorization of the cave as a dark—and hence subterranean—place that enables us to perceive its symbolism and its religious function, but the experience caused by entering a place whose sacredness makes it 'total', that is, a place that *constitutes a world-in-itself.*" After providing examples of the symbolic meaning of ritual caves, Eliade concludes: "It is only since the 'naturalistic' interpretation imposed by nineteenth-century scholars, who reduced religious symbolisms to their concrete, physical expressions, that the cosmic meaning of caves and underground cult dwellings have been reduced to a single value, that is, the abode of the dead and the source of telluric fertility."[16]

The Function of Unification

"This capacity of religious symbolism to reveal a multitude of structurally coherent meanings has an important consequence": "The symbol is thus able to reveal a perspective in which heterogeneous realities are susceptible of articulation into a whole, or even of integration into a 'system'. In other words, the religious symbol allows man to discover a certain unity of the World and, at the same time, to disclose to himself his proper destiny as an integrating part of the World."[17] Since religious language is symbolic, it is not surprising that this formulation closely resembles Eliade's analysis of the dialectic of the sacred and the relation of *homo religiosus* to nature and cosmos. And since myth is religious and mythic language is symbolic, it is not surprising that "myth" can be substituted for "symbol" in the above formulation, and we would be touching on characteristics of myth presented in the next chapter.

This "tendency to homologize the different planes of reality is of the essence of every archaic and traditional spirituality."[18] Religious symbolism plays the most important role in this process of homologization. One need only think of the snake, first as a purely natural and historical object and then as a religious lunar symbol, in order to understand how a symbol can be homologized with heterogeneous realities which reveal the fundamental structure deciphered in the lunar rhythms.

In this regard, Eliade's phenomenological method adheres closely to his understanding of the very activity of *homo religiosus* as *homo symbolicus* and the symbolic function of integration and unification. He attempts to empathize with and derive his method from the very nature of the religious life-world. The phenomenologist "should strive to grasp the symbolic meaning of the religious facts in their heterogeneous, yet structurally interlocking appearances." Eliade is often accused of oversimplifying the complexity of myth and other religious phenomena by reducing their meaning to his predetermined symbolic structures. But in emphasizing the symbolic function of integration and unification, he claims to be following an opposite procedure: "Such a procedure does not imply the reduction of all meaning to a common denominator. One cannot insist strongly enough that the search for symbolic structures is not a work of reduction but of integration. We compare or contrast two expressions of a symbol not in order to reduce them to a single, pre-existent expression, but in order to discover the process whereby a structure is likely to assume enriched meanings."[19]

In the illustration of lunar symbolism, symbols were seen to reveal a perspective in which heterogeneous realities were integrated into a "system." We presented Eliade's "logic of symbols" and his view of how structurally coherent meanings fit together to form a lunar "web." Intuitions and graspings of the religious meaning of the lunar rhythms allow for the homologization of different levels of existence. As a result, *homo religiosus* not only experiences a certain unity of the world but also understands how her or his mode of being participates in the constitution and destiny of the world. Such religious experience and creativity find symbolic expression through lunar and other myths.

The Expression of Paradoxical and Contradictory Aspects of Reality

Religious symbolism has the capacity to reveal structures of the world not evident on the level of immediate experience. Eliade develops this observation by asserting that symbols reveal "the deepest aspects" of reality "which defy any other means of knowledge." Symbols "respond to a need and fulfill a function, that of bringing to light the most hidden modalities of being."[20] These deepest aspects of symbolic revelation are often experienced as paradoxical and contradictory. It is the symbolic function of unification, the process of homologization and systematization based upon a logic and multivalence of symbols, that allows religious persons to integrate contradictory and paradoxical aspects of reality into a meaningful, coherent, structural whole.[21]

Robert Luyster summarizes some of Eliade's discussion of this symbolic revelation: "The symbol successfully brings to expression, furthermore, those aspects of reality to which the conceptualizing consciousness has been most insensible and which it has been most unable to articulate. It is in fact just these contradictory and mysterious features of the universe for which the very ambivalence (or, more properly, multivalence) of a symbol is most highly suited. A symbol is an image charged with many meanings simultaneously. And it is this very indeterminacy—whatever the logical or scientific disadvantages it may possess—that renders it uniquely able to preserve the richness and the paradox of experienced reality."[22]

It is just these features of reality—paradoxical, contradictory, mysterious—that, according to Eliade, most impress *homo religiosus* and that lead Eliade to emphasize a special revelatory capacity of religious symbolism. "Perhaps the most important function of religious symbolism—important above all because of the role which it will play in later philosophical speculations—is its capacity for expressing paradoxical situations, or certain structures of ultimate reality, otherwise quite inaccessible."[23] What Eliade wishes to emphasize here is such symbolisms as those of the "Symplegades" and the *coincidentia oppositorum*. He believes that such expressions reveal the most creative spiritual experiences and the highest religious attainments.

The conjunction of serpent and eagle in various myths illustrates this analysis. The serpent is usually a symbol of chthonian darkness, the nonmanifest, the fertilizing powers of Mother Earth, "the female principle," and the terrestrial waters. The eagle is usually a symbol of solar light, the manifest, the powers of Father Heaven, and the masculine celestial order. Serpent and eagle are "an archetypal pair of symbolical antagonists." In some myths, the opposition of the eagle and the serpent is emphasized. For example, in citing a scene from Homer's *Iliad,* Heinrich Zimmer observes that the "heavenly bird [an eagle] ravaging the serpent symbolized to him [Kalchas, the priest-soothsayer] the victory of the patriarchal, masculine, heavenly order of Greece over the female principle of Asia and Troy."[24] In many other myths, these symbolical antagonists or polar principles paradoxically coexist. Through the paradoxical conjunction of the serpent and the eagle, mythic persons attempt to express the mystery and unity of the "totality," the divinity, or the absolute.

Such paradoxical expression is seen in Eliade's analysis of the early chapters of Genesis. "The creation of woman from a rib taken from Adam can be interpreted as indicating the androgyny of the primordial man." "The myth of the androgyne illustrates a comparatively widespread belief: human perfection, identified in the mythical ancestor, comprises a unity that is at the same time a *totality.*" Eliade adds that "Divine bisexuality is one of the many formulas for the totality/unity signified by the union of opposed pairs: feminine-masculine, visible-invisible, heaven-earth, light-darkness, but also goodness-wickedness, creation-destruction, etc. Meditation on these pairs of opposites led, in various regions, to daring conclusions concerning both the paradoxical condition of the divinity and the revalorization of the human condition."[25] Such paradoxical and contradictory expressions found in myths of the androgyne and other symbolizations of unity/totality through the union of opposites are central to Eliade's interpretations of Yoga and Indian spirituality, Gnosticism, Hermeticism, and other religious phenomena, and are interpreted at length in his *Mephistopheles and the Androgyne.*

Another illustration of this symbolic revelation and expression of paradoxical and contradictory aspects of reality is Eliade's interpretation of the attempt by religious persons to unify sun and moon. One identifies all of experience with the valorizations of solar and lunar rhythms. Then the person endeavors to homologize these diverse levels of experience and unify the solar and the lunar rhythms in his or her living body. Finally, through such a unification that escapes rational or conceptual consciousness, the person aims at transcending the cosmos by realizing a primordial state of nondifferentiation, the primal unity, the original totality.[26]

> In accepting his presence in the world, precisely as man found himself before the "cipher" or "word" of the world, he came to encounter the mystery of the contradictory aspects of a reality or of a "sacrality" that he was led to consider compact and homogeneous. One of the most important discoveries of the human spirit was naively anticipated when, through certain religious symbols, man guessed that the polarities and the antinomies could be articulated as a unity. Since then, the negative and sinister aspects of the cosmos and of the gods have not only found a justification, but have revealed themselves as an integral part of all reality or sacrality.[27]

The "Existential Value"

Eliade examines myths and other religious documents and tries to interpret the nature and meaning of the religious experience that have given rise to these symbolic expressions. In this regard, he emphasizes "the *existential value* of religious symbolism, that is, the fact that a symbol always aims at a *reality or a situation in which human existence is engaged.*" "The religious symbol not only unveils a structure of reality or a dimension of existence; by the same stroke it brings a *meaning* into human existence. This is why even symbols aiming at the ultimate reality conjointly constitute existential revelations for the man who deciphers their message."[28]

Eliade's analysis of the existential dimension of religious symbolism is related to his formulations of the dialectic of the sacred and the relation of *homo religiosus* to nature and cosmos:

The symbol translates a human situation into cosmological terms; and reciprocally, more precisely, it discloses the interdependence between the structures of human existence and cosmic structures. This means that primitive man does not feel "isolated" in the Cosmos, that he is "open" to the World which symbolically is "familiar" to him. On the other hand, the cosmological valence of symbolism permits him to step out of a subjective situation, to recognize the objectivity of his personal experiences. Of course, it is not a question of reflections, but of intuitions, of immediate seizures of reality. . . . An important consequence proceeds from this cosmological valence of symbolism: we who understand symbols not only "open" ourselves to the objective world, but at the same time succeed in leaving our unique condition and acceding to a comprehension of the universal.[29]

Eliade continues: "the symbol 'explodes' a particular condition by revealing it as exemplary, i.e., indefinitely repeated in multiple and varied contexts. Consequently, 'to live' a symbol and to decipher the messages correctly is equivalent to gaining access to the universal. To transform an individual experience by symbolism is equivalent to opening it to the Spirit."[30]

This existential dimension of religious symbolism is directly relevant to the previous analysis of how symbolism "bursts open" the immediate reality of a particular, natural, profane, existential situation. The symbol is experienced as a "cipher" that points beyond itself and reveals hidden levels of reality or structures of the world. The religious symbol is experienced as a cipher of the sacred, relating the human and natural dimensions of existence to a mode of being "beyond" or "other than" the profane. "In general, symbolism brings about a universal 'porousness', 'opening' beings and things to transobjective meanings."[31]

This symbolic transformation of the world can be related to the previous analysis of the dialectic of hierophanies. Eliade claims that lunar symbolism adds new values and meanings to the snake appearing in myths without denying its immediate value. The snake, while remaining a natural phenomenon, "explodes" or "bursts" under the force of lunar symbolism to reveal many levels of profound existential meaning not evident on the level of immediate experience. The snake is no longer experienced as an isolated, conditioned phenomenon in a completely fragmented universe; it is experienced as one of countless valorizations of the moon and can be homologized with other phenomena revealing the structure of the lunar rhythms. "In application to objects or actions, symbolism renders them 'open'; symbolic thinking 'breaks open' the immediate reality without any minimizing or undervaluing of it: in such a perspective this is not a closed Universe, no object exists for itself in isolation; everything is held together by a compact system of correspondences and likenesses."[32]

We have uncovered two stages in this "bursting open" of ordinary, natural phenomena by religious symbolism. First, lunar symbolism functions as an extension of the dialectic of the sacred and the profane. Snakes are transformed into "something other" than what they appear to profane experience to be; as religious lunar symbols, they reveal sacred meanings. Then, by becoming symbols of a sacred transcendent reality, snakes "abolish their material limits, and instead of being isolated fragments become part of a whole [lunar] system; or, better, despite their precarious and fragmentary nature, they embody in themselves the whole of the system in question."[33]

In this double process of symbolic transformation, one observes the fundamental structure of the symbolic existential revelation. First, individual, profane, existential situations are transformed into spiritual experiences. Then, what was experienced as an "isolated," subjective, particular mode of existence now "opens out" to a world that appears unified and "familiar," to a system of meaningful structures that is recognized as "objective" and universal.

This existential dimension, as well as the multivalence, unification, and other aspects of religious symbolism, can be related to "the dialectical movement" analyzed as part of the dialectic of the sacred.[34] Eliade frequently states that the archetypal symbol or essential symbolic structure is continually incarnating and historicizing itself by embodying itself in particular objects and expressing itself through limited and relative symbolic forms; at the same time, the sacred is continually attempting to free itself from its particular, relative, historical symbolic forms, thereby approximating its essential symbolic structure. This dialectical movement of religious symbolism "translates a human situation into cosmological terms and vice versa; more precisely, it reveals the continuity between the structures of human existence and cosmic structures." This revelation allows the religious person to leave behind what was experienced as an isolated and subjective existence through mythic and other acts of new existential orientation founded on experiences of essential structures of the sacred.[35]

ARCHETYPES

In several of his most influential works, Eliade writes of "archetypes" and of "archetypal" symbols, images, myths, intuitions, structures, models, themes, and patterns. Eliade's use of these terms has created considerable confusion and misunderstanding. Many readers, when thinking of Eliade, immediately associate him with "archetypes" as well as "the sacred and the profane." And yet Eliade uses the term "archetype" extensively in only a few of his works. It appears often in two of his major scholarly works, both published in French in 1949: *Patterns in Comparative Religion,* his most important book for gaining an overall understanding of the theoretical framework of symbolic structural systems and probably the work that first established him internationally as a historian and phenomenologist of religion; and *The Myth of the Eternal Return,* his favorite and probably most discussed work.[36] Archetypal language is also prominent in several essays in *Images and Symbols.* Since Eliade often refers to archetypal symbols and since all archetypes are expressed symbolically, this may be the best place to clarify the uses and meanings of these terms.

Eliade's use of the term "archetype" is at times vague and ambiguous. For the most part, there are two primary meanings of archetype found in his works.[37] First, there are a minority of passages in which archetype and archetypal closely resemble Jungian uses and meanings. It is true that Eliade occasionally referred to archetypes before becoming familiar with Jung's writings, and he never endorsed a specific Jungian notion of "the collective unconscious." He explicitly distinguishes his use from the Jungian meaning when he defines the term "just as Eugenio d'Ors does, as a synonym for 'exemplary model' or 'paradigm', that is, in the last analysis, in the Augustinian sense."[38]

Nevertheless, there are Jungian-sounding passages in which he writes of atemporal, ahistorical, archetypal, "primordial," "imprinted," symbolic and mythic structures that persist in the unconscious. He later stopped using the term "archetype" in order to avoid Jungian and other misinterpretations.

Second, there is Eliade's primary use of archetype and archetypal that points to essential structures and meanings, exemplary models and paradigms. In *The Myth of the Eternal Return*, Eliade formulates an essential "'primitive' ontological conception: an object or an act becomes real only insofar as it imitates or repeats an archetype. Thus, reality is acquired solely through repetition or participation; everything which lacks an exemplary model is 'meaningless', i.e., it lacks reality." After asserting that this view of reality might be seen as having "a Platonic structure," Eliade formulates "a second aspect of this primitive ontology": the "abolition of profane time, of duration, of 'history,'" through "the imitation of archetypes and the repetition of paradigmatic gestures."[39] When one recalls Plato's philosophy, in which the philosopher gains an intuition or insight into the eternal, immutable Ideas that structure reality and in which we attempt to "imitate" and "participate" in these original pure Forms that function as exemplary normative models, the Platonic structure of Eliade's use of archetypes is evident.

While warning against the assimilation of Aranda and other mythic and initiatory Australian conceptions of *anamnesis* to Plato's more philosophical doctrine, Eliade emphasizes that the theories are "fairly close" and points out "the Platonic structure of Australian spirituality":

> For the Australians, to know means to remember. Initiation unfolds a long process of anamnesis: the neophyte learns not only the secret myths that explain and justify all existence, but he discovers himself, he *recognizes* himself in the mythical ancestor of whom he is the reincarnation. For Plato, philosophy helps you remember the Ideas; more precisely, to remember the situation of the soul in postexistence and preexistence when the soul contemplated the Ideas. For the Australians, initiation reveals to you that you *were already here,* in these places, in the dawn of time, *in illo tempore:* you were such-and-such civilizing hero. This mythical personage serves as a model: the

initiates must repeat what he did in the beginning. But, through the initiation, you discover that this mythical personage is *you yourself—* as you appeared for the first time. Ultimately, you are a repetition of yourself—as you were in the beginning, *exemplary.*[40]

In the above aspects of a "primitive ontology," it should also be evident not only why Eliade can speak of archetypal myths but also why myth itself serves such an archetypal function. As will be seen in the next chapter, myths symbolically disclose sacred truths and realities. They disclose the original paradigmatic models (the creation of the world, the creation of our human condition, and so forth), the exemplary structures to be imitated, the means for ritual reenactment and participation in the mythic realities. For Eliade, cosmogonic myths and other myths of origins are especially significant in providing such an archetypal function since they reveal the original, pure, exemplary models for all later, conditioned, limited acts of human creation.

In a few places Eliade uses "archetype" in a more specific, narrow variation of the second primary meaning of exemplary models and essential structures and meanings in order to get at very controversial ontological and metaphysical claims: his claims that there were certain momentous, foundational, "archetypal intuitions" when *homo religious* first experienced the structure of the sacred as revealing our true human place in the cosmos. Such archetypal intuitions have a permanent transcultural and transhistorical status, disclosing something essential about our human condition as such.

In this regard, Mac Linscott Ricketts, mainly using Romanian texts, focuses on "the moment man first became conscious of his position in the Cosmos"—a phrase sometimes associated with references to "archetypal intuitions"—as the key to understanding Eliade's use and meaning of archetype. Writes Eliade: "On every plane of human experience, no matter how low, the archetype continues to valorize existence, continues to create 'cultural values'. . . . Man can escape from anything except his archetypal intuitions, created at the moment when he became conscious of his position in the Cosmos."[41] Similarly, Eliade maintains that "man, whatever else he may be free of, is forever the prisoner of his own archetypal intuitions, formed at the moment when he first perceived his position in the cosmos."[42]

Ricketts finds the key to interpreting the meaning and significance of "the moment when man became conscious of his position in the Cosmos" in Eliade's Romanian publication *Mitul Reintegrării* in which the phrase is followed by this explanation:

> From the consciousness of his position in the Cosmos derives both his drama and his metaphysics. Because, this consciousness is, in a sense, a "fall." Man feels "separated" from something, and this separation is a source of continuous grief, fear, and despair. He feels weak and alone; whereas that "something," name it what you will, is *strong* and *total* (more precisely, "totalized," because it includes all that is *not* man, all that is *other* than he). He intuits the *power* (divinity) as a whole, as a great unity impermeable and perfect, sufficient unto itself. All that man thinks coherent and all that he does purposefully, from the moment he becomes conscious of his position in the Cosmos is directed toward a single end: the elimination of that "separation," the reestablishment of the primordial unity, his reintegration in the "all" (be it conceived as an impersonal power, as God, or whatever). Every religious act, however "primitive" it may be (ritual, adoration, liturgy, etc.) is an attempt at the reestablishment of the cosmic unity and the reintegration of man.[43]

This quotation makes clear that consciousness of "man's position in the Cosmos" gets at that archetypal intuition of being cut off from the Cosmos and yearning "to restore the *primal unity,* since he senses intuitively that he too once belonged to that Whole." "The primal religious experience is a sense of being separated from the Real, the All, the Cosmos perceived as a unity. Thus, the goal of all man's religious striving is to *reintegrate* himself into that Whole." Although Eliade's formulation of the human condition in the world seems strongly influenced by his exposure to Hinduism and expresses a kind of "nature mysticism," he intends it to be a "universally valid analysis of all religions: they are various attempts to restore the unity with the All which man lost when he became conscious of his position—of isolation—in the Cosmos."[44]

After citing passages from a number of Eliade's Romanian publications, especially *Comentarii la legenda Meşterului Manole,* Ricketts concludes "that while Eliade may speak of archetypal objects, myths, symbols, gestures, and so forth, *ultimately* the archetypes are the metaphysical principles of life, the 'intuitions' which accompanied man's awakening to consciousness of his unique and unhappy position in the universe. These constituents of the ultimate reality are 'archetypes' because man seeks to 'participate' in them, to conform his life to them."[45]

This insightful interpretation of archetypes gets at some of our formulations of the sacred structure of transcendence, the dialectic of the sacred and the profane (including the dialectical movement and crisis, evaluation, and choice), and the relation of *homo religiosus* to nature and cosmos. It also fits in with Eliade's analysis of essential symbolic structures and features of symbolism and myth, such as the symbolic function of unification and the capacity to express paradoxical and contradictory aspects of reality. And the kinds of passages cited by Ricketts are certainly similar to formulations found throughout Eliade's writings—for example, the passage from *The Myth of the Eternal Return* on the "primitive ontology" with its Platonic structure, and the studies on "the nostalgia for paradise" and other mythic themes.[46]

It should be obvious that this interpretation of archetypes commits Eliade to a universal, ahistorical, ontological and metaphysical position. He could never have arrived at such a position simply through a process of inductive generalization based on mythic and other empirical data. In my *Structure and Creativity in Religion,* most of Eliade's claims for universal, essential, archetypal, religious structures are analyzed as established through a process of "phenomenological induction." But I also maintain that his most controversial claims about the true human mode of being in the world and the human condition as such involve ontological moves and normative judgments and function on the level of metaphysics and philosophical anthropology.[47]

Not all of Eliade's formulations of archetypal symbols, myths, and structures refer to this specific ontological and metaphysical interpretation of the primordial, archetypal intuition of the true human position in the cosmos. Many formulations of archetypes as essential structures and exemplary models have their own distinctive features. For example, Eliade interprets the meaning of myth and other religious phenomena primarily by reintegrating the particular phenomenon within its universal, coherent system of essential symbolic structures. To interpret mythic and other religious meaning as fully as possible, it is necessary for him to identify the symbolic archetype or "center" of a symbolism, that essential structure and meaning around which a complex web of symbolic associations has been woven.

David Cave, in *Mircea Eliade's Vision for a New Humanism,* probably emphasizes the priority of "archetypes" more than any major interpreter of Eliade's approach. He claims that the "notion of a new humanism is the central archetype to the Eliadean corpus" and that "the new humanism is the *Urpflanze,* the archetypal plant, the 'center' of Eliade's life and of his scholarly and literary oeuvre."[48] Eliade's new humanism is "a spiritual, humanistic orientation toward totality capable of modifying the quality of human existence itself." It is "a dialectical, incarnational, and cosmic spirituality wherein every person and culture is understood in relation to the whole." In carrying further its "variant archetype of authenticity," the primordial archetype of the new humanism involves a free, existential encounter of concrete experiences leading to understanding and attainment of the real.[49]

Cave's book is full of archetypal formulations with the central archetype of the new humanism. Eliade's recurring concepts, expressing his ambitions or goals, are archetypal variants on the primordial archetype of the new humanism. Cave extracts four such archetypal goals: humans as authentic, as free, as of culture, and as at the center. The challenges in the new humanism, like the goals, are themselves archetypes. Cave focuses on three such archetypal challenges: that humans be creative, that humans be initiated, and that the new humanism proceed scientifically. Cave presents the morphological forms or archetypes of the new humanism as an ensemble of different archetypes of symbol, myth, authenticity, freedom, culture, science, center, initiation, and creativity.[50]

Although such archetypal interpretations are often sensitively and creatively formulated and can make for exciting and challenging reading, their cumulative effect may be one of vagueness and confusion. Unlike Cave's interpretation of Eliade, it has been noted that Eliade himself emphasizes "archetypes" in only a few major scholarly works and then intentionally avoids this term. For the most part, following the example of Eliade, it seems better to analyze his interpretation of myth and religion in terms of essential structures and meanings, of exemplary models and paradigms, than in terms of archetypal formulations.

THE SYMBOLISM OF THE "CENTER"

Eliade's theory of myth and religion is dependent on the universal symbolism of the "center." This symbolism is essential for his descriptions of the structures and interpretations of the meanings of sacred mythic space.[51] There is no religion or mythic construction that does not incorporate aspects of this very complex, multivalent symbolism.

For mythic persons, space is not homogeneous. "Spatial nonhomogeneity finds expression in the experience of an opposition between space that is sacred—the only *real* and *really* existing space—and all other space, the formless expanse surrounding it." "When the sacred manifests itself in any hierophany, there is not only a break in the homogeneity of space; there is also revelation of an absolute reality, opposed to the nonreality of the vast surrounding expanse." The sacred manifestation "ontologically founds the world," revealing "an absolute fixed point, a center."[52]

In the religious world of myth, "every microcosm, every inhabited region, has what may be called a 'Centre'; that is to say, a place that is sacred above all." Since this "place" is a "sacred space" and not a "profane, homogeneous, geometrical space," there is no contradiction in recognizing many "centers" within a single inhabited region. The symbolism of a center points to a sacred, mythic geography. "In mythical geography, sacred space is the essentially *real space,* for . . . in the archaic world the myth alone is real. It tells of manifestations of the only indubitable reality—the *sacred.* It is in such space that one has direct contact with the sacred—whether this be materialised in certain objects . . . or manifested in the hiero-cosmic symbols (the Pillar of the World, the Cosmic Tree, etc.). In cultures that have the conception of three cosmic regions—those of Heaven, Earth and Hell—the 'centre' constitutes the point of intersection of those regions. It is here that the breakthrough on to another plane is possible and, at the same time, communication between the three regions."[53]

Eliade summarizes the symbolism of the "center" as expressing itself in three connected and complementary things: the "sacred mountain," where heaven and earth meet, is situated at the sacred center of the world; every temple or palace, and by extension every sacred town or residence, is assimilated to a sacred mountain, thus becoming a center; and as an *axis mundi,* the sacred temple or city is held to be a meeting point between heaven, earth, and hell.[54]

Focusing on the widespread image of the three cosmic regions connected in a sacred center along one axis, Eliade provides mythic illustrations from Indian, Chinese, Babylonian, Hebrew, Christian, Roman, and other civilizations. Mythic "cities, temples or palaces, regarded as Centres of the World are all only replicas, representing *ad libitum* the same archaic image—the Cosmic Mountain, the World Tree or the central Pillar which sustains the planes of the Cosmos." Eliade formulates this "essential schema" in shamanism: "[T]here are three great cosmic regions, which can be successively traversed because they are linked together by a central axis. This axis, of course, passes through an 'opening', a 'hole'; it is through this hole that the gods descend to earth and the dead to the subterranean regions; it is through the same hole that the soul of the shaman in ecstasy can fly up or down in the course of his celestial or infernal journeys."[55]

Mountains, trees, columns, and other widely distributed symbols situated at the center of the world have endless potential for creative symbolic revalorization.[56] They not only revalorize the essential structures of the symbolism of the center but also participate in other structural systems of symbolic associations. For example, Eliade devotes many studies to the mythic Cosmic or World Tree, which is the most widely distributed variant of the symbolism of the center. Sacred and ritual trees and posts, sacrificial stakes, and mythic bridges and ladders can be homologized with the essential symbolic structure of the

Cosmic Tree at the center of the universe. Eliade's morphological, structural classification of sacred trees, representing "the *living cosmos, endlessly renewing itself*," discloses not only the tree as a center of the world but also the tree as image of the cosmos, as cosmic theophany, as symbol of life, as mystical bond with humans, and as symbol of resurrection of vegetation. Therefore, to interpret the meaning of a sacred tree in some myth, the interpreter must not only recognize the tree as a particular valorization of the symbolism of the center, but must also situate that symbol within other coherent systems of religious symbols.[57]

A far from obvious illustration of the symbolism of the center is the Central and North Asian shamanic drum, a replica of the Cosmic Tree at the center of the world.[58] Writes Eliade:

> It is above all by the aid of their drums that shamans attain to the ecstatic state. And, when we think that *the drum is made of the very wood of the World Tree,* we can understand the symbolism and the religious value of the sounds of the shamanic drum—and why, when he beats it, the shaman feels himself transported in ecstasy near to the Tree of the World. Here we have a mystical journey to the "Centre," and thence into the highest heaven. Thus, either by climbing up the seven or nine notches of the ceremonial birch-tree, or simply drumming, the shaman sets out on his journey to heaven, but he can only obtain that rupture of the cosmic planes which makes his ascension possible or enables him to fly ecstatically through the heavens, because he is thought to be already at the very Centre of the world; for, as we have seen, it is only in such a Centre that communication between Earth, Heaven and Hell is possible.[59]

This specific shamanic illustration of the symbolism of the center obviously introduces other widespread symbolisms, such as the universal system of symbols of ascension, the topic of many of Eliade's studies.[60] Here we find myths about shamanic and other rituals and myths about posts, creepers, cords, spider-web threads, ladders, staircases, and other symbolic variants. These myths of ascension symbolism, with symbolic images situated at the center of the cosmos, also introduce another of Eliade's favorite symbolisms: that of initiation, the subject of *Birth and Rebirth (Rites and Patterns of Initiation)* and many other studies.[61] The staircase (or shamanic drum and tree) symbolizes acts of ascension and initiatory rites for transcending the profane human condition because such a mythic symbol is thought to be at a sacred center, thus making communication possible between different levels of reality and becoming a "concrete formula for the mythical ladder, for the creeper or the spiderweb, the Cosmic Tree or the Pillar of the Universe, that connects the three cosmic zones."[62]

If we stop here without developing the symbolic extensions and variations necessary for a greater understanding of Eliade's interpretation of these mythic examples, we already have some sense of the hermeneutical framework of religious symbolism underlying Eliade's interpretation of myth and religion. When myths incorporate shamanic drums, ritual trees, staircases, or other religious symbols, Eliade, while sometimes reaffirming that it is necessary to do justice to the particular datum in its historical and cultural specificity, proceeds to interpret myth through morphological and structuralistic classification and analysis. One deciphers the meaning of such particular symbolic expressions by reintegrating them within their dynamic, complex, "logical," coherent, multivalent, unified, vegetation, ascension, initiation, and other structural systems of symbolic associations.

Eliade knows that myths and symbols necessarily involve the construction of one or more sacred centers. It is at such a mythic center that one locates key hierophanies, ritual constructions, and other sacred revelations and communications. Located at a sacred center, a drum or tree or staircase becomes assimilated to a World or Cosmic Tree or other archetypal symbol of the center. What may at first appear as an isolated, particular, mythic image is now seen to incorporate a rich world of symbolic meanings. This allows for the unification of different cosmic regions and for structures of transcendence.

By recognizing the invariant core or essential structure of the symbolism of the center and by reintegrating specific symbols within their structural systems of symbolic meanings, one may interpret the drum and other particular variants as revealing meanings not apparent on the level of immediate experience; as fitting together with other symbols to form logically coherent structural systems; as being particular variations of multivalent symbolic systems that allow for the unification of diverse aspects of reality; as allowing mythic beings to relate to seemingly paradoxical and contradictory aspects of reality; and as providing religious persons with a meaningful existential orientation in which there is a dynamic symbolic interaction between one's specific situation in the world and a transcendent universe of sacred meanings.

Finally, we may contrast our focus on the symbolism of the center to Carl Olson's more ambitious focus on the center as key to Eliade's theology and philosophy. As seen in the subtitle of his book, "A Search for the Centre," Olson claims that an understanding of Eliade's scholarship must be related to his interior personal quest for meaning and for his own sacred centre. "[Eliade] spent his creative career searching for the centre of his own existence. And this quest for a meaningful centre of existence is a theme that runs throughout his scholarly and literary publications. . . . Eliade's literary and scholarly work in the history of religions were part of his quest for personal meaning."[63] Olson tells us that the center is a place where the sacred is located and that Eliade is convinced that an absolute truth grounded in myth is possible. He then presents the following formulation that gets at his focus on the personal, theological, and philosophical nature of Eliade's approach and at the linkage between Eliade's personal quest and literary and scholarly studies:

> What does it mean to find and be located at the centre for Eliade? To be at the centre means that one can see everything as interconnected; it is to see unity or to have cosmos rather than the chaos typical of historical flux. By having access to cosmic experiences, one becomes open to the cosmos, one shares in its sanctity, and one actively communicates with divine being. When one finds the centre one is at the meeting-point of the levels of the cosmos, one is near heaven, and one can move from one cosmic region to another. This is to live in absolute reality. It is now possible to acknowledge, free from the terror of history, that life is meaningful. To have arrived at this meaningful centre is to be transported back to the beginning of time and to have successfully abolished it.[64]

If Olson had claimed that such a formulation expresses Eliade's interpretation of the orientation of religious mythic persons, few readers would have been surprised. If he had speculated that such a formulation also expresses Eliade's own personal orientation, there might have been considerable agreement. What is controversial is Olson's further claim that Eliade's scholarly studies of mythic and religious phenomena of others are so intimately linked with and necessarily dependent on his own personal religious path, his own personal quest for the sacred center, and his own theological and philosophical commitments. At the end of chapter 4, we noted some of the dangers in collapsing legitimate scholarly distinctions and rendering Eliade's scholarly interpretations of myth and religion so dependent on personal religious commitments.

NOTES

1. *Images and Symbols*, pp. 9, 177; "Methodological Remarks," p. 105. See also Robert Luyster, "The Study of Myth: Two Approaches," *Journal of Bible and Religion* 34 (1966): 235.

2. See, for example, *Patterns*, p. 450.

3. *Journal 1*, pp. 3-4.

4. "Methodological Remarks," pp. 97-103.

5. Reno, "Eliade's Progressional View of Hierophanies," p. 153.

6. There are several other essays that shed light on Eliade's general theory of religious symbolism, such as "Le symbolisme des ténèbres dans les religions archaïques" in *Polarités du symbole*, *Études Carmélitaines* 39 [1960], pp. 15-28. This essay has been translated as "The Symbolism of Shadows in Archaic Religions" in Eliade, *Symbolism, the Sacred, and the Arts*, pp. 3-16. Most chapters in *Patterns* are studies of specific systems of religious symbols and an entire chapter is on the structure of symbols. Several of Eliade's books, such as *Mephistopheles and the Androgyne: Studies in Religious Myth and Symbol* and *Images and Symbols: Studies in Religious Symbolism*, are collections of studies of religious symbolisms.

7. *Patterns*, p. 453; *Images and Symbols*, p. 37.

8. Ricoeur, *The Symbolism of Evil*, p. 353.

9. This is one of the major concerns in *Structure and Creativity in Religion*, especially in chapter 7: Descriptive Evaluations and Levels of Meaning. I try to show that Eliade's logic of symbols, in particular, and his phenomenology of religion, in general, are based on a recognition of a vertical differentiation of different planes of symbolic expression. I also try to show that most of the dismissals of Eliade approach as based on his own subjective

assumptions and normative judgments of levels of reality can be countered by constructing Eliade's complex methodological framework in which most judgments can be analyzed as "descriptive evaluations" based on his theory of religious symbolism with its logic of symbols. At the same time, it must be granted that some of Eliade's judgments of levels of symbolic manifestation as "elevated" and "highest" take him beyond any descriptive analysis, beyond the limits of any phenomenology of religion, and involve an assumed ontology and philosophical anthropology.

10. "Methodological Remarks," p. 98.

11. See *Patterns,* pp. 164-71, 182-83.

12. "Methodological Remarks," p. 99.

13. See *Images and Symbols,* pp. 15-16.

14. In the original French text, this sentence continues: "the attraction exercised on 'Spirit' by 'Matter,' the nostalgia for primordial unity and, therefore, the desire to abolish opposites, polarities, etc."

15. *Images and Symbols,* pp. 14-15.

16. *Zalmoxis, The Vanishing God,* pp. 29, 30.

17. "Methodological Remarks," pp. 99-100.

18. *Yoga,* p. 123.

19. "Methodological Remarks," p. 97. See also John E. Smith's analysis in "The Structure of Religion," *Religious Studies* 1 (1965): 65-66.

20. *Images and Symbols,* p. 12.

21. Paul Tillich often makes similar observations when describing the general nature of all symbols. Symbols "make accessible to our minds levels of experience from which we otherwise would be shut off; we would not be aware of them. This is the great function of symbols, to point beyond themselves in the power of that to which they point, to open up levels of reality which otherwise are closed, and to open up levels of the human mind of which we otherwise are not aware." Paul Tillich, "Theology and Symbolism," in *Religious Symbolism,* ed. F. Ernest Johnson (New York: Harper & Brothers, 1955), p. 109. See also Tillich, "The Meaning and Justification of Religious Symbols," pp. 4-5.

22. Luyster, "The Study of Myth," pp. 235-36.

23. "Methodological Remarks," p. 101.

24. Heinrich Zimmer, "The Serpent and the Bird," *Myths and Symbols in Indian Art and Civilization,* ed. Joseph Campbell (New York: Harper Torchbooks, 1962), pp. 72-76.

25. *History 1,* p. 165 and p. 165 n. 7.

26. See *Yoga,* pp. 236-41, 253-54, 267-73; *Patterns,* pp. 178-81, 419-20.

27. "Methodological Remarks," p. 102.

28. Ibid., pp. 102-3.

29. *Symbolism, the Arts, and the Sacred,* p. 13.

30. Ibid.

31. *Yoga*, pp. 250-51.

32. *Images and Symbols*, p. 178. See also *Patterns*, p. 455.

33. *Patterns*, p. 452. This distinction of two stages is for the sake of analysis and is not intended to indicate a temporal sequence.

34. See Dudley, *Religion on Trial*, pp. 56-59, 62-63, 81-82.

35. "Methodological Remarks," p. 103.

36. See *Autobiography 2*, pp. 125 and 134. In *Eliade: Romanian Roots*, 2, pp. 1142, 1149-57, Ricketts notes that Eliade made frequent use for the first time of the term "archetype" in the Romanian publication *Comentarii la legenda Meșterului Manole* (Bucharest: Publicom, 1943).

37. This ambiguity is significant because each meaning of archetype has different methodological consequences for Eliade's study of myth and other religious phenomena. See Allen, *Structure and Creativity in Religion*, esp. pp. 145, 210-12. Studies of Eliade's concept of archetypes include Ricketts, "The Nature and Extent of Eliade's 'Jungianism'"; Ricketts, *Eliade: Romanian Roots*, 2, esp. pp. 1149-57, Wilson M. Hudson, "Eliade's Contribution to the Study of Myth," in *Tire Shrinker to Dragster*, ed. Wilson M. Hudson (Austin: The Encino Press, 1968), p. 237; Ira Progoff, "The Man Who Transforms Consciousness," *Eranos-Jahrbuch 1966*, Band 35 (1967): 126-30, 133. See nn. 48-50 in this chapter for references to Eliade on archetypes in David Cave's *Mircea Eliade's Vision for a New Humanism*.

38. Mircea Eliade, "Preface to the Torchbook Edition," *Cosmos and History: The Myth of the Eternal Return* (New York: Harper & Row, Torchbooks, 1959), pp. viii-ix. Except for the addition of this Preface, *Cosmos and History* is the same as *The Myth of the Eternal Return*.

39. *Eternal Return*, pp. 34-35. While Eliade's references here and elsewhere to this "Platonic structure" are very revealing of his interpretation of myth, archetype, and religion, there are significant differences between Plato's philosophic and Eliade's mythic religious orientations.

40. *No Souvenirs*, p. 182; *Australian Religions*, p. 59. This quotation not only focuses on the above mentioned Platonic structure of the "primitive ontology," which involves imitation, repetition, and participation in exemplary, archetypal models, but also provides a more specific Platonic orientation in terms of the doctrine of anamnesis. This quotation illustrates many of the basic functions and structures of myth considered in the next chapter.

41. *Comentarii la legenda Meșterului Manole*, pp. 142-43. Eliade writes: "The models transmitted by archaic spirituality do not disappear, nor do they lose their capacity for reactualization, for the simple reason that they are archetypal intuitions, universal primordial visions, which were revealed to man at the moment he became conscious of his position in the Cosmos" (p. 140). See Ricketts, *Eliade: Romanian Roots*, 2, pp. 1124, 1151, 1156-57.

42. *Patterns,* pp. 433-34.

43. Mircea Eliade, *Mitul Reintegrării* (Bucharest: Vremea, 1942), p. 62.

44. Ricketts, *Eliade: Romanian Roots,* 2, pp. 1137-38.

45. Ibid., p. 1151.

46. Eliade's *Yoga* contains many of these formulations. For example, the yogic techniques aim at the goal "to abolish multiplicity and fragmentation, to reintegrate, to unify, to make whole" (p. 97). "Like all paradoxical states, *samādhi* is equivalent to a reintegration of the different modalities of the real in a single modality—the undifferentiated completeness of precreation, the primordial Unity" (pp. 98-99). The yogin who attains to the highest "undifferentiated stasis," according to Eliade, "also realizes a dream that has obsessed the human spirit from the beginnings of its history—to coincide with the All, to recover Unity, to re-establish the initial nonduality, to abolish time and creation (i.e., the multiplicity and heterogeneity of the cosmos); in particular, to abolish the twofold division of the real into object-subject" (pp. 98-99).

47. See, for example, my *Structure and Creativity in Religion,* pp. 190-200, 231-46. Eliade began his teaching in the 1930s as assistant to philosopher Nae Ionescu and taught his own philosophy courses at the University of Bucharest. While he resisted the urging of others to go beyond his "scientific" studies and present his own philosophical position, he occasionally stated that his scholarship should be of particular value for the philosophy of religion.

48. Cave, *Mircea Eliade's Vision for a New Humanism,* pp. 105, 140, 192. Cave submits that "the new humanism, taken as the Goethian primordial plant, is the archetype for all the variants throughout Eliade's life work" (p. 23).

49. Ibid., pp. 27-28, 32-33, 105. Obviously, most historians of religion will be uncomfortable with such ontological and metaphysical formulations as key to understanding Eliade's scholarship.

50. Ibid., pp. 103-104, 169-170, 194.

51. See, for example, "Sacred Space and Making the World Sacred," in *Sacred and Profane,* pp. 20-65; and "Sacred Places: Temple, Palace, 'Centre of the World'," in *Patterns,* pp. 367-87.

52. *Sacred and Profane,* pp. 20-21.

53. *Images and Symbols,* pp. 39, 40. Eliade then relates the loss of such communication to another of his favorite mythic themes: the myth of a primordial paradise lost on account of some fault. "Formerly, communication with Heaven and relations with the divinity were easy and 'natural'; until, in consequence of a ritual fault, these communications were broken off, and the gods withdrew to still higher heavens. Only medicine-men, shamans, priests, and heroes, or the sovereign rulers were now able to re-establish communication with Heaven, and that only in a temporary way and for their own use" (pp. 40-41). Variations of this mythic theme are found throughout Eliade's writings.

See, for example, *Shamanism,* pp. 265-66; *Myths, Dreams and Mysteries,* pp. 59-72.

54. *Eternal Return, p. 12; Patterns,* p. 375.

55. *Shamanism,* p. 259. Under "The Three Cosmic Zones and the World Pillar," pp. 259-66, and throughout *Shamanism,* Eliade provides numerous illustrations of this schema. See also Mircea Eliade, *A History of Religious Ideas.* Vol. 3: *From Muhammad to the Age of Reforms,* trans. Alf Hiltebeitel and Diane Apostolos-Cappadona (Chicago: University of Chicago Press, 1985), pp. 6-8 (hereafter cited as *History 3*).

56. For many examples of such symbols of the center, see *Patterns,* pp. 374-79; *Eternal Return,* pp. 12-17; *Images and Symbols,* pp. 37-56; and *Sacred and Profane,* pp. 36-47.

57. See *Patterns,* pp. 266-71; *Shamanism,* pp. 269-74.

58. See *Shamanism,* pp. 145-88.

59. *Images and Symbols,* pp. 46-47. See *Shamanism,* pp. 168-76 for more detailed analysis and many illustrations of this interpretation of the shamanic drum as symbol of the center.

60. See, for example, *Myths, Dreams and Mysteries,* pp. 99-122; *Patterns,* pp. 102-8.

61. For a detailed analysis of initiation directly relevant to our shamanic illustration, see *Shamanism,* pp. 110-44; *History 3,* pp. 11-15.

62. *Images and Symbols,* pp. 47-51.

63. Olson, *The Theology and Philosophy of Eliade,* p. 157. See also pp. ix, 1, 7, 161, 157-73.

64. Ibid., p. 166.

CHAPTER 7

The Structure of Myth

Earlier chapters have referred continually to myth, with many formulations analyzing Eliade's theory of myth and with numerous examples of myth illustrating Eliade's analysis of reductionism, religion, and symbolism. Most of what has been presented has not been unique to myth. For example, one cannot grasp Eliade's theory of myth without appreciating his antireductionist approach. It is necessary to be cognizant of the fact that whenever Eliade writes about myth, he is assuming the irreducibility of the sacred, thus focusing on certain religious dimensions of his data while ignoring, devaluing, and sometimes attacking and dismissing other aspects emphasized by reductionist theorists of myth. But Eliade's antireductionism is not restricted to myth. He assumes the irreducibility of the sacred and claims to be giving antireductionistic interpretations of nonmythic religious, as well as mythic, phenomena.

 To understand Eliade's theory of myth, it is necessary to understand his general theory of religion. For Eliade, myth is religious myth. Nonreligious narratives may at times resemble myth, but without any evidence of structures of the sacred, they are not fully mythic. One cannot grasp Eliade theory of myth without appreciating his concept of hierophany and especially his formulation of a universal process of sacralization. In their essential structure and function, myths disclose, often in complex and hidden ways, the universal structures of the dialectic of the sacred and the profane. But Eliade's general theory of religion is not restricted to the mythic. Although he places a primary emphasis on myth, the dialectic of the sacred refers to all religious phenomena, nonmythic as well as mythic.

Similarly, one cannot understand Eliade's theory of myth without understanding his general theory of symbolism. For Eliade, myth is symbolic, and symbols are the language of myth. Myths are specific ways that symbols are put together to form sacred narratives. One cannot grasp the structure and function of myth without appreciating how myths are multivalent, unify heterogeneous phenomena on different levels of experience, express contradictory and paradoxical aspects of reality, and are specific valorizations of complex, coherent, structural systems of religious symbols. But Eliade's theory of symbolism is not restricted to myth. Although he is especially attracted to symbolic expressions that appear in myth, Eliade's general formulation of symbolism applies to all religious phenomena, nonmythic as well as mythic.

Eliade was always attracted to narrative. In his *Journals* and *Autobiography* and other personal writings, he often discusses his "dual vocation" as fiction writer and scholar. Long before his recognition as an internationally renowned scholar of myth and symbolism, Eliade had emerged as an influential literary figure in his native Romania in the 1930s, especially after the publication of his hugely successful and controversial novel *Maitreyi* in 1933. Throughout his career, Eliade identified himself not only as an interpreter of myths—the sacred narratives of religious persons—but also as the creator of his own narratives.

At times Eliade emphasizes that the literary creation of narrative and the scholarly interpretation of narrative are autonomous and separate activities; at other times, he emphasizes that these concerns are complementary, necessary for his "spiritual equilibrium," separate but interdependent parts of the same universal cultural creativity.[1] Many of the assumptions, methods, and concerns already seen to define his scholarly work on myth also define his attitude toward the creation and interpretation of literary narrative: an autonomous creation of the literary imagination, interpreted on its own plane of reference, with its own irreducible structures and meanings, revealing but at the same time concealing hidden, transhistorical meanings. Indeed, Eliade views both oral and written literature as the offspring of mythology and as fulfilling the same mythic functions.

In appreciating why Eliade is so drawn to myth, one recognizes not only the primary importance he grants the sacred and the symbolic but also the remarkable status he accords narrative. "I must write a long article, which could be entitled 'On the Necessity of the "Novel-Novel,"' showing the autonomous, glorious, irreducible dimension of *narration*, the formula of myth and mythology readapted to the modern consciousness. Showing that modern man, like the man of archaic societies, cannot exist without myths, without exemplary stories."[2]

 Twenty-five years later, Eliade writes in his *Journal* that he would have liked to have commented in more depth in his preface to the English translation of *The Forbidden Forest* on the "necessity of narration." "In my journal, but also in lectures, I've already made numerous allusions to this *existential need* to listen to or to read a 'tale,' whether it is a myth, a fairy tale, a history, a short story, or a novel." Several months later, Eliade discusses the fashionable proclamation of the "death of the novel" as at most pointing to the death of outdated models or kinds of novels. "But true epic literature—that is, the novel, the story, the tale—cannot disappear as such, for the literary imagination is the continuation of mythological creativity and oneiric experience."[3]

In his "Preface" to *The Forbidden Forest*, Eliade mentions experiments on the phase of sleep called REM (Rapid Eye Movement) and concludes that there is an "organic need" for dreaming, mythology, and narration. "A closer analysis of this organic need for narration would bring to light a dimension peculiar to the human condition": that the human is *par excellence* "a historic being," not in the sense of the modern, historicist philosophies but more in the sense of mythic, sacred histories that are revealed through the structure and function of the mythic narratives.[4]

When one recognizes Eliade's primary concern with the sacred, the symbolic, and the narrative, it is not surprising that he devoted so many books and articles to the interpretation of myth. Since Eliade placed such a central priority on the meaning and significance of these sacred symbolic narratives, it will not be possible to consider all of the mythic themes and variations found throughout his writings. Instead, we shall focus on the essential mythic structures, functions, and general characteristics, together with a few illustrations.

In his insistence on the irreducibility of the sacred, Eliade often cites the principle that "the scale creates the phenomenon." In describing and interpreting myth, Eliade asserts that the historian of religions must be "too conscious of the axiological difference of his documents to marshal them on the same level. Aware of nuances and distinctions, he cannot ignore the fact that there exist great myths and myths of less importance; myths which dominate and characterize a religion, and secondary myths, repetitious and parasitical. *Enuma elish,* for example, cannot figure on the same plane with the mythology of the female demon Lamashtu; the Polynesian cosmogonic myth has not the same weight as the myth of the origin of a plant, for it precedes it and serves as a model for it." In terms of such an axiological scale, he reproaches Western scholars "for their indifference to the scale of values *indigenous* to" mythic, traditional societies. "I do not think that we can grasp the structure and function of mythical thought in a society which has myth as its foundation if we do not take into account the *mythology in its totality* and, at the same time, the *scale of values* which such mythology implicitly or explicitly proclaims."[5] Therefore, in defining myth and analyzing its structure and function by examining "mythology in its totality," Eliade not only assumes the irreducibility of the religious and the mythic but is also guided by the principle that within the mythic, there is a hierarchical scale of values. Most significantly, this allows him to account for the essential structure and function of myth in terms of the primary ontological status of the cosmogonic myth and the key importance of origin myths.

THE DEFINITION OF MYTH

In attempting to define myth, Mircea Eliade departs from a common Western tradition of privileging documents of Greek mythology.

> From Plato and Fontenelle to Schelling and Bultmann, philosophers and theologians have proposed innumerable definitions of myth. But all of these have one thing in common: they are based on the analysis of Greek mythology. Now, for a historian of religions this choice is

not a very happy one. It is true that only in Greece did myth inspire and guide epic poetry, tragedy, and comedy, as well as the plastic arts; but it is no less true that it is especially in Greek culture that myth was submitted to a long and penetrating analysis, from which it emerged radically "demythicized." If in every European language the word "myth" denotes a "fiction," it is because the Greeks proclaimed it to be such twenty-five centuries ago. What is even more serious for an historian of religion: we do not know a single Greek myth within its ritual context. Of course this is not the case with the paleo-oriental and Asiatic religions; it is especially not the case with the so-called primitive religions.[6]

Eliade concludes that "our best chance of understanding the structure of mythical thought is to study cultures where myth is a 'living thing', where it constitutes the very ground of the religious life; in other words, where myth, far from indicating a *fiction*, is considered to reveal the *truth par excellence.*"[7]

Already introduced in Eliade's attempt to define myth is the key distinction between a true and a false story. In societies where myth is still alive, mythic people distinguish myths, or "true stories," from fables, tales, and legends, called "false stories." Because myths are true stories, they can be related only under certain circumstances, such as only to those who are initiated or only during periods of sacred time. For mythic people, both the true and the false stories are narratives that present "histories" and contain actors not of the everyday, profane world. But myths are evaluated differently from other stories by the mythic believers. "For everything that the myths relate *concerns them directly* . . . . Myths, that is, narrate not only the origin of the World, of animals, of plants, and of man, but also all the primordial events in consequence of which man became what he is today." For the archaic person, "myth is a matter of primary importance, while tales and fables are not. Myth teaches him the primordial 'stories' that have constituted him existentially; and everything connected with his existence and his legitimate mode of existence in the Cosmos concerns him directly."[8]

Before presenting Eliade's general definition of myth, it is important to note that there is no scholarly agreement as to the definition, nature, structure, function, meaning, or significance of myth and its relation to nonmythic phenomena. This is evident when examining any of the anthologies of scholarly writings on myth, such as *Sacred Narrative: Readings in the Theory of Myth,* in which twenty-two scholars, including Eliade, present radically different, often conflicting, approaches and interpretations of myth.[9] William Bascom, for example, attempts to formulate many formal features for distinguishing prose narratives: myth, legend, and folktale. Lauri Honko, in analyzing "The Problem of Defining Myth," provides a brief classification distinguishing twelve modern approaches to myth. G. S. Kirk, in his study "On Defining Myth," rejects all universalistic theories of myth, arguing that each theoretical approach and definition, including Eliade's, receives support from certain mythic data but that each universalistic formulation can easily be negated by citing other instances of myth that do not accord with the assigned origins, functions, explanations, or definitions.[10]

Eliade's most developed definition of myth appears in *Myth and Reality.* After indicating that myth is an extremely complex cultural reality and that it is difficult, if not impossible, to formulate one, generally acceptable definition, he attempts the following definition.

> Speaking for myself, the definition that seems least inadequate because most embracing is this: Myth narrates a sacred history; it relates an event that took place in primordial Time, the fabled time of the "beginnings." In other words, myth tells how, through the deeds of Supernatural Beings, a reality came into existence, be it the whole of reality, the Cosmos, or only a fragment of reality—an island, a species of plant, a particular kind of human behavior, an institution. Myth, then, is always an account of a "creation"; it relates how something was produced, began to *be*. Myth tells only of that which *really* happened, which manifested itself completely. The actors in myths are Supernatural Beings. They are known primarily by what they did in the transcendent times of the "beginnings." Hence myths disclose their creative activity and reveal the sacredness (or simply the "supernaturalness") of their works. In short, myths describe the
> various and sometimes dramatic breakthroughs of the sacred (or the

"supernatural") into the World. It is this sudden breakthrough of the sacred that really *establishes* the World and makes it what it is today. Furthermore, it is as a result of the intervention of Supernatural Beings that man himself is what he is today, a mortal, sexed, and cultural being.[11]

In this definition and its elaboration, there are characteristics of myth that were either analyzed at great length or suggested in earlier chapters: the central focus on the sacred (transcendent structure, Supernatural Beings, etc.); the dynamic, creative process of sacralization (by which the sacred establishes and is manifested in the world); the narration of a sacred history that takes place in sacred time; a sacred account of how things were created, whether the entire Cosmos, human beings, or specific phenomena; true stories revealing the deepest realities; and the disclosure of paradigmatic models explaining and justifying the nature of the Cosmos and the world of the mythic believers, including the specific nature of human existence.

Although critics and some defenders emphasize Eliade's personal assumptions and beliefs about reality as central to his description and interpretation of myth and religion, at this stage it seems best to accept the above definition and elaboration as intended to be descriptive and phenomenological. Eliade is claiming that *for the believers in myth,* myths are sacred narratives that reveal ultimate truths and realities.

THE SACRED AND THE SYMBOLIC

As has been repeatedly emphasized, for Eliade myth is irreducibly religious. His interpretations of myth consist of identifying and analyzing the deep structures and meanings, often hidden and camouflaged, of the mythic disclosures of the sacred. As will be seen in chapter 10, Eliade does devote considerable time to modern, "secular myths," but these are invariably analyzed as responding to deeper religious nostalgias and desires for the sacred, as revealing hidden or repressed religious structures and meanings, as inadequate substitutes for the fully mythic sacred, or as superficial, transitory, pseudoreligious creations.

Since so many illustrations of Eliade's focus on the sacred have already been provided and will be provided, one typical, brief mythic reference to the sacred should suffice. In his study on "Greatness and Decadence of Myths," Eliade writes that for the archaic person, religion maintains the "opening" toward a sacred world of absolute values, and myths convey these paradigmatic models of absolute, sacred values. "Myths are the most general and effective means of awakening and maintaining consciousness of another world, a beyond, whether it be the divine world or the world of the Ancestors. This 'other world' represents a superhuman, 'transcendent' plane, the plane of *absolute realities.*"[12]

It has been evident in Eliade's conception of religion that he interprets *homo religiosus* as emphatically rejects Sartre's notion that "existence precedes essence."[13] Religious persons, whether of archaic, Asian, or Western traditions, believe that the essential sacred precedes and gives meaning, significance, and reality to their existence. Eliade's interpretation of how "the essential precedes existence" is seen in his analysis of how myth reveals the sacred in cultures where myth is a "living thing." "Man is what he is today because a series of events took place *ab origine.* The myths tell him these events and, in so doing, explain to him how and why he was constituted in this particular way. For *homo religiosus* real, authentic existence begins at the moment when this primordial history is communicated to him and he accepts its consequences. It is always sacred history, for the actors in it are Supernatural Beings and mythical Ancestors." Eliade goes on to mention that the content of the essential—which was determined in primordial time, precedes human existence, and is revealed through myths—varies according to different religious visions.[14]

As has also been repeatedly emphasized, for Eliade myth is irreducibly symbolic. Symbolism is the language of myth, and myth is necessarily symbolic. Symbolic structures provide the hermeneutical framework for Eliade's interpretation of myth and religion. All of the characteristics of symbolism elucidated in the previous chapter apply to Eliade's interpretation of myth: "the logic of symbols" that allows them to fit together to form coherent, structural systems; the symbolic as an autonomous mode of cognition; the capacity of symbols to reveal structures and meanings not evident on the level of immediate experience; the multivalence of symbols, revealing a multitude of structurally coherent meanings on different levels of reality; the function of unification, allowing symbols to homologize the different levels of reality and integrate them within a coherent system or whole; the capacity of symbols to express paradoxical and contradictory aspects of reality; and the existential value of the symbolic that aims at a reality and discloses a meaning of human existence. Eliade is fully cognizant of these and other characteristics of religious symbolism whenever he is describing and analyzing the function, structure, meaning, and significance of myth.

Since Eliade's theory of symbolism is essential to all of his interpretations of myth, only one passage from his *Journal* will be cited in which he emphasizes the major significance of symbolism in interpreting myths:

> Myths on the origin of man: he was made (by the Creator or by a Supernatural Being) from a *materia prima*: clay, stone, wood. This *materia prima* is obviously connected with the structures of the respective cultures: the megalithic peoples emphasized stone (but the myth is found elsewhere also), the agricultural ones, earth or dust (the fertility of the soil, etc.). But that is not where the significance lies— it lies in the symbolism implied by these substances. Rock, stone, is the plastic expression of perenniality: when man was made (or extracted) from stone, he partook of the mode of being of rock. He endured; he did not know death. On the other hand, the perenniality of life in a periodic, eternal regeneration is expressed by the fertile earth, the wood of trees.[15]

As polyvalent, symbols function on all levels of experience and reality: from undeveloped "ciphers" that key into immediate experience on prereflective levels of existence to very complex and sophisticated symbolic expressions found in elaborate forms of mysticism and highly developed systems of metaphysics and theology. Because of the logic, the multivalence, and the unification of symbols, Eliade maintains that there is a structural continuity from the foundational, prereflective, symbolic manifestation to the elaboration of complex symbolic formulations in the major forms of religious mysticism. But it is important to recognize that the symbolic sacred is manifested and expressed on very different levels of reality. The symbolic formulation of an elaborate ontological system is many levels removed from the immediacy of the foundational experience of the sacred.

In this regard, myth is a rather complex and sophisticated symbolic expression. Religious symbols are put together in narrative form so that these true stories reveal a sacred history of events that took place in sacred time and provide exemplary models for allowing mythic beings to make sense of their mode of being in the world. Mythic symbols, while keying into the immediate experiences of believers, form sacred narratives that function on mythic levels of varying "distances" from the prereflective level of the symbolic cipher.

At the same time, one must guard against interpreting such observations as meaning that mythic people "put together" their religious symbols in narrative form in some arbitrary or completely deliberate and controlled manner; or through some highly rational and intellectual process. The most sophisticated, complex, highly elaborated, even "rational," symbolic myths function on prereflective and nonrational levels of experience. They involve the "total person," including unconscious, conscious, and transconscious levels of experience. They cannot be reduced completely to rational or conceptual analysis. They preserve their own irreducible symbolic "logic," even when not understood by mythic persons. And they express an irreducible symbolic mode of cognition, with the mythic functioning as an autonomous act of creation and revelation.[16] Myths not only are sacred narratives that express symbolically the experiences of the sacred. At times they are themselves hierophanic, founding and revealing sacred meanings and, through a process of mythicization, extending the symbolic process of hierophanization.

THE GENERAL STRUCTURE AND FUNCTION OF MYTH

Most of the major points in Eliade's formulations of the most general structure and function of myth have already been noted in his general definition of myth. He proposes the following five characteristics of myth:

> In general it can be said that myth, as experienced by archaic
> societies, (1) constitutes the History of the acts of the Supernaturals;
> (2) that this History is considered to be absolutely *true* (because it is
> concerned with realities) and *sacred* (because it is the work of the
> Supernaturals); (3) that myth is always related to a "creation," it tells
> how something came into existence, or how a pattern of behavior, an
> institution, a manner of working were established; this is why myths
> constitute the paradigms for all significant human acts; (4) that by
> knowing the myth one knows the "origin" of things and hence can
> control and manipulate them at will; this is not an "external,"
> "abstract" knowledge but a knowledge that one "experiences" ritual-
> ly, either by ceremonially recounting the myth or by performing the
> ritual for which it is the justification; (5) that in one way or another
> one "lives" the myth, in the sense that one is seized by the sacred,
> exalting power of the events recollected or re-enacted.[17]

This "living" a myth implies a genuinely "religious" experience: "The
'religiousness' of this experience is due to the fact that one re-enacts
fabulous, exalting, significant events, once again witnesses the creative
deeds of the Supernaturals; one ceases to exist in the everyday world
and enters a transfigured, auroral world impregnated with the Supernaturals' presence." "In short, myths reveal that the World, man, and
life have a supernatural origin and history, and that this history is
significant, precious, and exemplary."[18]

This last statement points to Eliade's formulation of the major
function of myth: "The main function of myth is to determine the
exemplar models of all ritual, and of all significant human acts."[19] "Its
function is to reveal models and, in so doing, to give a meaning to the
World and to human life. This is why its role in the constitution of man
is immense. It is through myth . . . that the ideas of *reality, value,
transcendence* slowly dawn. Through myth, the World can be
apprehended as a perfectly articulated, intelligible, and significant
Cosmos. In telling how things were made, myth reveals by whom and

why they were made and under what circumstances. All of these 'revelations' . . . make up a Sacred History."[20]

As was seen in Eliade's definition of myth and his formulation of the general structure and function of myth, as well as in numerous interpretations of myth presented in earlier chapters, time and history are central to his theory of myth. Mythic time is sacred time, mythic history is sacred history, and as was presented in the illustration of "the symbolism of the center," mythic space is sacred space. The following sections and chapters 8 and 9 will provide a more detailed consideration of Eliade's interpretation of myth, time, and history.

For now we may note a key feature of Eliade's interpretation of mythic time and history that many modern, Western persons, including religious believers, may have difficulty in fully appreciating. In Eliade's interpretation of the nature, structure, function, and meaning of myth, mythic believers actually become contemporaneous with the supernatural beings and other sacred realities described in their myths. We may contrast a typical, less controversial, non-Eliadean interpretation to Eliade's dramatic claim.

It is not difficult to grant that for believers in myth their myths "symbolize," "represent," and "commemorate" events believed to have taken place in mythic time, space, and history. Mythic believers establish complex and widely divergent relations with such represented mythic realities and relate such symbolically expressed events to "ordinary" time and history in various ways.

If we examine mythic traditions interpreted by Eliade as radically ahistorical and even antihistorical, it may be irrelevant or even completely meaningless to some archaic mythic culture for scholars to try to establish precisely when some Supernatural Being or mythical Ancestor performed some exemplary act. It seems a waste of time to try to establish precisely when and where the Polynesian Io uttered the cosmogonic words that brought the world into existence; or when or where New Guinean *dema* type divinities were murdered by mythical Ancestors leading to the creation of the human world and the human condition. Similarly, it may be irrelevant or completely meaningless to some antihistorical or nonhistorical, Hindu, mythic culture for historians and archaeologists to try to establish precisely when and where Lord Śiva was born, when and where or if the famous battle in the *Bhagavad Gītā* actually took place, and whether there is historical evidence that Lord Kṛṣṇa really was Arjuna's charioteer, as represented in the *Gītā*. This is not to deny the complexity of temporal and historical relations within such mythic cultures. Even within those mythic cultures that seem to devalue or dismiss the significance and reality of nonmythic time and history, there is often a dynamic, changing, contextual relation between the disclosure of mythical events and "ordinary," secular time and history. The relations vary not only between different religious mythic cultures, but may even change significantly within the same mythic culture in response to changing historical, economic, social, and other conditions.

For example, the usual scholarly approach to Hindu myth and religion, frequently presented by Eliade and other interpreters, has included the assumption that Hindus—unlike Jews, Christians, and Muslims—have little or no interest in empirical, historical, and scientific questions regarding the "factual" basis of the mythical disclosures represented in their sacred narratives. Such questions as to whether Rāma, Kṛṣṇa, or Śiva were "actually" born and engaged in activities at the "historical" times and geographical locations described in myths are usually seen as irrelevant to Hindu, mythic spirituality. But as became evident from the destruction of the mosque at Ayodhya in December 1992 and from numerous other episodes of communal death and destruction, millions of contemporary Hindu "fundamentalists" are willing to kill and die over, say, historical claims that the Rāma of their myths was born at a certain place located in the present state of Uttar Pradesh on the same site where a mosque was later constructed.[21]

If we examine the dominant, Western religious traditions usually interpreted as more historical—not the ahistorical, archaic, cosmic structures within Western religions often emphasized by Eliade—chronological, irreversible history is sanctified and taken very seriously in the sacred narratives. It would not be irrelevant to the faith of Orthodox Jews if they learned that Moses was an ahistoric mythic creation or that scientific evidence made highly improbable the claim that Moses had received the Ten Commandments from God on Mt. Sinai at a precise time in the unfolding of historical events, as represented in the Hebrew Bible. Similarly, when serious doubts have been cast on the historical veracity of events portrayed in the sacred narratives of the New Testament and the Koran, traditional Christians and Muslims have usually not ignored or dismissed such questioning as completely irrelevant to their religious beliefs. Indeed, this is evident from the many actions taken by religious authorities over the centuries against perceived dissidents and heretics. This concern continues to be evident from recent cases, such as the Ayotollah Khomeini's issuance of the death sentence on Salman Rushdie's life after the publication of *The Satanic Verses* or steps taken by the Vatican and conservative Protestant institutions to silence liberal clergy and theologians. Millions of people raising questions about some of the factual basis of the Christian and Islamic historical accounts as represented and commemorated in the sacred narratives have been persecuted, excommunicated, and even put to death.

Nevertheless, it is easy to grant that all mythic expressions, in both ahistorical and more historical mythic cultures, point to eternal, transhistorical, sacred truths and realities—regardless of how differently religious cultures view and evaluate time and history—and that myths symbolize, represent, and commemorate those mythic creations and events revealing the sacred.

What makes Eliade's interpretation more striking and controversial is his frequent, dramatic assertions that this approach does not really get at the mythic mode of being in the world and the mythic experience and view of time and history. Repeatedly, Eliade emphasizes that myths do not "represent" or simply "commemorate" the primordial time and the sacred history. In living myths, mythic persons break through and abolish the limits of profane time, space, and history. Mythic believers, through the "reiteration" and "reenactment" of myths, through their participation in rituals and other significant activities based on their superhuman, exemplary mythic models, *actually become contemporaneous* with the Supernatural Beings, Ancestors, and sacred events described in the myths. "What is involved is not a commemoration of mythical events but a reiteration of them." The mythical actors "are made present, one becomes their contemporary. This also implies that one is no longer living in chronological time, but in the primordial Time, the Time when the event *first took place.*" This is the "strong time" of myth, the sacred time "when something *new, strong,* and *significant* was manifested. To re-experience that time, to re-enact it as often as possible, to witness again the spectacle of the divine works, to meet with the Supernaturals and relearn their creative lesson is the desire that runs like a pattern through all the ritual reiterations of myths."[22]

In reciting the cosmogonic myth, the Polynesian, American Indian, or southeastern European peasant "returns to the origin," is present at the moment of creation or at the primordial precosmic time before creation, and is renewed by "the perfection of beginnings." The medicinal herb has magico-religious efficaciousness in curing illness because one has knowledge of and participates in the mythic time when supernatural beings first created the sacred plant. The Hindu peasant, when participating in the sacred history narrated in the epic the *Rāmāyaṇa,* relives and becomes contemporaneous with the mythical events describing the dramatic rescue of Sītā by Lord Rāma from the demon Rāvaṇa on the island Lanka. The Jew doesn't simply symbolize and commemorate the Exodus from Egypt; the Jew is spiritually renewed by reenacting and becoming a participant in that sacred history of freedom from slavery. Periodic recurrence signifies that "mythical time is *made present* and then used indefinitely." The time of the mythical event, reenacted through the ritual, "is made *present,* 're-presented' so to speak, however far back it may have been in ordinary reckoning. Christ's passion, death and resurrection are not simply *remembered* during the service of Holy Week; they really happen *then* before the eyes of the faithful. And a convinced Christian must feel that he is *contemporary* with these transhistoric events, for, by being re-enacted, the time of the theophany becomes actual."[23]

These and similar formulations throughout Eliade's writings on myth raise a basic question: to what extent is Eliade presenting the view of the religious believer in myth and to what extent is he imposing his own value judgments? In the last citation, he clearly indicates that for "a convinced Christian" the mythic time is made present and the mythic events are relived. Leaving aside the obvious objection that many, if not most, modern Christians will more easily accept an interpretation that they are recalling or commemorating rather than actually being present at Christ's death, many of Eliade's interpretations do not have the explicit qualification "from the mythic person's point of view." Therefore, it is not always clear precisely what Eliade intends when he frequently claims that the mythic person "actually" returns to the perfection of beginnings and is present at the act of primordial creation or "really" meets with the supernatural beings and participates in the original mythical events.

What complicates such questions is the fact that it is clear from his autobiographical and journalistic writings, his often autobiographical literary creations, and his personal observations in scholarly works that Eliade himself believes in not only the possibility but even the necessity of transcending the "ordinary" temporal and historical dimension of existence. Human beings have a desire, need, and capacity to live in the transhistorical, nontemporal, qualitatively different universe of myth, symbol, and the sacred. Eliade frequently makes negative judgments about modern attempts to identify fully with the temporal and the historical and to deny mythic exemplary models of transcendence. Such a mode of existence is evaluated as inhuman, antihuman, alienated, meaningless, and self-defeating.

Nevertheless, it seems best, at least initially, to examine Eliade's interpretations of myth on a descriptive, phenomenological level; to approach Eliade's interpretations as claiming that these are the essential assumptions, beliefs, rituals, significant activities, metaphysics, and ontologies of archaic and other mythic cultures. None of this is meant to deny that in his theory of the structure of myth Eliade presents interpretations that repeatedly go far beyond the perspectives of real, particular, historical, religious, mythic human beings.

THE COSMOGONIC MYTH

Mircea Eliade places a primary significance on "creation," "origins," and "the perfection of beginnings." Focusing primarily, but not exclusively, on archaic myth and religion, he claims that mythic documents reveal a hierarchical scale of values granting primary ontological status and central structural and functional role to cosmogonic myths. Eliade's selection, arrangement, description, and interpretation of myths are dependent on the paramount importance that he attributes to the cosmogonic myth, and the key importance he grants other creation and origin myths, usually interpreted as continuing, completing, and often imitating the cosmogony. Eliade claims that "in every case in which we have access to a still living tradition" of a tribal society, what immediately strikes us is not only that the mythology constitutes a "sacred history" but also that "it reveals a hierarchy in the series of fabulous events that it reports. In general, one can say that any myth tells how something came into being, the world, or man, or an animal species, or a social institution, and so on. But by the very fact that the creation of the world precedes everything else, the cosmogony enjoys a special prestige. In fact . . . the cosmogonic myth furnishes the model for all myths of origin. The creation of animals, plants, or man presupposes the existence of a world."[24] As he illustrates:

> There is a great variety of cosmogonic myths. However, they can be classified as follows: 1. creation *ex nihilo* (a High Being creates the world by thought, by word, or by heating himself in a steam-hut, and so forth); 2. The Earth Diver Motif (a God sends aquatic birds or amphibious animals, or dives, himself, to the bottom of the primordial ocean to bring up a particle of earth from which the entire world grows); 3. creation by dividing in two a primordial unity (one can distinguish three variants: a separation of Heaven and Earth, that is to say of the World-Parents; b. separation of an original amorphous mass, the "Chaos"; c. the cutting in two of a cosmogonic egg); 4. creation by dememberment of a primordial Being, either a voluntary, anthropomorphic victim (Ymir of the Scandinavian mythology, the Vedic Indian Purusha, the Chinese P'an-ku) or an aquatic monster conquered after a terrific battle (the Babylonian Tiamat).[25]

In several of his books, Eliade uses the example of the Maori, Polynesian cosmogonic myth. "According to this myth, in the beginning there were only the Waters and Darkness. Io, the Supreme God, separated the Waters by the power of thought and of his words, and created the Sky and the Earth. He said: 'Let the Waters be separated, let the Heavens be formed, let the earth be!' These cosmogonic words of Io's, by virtue of which the World came into existence, are creative words, charged with sacred power. Hence men utter them whenever there is something to *do, to create.*" Io's cosmogonic words, by which he created the World and brought light from darkness, are repeated by Polynesians during all kinds of rites and activities requiring the creation of light from darkness: implanting a child in a barren womb, curing bodily and mental illness, and overcoming despair on the occasion of death or war.[26]

For Eliade, this "presents direct and incontrovertible testimony concerning the function of the cosmogonic myth in traditional society." This cosmogonic myth serves as the model for every kind of creation. As multivalent, the central myth can be applied on different planes of reference and has the capacity to transform diverse, fragmented experiences of despair into a meaningful, hopeful, creative, unified mythic mode of existence. "An unsuccessful war can be homologized with a sickness, with a dark, discouraged heart, with a sterile woman, with a poet's lack of inspiration, as with any other critical existential situation in which man is driven to despair. And all these negative, desperate, apparently irremediable situations are reversed by recitation of the cosmogonic myth, especially by the words by which Io brought forth the Universe and made light shine in the darkness. In other words, the cosmogony is the exemplary model for every creative situation: whatever man does is in some way a repetition of the preeminent 'deed', the archetypal gesture of the Creator God, the Creation of the World." Eliade adds that the Polynesian cosmogony is the exemplary model for every kind of "doing" not only because it is the ideal model for every creation "but also because the Cosmos is a divine work; hence it is sanctified even in its structure. By extension, whatever is perfect, 'full', harmonious, fertile—in short, whatever is 'cosmicized', whatever resembles a Cosmos—is sacred."[27]

Eliade writes of a lecture he gave at the Philosophers' Congress in Geneva in 1966, in which he presented two cosmogonic myths, the Indonesian and the Australian. He hopes that "the cosmogonic myth's role of exemplary model" was understood. Although he avoided translating "the lesson of archaic cosmogonic myths" into the language of the philosophers, he states that it is "a matter, naturally, of ontophany, for cosmogony means this: *Being which comes into being.* The birth, the creation of the world is, above all, the appearance of Being, ontophany. This is why the cosmogonic myth is an exemplary model for all types of *creation*—from the construction of a village or of a house, to the celebration of a marriage or the conception of a child. It is always a matter of a new creation of the world, that is, of a new epiphany of Being." Eliade concludes that this is "a matter, obviously, of a 'primitive' ontology, of a rudimentary metaphysics, if you will—because it reveals the world as an exemplary model of all forms of reality."[28]

Not only is there a great variety of cosmogonic myths, some presented in the relative simplicity and clarity of the Polynesian myth and others highly complex and ambiguous, but mythic peoples evaluate the nature and significance of their own cosmogonic myths and their own sacred histories in radically different ways. An excellent illustration of the complexity and ambiguity of cosmogonic myths can be found in Eliade's lengthy investigation of "The Devil and God: Prehistory of the Romanian Folk Cosmogony."[29] Starting with a Romanian version, Eliade examines numerous variations of the myth of the cosmogonic dive which constitutes the only "folk" cosmogony of southeastern Europe. The interpreter must attempt to make sense of dualistic versions in which God, deciding to create the Earth, sends his adversary, Satan, to the bottom of the primordial waters to bring back to the surface some of the seed of Earth. As cosmogonic diver, Satan subverts God's instructions, finally surfaces with a little mud under his fingernails, and even attempts to drown God. All of these events are essential for the creation of the Earth and the subsequent nature of the world and the human condition.

Different evaluations of the nature and significance of cosmogonic myths are illustrated by how the Ngaju Dayak of Borneo and other mythic peoples express their deepest nostalgia for reintegration with the primordial totality that existed *before* the creation of the world. Their cosmogonic myth is necessary for breaking up the primeval plenitude and unity and establishing the exemplary sacred history that gives meaning to life in this world. But their major longing is to be reintegrated with the original perfection, the precosmic unhistorical primordiality.[30] Many of Eliade's favorite myths and symbolisms—as expressed in the *coincidentia oppositorum,* the Symplegades, certain contradictory and extremely paradoxical rites of passage and initiations, and certain forms of mysticism—have the goal of abolishing and transcending the dualisms and other manifestations of creation and becoming unified or one with precosmic or acosmic absolute reality.

Eliade admits that not all myths of the creation of the world look like a cosmogonic myth as found in the Polynesian example, the Viṣṇu and other Hindu creation myths, the Akkadian (Mesopotamian) *Enuma Elish,* and the Hebraic narrative in Genesis. But Eliade claims that even in traditions where there is not such a cosmogonic myth, there is always some central myth that describes a primordial history that has a beginning; mythical events that account for how and why the world began and became what it is today.

There are relatively few cosmogonic myths compared with the huge number of mythical portrayals of the bringing into existence of other creations: the origins of human beings, different animal species, plants and trees and mountains, hunting and agriculture, birth and death, social relations and institutions, the prestige of religious specialists, rites of initiation and all kinds of other significant activities. Eliade often presents such myths of the origins as constituting sacred histories and providing paradigmatic models for anything viewed as significant and meaningful in the life world of mythic believers. Typically, in a hierarchical structural manner, Eliade relates the large number of origin myths to the primacy of the cosmogonic myth.

> Every mythical account of the *origin* of anything presupposes and continues the cosmogony. From the structural point of view, origin myths can be homologized with the cosmogonic myth. The creation of the World being *the* pre-eminent instance of creation, the cosmogony becomes the exemplary model for "creation" of every kind. This does not mean that the origin myth imitates or copies the cosmogonic model, for no concerted and systematized reflection is involved. But every new appearance—an animal, a plant, an institution—implies the existence of a World. Even when it is a matter of explaining how,

starting from a different state of things, the present situation was reached (for example, how the Sky was separated from the Earth, or how man became mortal), the "World" was already there, even though its structure was different, though it was not yet *our* world. Every origin myth narrates and justifies a "new situation"—new in the sense that it did not exist *from the beginning of the World.* Origin myths continue and complete the cosmogonic myth; they tell how the world was changed, made richer or poorer.[31]

Eliade attempts to substantiate his interpretation by citing a variety of origin myths employed in healing rituals. In the healing ritual of the tribal Bhils of India, a *mandala,* which is primarily an *imago mundi* representing the Cosmos in miniature and the pantheon, is drawn by the religious specialist or "magician" by the bedside of the patient. The construction of the *mandala* is equivalent to a magical re-creation of the world. The therapeutic value of this ritual operation arises from the fact that the patient is made contemporary with the Creation of the World and "is immersed in the primordial fullness of life; he is penetrated by the gigantic forces that, *in illo tempore,* made the Creation possible." Eliade provides other illustrations of the close connection between the cosmogonic myth, myths of the origin of a sickness and its cure, and rituals of healing among the Navahos, the Tibetan Nakhi, the Assyrians, and other mythic peoples. "As the exemplary model for all 'creation', the cosmogonic myth can help the patient to make a 'new beginning' of his life. The *return to origins* gives the hope of rebirth. Now, all the medical rituals we have been examining aim at a return to origins. We get the impression that for archaic societies life cannot be *repaired,* it can only be *re-created* by a return to sources. And the 'source of sources' is the prodigious outpouring of energy, life, and fecundity that occurred at the Creation of the World."[32]

Eliade summarizes the relations between cosmogonic and origin myths: "First and most important is the fact that the origin myth frequently begins with a sketch of the cosmogony: the myth briefly summarizes the essential moments of the Creation of the World and then goes on to relate the genealogy of the royal family or the history of the tribe or the history of the origin of sicknesses and remedies, and so on. In all these cases the origin myths continue and complete the cosmogonic myth." Origin myths are dependent on the cosmogonic myth because of the relation of "beginnings," with the absolute "beginning" being the Creation of the World. "It is not enough to *know* the 'origin', it is necessary to re-establish the moment when such-and-such a thing was created. This finds expression in 'going back' until the original, strong, sacred Time is recovered." And "recovering the primordial Time, which alone can ensure the complete renewal of the Cosmos, of life, and of society, is brought about primarily by re-establishing the 'absolute beginning', that is, the Creation of the World." In short, cosmogonies "serve as the model for all kinds of 'creations.'"[33]

MYTHS OF ORIGINS

The relation of origin myths to the cosmogonic myth is usually not so simple as has just been presented. Eliade acknowledges that many mythic cultures, including some with clear cosmogonic myths, actually show little interest in the cosmogony. This is clear from his numerous studies of the phenomenon of the *deus otiosus* in which the Creator God withdraws, becomes passive, and is devalued and even forgotten by the mythic believers. For example, what interests the Aranda of Central Australia and many other mythic peoples is what occurred in mythic time and history *after* the "original" creation. The later creations by mythical ancestors, heroes, and other supernatural beings constitute sacred histories that have more of an existential primordiality and relevance. Such sacred histories provide paradigmatic models that relate directly to the desires, needs, crises, rites, and activities of the lived world of *homo religiosus*. What the mythical ancestors did constitutes a cosmogony, although not a cosmogony properly speaking in the strict sense of the original creation of the world. Instead, one has the sense of later mythic creations that brought into existence worlds that look more like the worlds in which the mythic believers live. In such cases, believers are concerned with the recovery, through the exemplary models and their periodic reenactments, of what occurred in the sacred histories after creation.[34]

This same general mythic structure—in which the original cosmogonic myth becomes devalued or forgotten and more existentially relevant myths focus on what occurred after the creation of the world—applies also to sacred histories that account for the origin of human beings. Eliade sums up his examination of the majority of primitive myths relative to the creation of the human being: "Everywhere, the myth presents the creation (or the appearance: in a subterranean region, in the sky, etc.) of a primordial man, more or less perfect (that is, at first, immortal). But the origin of man does not explain the current situation of humanity. Man becomes mortal, sexed, in conflict with the animal world, condemned to work, etc.—following an event or a series of events that took place in the mythical epoch. That means that for primitives, as for the Judeo-Christian tradition, man as he is now is not only the work of God, but also the result of certain events that constitute a history ('mythical', to be sure, but history all the same)."[35]

In this regard, Eliade emphasizes "distinctions made by the primitives between the two sorts of *primordiality:* the *primordium* dominated by the Supreme Being (who is often transformed into *deus otiosus)* and the primordial in which the mythical ancestors or other inferior beings are manifested and created. Archaic man (not only he) is interested especially in this second *primordium:* what took place then marked him profoundly; he is the result of the events of this mythical period." Already in archaic mythic culture, the mythic believer thus feels "linked with a mythical history, and tends to forget, or neglect, the ontophanies, the creative manifestations of the supreme Gods which reveal being."[36]

Some of the most interesting mythic illustrations of the primary focus on what occurred after the cosmogony can be seen in Eliade's treatment of myths of "the murdered divinity," a genre especially characteristic of myths of the palaeo-cultivators of tubers. Eliade's most detailed illustration is from A. E. Jensen's interpretation of the famous New Guinean myth of Hainuwele and the *dema* type divinities. Without describing the specific myths of the murdered divinities, we may simply mention a few of their major features. Unlike the Creator Gods who become *dei otiosi,* disappear, and leave a gap to be filled by other mythical figures, the violent death of these divinities at the hands of mythical Ancestors is creative: "Murdered *in illo tempore,* the divinity survives in the rites by which the murder is periodically re-enacted; or, in other cases, he survives primarily in the living forms (animals, plants) that sprang from his body." The murder of these divinities is not cosmogonic, since they appeared on earth after the creation of the world. These divinities were then murdered after a very limited existence in mythic time, and their violent tragic death became creative and was essential for constituting the human world and the human condition.[37]

These origin myths account for the human condition, plants and animals, death, puberty initiations, blood sacrifices, and other significant aspects of the mythic culture. What is "essential" is fixed not at the cosmogony but at a later moment in the sacred history: "A mythic Time is still involved, but it is no longer the 'first' Time, what we may call the 'cosmogonic' Time. The 'essential' is no longer bound up with an *ontology* (how the World—the real—came into being) but with a *History*. It is a History at once divine and human, for it is the result of a drama acted out by the Ancestors of men and by Supernatural Beings different in type from the all-powerful, immortal Creator Gods." These divinities "die," but they survive in their creations. Their "death at the hands of the mythical Ancestors changed not only *their* mode of being but the mode of being of *mankind*. From the time of the primordial murder an indissoluble relation arose between Divine Beings of the *dema* type and men."[38]

Stating that these are "the first pathetic and tragic myths," later followed by other pathetic and violent mythologies of the ancient Near East, Eliade makes the striking claim that "the celestial Supreme Being and Creator recovers his religious activity only in certain pastoral cultures (especially among the Turco-Mongols) and in the monotheism of Moses, in the reform of Zarathustra, and in Islam." "What must be stressed is the fact that the great mythologies of Euro-Asiatic polytheism, which correspond to the first historical civilizations, are increasingly concerned with what happened *after* the Creation of the Earth, and even after the creation (or the appearance) of man. The accent is now on what *happened to* the Gods and no longer on what they *created*."[39]

We have presented a few of the numerous passages from Eliade that emphasize the primary mythic focus on origins, but not on the primacy of the creation of the world. This can easily lead to the criticisms raised by other theorists of myth that Eliade overemphasizes the paramount role of the cosmogonic myth as the exemplary model for all significant deeds and creations; that he has granted to the cosmogonic myth an ontological status, structure, and function not justified by the totality of the mythic data. One wonders, for example, about the fundamental, axiomatic teachings of Siddhartha Gautama, the Buddha, in the Pali Canon in which he shows little interest in cosmogonies. Indeed, he warns that such metaphysical and theological speculations about the origin of the world are a waste of time and "tend not toward edification." One may also question whether the Indian and Gnostic eschatologies or the Hebraic eschatology considered in the next section can be interpreted primarily as "moving" the cosmogony to the future.

ESCHATOLOGICAL MYTHS

An obvious objection to Eliade's structural emphasis on the paramount, exemplary, mythic significance of the cosmogony and his focus on other myths of origins is that many religions seem to emphasize eschatological myths. Not only is there a shift from the cosmogonic myth to other myths of origins revealing what occurred in mythic time after the creation of the world. There are religious cultures in which the primary mythic emphasis is not so much on what occurred in the past as on what will occur in the future; not so much on the creation of the world as on the end of the world. Eliade devotes considerable time to interpreting these end-of-the-world myths and to establishing a relation between cosmological and eschatological myths so that he can maintain his theory of the structural and functional primacy of the cosmogony.

To put Eliade's position in somewhat oversimplified terms: the mythic focus on the cosmogony and origins, with the idea of the "perfection of beginnings," becomes "movable" and is shifted from the primordial past to the timeless future. Without denying that something radically new has occurred, he maintains that the same, essential mythic intuitions and constructions of exemplary meaningful worlds seen in the symbolic narrative reenactments of sacred cosmogonies, with renewal through the recovery of the primordial sacred, may be detected in eschatological myths. Eschatologies, in their essential structures, can be understood as cosmogonies of the future.

In New Year and other cosmogonic and origin mythic-ritual scenarios, there is the idea that the sacred "beginning" can be recovered only through the destruction or end of the old, worn out, degenerate, corrupt world:

> In proportion as the cosmic cycle became longer, the idea of the perfection of the beginnings tended to imply a complementary idea: that, *for something genuinely new to begin, the vestiges and ruins of the old cycle must be completely destroyed.* In other words, to obtain an *absolute* beginning, the end of a World must be total. Eschatology is only the prefiguration of a cosmogony to come. But every eschatology insists on this fact: the New Creation cannot take place before this world is abolished once and for all. There is no question of regenerating what has degenerated; nothing will serve but to destroy the old world so that it can be re-created *in toto.* The obsession with the bliss of the beginnings demands the destruction of all that has existed—and hence has degenerated—since the beginning of the World; there is no other way to restore the initial perfection.[40]

Eliade attempts to substantiate this thesis through his interpretation of many myths of the End of the World. The end occurred in the mythic past or will occur in the mythic future.[41] In his general interpretation of archaic myths, there is the repetitious, cyclical structure of mythical beginnings followed by ends that are then followed by the renewal of new beginnings. This is usually seen as homologized and integrated with the "natural," cosmic cycles of the seasons, the lunar rhythms, and vegetation. In addition, archaic cultures have myths of the End of the World—not of a "natural end" of the World but of a catastrophe brought on by divine beings. Such catastrophes are most prevalent in flood myths, but there are many other archaic myths portraying cosmic cataclysms destroying the world and almost all of humankind. In archaic cultures, myths describing the End of the World in the past are much more prevalent than those describing some future end. In all cases, the end of the old degraded world, the return to some primordial chaos, is followed by the re-creation of a new world. In short, a new cosmogony recovers the perfection of the beginning.

After considering innovations in End of the World myths from India and other mythic cultures, Eliade turns to the obvious challenge of Jewish and Christian apocalyptic images in their eschatological visions. He readily grants that there is much that is radically different from the archaic mythic world. Just as the cosmogony occurred only once, so will the End of the World. No longer in the circular time of eternal return, sacred time has become linear and irreversible, and the eschatology will represent the final triumph of the sacred history. There will be a final divine judgment with the restoration of paradise and eternal bliss for those who have remained true to the sacred history. But for all of these radical innovations, Eliade reaffirms the same general structure: that the "Cosmos that will reappear after the catastrophe will be the same Cosmos that God created at the beginning of Time, but purified, regenerated, restored to its original glory." What is most essential is not the end of the world but the mythic certainty of a new beginning. Thus the primary mythic relation to the exemplary cosmogony is maintained.[42]

Many scholars have charged that here and elsewhere Eliade has partially acknowledged, but greatly underestimated, the radical changes and significance of the Hebraic views of myth, time, and history. His interpretations of Jewish and Christian apocalyptic visions of the End of the World are often seen by these critics as another example of privileging and generalizing an archaic mythic orientation.

MYTHIC RENEWAL

Renewal is central to Eliade theory of the essential structure and function of myth.[43] He maintains that "the periodical renewal of the World has been the most frequent mythico-ritual scenario in the religious history of humanity."[44] Eliade emphasizes how mythic persons long for spiritual renewal through the abolition of meaningless profane time and the total regeneration of sacred time.[45] The cosmogonic myth has ontological and structural primacy because it allows for total renewal through the recovery of the absolute perfection of the sacred beginning. Myths of origin, say, of medicinal plants have a special status among certain mythic cultures because returning to the strong time of the creation of the sacred plant is efficacious in allowing for the curing of disease and renewal of life. An end of the world myth has special prestige in a particular eschatology because such a complete destruction is necessary for the total renewal of a new cosmic creation including the spiritual renewal of human beings.

The theme of renewal is central to Eliade's critique of modernity. As will be seen in chapter 11, he claims that Western, secular life, in consciously denying the mythic and the sacred, is in a state of profound crisis, unable to cope with its experiences of meaninglessness, anxiety, death, and "the terror of history." At the same time, modern human beings have the possibility for dealing with their existential crises and for experiencing a cultural renewal if they open up to and revalorize the essential symbols and myths of the sacred that allow for the constitution of meaningful, significant, coherent life worlds.

In his analysis of hierophanies and the dialectic of the sacred, the structures of religious symbolism, the structure and function of myth, and the theme of mythical renewal, Eliade has presented some strong judgments involved in the mythic view of history. In Eliade's interpretation, the mythic person views homogeneous, irreversible, ordinary, profane time and history as without significant meaning. By contrast, the sacred time and history of myth and religion are significant and meaningful. What is ordinarily part of profane time and history can become part of a coherent, significant world of meaning only when it is experienced through superhuman, exemplary, transcendent, mythic and other sacred structures.

Such strong judgments have proven controversial. The next chapter will explore Eliade's attitudes toward and interpretations of time and history, especially in relation to his theory of myth, as well as criticisms of his treatment of the historical dimension of myth.

NOTES

1. For example, Eliade writes in his preface to the English edition of *The Forbidden Forest,* "I said to myself that my spiritual equilibrium, the condition indispensable to any creativity, is assured by this oscillation between research of a scientific nature and literary imagination" (p. vi).

2. *Journal 1*, p. 150. Eliade continues with the observation that "psychologizers," "realists," and other commentators and analyzers have ignored the "metaphysical dignity" and theology "revealed by narration as such." Eliade writes: "I maintain, as on so many other occasions, the 'irreplaceability' of the narrative novel, the so-called novel-novel, which fills the place of myths for the modern world" (p. 145).

3. *Journal 3*, pp. 278, 283-84.

4. "Preface," *The Forbidden Forest*, pp. vii-viii.

5. "Cosmogonic Myth and 'Sacred History'," *Quest*, pp. 74-75. This chapter in *Quest* was first published in *Religious Studies* 2 (1967): 171-83.

6. *Quest*, pp. 72-73.

7. Ibid., p. 73.

8. *Myth and Reality*, pp. 8-12.

9. *Sacred Narrative: Readings in the Theory of Myth*, ed. Alan Dundes (Berkeley: University of California Press, 1984).

10. William Bascom, "The Forms of Folklore: Prose Narratives," in *Sacred Narratives*, pp. 5-29; Lauri Honko, "The Problem of Defining Myth," in *Sacred Narrative*, pp. 41-52; G. S. Kirk, "On Defining Myth," in *Sacred Narratives*, pp. 53-61.

11. *Myth and Reality*, pp. 5-6.

12. Ibid., p. 139.

13. Of course, Jean-Paul Sartre and other existentialists would fully agree with Eliade's interpretation that for traditional, religious, mythic persons "essence precedes existence." Their disagreement arises from diametrically opposed evaluations. For the secular existentialists, the traditional, essentialized metaphysical and religious views are illusory and express human self-alienation, inauthentic existence, and escapes from reality. Sartre's most famous formulation of existence precedes essence appeared in a 1945 lecture which was published the next year as *L'Existentialisme est un humanisme* and *Existentialism and Humanism*. This lecture has been reproduced in numerous anthologies and edited texts. See, for example, Jean-Paul Sartre, *Existentialism*, trans. Bernard Frechtman (New York: The Philosophical Library, 1947), pp. 14-38.

14. *Myth and Reality*, pp. 92-93. In *The Myth of the Eternal Return*, Eliade writes: "We must add that, for the traditional societies, all the important acts of life were revealed *ab origine* by the gods or heroes. Men only repeat these exemplary and paradigmatic gestures *ad infinitum*" (p. 32).

15. *No Souvenirs*, p. 208.

16. See, for example, *Patterns*, p. 426, for Eliade's analysis of myth as an autonomous act of creation and revelation.

17. *Myth and Reality*, pp. 18-19.

18. Ibid., p. 19.

19. *Patterns*, p. 410. In *Myth and Reality*, Eliade asserts that "the foremost function of myth is to reveal the exemplary models for all human rites and all significant human activities—diet or marriage, work or education, art or wisdom." (p. 8).

20. *Myth and Reality*, pp. 144-45. *The Myth of the Eternal Return* contains many illustrations of the claim that the primary function of myth is to reveal the exemplary models for all rituals and all significant human activities.

21. In a similar way, I was not prepared for major mythic responses I encountered in Sri Lanka in 1985-1986. Sinhala Buddhist myths such as stories of the Buddha coming to Sri Lanka as a conqueror and mythical incidents in the Sri Lankan Chronicles were presented as historical fact, were used to legitimate the killing of Tamil Hindus in the civil war, and often seemed to contradict what I had always accepted as the basic teachings of the Buddha. The Sinhala Buddhist mythic constructions, identifying language with race with nationality with religion, made historical claims but seemed insulated from historical, archaeological, and scientific counterevidence presented by modern scholars. In my chapter in *Religion and Political Conflict in South Asia*, I analyzed the nature, meaning, and significance of such Buddhist mythic constructions and their complex and often contradictory relation to history. See Douglas Allen, "Religious-Political Conflict in Sri Lanka: Philosophical Considerations," in *Religion and Political Conflict in South Asia: India Pakistan, and Sri Lanka*, ed. Douglas Allen (Westport, Conn.: Greenwood Publishers, 1992; New Delhi: Oxford University Press, 1993), pp. 181-203. For an excellent study of complex mythic-historical relations, see Gananath Obeyesekere, "Duṭṭhagāmaṇī and the Buddhist Conscience," in *Religion and Political Conflict in South Asia*, pp. 135-60.

22. *Myth and Reality*, p. 19.

23. *Patterns*, pp. 392-93. "This contemporaneity with the great moments of myth is an indispensable condition for any form of magico-religious efficaciousness" (p. 393).

24. *Quest*, p. 75.

25. Mircea Eliade, *From Primitives to Zen: A Thematic Sourcebook of the History of Religions* (New York: Harper and Row, 1967), p. 83. (The one-volume paperback edition was published in 1977 as *From Primitives to Zen* and later as *Essential Sacred Writings From Around the World.*)

26. *Myth and Reality*, pp. 30-31. For this Polynesian cosmogonic account, Eliade cites E. S. C. Handy, *Polynesian Religion* (Honolulu: Bernice P. Bishop Museum Bulletin 34, 1927), pp. 10-11. A more complete version of Io and the Maori cosmogony appears in *From Primitives to Zen*, pp. 86-87, in which Eliade uses Hare Hongi, "A Maori Cosmogony," *Journal of the Polynesian Society* 16 (1907): 113-14. See also *From Primitives to Zen*, pp. 14-15, *Eternal Return*, pp. 82-83, *Sacred and Profane*, p. 82, and *Patterns*, p. 410.

27. *Myth and Reality,* pp. 31-33.
28. *No Souvenirs,* pp. 290-91.
29. See *Zalmoxis: The Vanishing God,* pp. 76-130.
30. See *Quest,* pp. 77-81. Eliade's source is Hans Schärer, *Ngaju Religion: The Conception of God among a South Borneo People,* trans. Rodney Needham (The Hague: M. Nijhoff, 1963). See the selections on Ngaju Dayak religion in *From Primitives to Zen,* pp. 155-58, 165-70, 170-73. For Eliade's emphasis on the desire for reintegration with the primordial totality, see esp. pp. 169-70, 170-73.
31. *Myth and Reality,* p. 21.
32. Ibid., pp. 24-30.
33. Ibid., pp. 36-38.
34. *Quest,* pp. 82-87. In providing this interpretation of the Aranda, Eliade primarily uses the writings of T. G. H. Strehlow, esp. "Personal Monototemism in a Polytotemic Community," *Festschrift für Ad. E. Jensen,* Vol. 2. ed. Eike Haberland (Munich: K. Renner, 1964), pp. 723-54, and *Aranda Traditions* (Melbourne: Melbourne University Press, 1947). Eliade's *Australian Religions: An Introduction* contains numerous illustrations of this primary focus on sacred histories describing later mythic creations. Key sections focusing on the Aranda illustration appear in *Australian Religions,* pp. 29-34, 39-41, 44-53, 57-59.
35. *No Souvenirs,* p. 207.
36. Ibid., pp. 287-88. Eliade writes: "Just as the 'primitives' considered themselves the result not of creation by the gods but of the activity of primordial heroes (the mythical Ancestors, the civilizing Heroes)," mythic persons of Greek culture situated themselves as dependent "on what had happened to certain heroes in the fabled times of the beginnings, Theseus, Oedipus, Creon, and the others" (pp. 284-85).
37. *Myth and Reality,* pp. 99-107. See Mircea Eliade and Ioan P. Couliano, *The Eliade Guide to World Religions* (San Francisco: HarperCollins Publishers, 1991), pp. 53-54, 189-90.
38. *Myth and Reality,* p. 108.
39. Ibid., pp. 108-11.
40. Ibid., p. 52.
41. See chap. 4, "Eschatology and Cosmogony," in *Myth and Reality,* pp. 54-74.
42. Ibid., pp. 64-67.
43. See chap. 3, "Cosmic and Eschatological Renewal," in *Mephistopheles and the Androgyne,* pp. 125-59.
44. *Mephistopheles and the Androgyne,* p. 158. This theme of renewal appears in all of Eliade's writings on myth. See chap. 3, "Myths and Rites of Renewal," in *Myth and Reality,* pp. 39-53.

45. See chap. 2, "Sacred Time and Myths," in *Sacred and Profane,* pp. 68-113; chap. 9, "Sacred Time and the Myth of Eternal Renewal," in *Patterns,* pp. 388-409.

CHAPTER 8

Eliade's Antihistorical Attitudes

Central to Eliade's interpretation of myth is his interpretation of history. Mythic history is sacred history and is distinguished from profane, temporal, irreversible history. Chapters 8 and 9 on "myth and history" could just as easily be entitled "myth, time, and history." Eliade often uses "history" and "time," "historicity" and "temporality," interchangeably. His interpretation of the sacred mythic view of profane history emphasizes its reaction to the view of humans as limited, conditioned, temporal beings.[1]

We have already seen many formulations of Eliade's interpretations of myth, time, and history. For example, Eliade analyzes the sacred-profane relation and the dialectic of the sacred as disclosing universal structures in terms of which a natural, temporal, historical phenomenon is transformed and burst open to reveal supernatural, eternal, trans-historical dimensions of reality. He analyzes the structure and function of myth, the primacy of the cosmogonic myth, and the importance of origins as ways that mythic peoples renew their lives and the world by abolishing limiting conditions of profane time and history.

Chapters 8 and 9 present different aspects of Eliade's approach to myth, time, and history. In the present chapter, I examine his personal attitudes toward history and historical time, dividing the presentation into two parts. First, Eliade's autobiographical reflections are presented: antihistorical expressions about his own life; his own experiences, fears, goals, and attitudes toward myth, history, and historical time. Second, Eliade's personal scholarly interpretations are considered: his interpretation of the antihistorical attitudes of mythic persons toward myth, time, and history. Finally, I examine interpretations of Eliade's approach to myth and history by other scholars. Most critics and some supporters have emphasized the antihistorical foundation of Eliade's approach to myth and religion. In the next chapter, I shall document and analyze in a more systematic manner and in greater depth the primacy of nonhistorical structures and meanings in Eliade's history and phenomenology of myth and religion.

ELIADE'S PERSONAL ATTITUDES TOWARD TIME AND HISTORY

In light of the concluding section to chapter 4, "Eliade's Personal Faith and His Scholarship," it may seem surprising that this first section is devoted to Eliade's "personal attitudes." I warned against interpretations that collapse flexible but important distinctions such as those between the personal and the scholarly. For example, I criticized scholarly interpretations that saw the key to Eliade's scholarship in terms of some largely hidden, personal, Christian faith. At the same time, I also noted that such warnings were not intended to endorse some clear-cut separation of the personal Eliade from Eliade the scholarly interpreter of myth and religion. Indeed, it has repeatedly been emphasized that Eliade's assumptions, beliefs, and priorities are an essential part of his scholarly interpretation of myth and religion. Chapters 10 and 11 will emphasize Eliade's personal assumptions and normative judgments that often go far beyond the scholarly boundaries of the history and phenomenology of religion.

Unlike speculations about some hidden faith, imputing to Eliade positions that he refused to embrace in his scholarly writings, Eliade had no reluctance in expressing his personal attitudes about history and historical time. These views are expressed explicitly in scholarly works, in which he clearly goes beyond the evaluations of *homo religiosus* and presents his own normative judgments, through his literary characters, and most clearly in autobiographical and journal entries.

Recognizing legitimate distinctions between the personal and the scholarly in no way means that Eliade's extensive, personal reflections on myth and history are not instructive in gaining insight into his scholarly interpretations of myth and history. Indeed, there is a remarkable overlap between Eliade's scholarly treatment of the mythic view of history and his personal reflections on history. In his autobiographical passages on his own fears, resistances, hopes, and experiences of time and history, one has the distinct impression that Eliade is viewing himself mythically; that he is attempting to cope with the threat of arbitrary, meaningless, profane, historical time by re-enacting and revalorizing exemplary, transhistorical, mythic models and opening himself to more meaningful mythic time and history.

Not so long ago, when there was more widespread acceptance of traditional standards of rationality and objectivity, formulations regarding a scholar's personal attitudes and other contextual considerations might have been regarded as anecdotal and of interest only for biographical and psychological studies and the history of ideas. Such a "personal" approach was typically dismissed as irrelevant or fallacious when it came to analyzing the nature and truth claims of various scholarly theories. But with the contributions of Kuhn and Feyerabend in philosophy of science, Derrida and Foucault, Rorty and the revival of pragmatism, and feminist and post-modernist scholars with their critiques of traditional theory-making, a contextual approach, maintaining that personal religious, political, cultural, and other factors are central to understanding why theories are produced in certain ways and why some gain hegemony, has considerable merit. Situating Eliade's scholarly productions within their contexts of his personal values and the larger economic, political, religious, and cultural structures of his society will help others better to understand the origin, nature, meaning, and significance of his writings.[2]

Nevertheless, it is important to distinguish two senses of "the personal" involved in Eliade's observations on myth and history. First, there are passages in which Eliade is clearly reflecting on his own personal life and is revealing his personal experiences, fears, goals, and attitudes toward myth and history. Second, there are Eliade's scholarly interpretations of religious data of mythic peoples. His interpretations may be highly personal—with personal assumptions, priorities, and privileging of certain phenomena—but Eliade is claiming that this is what, say, the Polynesian, Hindu, or Romanian cosmogonic myths reveal. In other words, his intention is to describe and interpret the religious meaning of myth for *homo religiosus*. This distinction is not intended to deny that the clearly autobiographical observations and the scholarly analysis often overlap, and the personal, autobiographical reflections on time and history are often helpful for grasping some of the motives behind and features of Eliade's scholarship.

What must be emphasized in maintaining legitimate distinctions is that there are important differences in these two senses of the personal. This is clearly seen in different approaches to the verification or falsification of Eliade's claims about myth and history. In the first sense of Eliade's personal, autobiographical reflections, a scholar doing a historical or biographical study might examine Eliade's other writings for possible inconsistencies; the writings of his Romanian and other contemporaries about him and the events he describes; and scholarship by others on the overall historical and cultural contexts within which he is expressing his views. A scholar might then attempt to confirm whether Eliade really had the motives and did the things he attributes to himself and whether the events he depicts are accurately portrayed. For example, a number of critics, focusing on Romanian fascism, have claimed that the nonpolitical, nonhistorical, spiritual Eliade portrayed in his writings reflects intentional omissions, silences, misrepresentations, and distortions of Eliade's real, historical motives, actions, and commitments. In the second sense, a scholar interested in determining the value of Eliade's personal, *scholarly* studies of the mythic views of history of, say, Australian aborigines or Eskimo shamans would employ different methods of verification: whether Eliade includes all of the relevant data; whether he approaches the data with methodological rigor; whether he reads all sorts of profound mythic meanings into the data; and whether he is guilty of uncritical, subjective generalizations.

Once again, this is not intended as an absolute, clear-cut dichotomy since Eliade's highly personal views about himself often enter into his scholarly interpretations of myth and history. Nevertheless, there is a legitimate, albeit flexible, distinction between Eliade's views on history that are presented as highly personal reflections and his interpretations of profane and mythic history that make scholarly claims and should be judged by appropriate scholarly criteria. In short, even when Mircea Eliade's personal fears, desires, and attitudes help one to understand motivations behind and specific directions taken by his scholarship on

myth, time, and history, there still remains the question of determining
the adequacy of his scholarly interpretations.

Personal Autobiographical Reflections

Eliade's personal attitudes toward history and historical time are
expressed frequently in his *Autobiography* and his *Journal.* His strong
language reveals his fears, needs, and hopes. He frequently asserts that
he and we are "condemned" to live in history, must "defend" ourselves
against history, and must learn to "escape" history. Typically, Eliade
writes: "My essential preoccupation is precisely the means of escaping
History, of saving myself through symbol, myth, rites, archetypes."[3]

Many incidents in Eliade's *Autobiography* express his need and
capacity to escape time and history. After describing earliest
recollections of an experience at age three or four of a green fairyland
with incomparable light, he indicates that for many years he practiced
"an exercise of capturing the epiphanic moment," always discovering
the "same plenitude," slipping into "a fragment of time without
duration." At age nine, he lived in an imaginary world of his own secret
army. A few years later, he discovered how to write "inspired," with
"no sense of duration" while existing in "another space." By age
eighteen, after the publication of his one hundredth article and as he
was about to take his baccalaureate examination, he used a "spiritual
exercise" that he says fortified him inwardly and make him invulner-
able. He would lie on the bed, close his eyes, and imagine himself in
one of the worlds that fascinated him. He would feel that he "had
become completely *present* in one of those extraterrestrial or lost
worlds. Then I would begin to live there, to move in a landscape that, to
me, seemed entirely *real,* meeting extraordinary beings who were
excited over truly *interesting* problems. . . ."[4]

In his attempt to escape or transcend Western history and culture,
Eliade describes two "failures" in India. First, while living in his
teacher Surendranath Dasgupta's house in Calcutta, he was "forbidden"
the "historical" India after his sexual relations with Dasgupta's
daughter Maitreya.[5] Then, while living at Swami Shivananda's ashram
in the Himalayas, he lost his chance for "eternal, trans-historical India"
after his tantric experiments with the South African Jenny. Eliade

concludes that his historical and transhistorical Indian existence represented an attempt at premature renunciation of Western culture and history. "To believe that I could, at twenty-three, sacrifice history and culture for 'the Absolute' was further proof that I had not understood India. My vocation was culture, not sainthood."[6]

Writers have commented on Eliade's extreme experiments in self-discipline, as seen in his determination to "rob sleep." Driven by an obsession that "time passes" and that there is "limited time," Eliade experimented for years in cutting back on his sleep to a minimum in order to free more time for his reading and writing. Later, sometimes describing this as his "Faustian ambition," Eliade commented that he "believed such self-discipline was the gateway to absolute freedom. The struggle against sleep, like the struggle against normal modes of behavior, signified for me a heroic attempt to transcend the human condition." Only later did he realize that the "freedom I thought I could obtain by doing the opposite of the 'normal' signified the surpassing of my historical, social, and cultural condition."[7]

Throughout his life, Eliade experienced "attacks of melancholia," often brought on by the realization that historical, irreversible "time passes, and in its passing something essential in us is irretrievably lost." In a journal entry of 8 September 1950, he recalls a letter he sent to Buonaiuti from India in which he "spoke of the terror I was suffering then—it was the summer of 1929—as I was experiencing, *sensing,* 'how time passes' (. . . that experience, the importance of which I did not understand until much later)." *Journal I, 1945-1955* contains many references to this oppressive, terrifying sense of time passing. There is never enough time. Eliade is often in a frenzy, bemoaning the fact that so much of his time has been wasted, even when to others he seemed so incredibly productive. In 1946, in a fit of despondency, reflecting on his estrangement as a Romanian writer, Eliade writes that the last "six years are irretrievably lost" and that he feels the "terror of the irreversible! For the first time in my life I could *see* and *accept* myself as a failure. . . ." Indeed, even *Journal IV, 1979-1985* contains many references by Eliade to his "melancholy" brought on by the oppressive sense of time passing; by his extremely self-critical attitude that he has wasted time and his ill health, especially his painful and debilitating arthritis, will not allow him the time to complete his scholarly work.[8]

"We Must Hurry . . ." is a chapter in Eliade's *Autobiography*. His writings contain many references to how he and his generation were condemned by the historical moment; how irreversible, historical time was against them. He had a "premonition . . . that we would *not have time.*" He "wrote hastily," "produced so much, so fast" because he knew that the freedom history allowed his generation was limited. He knew "that there would come a day when history would prevent me from growing and becoming myself." "I saw here the destiny of our generation: ten years of freedom . . . and then again to be 'conditioned' by the historical moment." He was obsessed by the fear that his generation would not have sufficient time to accomplish its "mission." "I sensed now not only that time was limited, but that soon there would come a terrifying time (the time of the 'terror of History')."[9]

Eliade views his journal as a defense against his enemy of historical time. The "special function" of a personal diary is the possibility of "saving and preserving time." He "saves" by "freezing" "fragments of *concrete time.*" "I write to find myself again later, to remind myself of times uselessly lost *(all* 'times' are irreparably condemned, however much we may endeavor to save them)."[10]

Eliade's journal reveals his attitude toward time and history in his selection and omission of possible subject matter. For example, he offers many personal reflections on students at the University of Chicago in the 1960s and 1970s. But from his entries, one would never guess that Vietnam/Indochina antiwar activism was dominating much of student life at the University of Chicago and throughout the United States. His few comments on the student antiwar movement tend to be very critical. But this is not the case of a conservative professor who enthusiastically supports the war, endorses the status quo, and denounces all rebellious students. He is attracted to hippies and other countercultural students who reject the status quo and are often quite rebellious. As with his own youth, he finds their alternative cultural spiritual experiments, their ritual nudity and other forms of behavior, fascinating, even encouraging, and open to ahistoric and nontemporal mythic interpretations, such as the desire to return to some prefallen paradise and to a relation of harmony with nature. For example, in a journal entry of 27 February 1974, Eliade does not denounce the "parody of copulation in public," which he sees as a "deliberate will to provoke public disgrace and collective indignation" and as reflecting a rebellious "down with the Establishment" attitude. Instead, he interprets it as part "of a much vaster and otherwise important phenomenon, that is, the rediscovery by certain young people—and not only hippies—of cosmic religiosity. Ritual nudity, free and spontaneous sexual union, belong to a syndrome in which one guesses the yearning for lost Paradise, for a return to the state before original sin, before the knowledge of good and evil."[11]

In many passages Eliade expresses attitudes that reveal that an overly simplified identification with some antihistorical, antitemporal orientation misrepresents his personal views. For example, in the 1930s, after realizing that he could not identify his life and "vocation" with some eternal, transhistorical India and after a number of personal "ordeals" in Romania, he began to understand his "destiny, which demanded that I live 'paradoxically,' in contradiction with myself and my era; which compelled me to exist concurrently in 'History' and beyond it; to be alive, involved in current events, and at the same time withdrawn, occupying myself with apparently antiquated extra-historic problems and subjects; to assume the Romanian mode of being in the world and at the same time to live in foreign, far-off, exotic universes; to be simultaneously an 'authentic Bucharestian' and a 'universal man.'"[12] Eliade goes on to describe such a "religious mode of being in the world" as a *coincidentia oppositorum,* one of his favorite mythic and symbolic structures. This description of his "destiny" will also be seen to illustrate some of the dynamic, complex historical-nonhistorical relation in Eliade's interpretation of myth and history.

Personal Scholarly Interpretations
In a journal entry of 26 September 1952, Eliade writes that for the past five or six years, when he has been wrestling with the meaning of "history," he has returned to his study of Hegel. He uses his reflections on Hegel to point to his "proper vocation" as an intellectual and to validate his philosophical "method":

I observe that Hegel's decision (on 14 September 1800) to reconcile himself with his time, to transcend the scission between the "absolute finitude" of interior existence and the "absolute infinitude" of the objectivity of the exterior world—I observe that this "virile unification with time (=history)" closely resembles the decision of my generation to "adhere" to politics in order to integrate itself into the historical moment and to defend itself from the "abstract," to avoid retreat into unreality. The same explanation seems to me valid for understanding the adherence of intellectuals to communism. The interpretation Hegel gives to the destiny of Hölderlin and to the Romantics in general—that "not to live in your own house in the world is more than a personal misfortune; it is a 'nontruth'" and that "the most terrible destiny consists in not having a destiny"—reminds me of the polemics of the "historicists" against the intellectuals who did not "adhere" during 1935-38. I find the same positions restated in the polemics of the French Communists and Existentialists, and they are, probably, attested everywhere.[13]

Eliade then rejects this Hegelian view as reflecting "the great temptation of the Spirit, which very few resist." "You 'adhere' in order to save yourself, in order to remain in 'life,' in 'history.'" Eliade's personal view is the exact opposite: I can "save myself" only by freeing myself from and transcending time and history. "I must analyze someday this grave error, validated and transfigured by Hegel, which drives intellectuals to renounce their proper vocation. Show the limits within which the 'historical moment' can be accepted."[14]

Eliade continues his personal reflections on Hegel by asserting that he was "pleasantly surprised" to learn that Hegel had not begun by engaging his philosophical problems head on. Instead he prepared for his later phenomenology and philosophical vision by devoting many years to historical research of "religion and history directly, from their sources; his principal preoccupation was the *historically concrete,* the life of the peoples, the 'spirit' that manifests itself directly in that life." Eliade concludes that "this makes me happy, because it validates my own philosophical 'method'. I've devoted almost thirty years of my life to 'concrete' studies: philology, history, folklore, religions. Always, however, I have had as my final objective the understanding of the spiritual meaning of the materials I was studying."[15]

There is certainly room for debate concerning the extent to which Mircea Eliade's personal attitudes toward time and history, reflecting antihistorical and nonhistorical views, influence his selection and interpretation of myth. Most of the religious phenomena cited by Eliade in his scholarly interpretations of myth are taken from archaic religions. He usually focuses on an underlying, antihistorical "archaic ontology": through the repetition of sacred, exemplary, transhistorical, mythic models, an object or act becomes real and profane time and history are abolished. This mythic behavior reveals the desire of archaic human beings to escape historical time and experience the sacred, mythic, non-historical mode of being as meaningful and real. In Eliade's analysis, such an antihistorical mythic orientation is not restricted to "primitive" societies. As has been noted, in Indian mysticism and some other forms of Eastern spirituality, he finds the most radical attempts to go beyond even the antihistorical archaic integration with rhythms of nature and the cosmos; to transcend all that is limited, finite, temporal, and histor-ical; and to realize a spiritual consciousness of unconditioned freedom that exists nowhere in time, history, or even the cosmos.

There is considerable evidence—found throughout Eliade's scholar-ly studies of myth and in his analysis of the general structure and function of myth—that he shows a personal preference, both in his selection and interpretation of religious phenomena, for such an antihistorical archaic and Indian orientation.

As was seen in chapter 4, this is also the case when it comes to Eliade's interpretation of Christian and other Western, "historical," religious phenomena. The myths in Christian and Western tradition toward which he is personally most sympathetic and which receive the major emphasis in his scholarly interpretations are those that are most similar structurally to the antihistorical archaic and Hindu and other Eastern religious phenomena. The volumes of Eliade's *Autobiography* and *Journal* and even his scholarly studies are full of personal reflec-tions and judgments expressing his extreme alienation from the dominant spirit of historical Christianity and other Western religions. What most interests him are such Western mythic and religious manifestations as are found in mysticism, alchemy, and the "cosmic religion" of eastern European peasants; those Western myths and other religious phenomena outside the mainstream of the Western historical religions. In short, those manifestations which have devalued or totally ignored the historical dimension of the so-called historical religions.

In general, Eliade is very critical of a Judaeo-Christian tradition which attacked cosmic religiosity and emptied nature of the sacred. He sees the roots of many contemporary crises in terms of such a historical development; he rejects dominant characteristics and structures of the historical religions as dangerously outmoded and fossilized; and he often expresses a hope that Christianity and the modern West can renew themselves by regaining this cosmic dimension of reality. In this regard, Eliade feels a close personal attraction to Romanian and other European forms of peasant "cosmic Christianity." As has been seen, this nature-oriented, antihistorical Christianity embraced an archaic ontology and resisted much of dominant historical Christianity. Such a cosmic Christianity is not attracted to the historical, but instead to cosmic and nature-oriented symbols and myths. Christ is not the historical hierophany of historical Christianity, but is imbued with cosmic symbols and experienced through antihistorical, archaic, universal, nature-oriented myths, such as the yearning for a prefallen paradise or cosmic nature-based defenses against the terror of history.

Once again, Eliade's personal, antihistorical attitudes, as seen in his alienation from historical Christianity and his attraction to cosmic religion, in general, and cosmic Christianity, in particular, greatly influence his scholarship. This is evident in his focus on antihistorical mythic data, in his deemphasis on or omission of religious phenomena of the so-called historical religions, and in his specific interpretations of the essential nonhistorical meaning of myths and other religious phenomena.

While acknowledging such a personal preference in his focus and interpretations, Eliade sometimes defends himself against criticisms by explaining this antihistorical approach to mythic data. In chapter 4, we noted his explanation that he focused on archaic religious phenomena because other scholars had devalued or ignored their deeper meaning. In chapter 7, we noted his admonition that it is best to study myths in those cultures, such as the cosmic religion of eastern European peasants, in which myths are still "alive"; in which mythic peoples are actually, consciously "living the myths." By contrast, Eliade maintains that in modern, historical, Western religions, myths have been largely demythicized and are at best lived on the level of the unconscious.

Nevertheless, it seems evident that Eliade's personal attitude toward time and history influences selections and interpretations in even his most historical works. The best illustration is his ambitious three-volume *A History of Religious Ideas* in which Eliade's project was to attempt a historical work involving a herculean synthesis of mythic and other religious data from the entire history of humanity, from the earliest prehistory to the present.[16] But even this most historical of Eliade's major works is often a very personal historical study with the selectivity of religious documents, the integration and interpretation of diverse data, the structural comparisons and bold syntheses reflecting Eliade's nonhistorical assumptions, sympathies, and evaluations. Although seven of the nine chapters of the third volume, *From Muhammad to the Age of Reforms,* are on the "historical religions" of Judaism, Christianity, and Islam, Eliade's presentation of their historical nature and historical theologies is rather minimal and his interpretations are far from original. As Eliade writes, "I have concentrated less on the familiar creations of Occidental thought (e.g., Scholasticism, Reformation) than on certain phenomena which have largely passed into silence or been minimized in the manuals: heterodoxies, heresies, mythologies, and popular practices such as sorcery, alchemy, and esotericism."[17] One feels that with the dominant, Christian, and other Western, historical religious phenomena, Eliade is not especially at home.[18]

In discussing Marsilio Ficino, Pico della Mirandola, Giordano Bruno, and Hermeticism, Eliade writes of "the profound dissatisfaction left by scholasticism and the medieval conceptions of man and the universe. It was a reaction against what one could call a 'provincial' Christianity, that is, one that was purely *western,* as well as an aspiration to a universal, transhistorical, and 'primordial' religion."[19] Mircea Eliade might have been describing himself. As will be seen, even with respect to the so-called historical religions, Eliade, while not denying historical innovations, interprets "historical," mythic, religious phenomena as essentially nonhistorical and even antihistorical.

Eliade's personal attitudes toward time and history greatly influence his generally unsympathetic formulations of nonreligious historical approaches, which, as Ricketts correctly describes, he tends to "lump together, ignoring their differences" and vaguely labels as "positivism, historicism, existentialism, and materialism."[20] The reader cannot fail to notice the contrast between Eliade's sensitive and generous attitude toward archaic religious phenomena, to the extent of interpreting profound spiritual meanings even when they are not understood by *homo religiosus,* and the many oversimplified and unsympathetic formulations attributed to nonreligious positions.

One can certainly understand Eliade's strong reaction against such nonreligious "historical" approaches which he views as narrow-minded and intolerant toward myth and religion and which he even describes as inhuman and antihuman, "inane," "neurotic," and leading humanity to mass suicide or obliteration. On scholarly grounds, such a strong personal reaction by itself does not justify highly personal interpretations that involve one-sided negative formulations and the uncritical lumping together of such diverse positions. To use one of Eliade's frequent illustrations, he is justified in criticizing "vulgar" or "mechanistic" materialists, narrow-minded historicists, positivists, and other "reductionists" who claim to explain the total meaning and significance of *Madame Bovary* and other literary creations on the basis of the specific historical, economic, and other conditionings of the author. There certainly are such scholars, just as there are religious persons who explain the meaning and significance of their myths and rituals—and present negative formulations and explanations of nonreligious phenomena—in crude mechanical terms. But it is not difficult to point to sensitive and sophisticated scholars who provide nonreligious interpretations and explanations of their data. One can cite "materialists," even "historical materialists," who attempt to "interpret meaning" and know that this consists of more than simply uncovering historical and economic conditionings. They recognize complex, interacting, multiple determinants and avoid the crude, narrow, causal reductionism Eliade attributes to them. When it comes to nonreligious historical (and nonreligious nonhistorical) approaches, Eliade's personal attitudes toward time and history shape his nonhistorical and antihistorical interpretations of meaning and significance.

In the second volume of *A History of Religious Ideas,* Eliade presents some of the approach of the *Bhagavad Gītā* toward time and history:

> By the fact that it puts the emphasis on the historicity of man, the solution that the *Gītā* offers is certainly the most comprehensive one and, it is important to add, the one best suited to modern India, already integrated into the "circuit of history." For, translated into terms familiar to Westerners, the problem in the *Gītā* is as follows: how is it possible to resolve the paradoxical situation created by the twofold fact that man, on the one hand, finds himself existing in time, *condemned to history,* and, on the other hand, knows that he will be "damned" if he allows himself to be exhausted by temporality and by his own historicity and that, consequently, he must at all costs find *in the world* a way that leads into a transhistorical and atemporal plane?[21]

This complex, dynamic orientation of the *Gītā* toward time and history recognizes one's specific, conditioned, historical situation with its corresponding historical and temporal obligations. But it views one's historical situation in terms of ultimate nontemporal, transhistorical values. We have no choice but to act historically, but we should adopt an attitude of nonattachment to the results of our conditioned, limited worldly actions, while striving to realize ultimate transhistorical and atemporal reality.

In *Myths, Dreams and Mysteries,* Eliade's comments on this attitude in the *Gītā* "of remaining in the world and participating in History, but taking good care not to attribute to History any absolute value. Rather than an invitation to renounce History, what is revealed to us in the *Bhagavad Gītā* is a warning against the *idolatry* of History. All Indian thought is insistent upon this very point, that the state of ignorance and illusion is not that of *living* in History, but of *believing in* its ontological reality." The world may be illusory, but it is sacred as divine creation and as divine play. "The ignorance, and hence the anxiety and the suffering, are perpetuated by the absurd belief that this perishable and illusory world represents the ultimate reality." "One is devoured by Time, by History, not because one lives in them, but because one thinks them *real* and, in consequence, one forgets or undervalues eternity."[22]

Mircea Eliade, I would submit, finds such an approach to time and history personally attractive, and this personal attitude is reflected in his methodology and his history of religions. That such a personal attitude toward time and history shapes Eliade's scholarship will become clear in the following sections, as seen in his analysis of the complex historical-nonhistorical relation.

OTHER SCHOLARS: ELIADE IS ANTIHISTORICAL

As was seen in chapter 1, Eliade writes that twentieth-century scholars, in contrasting their approaches to Müller, Frazer, Tylor, and other earlier investigators of myth and religion, emphasize the irreducibly historical nature of their documents. Mythic and other religious data are historical data. Eliade often affirms this, claiming that there are "no purely religious phenomena" and that a scholar must do justice to the specific historical conditionings of the data.

Nevertheless, one of the most frequent expressions of the general criticism that Eliade is methodologically uncritical is the claim that he is antihistorical and does not do justice to the historical nature of the myths and other religious data. Most scholars who have emphasized the antihistorical nature of Eliade's approach have been critics: historically-minded historians of religion, various specialists who are critical of universal structures and sweeping generalizations, a few Christian theologians, and many anthropologists, such as Wallace, Raglan, Lessa, Leach, and Saliba.[23]

Eliade emphasizes archaic myth and religion. According to the historically oriented empiricist Robert D. Baird, Eliade assumes this ahistoric archaic model for all religious experience. His method, with its search for structures, is not historically falsifiable and becomes a "barrier to the attainment of authentic religio-historical understanding." Eliade's phenomenology is "as normative as theology because it is based on an assumed ontology which is neither historically derived nor descriptively verifiable."[24]

Several scholars have assumed that Eliade's approach is theological and privileges an antihistorical theology, as seen in the archaic ontology. Theologians such as Kenneth Hamilton charge that Eliade's theology, while it may do justice to much of nonhistorical archaic myth and religion, is inadequate for understanding Christianity and other "historical religions."[25] According to Thomas Altizer, Eliade's method is "mystical" and "romantic," not "rational" and "scientific." His interpretations of archaic religion may have great merit, but his phenomenology is insufficient for interpreting the "higher religions" and religious phenomena in the modern Western world. Altizer submits that Eliade's approach, which has nothing to do with historical Christianity, favors a return to some archaic mode of being and is therefore inconsistent with his "Christian ground."[26]

Similarly, Carl Olson, while generally sympathetic to Eliade's interpretations and critical of Eliade's critics, also claims that Eliade's approach is based on an antihistorical theological orientation. In Olson's interpretation, Eliade's personal theology is at the foundation of his scholarly approach and is based on the acceptance of a Christian theology. But this is the antihistorical, premodern theology of the cosmic Christianity of Romanian peasants. Eliade's antihistorical theology advocates abolishing time and history through an eternal return to a primordial sacred history embodied in myths. Olson criticizes it for rejecting what is positive in historical progress and for failing to see the need for integrating history and nature.[27]

According to Ivan Strenski, the numerous statements by Eliade "giving an impression that the history of religions is an inductive study, which grounds its conclusions on historical fact, are rendered nugatory." Eliade's history of religions is based on a priori truths, which stand in an a priori relation to the historical data both logically and chronologically. These "truths" may sometimes be confirmed "in historical materials, but falsification from these materials seems ruled out."[28] Strenski maintains that Eliade first reduces history to false, limited, and impoverished senses of "history." Then, having formulated such an easy and vulnerable target to attack, Eliade can argue for the need of investigators to go beyond such a "history" of the sacred.[29]

Strenski claims that Eliade uses and criticizes three senses of history. First, there is history as nothing more than a "chronicle," as if the task of the historian was merely to piece together events or series of events. Second, there is "positivist history," which neglects human intentions and internal meanings, thus leading to Eliade's false dichotomy of giving a historical account versus interpreting meaning. Third, and most interesting, there is "plenary history," which is an explanatory and meaning-giving sense of history, but which has limited value since it can only help us to grasp the particular historical meaning of the sacred as it was understood and lived in a specific culture. Such a plenary history is insufficient since it does not allow the historian of religions to decipher the primary "transhistorical" meanings of the sacred; it falls short of the transcendent "prehistoric" meanings that "condition the lower or historical meanings."

Challenging Eliade's antihistorical position, Strenski argues that he forces upon his readers "false dilemmas" and then proposes "false solutions" for escaping from them. "Though positivist history or chronicle do not suffice to explain religious phenomena, and though the scrappiness of historical evidence in certain areas (especially the areas in which Eliade specializes) prevents extensive cross-cultural generalization, a rejection of a proper historical view is not thereby entailed. The nature of the issue of explaining and determining the meanings of religious phenomena, myths and symbols, respectively, does not change from a historic to a nonhistoric one because we *in fact* have insufficient means of dealing with the historical problems."[30] It may be true that we are unable to explain certain cross-cultural resemblances among various myths by reference to a common historical or geographical origin; but this "dilemma" does not legitimize our positing some origin and explanation "outside history," some ontologically transcendent condition (nonhistorical archetypes) of such historically inexplicable similarities. Eliade is not justified in assuming such an antihistorical normative position of "self-authenticating" intuitions of nonhistorical structures that are historically unverifiable and unfalsifiable.[31]

Not only have critics pointed to the antihistorical nature of Eliade's approach, but scholars who praise Eliade have also granted that he is antihistorical. Some of these have been scholars critical of historical and empirical approaches to religious phenomena; many have been literary figures or others with an interest in the mythical and fantastic dimensions of Eliade's literary works and with little concern for the historical dimensions of experience; and several have attempted to view Eliade as an antihistorical or transhistorical shaman or mystic.[32]

Guilford Dudley's interpretation is unusual in being one of the few "scientific" studies that both conclude that Eliade's history of religions is based on an antihistorical normative position and then suggest that such an "antihistory" be viewed sympathetically. Indeed, Dudley, who analyzes contemporary history of religions as being in a state of severe crisis and confusion, proposes Eliade's antihistory theory of religion as the leading candidate to bring some sense of unity and future development to the discipline.

After noting Eliade's frequent claim that he uses an empirical and historical approach, Dudley shows that Eliade has been continually criticized and dismissed by empiricists. He agrees with the critics that Eliade cannot meet their minimal empirical, historical, inductive criteria for a "scientific" approach, such as criteria for empirical verification or falsification.[33] Dudley goes on to argue that Eliade's history of religions is highly normative, since it rests on a privileged ontological status granted to the antihistorical "archaic ontology." Eliade's polemic favors this archaic ontology, which he takes as constituting the basis of all religions and which has its clearest and most developed roots in Indian religion and, more particularly, in Patanjali's Yoga.[34]

In the final chapter of *Religion on Trial*, Dudley argues that the empiricist approach does not provide an adequate model for being "rational" or "scientific" since sophisticated thinkers have totally undermined its methodological criteria. Using the terminology and formulations of Imre Lakatos, Dudley submits that Eliade and his followers must now clarify his comprehensive theoretical system so that we can examine its potential as a viable "research program." Dudley concludes that Eliade is really an "antihistorian" of religions, who should be placed within the tradition of French, deductive, synchronic, systematic approaches, sharing many similarities with such scholars as Foucault and Dumézil. Eliade should avoid the "ambivalence," confusion, and contradictions in his writings arising from his insistence that he is using an empirical and historical method. There are problems with this "sympathetic" simple identification of Eliade's approach as "antihistorical." There can be little doubt of the centrality of structural analysis and synchronicity in Eliade's systematic approach. But to accept Dudley's interpretation, one would have to throw out important assertions found throughout Eliade's writings in which he insists that his approach is in some sense "empirical" and "historical." More important, as we shall see, Eliade often insists that the very "ambivalence" Dudley wants to eliminate is essential to an adequate interpretation of myth and religion. He submits that the "tension," expressed in the conflicting methodological claims of historical and phenomenological approaches and in the dynamic historical-nonhistorical interaction, is in fact a "creative" and necessary tension for any adequate comprehensive hermeneutics.[35]

Among the scholars of Eliade's works, there is an extreme exception to the interpretation of Eliade as antihistorical. David Cave attempts to establish the morphological structure of Eliade's foundational, unifying "notion of a new humanism." We noted a startling conclusion in Cave's morphological approach: Eliade favors Christianity and accepts the superiority of Christianity because it is the most historical religion. One might expect Cave's morphological, structural approach to lead to the typical interpretation of Eliade as devaluing historical change, but the opposite is the case. Critics and supporters have misinterpreted Eliade as emphasizing the ahistorical or nonhistorical. Eliade is obsessed by history. His "method is ruled by history"; his morphology is "limited to its governing paradigm . . . of history."[36] Cave claims: "It is short-sighted, therefore, to say that Eliade is unconcerned with history or that he is "anti-history" when in fact history—existential, chronological, sacred, and secular—is all-important to him, either in a positive or negative way." Indeed, Eliade's new humanism may be limited because it is too historical. "In a sense, if the new humanism is to be more universal, it is not *more* historical consciousness that is needed, but less."[37]

It seems to me an almost impossible task to present in a convincing manner an interpretation of Eliade as so emphasizing a historical method and paradigm. Cave is correct that Eliade, in his personal life and in his scholarship, was obsessed with the "problem of history." But this obsession usually took the form of his desire and need to overcome or escape from the conditionings and terror of history. Cave is also correct that Eliade maintains that in actual religious experience the sacred is manifested in history; that sacred structures are incarnated in relative imperfect forms and limited by historical conditionings. But this in no way negates the lofty methodological, phenomenological, and ontological status Eliade grants his nonhistorical, nontemporal sacred structures and meanings.

Finally, we note only briefly a bold interpretation by Bryan Rennie. Scholars have not appreciated that Eliade has a personal idiosyncratic meaning of "history" which he equates with personal experience, personal event, actual lived experience. Eliade also uses "history" to refer to a record of past events, the history of antecedent events, and he does not distinguish this common usage from his idiosyncratic meaning of history as personally experienced actuality. Scholars have misinterpreted Eliade's approach as antihistorical. Eliade is antihistoricist, not antihistorical. What he opposes are narrow, modern, reductionist, historicist explanations that attempt to reduce the whole meaning and significance of the sacred, ideals, norms, the imagination, dreams, etc., to physical determinants within a narrowly defined historical-temporal-spatial reality.[38]

Eliade does sometimes use the term "history" to refer to personal, actually lived experience, but as has been seen and will be emphasized in the next chapter, he usually focuses on the *nonhistorical* dimension of such personal experience. The personal, actually lived experience is often interpreted as a way of defending oneself against history and escaping history. Eliade provides such an antihistorical emphasis in his interpretations of traditional mythic and religious data, his reflections about himself, and his hopes for the cultural and spiritual renewal of modern human beings. And it is certainly true that historicism, which

Eliade characterizes in very narrow reductionist terms, is one of his major targets. But Eliade's theory of religion and myth and his methodological approach reveal a much broader and more radical antihistorical orientation than such a critique of historicism. Many scholars are critical of extreme historicist explanations, but they see value in various modern historical interpretations and explanations that Eliade devalues and often dismisses. At his most controversial, Eliade makes antihistorical ontological claims and normative judgments about history, time, the human condition, and reality that go far beyond a critique of historicism.

NOTES

1. The next two chapters utilize material that appeared in Allen, "Eliade and History."

2. See my review of Ivan Strenski's *Four Theories of Myth in Twentieth-Century History* in *Journal of the American Academy of Religion* 59 (Winter 1991): 874-77.

3. Mircea Eliade, "Fragmente de Jurnal," *Caete de Dor* 8 (1954): 27. This and other personal statements by Eliade are quoted by Virgil Ierunca, "The Literary Work of Mircea Eliade," in *Myths and Symbols: Studies in Honor of Mircea Eliade,* ed. Joseph M. Kitagawa and Charles H. Long (Chicago: University of Chicago Press, 1969), pp. 343-63.

4. See *Autobiography 1,* pp. 6-7, 27-30, 48-49, 97.

5. Radically different accounts of this relationship appear in Mircea Eliade, *Maitreyi* (Bucharest: Cultura Nationala, 1933), which gained Eliade recognition in Romania as a major literary figure, and Maitreyi Devi, *It Does Not Die: A Romance,* trans. from the 1974 Bengali *Na Hanyate* (Calcutta: Writers Workshop, P. Lal, 1976 and Connecticut: Inter-Culture Associates, 1976). Recent English editions are Mircea Eliade, *Bengal Nights* (from the 1950 French trans. of *Maitreyi* entitled *La nuit bengali;* Chicago: University of Chicago Press, 1994), and Maitreyi Devi, *It Does Not Die: A Romance* (Chicago: University of Chicago Press, 1994).

6. *Autobiography 1,* pp. 189, 199-200.

7. Ibid., pp. 63-64, 110-11.

8. *Autobiography 1,* pp. 72-75; *Journal 1,* pp. 33, 116; *Journal 4,* pp. 10, 26. In one of my first meetings with Mircea Eliade, he bemoaned the fact that he "had wasted so much time" on the recently completed *From Primitives to Zen,* and that he feared that his health and limited remaining time would not allow him to complete his significant scholarly projects.

9. *Autobiography 1*, pp. 135-36, 292, 298-99, 269-305; *Autobiography 2*, pp. 13-14.

10. *No Souvenirs*, p. viii; *Journal 1*, pp. 42, 184. In his "Translator's Preface" to *Journal 1*, Ricketts writes that "His journal, then, was Eliade's first line of defense against his great enemy Time, his most effective weapon for resisting its destructive power. Or, put otherwise, it was his sacred history, his personal mythology—to be reread and relived" (p. x).

11. *Journal 3*, p. 148.

12. *Autobiography 1*, pp. 256-57.

13. *Journal 1*, pp. 174-75.

14. Ibid., p. 175. In *Journal 3*, Eliade writes: "Temporal cycles are shorter and shorter: geological, biological (life of the species); historical (duration of cultures); individual (the human person) cycles. But man alone knows their true 'significance,' and he alone is capable of freeing himself of Time" (p. 301).

15. *Journal 1*, pp. 175-76. Critics and most supporters may question how "historically concrete" Eliade's historical research was. Eliade's assumption and understanding of the essential nonhistorical "spiritual meaning of the materials" was always at the foundation of his "historical" studies.

16. In *Traité d'histoire des religions* (trans. as *Patterns in Comparative Religion*), Eliade wrote of a forthcoming, more historical "companion volume." Eliade's historical project developed into the three-volume *A History of Religious Ideas*. He proposed to write a history of religions "from the Stone Age . . . to contemporary atheistic theologies." Because of Eliade's ill health, the third volume was delayed and finally abbreviated to include religious phenomena between the fourth and seventeenth centuries. An uncompleted fourth volume was to have included not only religious developments from the seventeenth century to the present, culminating with the religious creativity of modern secular societies, but also archaic and traditional religions of America, Africa, and Oceania, as well as chapters on the expansion of Hinduism, medieval China, and Japanese religions.

17. *History 3*, p. xi.

18. For example, as was seen in chap. 4, Eliade largely ignores the influential theology of St. Thomas Aquinas and the Thomistic tradition. By contrast, he provides detailed descriptions and interpretations of profound mythic religious meaning of the folklore and popular cosmic religion of eastern European peasants. He often focuses on how these peasant "Christian" myths reveal pre-Christian, nonhistorical and antihistorical, structures and "survivals."

19. *History 3*, p. 253. Eliade wrote his master's thesis in Italy in 1928 on Italian Renaissance philosophy from Marsilio Ficino to Giordano Bruno.

20. Mac Linscott Ricketts, "In Defense of Eliade: Toward Bridging the Communications Gap between Anthropology and the History of Religions," *Religion: Journal of Religion and Religions* 3 (1973): 28.

21. *History 2*, pp. 242-43. See also Matei Calinescu, "Creation as Duty," *Journal of Religion* 65 (1985): 253.

22. *Myths, Dreams and Mysteries*, pp. 241-42.

23. See chap. 1, n. 2 for several of the studies summarizing attacks on Eliade for neglecting the historical dimension of his data. For critiques of Eliade by anthropologists and responses to the critics, see Brown, "Eliade on Archaic Religions"; Ricketts, "In Defense of Eliade"; Ioan P. Culianu, "Mircea Eliade at the Crossroads of Anthropology," *Neue Zeitschrift für systematische Theologie und Religionsphilosophie* 27, no. 2 (1985): 123-31; Allen, "Eliade and History"; and Rennie, *Reconstructing Eliade*. See part 2, "Works about Mircea Eliade," in Allen and Doeing, *Mircea Eliade: An Annotated Bibliography*, pp. 95-157.

24. Baird, *Category Formation and the History of Religions*, esp. pp. 86-87, 152-53. One could counter that Baird's notion of empirical and historical "verification" is too narrow and even outdated.

25. See Hamilton, "*Homo Religiosus* and Historical Faith, " pp. 213-22. Robert A. Segal, in "Eliade's Theory of Millenarianism," *Religious Studies* 14 (1978):159-73, submits that Eliade has a general theory that "given the meaninglessness which man *qua* man finds in history and the meaning which he finds in primordial time, he seeks instinctively to abolish history and return to primordial time." This theory of such an "innate" or "natural" yearning forces Eliade to deny the specific "Israelite sense of history" and to misinterpret Jewish eschatology.

26. See Altizer, *Mircea Eliade and the Dialectic of the Sacred*, esp. pp. 17, 30, 41, 59–80. Altizer's interpretation has been criticized by Eliade, "Notes for a Dialogue," pp. 234-41; Mac Linscott Ricketts, "Eliade and Altizer: Very Different Outlooks," *Christian Advocate* (Oct. 1967): 11-12; Ricketts, "Mircea Eliade and the Death of God," pp. 40-52; Allen, *Structure and Creativity in Religion*, pp. 126, 133; Rennie, *Reconstructing Eliade*, pp. 27-31.

27. See Olson, *The Theology and Philosophy of Eliade*, pp. 55-59, 153, 156, 167-70.

28. Ivan Strenski, "Mircea Eliade: Some Theoretical Problems," in *The Theory of Myth: Six Studies*, ed. Adrian Cunningham (London: Sheed and Ward, 1973), pp. 51-52.

29. See Strenski's section on "Eliade and the Study of Religion: Against History," ibid., pp. 43-52.

30. Ibid., pp. 58-59

31. Ibid., pp. 53-54, 58-59, 60-61. Criticisms of Strenski's interpretation are presented in Allen, *Mircea Eliade et le phénomène religieux*, pp. 198, 244-45.

32. The majority of scholars sympathetic to Eliade's history of religions, such as Matei Calinescu, Adriana Berger (in her early publications), Ricketts,

and Rennie, either do not regard him as antihistorical or, more often, do not focus on this question. In "Mircea Eliade and the Death of God," *Cross Currents* 29 (1979): 257-68, Thomas Altizer extols Eliade as an atheistic Christian theo-logian, whose dialectic and theology are adequate for understanding modern godless history and for grasping the camouflaged transcendent which, since the Christian Incarnation (equivalent to the death of God), can only be made fully present and real through radically profane history.

33. See chap. 1 of Dudley's *Religion on Trial.*

34. In chap. 3 of *Religion on Trial,* Dudley attempts to establish that this antihistorical "archaic ontology" serves as the normative foundation of Eliade's theory of religion; in chap. 4, he argues for the "Indian roots" of this ontology.

35. There are other difficulties with such an interpretation of Eliade as antihistorical. For example, one may question Dudley's easy acceptance of the clear-cut epistemological dichotomy: empiricist-inductive-historical versus rationalist-deductive-antihistorical. Much recent philosophy has been directed not only at criticizing classical empiricism but also at undermining such a sharp dichotomy.

36. Cave, *Mircea Eliade's Vision for a New Humanism,* p. 40. Note pp. 53, 131, 169, 191 n.53.

37. Ibid., p. 195.

38. Rennie, *Reconstructing Eliade,* esp. pp. 89-108, 110-11.

CHAPTER 9

The Primacy of Nonhistorical Structures

We have examined Mircea Eliade's attitudes toward time and history and how scholars regard his approach. Both in his personal autobiographical reflections and his scholarly interpretations, Eliade expresses a basic antihistorical orientation. Many scholars—primarily critics but also some supporters—focus on this antihistorical emphasis in his approach to myth and religion.

In this chapter, I document and analyze the primacy of the nonhistorical in Eliade's history and phenomenology of religion. First, Eliade will be seen to interpret myth and religion in general as displaying a basic antihistorical, atemporal essence. Not only are archaic and Eastern phenomena interpreted as essentially antihistorical, but Eliade even interprets the Western "historical religions" as basically antihistorical. Next, after briefly considering Eliade's analysis of the historical nature of mythic and religious data, his entire approach will be seen to rest upon the primacy of nonhistorical mythic and other religious structures. Third, a fundamental Eliadean dichotomy—interpreting religious and mythic structures and meanings versus uncovering historical conditionings and providing historical explanations—will be considered. Eliade focuses on the former and deemphasizes the significance of the latter. Fourth, a brief consideration of Eliade's bold, normative, antihistorical judgments will be used to illustrate the need to differentiate different levels of analysis in his approach to myth and religion. There is continuity but also significant difference between, say, Eliade's interpretations of the antihistorical universal structure of myth and religion in general or his judgments about the antihistorical essential nature of the human condition as such and his interpretations of the antihistorical meaning of a particular Polynesian cosmogonic myth or of a particular Romanian peasant ritual. In his normative antihistorical judgments, Eliade often makes ontological moves and goes far beyond the perspectival boundaries of the history and phenomenology of religion. Finally, it will be seen that a simple identification of Eliade's approach as antihistorical or nonhistorical misrepresents the complexity of his history and phenomenology of religion. To make sense of his interpretation of myth and religion, one must do justice to the complex, dynamic interaction of particular historical conditionings and general nonhistorical structures.

ANTIHISTORICAL ATEMPORAL ESSENCE OF MYTH AND RELIGION

According to Eliade, "the greatest difference between the man of the archaic societies and modern man" is "the irreversibility of events, which is the characteristic trait of History" for modern human beings, but is not accepted as true by archaic human beings.[1] What is "the meaning of historical man"? First, this means that "we are the result of events that can no longer be undone." We are what we are because of what happened in the past.

> But the so-called ahistorical man (the "primitive," the man of traditional civilizations) also considers himself the result of certain decisive events, which took place well before him, *in illo tempore*. Such events constitute the mythical history of the clan. Nevertheless, these represent two different ways of being constituted. For the primitive, myths unveil to him those exemplary events that have made him what he is today. Exemplary events; namely: the creation of the world and of man, the founding (by superhuman beings) of civil and religious institutions, etc. One could say that the primitive views himself as the result of a *cultural* history. Myths reveal to him how institutions were founded. Cultural history—and as such, paradigmatic history.[2]

Thus, both archaic and modern human beings view themselves as constituted by "history," but from the perspective of modern historical consciousness, the archaic, cultural, paradigmatic, sacred, mythic history is essentially nonhistorical.

It was seen that Eliade interprets archaic and Eastern myths and religion as disclosing essential antihistorical functions, structures, meanings, and significance. In the world of myth, the nonhistorical essence precedes historical existence. The transhistorical, atemporal, mythic essence is experienced as preceding and providing exemplary models for historical, temporal, ordinary existence. By living myths, *homo religiosus* participates in transhistorical structures that portray a mythic history of supernatural events. Through the repetition of sacred narratives and their reenactment through the repetition of sacred rituals, archaic human beings annul the irreversibility of historical events and experience a nonhistorical, atemporal, sacred reality.

In *The Myth of the Eternal Return* and other studies, Eliade analyzes the process of transfiguration of the historical into the nonhistorical mythic as seen in the mythicization of historical personages. According to Eliade, the popular collective memory is ahistorical, transforming specific historical individuals and events into exemplary, transhistorical categories and meanings. Specific historical figures and events are assimilated to mythic models, such as the paradigmatic mythic narrative of the mythic hero fighting with the monster. This process of mythicization discloses the structures of the dialectic of the sacred and the profane, as seen in the dialectical movement in which limited, finite, historical phenomena seek to realize their deeper, exemplary, transhistorical meanings.[3]

In some case, scholars can show that what mythic people attribute to historical persons and events is historically false or even impossible, although the reconstructed mythic history conforms to the exemplary images of mythic heroes and mythic norms. For example, Eliade cites the investigation by a Romanian folklorist, Constantin Brailoiu, into a rather recent, actual transformation of a historical event into myth. Villagers recounted a tragic narrative of love in which a young suitor had been bewitched by a mountain fairy. A few days before the young man was to be married, the jealous fairy threw him from a cliff.

Overcome by grief, his fiancée poured out a ritual funeral lamentation full of mythic allusions. Learning that the heroine of the myth was still alive, the folklorist was able to establish that what had actually occurred was a much more mundane tragedy: her lover had slipped and fallen over a cliff, and he had been carried to the village where he died.

What is most significant for Eliade is that the villagers, who had been contemporaries of this historical event, were not satisfied with the historical fact that the tragic death of this young man on the eve of his marriage was a simple death by accident. Within a few years, this historical accident had been completely mythicized. The tragedy had a deeper meaning that could only be revealed through the transhistorical categories of myth. The folklorist drew the villagers' attention to the authentic historical version, but they responded that the old woman in her grief had forgotten the true story. Eliade concludes: "It was the myth that told the truth: the real story was already only a falsification. Besides, was not the myth truer by the fact that it made the real story yield a deeper and richer meaning, revealing a tragic destiny?"[4]

In a summarizing formulation, Eliade points to "a common perspective: the need of archaic societies to regenerate themselves periodically through the annulment of time." The "regeneration rites always comprise, in their structure and meaning, an element of regeneration through repetition of an archetypal act, usually of the cosmogonic act."

> What is of chief importance to us in these archaic systems is the abolition of concrete time, and hence their antihistorical intent. This refusal to preserve the memory of the past, even of the immediate past, seems to us to betoken a particular anthropology. We refer to archaic man's refusal to accept himself as a historical being, his refusal to grant value to memory and hence to the unusual events (i.e., events without an archetypal model) that in fact constitute concrete duration. . . . Basically, if viewed in its proper perspective, the life of archaic man (a life reduced to the repetition of archetypal acts, that is, to categories and not to events, to the unceasing rehearsal of the same primordial myths), although it takes place in time, does not bear the burden of time, does not record time's irreversibility; in other words, completely ignores what is especially characteristic and

decisive in a consciousness of time. Like the mystic, like the religious man in general, the primitive lives in a continual present. (And it is in this sense that the religious man may be said to be a "primitive"; he repeats the gestures of another and, through this repetition, lives always in an atemporal present.)[5]

What is of particular interest in this quotation is not Eliade's typical formulation of the archaic attitude toward time and history, but rather the fact that he also identifies such an antihistorical, atemporal orientation with *"the religious man in general."* Eliade frequently writes of the "negative attitude toward history" found in "traditional" cultures. Sometimes "archaic" and "traditional" are used interchangeably. But Eliade often defines "traditional" as extending until the "modern," post-Hegelian conception of history.[6] The antihistorical, atemporal orientation defines mythic and religious life until the modern, Western, secular, historicistic alternative mode of being in the world. It includes myth and religion in general.

In noting that all of the redeemed in *The Last Judgment* by Fra Angelico have the same childlike faces, Eliade asserts that "Unlike all other modes of being, the spiritual life has nothing to do with the law of becoming, for it does not develop within time." In his exemplary symbolism of the "newborn," Angelico reveals that the essential child "will remain a child *in aeternum:* he will partake of the atemporal beatitude of the Spirit, and not of the flux of history. The second life— the life of the initiate—does not repeat the first, human, historical life: its mode of being is qualitatively different." Similarly, in another journal entry, Eliade submits that if religious experience "is authentic and deep, religion rediscovers the elementary, the fundamental, the primordial, in a word, the 'ahistorical.'"[7]

If an atemporal, antihistorical orientation defines myth and religion in general and not simply archaic and Eastern phenomena, then Eliade is committed to showing the essential antihistorical nature of the so-called historical religions. Eliade in no way denies that the Hebraic religions are innovative and place new value on history, but he contends that they are still basically antihistorical.

At first Eliade's description of the innovative Jewish historicization of the sacred seems to conform to the usual emphasis on the essential historical dimension of the Hebraic traditions. "Thus, for the first time, the prophets placed a value on history, succeeded in transcending the traditional vision of the cycle (the conception that ensures all things will be repeated forever), and discovered a one-way time." History was now regarded as theophany. For "the first time, we find affirmed, and increasingly accepted, the idea that historical events have a value in themselves, insofar as they are determined by the will of God. This God of the Jewish people is no longer an Oriental divinity, creator of archetypal gestures, but a personality who ceaselessly intervenes in history, who reveals his will through events (invasions, sieges, battles, and so on)." The "Hebrews were the first to discover the meaning of history as the epiphany of God, and this conception, as we should expect, was taken up and amplified by Christianity."[8]

The idea of revelation is found in all myth and religion. But in archaic myth and religion, the sacred revelations occur in nonhistorical mythical time. "The situation is altogether different in the case of the monotheistic revelation. This takes place in time, in historical duration." Moses receives the Ten Commandments on Mt. Sinai at a certain historical moment. This moment of revelation is "definitely situated in time. And since it also represents a theophany, it acquires a new dimension: it becomes precious inasmuch as it is no longer reversible, as it is a historical event." "Under the 'pressure of history' and supported by the prophetic and Messianic experience, a new interpretation of historical events dawns among the children of Israel. Without finally renouncing the traditional concept of archetypes and repetitions, Israel attempts to 'save' historical events by regarding them as active presences of Yahweh." History no longer appears as the traditional mythic cycle that repeats itself *ad infinitum*. History now appears as a series of theophanies, each of which "acquires a coefficient of irreversibility: Yahweh's personal intervention."[9]

If the Jewish innovations and later Hebraic developments are so historical, insisting on the uniqueness and irreversibility of the historical event as sacred revelation, how can Eliade maintain his interpretation of the antihistorical, atemporal essence of myth and religion in general? He does this by maintaining at least two general senses in which the historical religions are essentially antihistorical. First, he says that the prophetic and Messianic conceptions are exclusive creations of a religious elite. The popular religion of Jews and Christians often retains the traditional attitudes toward time and history. Neither in Judaism nor in Christianity does the innovative conception of history as theophany, with a unique faith based on historical interventions of a personal transcendent God, "produce a basic modification of traditional conceptions." "The great majority of so-called Christian populations continue, down to our day, to preserve themselves from history by ignoring it and by tolerating it rather than by giving it the meaning of a negative or positive theophany."

Second, even "the acceptance and consecration of history by the Judaic elites does not mean that the traditional attitude . . . is transcended. Messianic beliefs in a final regeneration of the world themselves also indicate an antihistoric attitude." Indeed, Eliade claims that the Hebraic attitude, while tolerating the irreversibility of historical events and time, is in a fundamental way even more antihistorical than the traditional, archaic, mythic and religious orientation. For the antihistorical archaic, history is ignored or abolished through the periodic repetition of nonhistorical mythic structures; for the Hebraic, irreversible history can be tolerated because it will finally end.

> [I]n the Messianic conception history must be tolerated because it has an eschatological function, but it can be tolerated only because it is known that, one day or another, it will cease. History is thus abolished, not through consciousness of living an eternal present (coincidence with the atemporal instant of the revelation of archetypes), nor by means of a periodically repeated ritual (for example, the rites for the beginning of the year)—it is abolished in the future. Periodic regeneration of the Creation is replaced by a single regeneration that will take place in an *in illo tempore* to come. But the will to put a final and definitive end to history is itself still an antihistorical attitude, exactly as are the other traditional conceptions.[10]

We may conclude that there is an antihistorical, atemporal essence to Eliade's general theory of myth and religion. There is something essentially antihistorical in his conception of *homo religiosus*. This is certainly the case for archaic myth and religion with its antihistorical archaic ontology: the repetitious reenactment of transhistorical exemplary structures; the periodic abolishing of profane time and history through the regeneration of sacred, mythic time and history. This is also clearly the case for Eastern cultures which, while maintaining archaic cyclical patterns of time and history, are even more radically antihistorical. No longer satisfied with regenerating the cyclical natural and cosmic rhythms, the antihistorical, atemporal spiritual goal becomes the need to free oneself totally from and absolutely transcend the archaic mythic and religious cycles.

When it comes to the Western historical religions—and not just the antihistorical, nature-oriented cosmic Christianity favored by Eliade—Eliade once again emphasizes an antihistorical, atemporal essence to *homo religiosus*. In many studies, Eliade emphasizes that Judaism, Islam, and especially Christianity, while incorporating innovative conceptions of history and the historicization of the sacred, maintain and revalorize pre-Hebraic cyclical and antihistorical patterns of myth and ritual. As was just seen, Eliade claims that the majority of religious persons in the Western religions have attempted to preserve themselves from history, rather than identify themselves as historical beings. And religious persons in the West have been able to tolerate history and give it provisional, irreversible value because of their antihistorical faith that history will be finally abolished once and for all.

NONHISTORICAL STRUCTURES
Eliade occasionally expresses his agreement with other scholars in affirming that historians of religions use an empirical method of approach toward myths and other religious phenomena and that they work exclusively with historical documents. Repeatedly Eliade states that his point of departure is historical data, and he acknowledges their irreducibly historical nature. In one's concern with religio-historical facts, the historian of religions "is attracted to both the *meaning* of a religious phenomenon and to its *history;* he tries to do justice to both

and not to sacrifice either one of them." The "historian of religions *sensu stricto* can never ignore that which is historically concrete."[11]

For Eliade, to affirm that all myths and other religious phenomena are historical is primarily to acknowledge that all religious data are conditioned. "For the student of religion 'history' means primarily that all religious phenomena are conditioned. A *pure* religious phenomenon does not exist." The sacred is always manifested in history; particular temporal, spatial, and cultural factors always condition the religious manifestation. A religious phenomenon "is always also a social, an economic, a psychological phenomenon, and, of course, a historical one, because it takes place in historical time and it is conditioned by everything which had happened before."[12] "A religious phenomenon cannot be understood outside of its 'history,' that is, outside of its cultural and socioeconomic contexts. There is no such thing outside of history as a 'pure' religious datum. For there is no such thing as a human datum that is not at the same time a historical datum. Every religious experience is expressed and transmitted in a particular historical context."[13] Thus, for example, without taking into consideration historical conditionings, Eliade could not analyze the paradoxical relation in the dialectic of the sacred: that which is finite and historical, while remaining a natural conditioned thing, manifests something supernatural, infinite, and transhistorical; that which is transcendent and transhistorical limits and historicizes itself by manifesting itself in some finite, conditioned, historical thing.[14]

Nevertheless, most scholars have not been impressed by Eliade's sensitivity to the particular historical conditionings of his data. Critics charge—and supporters sometimes grant—that Eliade does not do justice to both the history and meaning of mythic and other religious phenomena. He often ignores and sacrifices historical conditionings and that which is historically concrete. What stands out in Eliade's approach is the primary methodological emphasis he places on, and the lofty status he grants to, nontemporal and nonhistorical universal mythic and other religious structures.

Many of the criticisms attacking Eliade for being antihistorical initially came in response to *Traité d'histoire des religions (Patterns in Comparative Religion)*. This synchronic morphological study was not historical. Religious and mythic structures were detached from their historical and cultural contexts. In *Patterns* Eliade wrote of a forthcoming, more historical "companion volume," and over the next thirty years, he occasionally referred to this "historical companion," even describing it as the culmination of his career and as his *opus magnum.*

The three-volume *A History of Religious Ideas* is certainly Eliade's most historical major work. It adds to his previous structural and morphological studies a greater emphasis on historical change and development, on the inexhaustible newness of religious expressions and the irreducible differences in religious forms. There is a greater sense of structures in process, as part of an ever changing, dynamic, creative, spiritual history. Although Eliade presents a greater sense of historical differences and historical change, he certainly remains the generalist, comparativist, and synthesizer, emphasizing similarities, general structures and patterns, and his belief in the fundamental "unity of history and of the human mind and spirit."[15] Indeed, Eliade could not have written such a history of religions without his nonhistorical assumptions and principles, allowing for his hermeneutical framework of the dialectic of the sacred and structural systems of symbols and myths. In short, this historical study of existential crises and religious creativity from the entire history of humankind is guided by Eliade's morphological analysis of essential nonhistorical mythic and religious structures.

Those cultural historians, anthropologists, and other critics who have attacked Eliade for his antihistorical approach, for his sweeping nonhistorical generalizations and lack of sensitivity to the specific concrete historical dimension of the data, will not be satisfied with this "history" as presented in *A History of Religious Ideas.* In terms of their methodological orientations, most of these critics will view much of the three-volume history as a nonhistorical history or pseudohistory.

Eliade certainly accepts the necessity for historical research, but it is necessary primarily as a means to uncover and decipher transhistorical meanings. For example, in *Birth and Rebirth* and other works, Eliade describes in some detail the symbolism of initiation myths and rituals implying a *regressus ad uterum* or return to the embryonic state.[16] But it is usually clear that Eliade's primary concern is not with the historical details. His primary task is to interpret the deeper transhistorical and atemporal structures and meanings revealed by these particular myths and techniques for "going back" in order to overcome time.

> The initiation myths and rites of *regressus ad uterum* reveal the following fact: the "return to the origin" prepares a new birth, but the new birth is not a repetition of the first, physical birth. There is properly speaking a mystical rebirth, spiritual in nature—in other words, access to a new mode of existence (involving sexual maturity, participation in the sacred and in culture; in short, becoming "open" to Spirit). The basic idea is that, to attain to a higher mode of existence, gestation and birth must be repeated; but they are repeated ritually, symbolically. In other words, we here have acts oriented toward the values of Spirit, not behavior from the realm of psycho-physiological activity.[17]

While claiming that the essential "symbolism is the same" in the myths and rites of "return to the origin," including those of the *regressus ad uterum,* Eliade recognizes that "the contexts differ, and it is the intention shown by the context that gives us the true meaning in each case." Eliade homologizes the structure of the cosmogonic myth with the structure found in myths and rituals of initiatory rebirths, but "obviously this cosmogonic symbolism is enriched with new values in the case of the birth of the mythical Ancestor, the birth of each individual, and initiatory rebirth."[18] To show how the same symbolism of this "return to the origin" functions on very different planes, Eliade contrasts Hindu, Buddhist, and Taoist contexts with his previous formulations of archaic myth and religion.

In his interpretation of "curing oneself of the work of time," Eliade claims that Yoga and Buddhism developed psycho-physiological methods of "going back" to a degree unknown elsewhere. The goal was no longer the archaic therapeutic purpose of obtaining a cure or rejuvenation of life through the mythic and ritual abolishing of time and history with the reimmersion of the patient in the fullness of primordial sacred time. Yoga and Buddhism are on a different plane. "Their final goal is not health or rejuvenation but spiritual mastery and liberation. Yoga and Buddhism are soteriologies, mystical techniques, philosophies—and, naturally, pursue ends other than magical cures."[19] After stating that the Indian philosophies and mystical techniques show structural analogies with archaic therapies, since they also pursue the goal of curing human beings of the pain of existence in time, Eliade emphasizes differences in the Indian contexts. In Yoga, Buddhism, and various Tantric schools, there is the goal and specific techniques for attaining the beginning of Time and entering "the Timeless—the eternal present which preceded the temporal experience inaugurated by the 'fall' into human existence." Starting from any moment in temporal historical existence, one can "exhaust that duration by retracing its course to the source and so come out into the Timeless, into eternity. But that is to transcend the human condition and to regain the non-conditioned state, which preceded the fall into Time and the wheel of existences."[20]

Eliade concludes:

> To repeat: we have no intention of putting Indo-Chinese mystical techniques and primitive therapies on the same plane. They are different cultural phenomena. But it is interesting to observe a certain continuity of human behavior in respect to Time, both down the ages and in various cultures. This behavior may be defined as follows: *To cure the work of Time it is necessary to "go back" and find the "beginning of the World."* We have just seen that this "return to the origin" has been variously evaluated. In the archaic and paleo-Oriental cultures the reiteration of the cosmic myth had as its purpose abolishing past Time and beginning a new life with all vital forces intact. For the Chinese and Hindu "mystics" the goal ceased to be beginning a new life again here below, on earth, and became "going back" and reconstituting the primordial Great-One. But in these examples, as in all the others we have given, the characteristic and decisive element was always "returning to the origin."[21]

None of this is meant to deny that in his detailed illustrations of such phenomena in *Yoga: Immortality and Freedom* and other works, Mircea Eliade is often fascinated with particular historical and cultural variations. But even when he emphasizes cultural differences, Eliade is primarily concerned not with particular historical conditionings, but rather with "deeper" variations in nonhistorical structures and meanings. And even when Eliade emphasizes such structural variations, he is usually determined to uncover even deeper transhistorical similarities, homologies, structures and meanings, such as "curing the work of time" by "going back" and "returning to the origin."

To provide one other illustration of Eliade's primary goal, the uncovering and interpretation of transhistorical atemporal structures and meanings, Eliade indicates that there are many historical and cultural variations of the myth of human androgyny.[22] He considers many myths, such as those of the hermaphrodite god and bisexual ancestor or first human being. The deeper meaning of these myths of human androgyny is that the "need man feels to cancel periodically his differentiated and determined condition so as to return to primeval 'totalization' is the same need which spurs him to periodic orgies in which all forms dissolve, to end by recovering that 'oneness' that was before the creation. Here again we come upon the need to destroy the past, to expunge 'history' and to start a new life in a new Creation." Even the most bizarre variations seen in reenactments of the myth of human androgyny "never succeeded in abolishing their essential significance—of making their participants once more share in the paradisal condition of 'primeval man'. And all these rituals have as their exemplar model the myth of divine androgyny."[23]

Throughout his writings, Eliade maintains that fundamental mythic and religious structures are nonhistorical.[24] We cannot demonstrate that essential mythic structures are created by certain societies or at certain historical moments. We can only establish that particular historical conditions provide the opportunity for the manifestation or predominance of a specific nontemporal, nonhistorical, mythic structure. History does not basically modify the structure of an essential, exemplary, mythic symbolism. History does add new meanings. New valorizations are occasioned by particular historical situations. But the new valorizations are conditioned by the essential transhistorical structure of the symbolism expressed through myths.[25]

Not only is Eliade's primary task to interpret transhistorical meanings, but he also argues for "the ahistoricity of religious life." He notes the occurrence of certain essential, nonhistorical, mythic and symbolic structures and meanings in extremely diverse historical and cultural contexts. He interprets the recurrence of such transhistorical, atemporal structures as pointing to a spontaneity and reversibility of religious positions that eludes reductionistic historical explanations. Certain coherent mystical experiences "are possible at any and every degree of civilization and of religious situation. This is as much as to say that, for certain religious consciousnesses in crises, there is always the possibility of a historical leap that enables them to attain otherwise inaccessible spiritual positions."[26]

As will be seen, not only does Eliade interpret transhistorical mythic and other religious meanings by means of a hermeneutics grounded in nonhistorical structures, but he also maintains that primordial religious experiences, such as ecstasy or mystical ascension, are nonhistorical. Indeed, at the most universal level of normative judgments, far beyond the disciplinary boundaries of the history and phenomenology of religion, Eliade claims that our basic human mode of being in the world and our essential human nature are essentially nonhistorical.

Little wonder that Seymour Cain writes that "historical actuality and the living context of religious phenomena," which had been empha- sized by Eliade, "appear to be dismissed as banally meaningless, a mere naught besides the 'transhistorical' intentionality of the specific manifestations of the sacred in symbols, rites, myths, etc." For Eliade, it appears that "the systematic precedes the historical, structure comes before history, methodologically—if not also metaphysically- speaking."[27]

STRUCTURES AND MEANINGS VERSUS CONDITIONINGS AND EXPLANATIONS

In the methodologically important foreword to *Shamanism*, in *Myths, Dreams and Mysteries*, in *Images and Symbols*, and in other works, Eliade is determined to differentiate what he is doing from historical (psychological, causal) "explanation." One may explain the origin or diffusion of a particular myth in terms of historical, cultural, and temporal conditionings, but Eliade continually maintains that the task of the historian of religions is not completed by such historical research: one must still interpret the meaning of mythic and other religious data. "So at some point the historian of religion must become a phenomenologist of religion, because he tries to find meaning. Without hermeneutics, the history of religion is just another history—bare facts, special classifications, and so forth."[28]

Eliade repeatedly makes a key methodological distinction between uncovering mythic and religious structures and interpreting their irreducibly religious meaning versus uncovering particular historical and other conditionings and providing historical explanations. He not only emphasizes such a methodological dichotomy, but he usually affirms the primacy of the task of interpreting meaning. In some formulations, he simply leaves the task of providing historical, psychological, sociological, economic, and other explanations to other scholars. In other formulations, he devalues, as preparatory and secondary, historical and other explanations or even attacks them as nonreligious reductionistic accounts that distort the intentionality, meaning, and significance of myth and religion.

After presenting myths and rituals focusing on "the regeneration of time," Eliade makes statements typical of formulations in which he simply leaves the task of historical explanation to other scholars. "Our sole aim has been a summary phenomenological analysis of these periodic purification rites (expulsion of demons, diseases, and sins) and of the ceremonials of the end and beginning of the year." Eliade admits that in addition to his phenomenological analysis of similarities and general structures and meanings, there are problems requiring further study having to do with particular variations and differences and with historical questions of origins and dissemination. "It is for this very reason that we have avoided any kind of sociological or ethnographic interpretation and have limited ourselves to a simple exposition of the general meaning that emanates from all these ceremonies. In short, our ambition is to understand their meaning, to endeavor to see what they show us—leaving to possible future studies the detailed examination (genetic or historical) of each separate mythico-ritual complex."[29]

More typical is Eliade's formulation in *Shamanism*. After acknowledging the contributions of psychologists, sociologists, and ethnologists—such as the great services of historical ethnography in attempting "to establish the 'history' of one or another constituent element of shamanism"—Eliade focuses on the specific method and viewpoint that defines the history of religions: "to reveal the deeper meaning of all these religious phenomena, to illuminate their symbolism, and to place them in the general history of religions."[30] Eliade typically affirms that "the historical conditions are extremely important in a religious phenomenon (for every human datum is in the last analysis a historical datum)," and "the historian of religions, while taking historico-religious facts into account, does his utmost to organize his documents in the historical perspective—the only perspective that ensures their concreteness."[31] But what is most important is that historians of religions "must never forget that, when all is said and done," the primary "work of deciphering the deep meaning of religious phenomena rightfully falls to the historian of religions." "The historian of religions makes use of all the *historical* manifestations of a religious phenomenon in order to discover what such a phenomenon 'has to say'; on the one hand, he holds to the historically concrete, but on the other, he attempts to decipher whatever transhistorical content a religious datum reveals through history." And what myths and other religious phenomena "have to say" is primarily deciphered in terms of nonhistorical, atemporal, sacred structures and meanings.

While acknowledging that the "specific plane of manifestation [of religious facts] is always *historical,* concrete, existential, even if the religious facts manifested are not always wholly reducible to history" and "everything is in some sort conditioned by history," Eliade continues: "Yet in the humblest hierophany there is an 'eternal new beginning,' an eternal return to an atemporal moment, a desire to abolish history, to blot out the past, to recreate the world. All this is 'shown' in religious facts; it is not an invention of the historian of religions. Obviously, a historian bent on being only a historian has the right to ignore the specific and transhistorical meanings of a religious fact; an ethnologist, a sociologist, a psychologist may do likewise. A historian of religions cannot ignore them."[32] Eliade views his primary task as formulating a "creative hermeneutics" in which he interprets specific transhistorical meanings of mythic and other religious data.[33]

In distinguishing the interpretation of meaning from providing historical explanations and in repeatedly affirming that "[u]ltimately, what we desire to know is the meaning of the various historical modifications,"[34] Eliade, at the minimum, is making a claim frequently found in philosophical phenomenology: giving a historical or causal explanation does not exhaust the meaning of one's data. Phenomenology is concerned with finding "meanings," not with giving "explanations." "The primary aim of philosophical phenomenology is to investigate and become directly aware of phenomena that appear in immediate experience, and thereby allow the phenomenologist to describe the essential structures of these phenomena. In doing so phenomenology attempts to free itself from unexamined presuppositions, to avoid causal and other explanations, and to utilize a method that allows it to describe that which appears and to intuit or decipher essential meanings."[35] Interpreting mythic and religious meaning is not tantamount to uncovering historical conditionings and providing historical explanations.

In this regard, Eliade, along with many philosophical phenomenologists and phenomenologists of religion, often accepts two clear-cut dichotomies.[36] First, the historian and phenomenologist of religion adopts a clear distinction between the initial collection and description of empirical, historical, objective, uninterpreted, factual, mythic and religious data and the subsequent interpretation of the meaning of such data. In recent decades, however, many philosophers and other scholars have challenged this absolute dichotomy.[37] Second, this interpretation of meaning, the primary task for the history and phenomenology of religion, is clearly distinguished from historical and other causal explanation. To provide but one additional illustration, in his concluding critique of "historicity and historicism" in "The Quest for the 'Origins' of Religion," Eliade asserts that for scholars of religion "history" means primarily that all religious phenomena are conditioned and take place in historical time. But he then asks: "Are the multiple systems of conditioning a self-sufficient explanation of the religious phenomena?" Modern scholars, overly impressed by the discovery of the importance of history, have been carried away in their tendency to explain everything on a historical plane of reference and in terms of historical conditionings.

> But we must not confuse the historical circumstances which make a human existence what it actually is with the fact that there is such a thing as a human existence. For the historian of religions the fact that a myth or a ritual is always historically conditioned does not explain away the very existence of such a myth or ritual. In other words, the historicity of a religious experience does not tell us what a religious experience ultimately *is*. We know that we can grasp the sacred only through manifestations which are always historically conditioned. But the study of these historically conditioned expressions does not give us the answer to the questions: What is the sacred? What does a religious experience actually mean?[38]

As was seen, not only do critics challenge the claims to such unique, hermeneutical methods and goals, but they also question whether phenomenological understanding of (nonhistorical) meaning and non-phenomenological, historical explanation can be so completely separated.[39] Even in Eliade's formulations, the absolute dichotomy of interpretation versus explanation is blurred. Although Eliade usually formulates clear-cut contrasts between his interpretation of (trans-historical) meaning versus providing (historical) explanation, he sometimes "explains" myth and religion as fulfilling certain functions, responding to needs and desires and nostalgias, being more authentically human and more consistent with human nature. Sometimes he claims that his irreducibly religious explanations are more profound than explanations based on more surfacial, nonreligious, historical conditionings. In all such cases, one can see that there is an integral relation between Eliade's interpretations of structures and meanings and his explanations of mythic and religious phenomena.[40]

Although the phenomenological dichotomy of interpretation of meaning versus historical explanation may be controversial, Eliade often intends something far more controversial in his move beyond historical explanation. As should be evident from previous illustrations, Eliade sometimes makes definite nonhistorical and antihistorical ontological claims about reality, human nature, the human mode of being in the world, and the human condition as such.[41] Scholars providing historical and other causal explanations are not only doing something different from interpreting mythic and religious meaning. Their very approaches are inadequate for comprehending the deepest ontological levels of mythic and religious experience.

Eliade comments favorably on Christopher Mayhew's description of his experience with mescaline in "An Excursion out of Time." Eliade "trembled with joy" because in so many of his scholarly studies and short stories he had also "spoken of the possibility of abolishing time, and of putting oneself into a transtemporal condition." Mayhew's experience helps us to understand ecstatic experiences in which "time is left behind," a theme that is "so constant through the history of religions and the different mystical doctrines, and even in popular literature or folklore." Eliade believes "that similar ecstatic experiences base all their conceptions on the abolition of time. They are not aberrant or peripheral experiences without interest for everyday man. On the contrary, I would say that there exists in the soul of each of us a secret longing for this sort of ecstasy. One satisfies it as well as one can by dreams, fantasies, literature. This *imaginary* satisfaction does not mean that these ecstasies are not an integral part of our mode of being in the world (cf. what I wrote on "Symbolisms of Ascension," in *Myths, Dreams, and Mysteries*)."[42]

Particular historical and cultural conditionings cannot account for primordial existential experiences, for primordial mythic and religious phenomena that are constitutive of the human condition as such. "As an *experience,* ecstasy is a non-historical phenomenon; it is a primordial phenomenon in the sense that it is coextensive with human nature. Only the religious *interpretation* given to ecstasy and the *techniques* designed to prepare it or facilitate it are historical data." Eliade often writes of "the nonhistorical portion of every human being" and of how "primordial" phenomena exhibit dimensions that are "metacultural and transhistorical." A primordial phenomenon such as ecstasy, revealing an essential structure of celestial ascent, "belongs to man as such, not to man as a historical being; witness the dreams, hallucinations, and images of ascent found everywhere in the world, apart from any historical or other 'conditions.'"[43] Eliade acknowledges that he must consider particular historical conditions, but not all mythic and religious experiences are historically determined. Sometimes human beings transcend their specific historical context and have certain nonhistorical primordial experiences simply by virtue of their human mode of existence.

To summarize, in contrasting his interpretation of structures and meanings with scholars who uncover historical conditionings and provide historical explanations, Eliade is asserting something more than the noncontroversial claim that *homo religiosus* experiences religious mythic phenomena as revealing transhistorical atemporal meanings. He is asserting the primacy of the phenomenological, hermeneutical interpretation of mythic and other religious meaning for the history of religions. While acknowledging the importance of historical conditions, he makes the controversial claim that the interpretation of meaning is completely different from providing historical explanations and gets at a deeper level of myth and religion. Finally, in his most controversial assertions, his attempt to go beyond historical explanation incorporates implicit, and at time explicit, ontological moves. On the basis of primordial, nontemporal, nonhistorical mythic and religious structures and meanings, Eliade is making significant ontological claims about reality, about time and history, and about the true human mode of being in the world and the human condition as such.

NORMATIVE ANTIHISTORICAL JUDGMENTS
As was seen in his autobiographical reflections and personal scholarly attitudes toward time and history and in the above ontological moves, Eliade wishes to claim that it is more authentically human to live one's life in terms of transcendent exemplary mythic and religious models, nontemporal and nonhistorical structures, than to identify oneself fully with the temporal and historical dimension of existence. Historical persons, who refuse any "religious solution," cannot solve their most fundamental existential crises. There is something fundamentally inhuman, even antihuman, about modern historicism and materialism and other approaches that deny the basic mythic and sacred foundation of our human nature and human condition as such. Representative of

formulations found throughout Eliade's writings is the following: "I cannot limit his [the modern person who claims not to be religious] universe to that purely self-conscious, rationalistic universe which he pretends to inhabit, since that universe is not human."[44]

As was seen in chapter 1, Eliade is extremely critical of modern approaches labeled positivist, historicist, existentialist, Marxist, materialist, and reductionist, often lumping them together. In most contexts, he attacks their interpretations and explanations of myth and religion, but he is also severely critical of their general assumptions, treatments of history, and judgments about the human mode of being and the nature of reality. Eliade analyzes the sacred as a permanent structure of consciousness and as expressing a transhistorical structure of transcendence. He conceives of the study of *homo religiosus* as the study of the "total person," encompassing the unconscious, the conscious, and the transconscious; the prereflective and nonrational as well as the rational; the nontemporal and nonhistorical as well as the temporal and historical. Therefore, Eliade evaluates interpretations and explanations of existentialists, historicists, materialists, and others who identify what is truly human with the temporal and historical dimension of existence as denying an essential structure of consciousness of transcendence, as denying the total person, and hence as denying what is fully and authentically human.[45]

Without developing the illustrations of ecstasy, ascension, and other primordial mythic and religious phenomena or citing other normative claims found throughout Eliade's works, I shall simply focus on several antihistorical judgments from the analysis of "the terror of history" in *The Myth of the Eternal Return.* "Whatever be the truth in respect to the freedom and the creative virtualities of historical man, it is certain that none of the historicistic philosophies is able to defend him from the terror of history." When the modern experiences existential crises and historical tragedies, the "terror of history" must lead to "nihilism or despair" if the person completely makes oneself through historical conditions. "The man who has left the horizon of archetypes and repetition can no longer defend himself against that terror except through the idea of God." "Only such a freedom," grounded in the Judaeo-Christian "category of faith"—"for God everything is possible"—can defend the modern from the terror of history. "Every other modern freedom . . . is powerless to justify history."[46]

What concerns us is not the adequacy of Eliade's particular interpretations but the fact that he is no longer defining his analysis simply in terms of the general perspective of *homo religiosus*. Eliade has moved to a level of even greater generality beyond such perspectival limitations. In other words, Eliade is not claiming that from an antihistorical, mythic, religious perspective, no historicistic "solution" can defend us from "the terror of history"; but from some nonreligious historical perspective—which is not my concern as a historian of religions providing irreducibly religious interpretations— there may be a "solution" that can "justify" history and overcome nihilism and despair. Eliade is making general, normative, antihistorical judgments about the human mode of being in the world and the human condition as such. And on the basis of such antihistorical judgments, he is claiming that the "historicistic philosophies" of Hegel, Marx, Dilthey, and others cannot defend modern human beings from the terror of history.

Such a procedure clearly involves an ontological stance with normative antihistorical judgments.[47] Eliade assumes that the nonhistorical structures of mythic and religious experience, as seen in the refusal to identify oneself fully with the historical and temporal dimension of existence, reveal fundamental essential structures of the human mode of being generally. According to Eliade, such a level of ontological analysis reveals that only by experiencing the essential, nonhistorical, symbolic and mythic structures of the sacred can modern persons overcome their "terror of history" and their existential anxiety and live a truly meaningful and authentic human existence.

THE INTERACTION OF THE HISTORICAL AND NONHISTORICAL

On the basis of the antihistorical foundation of Eliade's interpretation of myth and religion, it is tempting simply to identify his approach as nonempirical, nontemporal, and nonhistorical as so many other scholars have done. But this would oversimplify and misrepresent the complexity of his history and phenomenology of religion. Such a simple identification fails to recognize the seriousness with which Eliade often regards the particular historical document. As seen in *Shamanism, Yoga,* and other scholarly works, Eliade is fascinated with the particular, historical, and cultural variations of more general, underlying structures and meanings. It is true that Eliade seems to approach his "historical" research with all kinds of *a priori* assumptions and with an assumed hermeneutical framework of essential nonhistorical mythic and symbolic structures. Such an assumed methodological framework is essential in allowing us to understand what mythic and religious data he selects and how he interprets their structures, meanings, and significance. Nevertheless, one should not completely dismiss the seriousness with which Eliade is attracted to and struggles with the new, historical, particular variations and revalorizations of deeper structures.

Although Eliade certainly interprets *homo religiosus* as determined to devalue and abolish the historical and temporal dimension of existence, we must avoid a misconception of identifying his approach with an antihistorical, atemporal otherworldly orientation in the manner that so many scholars have interpreted Hinduism, Buddhism, and other nonWestern religions. Eliade was always attracted to myth and religion because of their existential value. Transhistorical and atemporal mythic and other sacred structures are intended to sanctify, cosmicize, and make meaningful the most pressing, immediate, existential concerns. Thus in India, Eliade was most attracted to religious and mythic approaches that expressed not a renunciation of, but a zest for life. He had little interest in the abstract analysis found in Advaita Vedānta and other forms of Indian philosophy, including those commonly analyzed as devaluing the cycles of worldly existence as mere illusion. Instead, he was drawn to concrete techniques of spiritual transformation, as found in certain forms of Yoga and tantrism, and to the concrete, life-affirming religious and mythic world of Indian peasants. Similarly, in Romania and the West, Eliade was not drawn to rather abstract forms of argumentation found in Thomistic and other theologies. Instead, he was most attracted to the very concrete passions, existential concerns, and mythic and religious transfigurations of temporal and historical events in cosmic Christianity and other forms of peasant cosmic religion.

Indeed, what most attracts Eliade to mythic phenomena is not some abstract, detached, nonhistorical, theoretical formulation, but rather his belief that the nonhistorical, atemporal, exemplary, mythic and symbolic structures allow mythic peoples to concretely, existentially, "live the myths." None of this is meant to deny that in Eliade's interpretation of this concrete, existential, religious and mythic orientation, the profane *qua* profane, the temporal *qua* temporal, and the historical *qua* historical have little or no meaning and value. They only gain value and significant meaning when experienced in terms of transhistorical, atemporal, mythic, sacred structures.

The sense of a complex, dynamic historical-nonhistorical interaction is evident in several works in which Eliade accepts the historical-phenomenological "tension," formulated by Raffaele Pettazzoni, as defining "the history of religions" *(Religionswissenschaft).*[48] This tension between historical and phenomenological approaches is both necessary and creative. Eliade affirms this indispensable historical-phenomenological tension and the need to do justice to both the historical particular and the nonhistorical universal structure. But as we have established, his approach emphasizes the primacy of nonhistorical, atemporal structures, and he conceives his primacy task as the interpretation of transhistorical mythic and religious meanings.

In chapter 3, we saw Eliade's emphasis on permanent universal structures in his formulation of the dialectic of the sacred and the profane. It is through essential structures of sacralization that he is able to distinguish mythic religious phenomena from nonreligious phenomena. But it is also impossible to grasp fully this dialectic in its dynamic complexity without taking into consideration the particular historical nature of one's data and the interaction of historical conditions and phenomenological structures. We examined the essential universal structure of paradoxical coexistence revealed by the dialectic of the sacred: some ordinary historical thing, while remaining a stone or person or some other natural thing, manifests something transhistorical and supernatural; something transhistorical, atemporal, and transcendent limits itself by manifesting itself in some historical, temporal, finite, relative thing. In order to grasp the nature of hierophanies, one must appreciate the specific historical, temporal, natural medium through which the sacred is revealed.

To provide a second example, this paradoxical relation of the sacred and the profane expresses itself as a dynamic tension and dialectical movement. This essential universal structure of dialectical tension and movement may be expressed through two contrary, but equally necessary, interacting processes. On the one hand, there is the movement from essential, nonhistorical, sacred structure to particular, historical, temporal, conditioned thing. The sacred is manifested and incarnated in particular, temporal, historical objects. On the other hand, there is at the same time the "reverse" movement in which the particular sacred manifestation tends to free itself from its limited, finite, temporal, and historical conditions so that it can realize as fully as possible its transhistorical sacred structure or exemplary form. Without a recognition of the historical dimension of the data, there would be little appreciation of this dialectical movement; there would be little understanding of the structurally necessary dialectical tension existing between the contrary but interacting dialectical movements. In short, without the dynamic historical-nonhistorical interaction, there would be no process of sacralization as the universal structure of religious experience.

One could demonstrate the impossibility of comprehending other structures of the dialectic of the sacred, such as camouflage and concealment, without emphasizing the historical-nonhistorical relation. At the same time that it manifests itself, the transcendent transhistorical sacred conceals and camouflages itself in history; in ordinary, natural, temporal, historical phenomena. Without a careful analysis of the historical and temporal dimension of existence and the complex historical-nonhistorical relation, one would not be able to recognize the religious phenomenon, much less interpret its transhistorical meaning.

Even with regard to nonhistorical, universal, symbolic structures—those symbolic and mythic structures that enjoy such a privileged ontological status in Eliade's phenomenological approach—one could show the impossibility of fully understanding Eliade's interpretation of religious symbolism without taking seriously the historical dimension of existence. Nontemporal and nonhistorical mythic and religious structures do not by themselves constitute religious experience. Actual mythic religious experience consists of just what human beings do with these symbolic structures. These universal nonhistorical structures function as inexhaustible sources of meaning and offer virtually unlimited possibilities for historical actualization. Actual revalorization of a religious symbolism is the particular way mythic religious persons, situated in their particular historical and cultural world, relate to the symbolism in structuring and making sense of their world. And just what religious persons do with these nonhistorical structures must be seen in terms of their concrete, specific, historical conditions. What transhistorical structures we become aware of, how we respond to our discovery, what meaning they have for us, and how we use them to structure our world depend largely on historical, cultural, and other particular conditions. Once again, for Eliade, actual religious mythic experience and creativity always entail the dynamic interaction between the historical particular and the nonhistorical universal structure.

Even with regard to archaic religion, in which *homo religiosus* strives to abolish profane time and history, Eliade offers many interpretations of different senses in which these antihistorical societies are historical. In *Australian Religion* and other works, he stresses that archaic persons do live in history and are influenced by the historical. He sometimes shows that it is precisely the appeal to some transhistorical, mythical, sacred history, with the interaction of the transhistorical structures and historical events, that enables the archaic society "to live historically" and even to "make history."[49]

Eliade's approach does have an antihistorical normative basis. Not only is he primarily concerned with interpreting transhistorical mythic and religious meaning, but there is also something essentially nonhistorical about his hermeneutics: the methodological primacy of nonhistorical and nontemporal universal structures, as seen in the permanent, essential, universal structure of the dialectic of the sacred; in systems of essential symbolic and mythic structures at the foundation of his interpretations; and in the ontological moves beyond the historical involving all sorts of antihistorical normative judgments.

In this concluding section, without denying the antihistorical foundation and emphasis in Eliade's approach to myth and religion, I have tried to show that interpreters who simply classify Eliade's approach as antihistorical do not appreciate the complexity of the historical-nonhistorical interaction in his interpretations. To establish that Eliade interprets the ontology of *homo religiosus* as essentially antihistorical or to establish that Eliade's own normative position tends to be antihistorical does not mean that his phenomenological approach and hermeneutics simply dismisses the historical particular as insignificant or irrelevant to the interpretation of mythic and religious meaning. At the same time, while acknowledging Eliade's hermeneutical struggle over the historical particular, his fascination with historical variations of nonhistorical structures, and the complexity of historical-nonhistorical interactions in his phenomenological method, I in no way intend to deny that compared to most modern scholars of religion, Eliade does indeed emphasize the nonhistorical.

NOTES

1. *Myth and Reality*, p. 13.

2. *No Souvenirs*, p. 89.

3. *Eternal Return*, pp. 37-44. Although Eliade usually provides such mythic examples from archaic cosmic religion, he frequently illustrates this mythic transfiguration of historical individuals and events through Egyptian, Greek, Jewish, Christian, and other religious traditions. He also interprets this mythic ahistorical transformation as present in much of contemporary, secular, historical consciousness, often expressed indirectly on the level of the unconscious and through fantasies, dreams, and literary and artistic creativity. Indeed, he sometimes claims that this process of transformation of the concrete, particular, historical phenomenon into the ahistoric, exemplary, mythic deeper structure and meaning reveals something essential about human nature and the human condition as such.

4. *Eternal Return*, pp. 44-46.

5. Ibid., pp. 85-86.

6. See, for example, *Eternal Return*, pp. 141-42.

7. *No Souvenirs, pp. 23, 167.*

8. *Eternal Return*, p. 104. See also *Myth and Reality*, pp. 168-70, and *History 1*, pp. 355-56.

9. *Eternal Return*, pp. 104-7.

10. Ibid., pp. 107-12.

11. "Methodological Remarks," p. 88; "The Quest for the 'Origins' of Religion," p. 169 (which is reproduced as chap. 3 in *Quest*). See also *Eternal Return*, pp. 5-6; *Patterns*, pp. xiv-xvi, 2-3.

12. *Quest*, p. 52. See also *Quest*, p. 7, and *Images and Symbols*, pp. 30-32.

13. "Comparative Religion: Its Past and Future," p. 250. Eliade continues: "But admitting the historicity of religious experiences does not imply that they are reducible to nonreligious forms of behavior." See also *Patterns*, p. xiii, and Eliade, "History of Religions and a New Humanism," *History of Religions* 1 (1961): 6 (which appears as chap. 1 in *Quest*, p. 7).

14. This was discussed at length in chap. 3. See *Patterns*, pp. 26, 29-30; *Images and Symbols*, pp. 84, 178.

15. *Ordeal by Labyrinth*, p. 137. See also Adriana Berger, "Cultural Hermeneutics: The Concept of Imagination in the Phenomenological Approaches of Henry Corbin and Mircea Eliade," *Journal of Religion* 66 (1986): 141-56.

16. Mircea Eliade's *Birth and Rebirth: The Religious Meaning of Initiation in Human Culture*, trans. Willard R. Trask (New York: Harper and Brothers, 1958), based on the Haskell Lectures on "Patterns of Initiation" delivered at the University of Chicago in 1956, was reprinted as Mircea Eliade, *Rites and Symbols of Initiation: The Mysteries of Birth and Rebirth*, trans. Willard R. Trask (New York: Harper Torchbooks, 1965). See *Birth and Rebirth* or *Rites and Symbols of Initiation* for Eliade's presentation of the Australian Kunapipi ritual and other examples of the initiatory symbolism of return to the womb (pp. 49-53), this symbolism in Indian initiations (pp. 53-57), and the multiple meanings of initiatory myths and rites with this symbolic theme of return to the embryonic state (pp. 57-60).

17. *Myth and Reality*, pp. 79-81.

18. Ibid., p. 82.

19. Ibid., p. 85.

20. *Myths, Dreams and Mysteries*, p. 50. See also ibid., pp. 49-51. In *Yoga* Eliade provides many illustrations of such Indian goals and techniques from Yoga, tantrism, and other forms of Hinduism and Buddhism. See, for example, *Yoga*, pp. 270-73.

21. *Myth and Reality*, pp. 87-88.

22. Eliade's most extensive study of the myth of androgyny is "Mephistopheles and the Androgyne or the Mystery of the Whole," in *Mephistopheles and the Androgyne*, pp. 78-124. To get at the deepest meaning of androgynous mythic and symbolic structures, Eliade usually interprets androgyny as a structural variation or revalorization of an even more universal symbolism of *coincidentia oppositorum*.

23. *Patterns*, pp. 423-25. On p. 425 Eliade makes an important point found throughout his writings. The paradigmatic function of myth should not be restricted to serving as a paradigm for rituals. In addition to providing transhistorical models for reenactment through rituals, myths disclose paradigms for other religious and metaphysical experience as well. They often reveal

exemplary structures that some religious persons attempt to reenact outside the ritualistic and ceremonial life of the community.

24. See, for example, *Myths, Dreams and Mysteries,* pp. 107-8, 110, 178; *Sacred and Profane,* p. 137; *Images and Symbols,* pp. 159-61; Mircea Eliade, "Mythologie et histoire des religions," *Diogène* 9 (1955): 99-116.

25. In *Structure and Creativity in Religion* and *Mircea Eliade et le phénomène religieux,* I maintain that it is these essential, nonhistorical, symbolic structures, when integrated with the universal transhistorical structure of the dialectic of the sacred, that primarily constitute Eliade's hermeneutical framework and serve as the foundation for his phenomenological approach.

26. *Shamanism,* pp. xvi-xix, esp. p. xix.

27. Seymour Cain, "Mircea Eliade: Attitudes Toward History," *Religious Studies Review* 6 (1980): 14, 15.

28. Mircea Eliade, "The Sacred in the Secular World," *Cultural Hermeneutics* 1 (1973): 101, 103, 106-7. The title *Cultural Hermeneutics* was changed to *Philosophy and Social Criticism.*

29. *Eternal Return,* pp. 73-74.

30. *Shamanism,* pp. xi-xiii.

31. Ibid., pp. xiv-xv. As we have often seen and as will become even more evident later in this chapter and in chap. 10, Eliade does not really agree with his own formulations that "every human datum is in the last analysis a historical datum" or that he "does his utmost to organize his documents in the historical perspective."

32. Ibid., pp. xv-xvii.

33. See, for example, *Images and Symbols,* pp. 33-34, where Eliade asserts that the historian of religions, in one's concern with myths, symbols, and other religious phenomena, must affirm "that his business ought not therefore to be reduced to *recording the historical manifestations of that behaviour;* he ought also to be trying to gain deeper insight into its *meanings* and its articulation." Eliade continues that historians of religions will not be satisfied with ethnological and other historical research, because the basic questions of religious meaning and significance remain to be investigated.

34. Mircea Eliade, "On Understanding Primitive Religions," in *Glaube, Geist, Geschichte: Festschrift für Ernst Benz,* ed. Gerhard Müller and Winfried Zeller (Leiden: E. J. Brill, 1967), p. 501. Similar methodological claims are made in such articles as "History of Religions and a New Humanism" and "Crisis and Renewal in History of Religions" (both reproduced in *Quest)* and in methodological sections of Eliade's books.

35. Allen, "Phenomenology of Religion," p. 274.

36. Ibid., pp. 282-83.

37. Ibid., p. 282: "What is taken as objective and scientific is historically, culturally, and socially situated, based on presuppositions, and constructed in

terms of implicit and explicit value judgments. For example, how does one even begin the investigation? What facts should be collected as religious facts? One's very principles of selectivity are never completely value-free. Indeed, philosophical phenomenologists have never accepted this sharp dichotomy, since the entire phenomenological project is founded on the possibilities of describing meanings. The challenge to the phenomenology of religion is to formulate a phenomenological method and framework for interpretation that allows the description of essential structures and meanings with some sense of objectivity."

38. *Quest*, pp. 52-53.

39. For example, see p. 60 n. 23 in which we noted that Segal is correct in claiming that the clear-cut interpretation versus explanation dichotomy is often confusing and imposes an oversimplified and false methodological framework.

40. Similarly, it is incorrect to state that Marx, Freud, and other "reductionists" are concerned only with providing historical, economic, and psychological causal explanations and do not attempt to interpret the meaning of their data. Marxian and Freudian interpretations of meaning are integrally related to their explanations of phenomena. In challenging the absolute dichotomy of interpretation of meaning versus historical explanation, I do not want to deny that this is often a valuable methodological distinction in allowing us to understand differences in scholarly assumptions, methods, and goals.

41. See my *Structure and Creativity in Religion* for numerous illustrations of such nonhistorical and antihistorical ontological claims and normative judgments.

42. *No Souvenirs*, p. 157. Christopher Mayhew's "An Excursion out of Time" appeared in the *Observer* (28 October 1956). Eliade read it in *The Drug Experience*, ed. David Evin (New York, 1961), pp. 294-300. I have not been able to locate this book in any library.

43. Mircea Eliade, "Recent Works on Shamanism: A Review Article," *History of Religions* 1 (1962): 154; *Shamanism*, p. xiv. See also the foreword to *Images and Symbols*; *Myths, Dreams and Mysteries*, p. 106; *Rites and Symbols of Initiation*, pp. 130-31; "The Quest for the 'Origins' of Religion," p. 169.

44. "The Sacred in the Secular World," p. 104. As Ricketts has written in "Mircea Eliade and the Death of God," p. 43: "instead of choosing historicism, Eliade chooses the transhistorical or the religious mode of being as the more truly human."

45. As was seen in chap. 3, Eliade maintains that this universal structure of transcendence is an invariant structure of the sacred. Many of the "modern" scholars he attacks for denying such a structure of transcendence do in fact uphold a universal structure of transcendence. In the philosophies of Hegel, Marx, Sartre, and Simone de Beauvoir, among others, the universal structures of self-transcendence are key to their analyses of freedom and the development

of human consciousness and authentic human relations. But from Eliade's perspective, such modern formulations of transcendence are constituted within the horizon of temporal and historical conditions and deny the unique, irreducibly religious, transcendent structure of the sacred.

46. *Eternal Return*, pp. 141, 150, 159-62. Compare Eliade's similar level of analysis in "Religious Symbolism and the Modern Man's Anxiety," in *Myths, Dreams and Mysteries*, pp. 231-45. See also Eliade comments on "the terror of history" in *Ordeal by Labyrinth*, pp. 126-28.

47. In *Structure and Creativity in Religion*—in which my primary concern is to uncover, analyze, and assess Eliade's methodological approach—I analyze in great detail the nature of such ontological moves and normative judgments and how they are related to Eliade's more descriptive levels of phenomenological and hermeneutical interpretation.

48. See, e.g., Mircea Eliade, "Historical Events and Structural Meaning in Tension," *Criterion* 6 (1967): 29-31; "History of Religions and a New Humanism," pp. 7-8; "Methodological Remarks," p. 88. See also Raffaele Pettazzoni, "The Supreme Being: Phenomenological Structure and Historical Development," in *The History of Religion: Essays in Methodology*, ed. Mircea Eliade and Joseph M. Kitagawa (Chicago: University of Chicago Press, 1959), pp. 59-66, and Raffaele Pettazzoni, "History and Phenomenology in the Science of Religion," in his *Essays on the History of Religions*, trans. H. J. Rose (Leiden: E. J. Brill, 1954), pp. 215-19.

49. See, e.g., Mircea Eliade, "The Dragon and the Shaman: Notes on a South American Mythology," in *Man and His Salvation: Studies in Memory of S. G. F. Brandon*, ed. E. J. Sharpe and J. R. Hinnells (Manchester: Manchester University Press, 1973), pp. 99-105. Eliade provides illustrations of how archaic, largely nonhistorical, rural European peasants have "made" history and of how historians have generally overlooked the historical contributions of these peasants in "History of Religions and 'Popular' Cultures," *History of Religions*, pp. 1-26.

CHAPTER 10

Camouflage of Sacred in Modern Profane

Mircea Eliade distinguishes archaic, "traditional," mythic, religious human beings from "modern," nonmythic, nonreligious human beings. Eliade does not claim that every contemporary, Western human being is a "modern" person. He refers to two, general orientations or human modes of being in the world: two radically different ways of conceiving of human nature, the human condition, and how human beings are existentially, temporally, and historically related to reality. In presenting these two essential types, Eliade formulates clear-cut traditional versus modern contrasts and dichotomies: affirming or rejecting the reality of the sacred; affirming the mythic and living myths versus identification with a demythologized reality; devaluing or abolishing time and history and upholding atemporal, nonhistorical, exemplary, mythic and religious models versus identification with the temporal and historical dimensions of existence.

In most of his descriptions and interpretations involving traditional-modern contrasts, Eliade is primarily concerned with communicating the nature, meaning, and significance of irreducibly religious mythic orientations of traditional societies. In some writings, he goes on to establish an encounter, confrontation, and dialogue between traditional and modern perspectives and shows how mythic religious cultures might analyze and critique the existential crises, anxieties, and temporal and historical identifications of modern secular life. In such formulations of traditional-modern encounters, there is little doubt as to Mircea Eliade's personal sympathies and scholarly commitments.

In some passages, Eliade goes beyond this irreducibly religious, mythic perspective of premodern traditional societies. He makes highly normative judgments in which he attacks the modern rejection of the sacred reality and the identification with the temporal and the historical for denying the essential mythic and symbolic structures of reality and even for being inhuman or antihuman. He makes ontological moves in which he affirms a mythic religious orientation, not only as rejecting major characteristics of modernity, but also as more in touch with human nature and the transhistorical nature of reality. Previous chapters have provided scattered illustrations of such Eliadean assertions and judgments. They will be the major focus of our concluding chapters.

This chapter focuses on Eliade's frequent attempts to use his general theory of myth and religion to offer interpretations and make normative judgments about modern human beings, features of the contemporary world, and the nature of reality. Here we find levels of analysis, imaginative constructions, sweeping generalizations, and personal assertions that do not respect defining methodological features of specialized empirical and historical research. Eliade not only goes far beyond criteria of ethnologists and other social science specialists, but he also goes far beyond self-imposed disciplinary boundaries of almost all historians of religions and phenomenologists of religion. Here Eliade is at his most controversial. Such Eliadean formulations have delighted and inspired many supporters, but they have been the source of severe attacks on the part of critics.

For the most part, Eliade's interpretations and claims will be presented without my evaluation. The controversial nature of Eliade's position is usually obvious. In this introductory section, I shall offer a broad formulation as to my general position and evaluation regarding the controversial Eliadean interpretations and judgments that follow. On the one hand, Eliade's interpretations and judgments about modernity, the contemporary world, and reality—based on, but going far beyond his theory of myth and religion as seen in his interpretation of mythic and religious data—are often challenging, insightful, and serve as a catalyst for further reflection, creativity, and "bursting open" some of our self-imposed limitations and provincialism. This will be clear from what follows. On the other hand, the fact that Eliade is willing to take risks and has a remarkable imagination does not free his interpretations and claims from requirements of rigorous scholarly analysis. And to claim, as some supporters have done, that Eliade is a mystic or a shaman or a literary figure who is not bothered by inconsistencies in his writings or with other scholarly criteria does not mean that an assessment of Eliade the scholar, with his own claims to scholarly interpretations and judgments, is inappropriate.

In this regard, it is important to reaffirm that formulations found in this chapter go beyond disciplinary boundaries of the history and phenomenology of religion. Therefore, these interpretations and judgments will be judged negatively by many historians and phenomenologists of religion if they restrict themselves to methods of verification and other scholarly criteria of their disciplines. Scholars endorsing social scientific and other highly specialized approaches to myth and religion will be even more critical. The fact that Eliade's analysis often functions at the levels of metaphysics, ontology, and philosophical anthropology does not free his interpretations and judgments from all scholarly criteria, including the scholarly requirements of those normative disciplines and approaches. Often Eliade's metaphysical and ontological judgments are startling, suggestive, and sources for further reflection. But even on this level of interpretation and judgment, he usually has not developed a rigorous and complete analysis. As he occasionally states, this may be a project for others to undertake.

In addition, in my view, Eliade's controversial interpretations and judgments about the contemporary world and the future of humanity are sometimes downright reactionary. They may appeal to various traditional, hierarchical, scholarly orientations, but in terms of Eliade's own professed ideals and goals, they may fall far short. Eliade insists on the separation of planes of analysis and reality and the primacy of an irreducibly religious framework. But he does not hesitate to make personal and scholarly judgments about economic, political, social, and historical planes of reference. With his focus on religious and mythic cultures, on an irreducibly religious essence of reality, and on the truth of a largely nonhistorical and antihistorical mode of being in the world, Eliade ignores, deemphasizes, and even attacks legitimate economic, social, political, and historical values and struggles. Rather than leading to self-empowerment and liberation, many of his formulations—if left as stated—would reproduce hierarchical structures of domination and leave most human beings imprisoned in structures of powerlessness, poverty, class exploitation, gender and racial oppression.[1]

Therefore, Eliade presents many valuable challenges, insights, interpretations, and judgments that critique real dangers of modernity: Western provincialism and its domination over and denial of the reality of "the other"; tyranny and hegemony of a narrow-focused scientism, technology, instrumental reason, and rationalism; domination and exploitation of nature; fragmentation, alienation, and lack of meaningful relations; lack of awareness of profound symbolic and mythic structures for constituting a meaningful and significant mode of being in the world; repression and denial of the total human being and the diversity of reality; overspecialization and lack of creative synthesis. But even these valuable contributions usually need to be reformulated and integrated and synthesized with nonEliadean approaches to myth, religion, the contemporary world, and reality.

Eliade's approach can reveal hidden mythic and symbolic dimensions of much of contemporary secular life. In this respect, it is imperative, for example, that those struggling for peace with justice not restrict their analysis, methods, and goals to narrow economic or political perspectives. Their greater awareness of mythic and symbolic structures will increase their consciousness, provide more adequate analysis, and may even be invaluable in their struggles to transform the violent and unjust reality of the status quo. But this should not allow one to dismiss or devalue the contributions of nonEliadean modern approaches. Eliade's approach will tell us nothing about the specific, dynamic, economic structures and relations of class domination, monopoly capitalism, imperialism, and commodification defining much of contemporary life. And in some cases Eliade's prescriptions are reactionary and should be rejected. What is needed is for those concerned with peace and justice and with overcoming sexism and racism and environmental devastation not to renounce what is valuable in their own approaches, but instead to incorporate some of Eliade's valuable interpretations and judgments in their enlarged, reformulated, dynamic orientations.

Obviously, such a broad formulation oversimplifies the complexity and often contradictory nature of Eliade's interpretations and judgments about the contemporary world and reality. For example, a common demand by scholars and activists of leftist political and economic orientations is that we must reclaim the suppressed and silenced voices of Third World (African, Asian, Latin American) peoples, indigenous peoples, workers, women, the poor, the oppressed. This is necessary for more authentic, more egalitarian human relations and for the self-empowerment of those who have been marginalized by powerful forces that have "made history." As will be seen, in his attacks on Western provincialism and domination, both by nations and cultures and by scholarly approaches, Eliade also insists on the indispensable value of the voices of the nonWestern "other." He does not endorse a dominant, Western, religious, political, economic, cultural position extolling the superiority of its own positions and justifying its privileges and domination over others. And Eliade is certainly correct that the scholar or activist who claims to care about the plight of displaced peasants in Calcutta or impoverished Puerto Ricans in the South Bronx cannot be ignorant of or simply dismiss the central spiritual and mythic reality in the lives of these people. But my point is that Eliade, in his interpretations and judgments about such contemporary mythic and religious others, also cannot ignore or simply dismiss the centrality of economic, political, and historical factors in determining and structuring their lives. When he dismisses such "nonreligious," "modern" factors as secondary or irrelevant in interpreting the meaning and significance of the phenomena of the other, his interpretations are sometimes limited, at the minimum, and reactionary, at worst.

Since most of Eliade's writings contain numerous reflections on the demythologized contemporary world and its inadequate relation to reality, it would be possible to write an entire book on the topic of this chapter.[2] Therefore, it will be necessary to be selective in focusing on some of the key topics in Eliade's analysis of myth, reality, and the contemporary world. This chapter will examine Eliade's contention that the modern secular world is not what it appears to be. The mythic symbolic sacred is camouflaged and unrecognized in modern profane phenomena. The sacred is concealed in our dreams, yearnings, artistic creations, and in the banalities of everyday life. It is also manifested in hidden and disguised forms on the level of the modern unconscious. It is the unrecognizability of the camouflaged mythic symbolic sacred and the conscious denial of this sacred reality by modern human beings that has contributed to our ignorant and dangerous Western provincialism. Chapter 11 will then examine Eliade's more positive vision: that by recognizing and establishing dynamic relations with the mythic and symbolic structures of the sacred, modern human beings will have the opportunity for cultural, spiritual, and philosophical renewal.

CAMOUFLAGE OF SACRED IN MODERN PROFANE

Mircea Eliade's scholarly writings and journals are full of claims that modern, demythicized, desacralized, temporal, historical reality is not what it appears to be. Usually unrecognized and sometimes consciously denied are mythic and symbolic structures camouflaged and concealed in contemporary secular phenomena: dreams, fantasies, nostalgias, and other creations of the imagination; the unconscious; literary and artistic creations; the banality of ordinary life. Indeed, there is no more frequent theme in Eliade's literary works than the initial unrecognizability and gradual unconcealment of the sacred hidden in modern, secular, temporal, historical, natural, and cultural phenomena and in trivialities and banalities of everyday existence.

In the dialectic of the sacred, we noted "the fundamental idea" developed in *Patterns in Comparative Religion:* "hierophanies, i.e., the manifestation of the sacred in cosmic realities (objects or processes belonging to the profane world), have a paradoxical structure because they *show* and at the same time *camouflage* sacrality." Eliade continues: "By following this dialectics of hierophanies to its ultimate consequences," we could "identify a new camouflage in modern 'cultural' practices, institutions, and creations." After asserting that it is well known that important biological functions, the arts, occupations and trades, and techniques and sciences had a magico-religious function or value at their origin, Eliade concludes that he "wanted to show that even beneath its radically desacralized forms, Western culture camouflages magico-religious meanings that our contemporaries, with the exception of a few poets and artists, do not suspect."[3]

Eliade claims that anything is potentially hierophanic. Therefore, it is not surprising that he finds the camouflage of the dialectic of the sacred almost everywhere. Often he identifies and interprets common aspects of modern life that others regard as completely secular as revealing profound mythic and symbolic sacred structures and meanings. For example, in his "Notebook of a Summer Vacation (1937)," Eliade observes how his fellow travelers experience the passing of borders for the first time and the intensity of the first hours of a journey, of even the most insignificant happenings. He regards this "spectacle" as very reassuring: "The thirst for the fantastic, for daydreaming, for adventure has remained as unquenched as ever in the soul of modern man." "The adventure of which each one dreams, and which for some has begun with the crossing of the border, is, in any event, a desire for transcendence, for an anchoring in significant reality, in certain 'ontological centers.' People want, at all costs, to get out of neuter, non-significant zones. If I had the courage to carry my thought to its logical conclusion, I would say that people today, as always, long to go out of the 'profane,' neuter zones and attain the 'sacred,' that is, ultimate reality."[4] Any social "simplistic explanation" of such human desire does not satisfy Eliade, and he offers one of his highly normative judgments about reality. "It seems to me that in man's general tendency toward the concrete, the sacred—in a word, his ontological instinct— there is betrayed the very meaning of existence: the *unification* (total-ization) of the Cosmos, split in two (microcosm-macrocosm) by Creation. Only the One, the Whole, can be sacred, real."[5]

Although Eliade identifies sacred and mythic structures hidden everywhere in desacralized contemporary phenomena, he emphasizes the difficulty in detecting the camouflage. "In our time religious experience has become unrecognizable, for it is camouflaged in its contrary—in materialism, antireligion, etc. . . ."[6] The sacred is hidden in the desacralized appearance of history and in the historical moment. Eliade asserts that *"coincidentia oppositorum* confronts us today in certain principles of nuclear physics (for example, in Oppenheimer's principle of complementarity), but it is posed more and more insistently in the entire historical moment in which we live: for instance, how is freedom possible in a conditioned universe? How can one live in history without betraying it, without denying it, and nevertheless participating in a transhistorical reality? At bottom, the problem is this: how to recognize the *real* camouflaged in *appearances?*[7]

In uncovering the camouflage of the sacred in the modern profane, "it is necessary to apply a demythologization in reverse. Freud, like Marx, taught us to find the 'profane' in the 'sacred.'" Eliade finds the sacred, implicit and camouflaged, in the profane of the narrative novel, everyday characters, and common adventures. "And that is precisely what is significant in the situation of modern man: he satisfies his nonexistent religious life (nonexistent on the conscious level) by the imaginary universes of literature and art. And it is just as significant for literary critics who find religious significance in profane works."[8]

The sacred and mythic are camouflaged in the banalities of everyday contemporary life. Eliade compares this with the traditional Japanese tea ceremony which —"like all other 'paths' *(do):* painting, poetry, floral art, calligraphy, archery, etc.—also constitutes a spiritual technique, for it places he who practices it in a 'nirvanic' state in his everyday life." After providing some of the Japanese Buddhist context and how "the most natural and insignificant gestures become soterial actions," Eliade concludes with the contemporary character of such conceptions and techniques. "It has never been more essential than it is today to reveal the transhistorical meaning and importance that is hidden in the depths of an existence condemned to be carried out *exclusively* in immanent and opaque banality. Its spiritual and religious significance, and thus the 'salvational' message of all experience, is camouflaged in the profane, in the flow of daily activities. To discover a transhistorical significance in them would be to decode them, to decipher the message they conceal." The sacred is always hidden behind "the mask" of the profane, but today it is especially difficult to recognize this dialectic of the sacred. Today "the majority of contemporary religious currents insist on the necessity of accepting Nature, Life, and History such as we find them, and thus of looking for our own accomplishment—or our salvation, or our deliverance, or our beatitude—*in this world.* This is just exactly the role that has fallen to the tea ceremony, and to other Japanese 'arts.'"[9]

One of the keys to Eliade's claim that he can recognize and decipher camouflaged sacred manifestations hidden in the modern profane is the universal nature, meaning, and significance he grants to mythic and symbolic initiatory structures. Mythic and ritual structures of initiation are central to his interpretations of all traditional societies. He also claims that mythic, symbolic, initiatory structures appear in the lives of contemporary persons because initiation is constitutive of the human mode of being in world, traditional or modern. In our age of radical desacralization, it might appear that "initiatory scenarios survive only in oneiric and artistic realms." But Eliade does not believe that they only survive there. "If one agrees with what I've called the 'dialectic of the camouflaging of the sacred in the profane,' one must also admit another possibility: The initiatory phenomenon could well be perpetuated in our time, before our eyes, but in other forms, so well camouflaged in the 'profane' that it would be impossible for us to recognize them as such."[10]

Eliade's submits that "initiation is so closely linked to the mode of being of human existence that a considerable number of modern man's acts and gestures continue to repeat initiatory scenarios." "For every human existence is formed by a series of ordeals, by repeated experience of 'death' and 'resurrection.' And this is why, in a religious perspective, existence is established by initiation; it could almost be said that, in so far as human existence is fulfilled, it is itself an initiation." Eliade continues with one of his controversial claims: "In short, the majority of men 'without religion' still hold to pseudo religions and degenerated mythologies. There is nothing surprising in this, for, as we saw, profane man is the descendant of *homo religiosus* and he cannot wipe out his own history—that is, the behavior of his religious ancestors which has made him what he is today."[11]

To provide but one of many illustrations, Eliade interprets fairy tales as repeating, on an imaginary plane and by nonmythic means, "the exemplary initiation scenario." If the tale "represents an amusement or an escape, it does so only for the banalized consciousness, and particularly for that of modern man; in the deep psyche initiation scenarios preserve their seriousness and continue to transmit their message, to produce mutations." "Today we are beginning to realize that what is called 'initiation' coexists with the human condition, that every existence is made up of an unbroken series of 'ordeals,' 'deaths,' and 'resurrections,' whatever be the terms that modern language uses to express these originally religious experiences."[12]

Eliade's writings contain numerous interpretations of the survivals and camouflages of myths and other religious phenomena in the modern profane.[13] Many modern nationalistic histories and other political ideologies uphold mythic structures of the prestige of the noble origin and the return to origins, as well as eschatological and millennialist structures. Mythical structures are perpetuated by the mass media in mythical themes in comic strips and detective novels, the mythicization of public figures, and contemporary cultural images of success. There are many "myths of the elite," as seen in myths of the artist and writer and of artistic and literary creation.

As was seen, in his autobiographical reflections, literary works, and scholarly interpretations, Eliade is obsessed with the mythic theme of the need to escape from temporal and historical existence. In interpreting mythic survivals, "it is especially the 'escape from Time' brought about by reading—most effectively by novel reading—that connects the function of literature with that of mythologies." The time that a modern person "lives" when reading a novel is not the same as the mythic time reenacted by the traditional religious person "living the myth." "But in both cases alike, one 'escapes' from historical and personal time and is submerged in a time that is fabulous and trans-historical." Even though "the novelist employs a time that is *seemingly historical,*" Eliade asserts that, more strongly than in the other arts, "we feel in literature a revolt against historical time, the desire to attain to other temporal rhythms than that in which we are condemned to live and work." In this desire to transcend personal historical time, the modern person "preserves at least some residues of 'mythological behavior.'"[14]

We conclude this section on the camouflage of the sacred in the modern profane with a brief consideration of an illustration that appears in several of Eliade's writings: the sacred and the modern artist.[15] Living in the modern world, artists have found it impossible to express their experiences through traditional artistic and religious language.

"This is not to say that the 'sacred' has completely disappeared in modern art. But it has become *unrecognizable;* it is camouflaged in forms, purposes and meanings which are apparently 'profane.'"[16]

Eliade finds that some of the characteristics of modern art can be given religious interpretations based on hidden mythic and symbolic structures. The "destruction of the language of art" and the sense of destroying all forms and structures need not be interpreted simply as an expression of the chaos, alienation, and meaninglessness of the modern world. What may seem little more than nihilistic expressions of secular modern life may conceal deeper mythic and symbolic structures, meanings, and significance. In much of modern art, there is more than simple destruction; there is a reversion to chaos in which the artist seems to be searching for something new that hasn't yet been expressed. Comparing the attitude of many modern artists to archaic mythic religion, Eliade senses that this destruction of artistic language may be the first phase of a complex process of recreation of a new universe. Death is precondition for rebirth. The destruction of the old world is necessary in order to create a new, more meaningful world. In this regard, some creations by modern artists may anticipate radically new, cultural creations.[17]

By focusing on Brancusi, Chagall, nonfigurative painters, and other modern artists, Eliade interprets the destruction of artistic languages and forms as revealing a desire to return to a primordial plentitude; a desire to rediscover and experience the deeper structures underlying phenomenal appearances. In this he sees similarities between modern art and archaic cosmic religion. And by using initiatory and other mythic and symbolic structures, Eliade interprets "the end of the world" in modern art not as a final nihilistic phase but as a first phase necessary for rebirth, renewal, and new creativity. Eliade compares the modern artists' "destruction of worlds" (traditional artistic worlds) to "primitive" and paleo-Oriental ritual scenarios of the need for the periodic destruction and recreation of the cosmos. "The *religious* necessity for the abolition of old, tired, inauthentic forms ('illusory,' 'idolatrous'). All this corresponds in a certain sense to the death of God proclaimed by Nietzsche. But there is more: the passion for matter resembles the pre-Mosaic cosmic religiosity. The modern artist who can no longer believe in the Judeo-Christian tradition ('God is dead') is returning, without noticing it, to 'paganism,' to cosmic hierophanies: substance as such incarnates and manifests the sacred."[18]

THE MODERN UNCONSCIOUS

Mircea Eliade often asserts that "modern man's only real contact with cosmic sacrality is effected by the unconscious, whether in his dreams and his imaginative life or in the creations that arise out of the unconscious (poetry, games, spectacles, etc.)." [T]oday religious behavior and the structures of the sacred—divine figures, exemplary acts, etc.—are found again at the deepest levels of the psyche, in the 'unconscious,' on the planes of dream and imagination."[19]

Eliade frequently uses the mythic theme of a "fall," not only as an essential structure for grasping the fundamental mode of being of *homo religiosus,* but also for understanding the mode of being of modern human beings. The modern human condition is sometimes described as a "second fall." In describing the religious mythic life-world, the *Lebenswelt* of *homo religiosus,* the fall refers to the decisive event in the mythic history that essentially constituted human beings and their relations to the world and to reality as we know them. Sacred mythic histories refer to a prefallen primordial condition that does not resemble our human condition and our human mode of being in the world: an organic wholeness and harmony with nature and cosmos; no experience of ignorance, evil, sin, guilt, or alienation; a mythic sense of primal plentitude and blissful paradise. The fall describes the mythic event through which that primordial plentitude was ruptured and fragmented, and the prefallen paradise was lost. After the fall, beings were constituted as human beings as we know them: limited, finite, ignorant, suffering, alienated, temporal, historical beings. "Religion" really begins with the fall. Through its myths and rituals, religion expresses the desires and nostalgias for that prefallen paradise and means for overcoming our human condition and reconnecting with the sacred.

When Eliade describes modern life as a second fall, he usually refers to the unconscious and its functioning through dreams, nostalgias, fantasies, literary and artistic creativity, and other expressions of the imagination. In terms of mythic consciousness of the original fall, *homo religiosus* of traditional societies consciously experiences the tragic human condition of separation from the primordial plentitude; from the prefallen experience of sacred reality. And traditional religious persons consciously attempt to use transhistorical, exemplary, mythic models and other religious means to overcome their limited, finite, historical, human mode of being in the world. After the second fall, constitutive of the secular mode of being in the world, moderns have lost that consciousness of the sacred. They simply define themselves, on a conscious level, as limited, finite, temporal, historical, alienated, suffering human beings without recourse to transhistorical, atemporal, sacred structures and meanings. In terms of Eliade's ontological moves and normative judgments, the essential mythic symbolic structures, as permanent structures of consciousness, do not disappear. They are constitutive of the human condition as such. But they have "fallen" to the level of the unconscious. Not lived consciously, they are manifested indirectly through dreams and fantasies, through "para-religious" and "pseudo religious" creations, and through all sorts of imaginary phenomena camouflaged in the modern profane. In the modern mode of being in the world, the sacred is hidden but still functioning on the level of the unconscious.

What this means is that the sacred in the modern world is most submerged and hidden; the mythic and religious revelation of reality is most camouflaged. This is evident, in Eliade's general interpretation, when contrasting the level of manifestation of the sacred in traditional and modern human beings. In the universal process of sacralization, the sacred is always camouflaged; at the same time that it shows itself, it conceals itself. That is why even premodern, mythic, religious beings always have a limited consciousness of the sacred reality. After the original fall, human beings no longer have easy access to the sacred. That is why persons in traditional cultures need religion to establish meaningful relations with the sacred reality: truths about ultimate reality communicated through mythic histories and other transhistorical exemplary models; rituals and other means for reenacting mythic truths and other sacred realities; religious specialists who are more conscious of and have greater access to the sacred. In short, religion allows fallen human beings in limited conditioned ways to unconceal camouflages of the sacred in the profane and to gain access to the sacred reality.

With the second fall, sacred realities that are expressed through essential mythic and symbolic structures are "buried" on the level of the unconscious. Moderns are no longer aware of the primordial sacred-profane rupture. They no longer consciously express the need to recognize and reestablish meaningful relations with transcendent sacred structures that have become camouflaged in ordinary, natural, temporal, historical things. Just the opposite: they affirm their humanity and their relations to reality by consciously denying the transcendent sacred. Thus it is in modern secular life, in which human beings consciously identify themselves with the nonsacred, nonmythic, temporal and historical dimensions of existence, that the camouflage and concealment of the sacred is most perfected, most radical, most complete. Sacred, mythic, and symbolic structures—still functioning on the level of the unconscious—are completely reduced to and identified with natural, temporal, historical phenomena; to what, from a conscious religious point of view, is identical with the profane mode of being.

In claiming that the sacred is manifested on the level of the modern unconscious and that the contents and structures of the unconscious exhibit astonishing similarities to the mythic, Eliade does not maintain that the mythic is a "product" of the unconscious. This would be a reductionistic causal explanation. The mythic is an autonomous mode of cognition, an autonomous mode of being in the world. It reveals itself on unconscious and other levels of existence according to its irreducibly mythic structures and meanings.

> Yet the contents and structures of the unconscious are the result of immemorial existential situations, especially of critical situations, and this is why the unconscious has a religious aura. For every existential crisis once again puts in question both the reality of the world and man's presence in the world. This means that the existential crisis is, finally, "religious," since on the archaic levels of culture *being* and *the sacred* are one. As we saw, it is the experience of the sacred that founds the world, and even the most elementary religion is, above all, an ontology. In other words, in so far as the unconscious is the result

of countless existential experiences, it cannot but resemble the various religious universes. For religion is the paradigmatic solution for every existential crisis. It is the paradigmatic solution not only because it can be indefinitely repeated, but also because it is believed to have a transcendental origin and hence is valorized as a revelation received from an *other,* transhuman world.[20]

In this passage, typical of formulations found throughout Eliade's writings, one can detect a possible confusion and a clear ontological move. Eliade qualifies his formulation "on the archaic levels of culture," but he then goes on to make sweeping generalizations and normative judgments about every existential crisis, the sacred, and the unconscious as such. Certainly, for nonreligious nonmythic persons, religion is not "the paradigmatic solution for every existential crisis." Modern nonreligious persons do not accept religion as the paradigmatic solution because of some religious belief in its supernatural origin and transhuman revelation. If they did, they would be religious. Here and elsewhere Eliade makes universal judgments and makes ontological moves based on his assumption that the archaic, mythic, and general religious mode of being reveals essential truths about and essential structures of the unconscious as such, solutions to every fundamental existential crisis, and the nature of reality. Based on such a scholarly orientation, Eliade assumes both that his investigation into the myths, symbols, and images of the sacred will shed light on the structures and functioning of the modern unconscious and that an investigation of the modern, seemingly desacralized unconscious will disclose hidden and camouflaged mythic and other sacred structures and meanings.[21]

The modern unconscious with its hidden sacred structures is not equivalent to mythic religious experience. Modern "private mythologies," as expressed through dreams, fantasies, and the imagination, "never rise to the ontological status of myths, precisely because they are not experienced by the *whole man* and therefore do not transform a particular situation into a situation that is paradigmatic." The unconscious of modern human beings discloses deep meaningful symbols. But *homo religiosus* of traditional societies experiences such symbols in ways that allow for the homologization of diverse planes of existence and the transformation and integration of particular phenomena into unified, coherent, meaningful, religious perspectives. A person "of the premodern societies can attain to the highest spirituality, for, by understanding the symbol, *he succeeds in living the universal.*" For Eliade this "suffices to show in what way the nonreligious man of modern societies is still nourished and aided by the activity of his unconscious, yet without thereby attaining to a properly religious experience and vision of the world."[22]

Eliade uses the symbolism of "the Tree of the World" to distinguish psychological interpretations and the universe of the unconscious, which often has a "religious aura," from irreducibly religious interpretations and the universe of mythic religious phenomena. A psychologist may uncover an image of the tree expressed in dreams, and this may disclose how a person is coping with a deep psychological crisis, but this, by itself, does not constitute a religious experience. In religious experience, there is the revelation of the universal structure of the tree-symbolism: periodic and unending renewal, regeneration, immortality. "But not having been accepted in its symbolic sense, the image of the Tree [in dreams] has not succeeded in revealing the universal, and therefore has not lifted the man up to the plane of the Spirit, as religion, however rudimentary, always does."[23] "The dream image of the Tree was not genuinely religious, because it was manifested *only* on the plane of the unconscious; the symbolism of the Tree of the World was evaluated as religious, because it was manifested on all levels of reality and thus included the transconscious, which was, in fact, that higher consciousness which enabled *homo religiosus* to *unify* the diverse levels of manifestation, thereby experiencing "the totality" and "living the universal."[24]

If the sacred is camouflaged in the modern profane and is usually unrecognizable and if the sacred is manifested in disguised forms on the level of the modern unconscious, then it is a considerable task to identify, decipher, and interpret the meaning and significance of these hidden mythic and symbolic structures. Here Eliade emphasizes the special role of the history and phenomenology of religion in formulating a creative hermeneutics and the need for encounters and dialogues with the nonWestern other, for whom the mythic and sacred is not so hidden and concealed. The need for the renewal of modern human beings through creative hermeneutics, including the dynamic encounter and dialogue with the mythic religious other, will be the major focus of the next chapter.

MODERN WESTERN PROVINCIALISM

Eliade's journals and scholarly writings contain numerous criticisms of the arrogant, ignorant, and dangerous "provincialism" of the modern West. This is a reversal of a typical, Western, condescending attitude in which it is assumed that the nonWestern, premodern "other" is hopelessly provincial (unsophisticated, limited, ignorant, backwards) and incapable of coping with the sophisticated demands of the contemporary world.

Often this modern orientation is used to justify the assumption that only sophisticated, enlightened, Western paradigms, explanations, values, and concerns will enable nonWestern societies, cultures, and economies to move into the twentieth and twenty-first centuries and become participants in shaping the contemporary world. If these "primitive," backward peoples would only stop believing their false, outdated, irrelevant myths, they would be able to relate to contemporary reality. More often there is little need felt to invoke this appearance of concern or ideological benevolence. The modern orientation is used to justify economic, political, cultural, asymmetrical relations of domination and exploitation. Gross inequalities, domestically and globally, reflect the "natural," rational, objective, scientific, technological reality of relations between the modern sophisticated West and the provincial, nonWestern, premodern other.

Eliade reverses all of this. The modern West has defined itself and imprisoned itself within the narrow horizons of temporality, historicism, the economic, the political, the idols of science and rationalism, and demythicized secularism. Eliade usually evaluates modern cultures negatively, describing contemporary phenomena by such terms as "impoverished" and "degenerate." What is desperately needed is a deprovincialization of Western cultures. In order to cope with contemporary realities, deal with existential and historical crises, and experience the deepest transhistorical, universal, human reality, we must transcend the present cultural provincialism of the modern West.[25]

In addition to scholarly formulations of Western provincialism and the need for deprovincializing cultural renewal, this is one of the most common themes in Eliade's literary works. He writes of temporally and historically defined, seemingly sophisticated bureaucrats and other modern Western characters, who are gradually exposed as narrow, unsophisticated, and provincial, since they are unable to recognize and understand the deeper, wider universe of myth, symbol, and the sacred. By contrast, characters who initially appear simple, unsophisticated, strange, and provincial in terms of a modern scale of values, prove to be more in touch with the enigmas, contradictions, and signs of a deeper, more meaningful, mythic spiritual reality; they often elude or overcome the oppressive, nonmythic, desacralized structures of domination of an impoverished, provincial, modern plane of reference.[26]

Although Eliade repeatedly claims that the history of religions, through creative hermeneutics, offers the best possibility for overcoming such Western provincialism and for realizing a cultural renewal, many of his passages express a sobering pessimistic attitude about whether this will be accomplished. Once again, Eliade is not some premodern romantic, who identifies uncritically with some joyful optimism of mythic cosmic religion. His personality is complex, he goes though tremendous mood swings, and he frequently describes his outlook in such terms as "melancholy" and "despair."

In 1960, Eliade writes: "After a long mythological period, and a short historical period, we are on the threshold of a biological (economic) period. Man will be reduced to the condition of a termite, an ant. It is impossible for me to believe that this phase will succeed. But for several generations, or, perhaps, several thousand years, men will live like ants."[27] Four years later, he records how "I find myself suddenly sad, depressed: I no longer know which way to look for courage. *Whatever happens, we are lost.* Our world, my world, is irremediably condemned." After noting the rapid growth in China's population, Eliade continues: "There will be born another world which could be just as creative and interesting as the one that came into being in Greece around the seventh century B.C. But it is no less true that *our world* will disappear, and in a manner perhaps even more tragic than the way the worlds of the Near East and Greece disappeared." He can "imagine Europe inhabited by Asiatic or African populations; intelligent and cultured people walking in the old cities or among the ruins, without even looking at them, without understanding them (like the Anglo-Indians of Calcutta who would pass Hindu temples every day without giving them a glance, from scorn or from hate)."[28]

Here and in other passages Eliade seems to identify with Western culture and civilization and is depressed over the terrifying and dreaded image that the future belongs to nonWestern peoples. Focusing on these passages, one could conclude that Eliade, although in disagreement with much of the modern orientation, is at heart Eurocentric. This contrasts with his more frequent formulations of the provincialism and decadence of Western culture and the need for its transcendence through the embracing of nonWestern mythic and spiritual worlds of meaning.[29]

In a dramatic controversial passage reflecting Eliade's personal and scholarly attitudes toward history seen in chapter 8, Eliade writes:

> Today, I'm thinking of this detail: *here* too, I mean in this eventual catastrophic disappearance of humanity, the Jews were the precursors. The millions of Jews killed or burned in the Nazi concentration camps constitute the avant-garde of humanity which is waiting to be incinerated by the will of "History." Cosmic cataclysms (floods, earthquakes, fires) are also known in other religions. The cataclysm provoked by man, as a *historical being,* is the contribution of our civilization. The destruction, it is true, will be possible only thanks to the extraordinary development of Western science. But the *cause or pretext* of the cataclysm is found in man's decision to "make history." Now, one must remember, "History" is the creation of the Judeo-Christian tradition.[30]

When Eliade is feeling most in despair about the prospects for overcoming Western provincialism and accomplishing a cultural renewal, his attitude is similar to his journal entries and scholarly interpretations of the tragic history of Romanian and other eastern European peasants. Romanian peasants had their mythic cosmic religion, but they were still "condemned by history," a history not of their own making. They found themselves surrounded by more powerful political and military forces. They could use their myths, symbols, and rituals to defend themselves against the "terror of history," but this did not allow them to avoid being invaded and conquered by outsiders. At most, they could give mythic and spiritual meaning to the powerlessness, suffering, and tragedy of their historical condition.

Similarly, Eliade believes that the archaic and nonWestern others, with their myths, symbols, and worlds of spiritual meaning, offer the modern West possibilities for creative dialogue, cultural renewal, more adequate ways for dealing with existential and historical crises, and openings to a greater reality. But Eliade knows that the archaic and nonWestern others have been repeatedly and tragically invaded, conquered, colonized, and exploited by the historical, political, economic, military, scientific, modern West. The contemporary world is defined by asymmetrical power relations that destroy the mythic religious cultures of the other rather than changing a provincial West. Will modern human beings listen and learn from the archaic and nonWestern voices before it is too late? Eliade holds out the hope, but one often has the sense of a troubling pessimism about the future of the West and of humanity.

Eliade is usually not so pessimistic. Most often, he simply presents the extreme urgency of the present situation and the great opportunities for cultural renewal without minimizing his negative evaluations of the modern mode of being in the world. He sometimes suggests that prospects for creative encounter and cultural renewal may be realized, not because moderns will suddenly become aware of the errors and dangers of their nonmythic desacralized approaches, but rather because they will have no choice. Like it or not, historical developments will force Westerners to relate more authentically to Asian and other nonWestern cultures and to redefine themselves as global beings.[31]

And in a minority of passages, Eliade seems full of optimism, envisioning a glowing future of spiritual creativity and cultural renewal. Mythic religious human beings will be spiritually centered: transcending both the provincialism of secular modernity and outdated religious forms; dealing with their particular, historical, cultural, existential crises in terms of transhistorical, atemporal, universal, exemplary models, structures, and values; conceiving of themselves as global beings, as part of a universal spiritual history, and as creators of a new humanism; experiencing the deepest structures of human nature and reality and opening out to the universal values of the Spirit. We examine this potential for mythic spiritual creativity and cultural renewal in the final chapter.

NOTES

1. There is a tradition of European intellectuals who have romanticized and idealized "the primitive" or "the native," often accompanying this with a nostalgia for that lost premodern mode of being in the world. But such intellectuals—even if unintentionally—have tended to reinforce structures of domination and, in any case, have done little toward the greater empowerment and self-determination of these "more authentic," "more human," "fortunate," oppressed peoples.

2. In *Sacred and Profane,* Eliade writes: "A whole volume could well be written on the myths of modern man, on the mythologies camouflaged in the plays that he enjoys, in the books that he reads" (p. 205). Eliade goes on to mention the mythical motifs in movies, the mythological function of reading, the mythological structures of political ideologies and psychoanalysis, and other illustrations to substantiate his claim: "Strictly speaking, the great majority of the irreligious are not liberated from religious behavior, from theologies and mythologies" (pp. 205-6).

3. *Autobiography 2,* pp. 84-85.

4. Ibid., p. 17.

5. Ibid., pp. 17-18.

6. *Journal 3,* p. 149.

7. *Autobiography 2,* p. 198. See also ibid., pp. 152-53.

8. *No Souvenirs,* pp. 229-30. In *No Souvenirs* Eliade writes of "Marxist or Freudian 'explanations': they are true if they are considered as imaginary universes." "All these global and systematic interpretations, in reality, constitute mythological creations, highly useful for understanding the world; but they are not, as their authors think, 'scientific explanations'" (p. 291).

9. *Journal 3,* pp. 133-36.

10. Ibid., pp. 227-28.

11. *Sacred and Profane,* pp. 208-9. In *Journal 1,* Eliade submits that "initiation is equivalent of philosophy." Initiation represents "death" to profane experience and access to metaphysical knowledge. Obstetric symbolism is found in both initiatory rituals and Socratic maieutics. In Husserl's

phenomenology, the "natural attitude" is the profane preinitiatory condition, and the phenomenological reduction, allowing for access to the real, can be compared with means of initiation through which "one penetrates into the sacred plane; that is, the spirit gains access to the absolute (= the real)" (p. 203). See also "Initiation and the Modern World," in *Quest,* p. 125; *Rites and Symbols of Initiation,* p. 114.

    12. *Myth and Reality,* pp. 201-2. In *Ordeal by Labyrinth* and other writings, Eliade uses the mythic and symbolic image of a "labyrinth" as a model for describing his personal life, his scholarly pursuits, and the human mode of being in general. A human existence involves a "wandering in a labyrinth," really in many labyrinths; a journey marked by the need to pass through many ordeals, often by means of mythic and symbolic structures of initiation. See, for example, *Ordeal by Labyrinth,* esp. pp. 185-89; *Journal 1,* pp. 22-23, 59; *No Souvenirs,* pp. 74-75, 97; *Journal 3,* p. 34. See also David Carrasco, "Prologue: Promise and the Labyrinth," in *Waiting for the Dawn: Mircea Eliade in Perspective,* ed. David Carrasco and Jane Marie Law (Boulder, Colo.: University of Colorado Press, 1991), pp. xv-xx.

    13. See, for example, "Survivals and Camouflages of Myths," in *Myth and Reality,* pp. 162-93; and "The Myths of the Modern World," in *Myths, Dreams and Mysteries,* pp. 23-38. Typical of claims found throughout Eliade's writings is the following: "cosmic rhythms, although ignored or considered negligible by men who want to be 'modern,' end up reappearing by way of the imagination" *(Journal 3,* p. 204).

    14. *Myth and Reality,* p. 192.

    15. E.g., see Mircea Eliade, "The Sacred and the Modern Artist," *Criterion* 4 (1965): 22-24; *Myth and Reality,* pp. 72-74, 187-93; *No Souvenirs,* pp. 15, 218-19; "Brancusi and Mythology," in *Ordeal by Labyrinth,* pp. 193-201; "Crisis and Renewal in History of Religions," *History of Religions* 5 (1965): 11-12 (whilch is reprinted in *Quest,* pp. 65-66); "Cultural Fashions and History of Religions," in *Occultism, Witchcraft, and Cultural Fashions,* pp. 1-3, which is reproduced from *The History of Religions: Essays on the Problem of Understanding,* ed. Joseph M. Kitagawa (Chicago: University of Chicago Press, 1967); *Quest,* pp. 123-25. Several of the above articles and other relevant selections are reproduced in Eliade, *Symbolism, the Sacred, and the Arts.*

    16. "The Sacred and the Modern Artist," p. 22.

    17. See *Myth and Reality,* pp. 72-74.

    18. *No Souvenirs,* pp. 218-19.

    19. Ibid., pp. 77 n. 1 and 201. Since Eliade's scholarly books contain many studies of mythic and symbolic structures of the sacred as found in the unconscious, both in traditional and modern societies, I shall present a summarizing formulation in this section without much documentation.

    20. *Sacred and Profane,* p. 210.

21. E.g., Eliade writes in Journal *1:* "The reason I am so eager to decipher symbols and specify the modalities of these [traditional, religious, mythic] societies is because I rediscover in them, diminished and 'interiorized,' all the nostalgias and enthusiasms I find in modern man" (p. 24).

22. *Sacred and Profane,* pp. 211-13.

23. *Myths, Dreams and Mysteries,* pp. 18-20.

24. Allen, *Structure and Creativity in Religion,* p. 219.

25. See *Autobiography 2,* pp. 108 and 166 for typical expressions of Eliade's emphasis on modern, Western provincialism and the need to overcome this provincialism through cultural renewal. Eliade makes such contentions in *No Souvenirs* and other journal entries. They are prominent in several of the chapters in *Quest.* They are also central to Eliade's prefaces and forewords to *Myths, Dreams and Mysteries, Mephistopheles and the Androgyne,* and *Images and Symbols,* and to chapters in *Eternal Return* and other scholarly works.

26. For example, see Mircea Eliade, *The Old Man and the Bureaucrats,* trans. Mary Park Stevenson (Chicago: University of Chicago Press, 1988); Mircea Eliade, "The Cape" and "Nineteen Roses," in *Youth Without Youth and Other Novellas.* ed. Matei Calinescu and trans. Mac Linscott Ricketts (Columbus, Ohio: Ohio State University Press, 1988).

27. *No Souvenirs,* p. 89. Eliade even interprets some of the significance of recent Western discoveries, translations, and fascination with Egyptian, Tantra, Taoist, Iranian, and other esoteric texts in a pessimistic manner. In *Journal 3,* in commenting on this "process of 'de-occulting' esoteric and initiatory traditions," Eliade observes that traditionally "esoteric texts are only brought to light, and only become accessible to the public, to all publics, on the eve of great historical cataclysms, when the 'end of the world,' is near, the end of *our* world, of course" (p. 154).

28. *No Souvenirs,* p. 222.

29. One can understand why Edward Said in his critique of Orientalism and other scholars maintain that what appears to be an inclusivistic, universalistic approach often disguises an essentially Western project, with hidden agendas, and with the "embracing" and redefining of the other in ways that reinforce the superiority and dominance of the West. Indeed, there is a long intellectual and cultural tradition of romanticizing and elevating the other in such ways that one need not relate authentically to the reality of the other. My own view is that while Eliade's attitude is often complex and contradictory, he usually has a positive attitude toward the archaic and nonWestern other.

30. *No Souvenirs,* pp. 145-46. What makes this pessimistic vision of the future even more controversial is not only the use of the Nazi Holocaust but its formulation in such a way that anti-Semites, at least, could read this as stating or implying that the Jews themselves created the preconditions of their own destruction and of the future destruction of humanity.

31. E.g., in *Myths, Dreams and Mysteries,* Eliade maintains that "Western culture will be in danger of a decline into a sterilising provincialism if it despises or neglects the dialogue with the other cultures. Hermeneutics is Western man's response—the only intelligent response possible—to the solicitations of contemporary history, to the fact that the West is forced (one might almost say, condemned) to this encounter and confrontation with the cultural values of 'the others'" (p. 8).

CHAPTER 11

Cultural and Spiritual Renewal

The mythic and symbolic sacred is camouflaged and unrecognized in the modern profane. This unrecognizability and the conscious rejection of the sacred by modern culture have resulted in impoverished dangerous forms of Western provincialism. The West is desperately in need of renewal. Eliade proposes that moderns can achieve this cultural, spiritual, and philosophical renewal through creative hermeneutics, by rediscovering essential symbolic and mythic structures, and through a creative encounter and dialogue with the mythic sacred other.

THE RENEWAL OF MODERN HUMAN BEINGS

Not only does Eliade contend that modern, Western, historicistic and other reductionistic approaches are inadequate for grasping the intentionality, deeper meaning, and ultimate significance of irreducibly mythic and irreducibly religious data; he also contends that modern human beings and their Western cultures are in a condition of the most severe crisis. These two contentions are interrelated. As a reflection of the overall modern desacralized orientation, scholarly approaches that are inadequate for deciphering profound mythic, symbolic, religious structures and meanings exhibit the very same characteristics that define the ways moderns have repressed and denied much of their humanity and cannot solve their basic existential and historical crises. Both modern human beings, in general, and modern scholarly approaches, in particular, are in need of radical renewal.

Creative Hermeneutics

Mircea Eliade maintains that the history of religions has a special role, even the most important role, to play in challenging Western provincialism and serving as an indispensable means for cultural renewal. The following passage is typical of Eliade's formulations:

> I see the history of religions as a total discipline. I understand now that the encounters, facilitated by depth psychology, with the stranger within, with that which is foreign, exotic, archaic in ourselves, on the one hand—and, on the other, the appearance of Asia and of exotic or "primitive" groups in history—are cultural moments which find their ultimate meaning only from the perspective of the history of religions. The hermeneutic necessary for the revelation of the meanings and the messages hidden in myths, rites, symbols, will also help us to understand both depth psychology and the historical age into which we are entering and in which we will be not only surrounded but also dominated by the "foreigners," the non-Occidentals. It will be possible to decipher the "Unconscious," as well as the "Non-Western World," through the hermeneutic of the history of religions.[1]

Similarly, in the foreword to *Mephistopheles and the Androgyne*, Eliade submits: "Hermeneutics—the science of interpretation—is the Western man's reply—the only intelligent reply—to the demands of contemporary history, to the fact that the West is committed (one might be tempted to say 'condemned') to a confrontation with the cultural values of the 'others.' Now in this present situation, hermeneutics will find its most valuable ally in the history of religions." When the history of religions assumes its proper hermeneutical role, it will allow us to recognize and interpret the deep structures and meanings of the "strange worlds" of two "others": the world of the unconscious—which is the plane of camouflaged mythic and sacred manifestation in modern consciousness—and the world of mythic, symbolic, sacred phenomena of archaic, Asian, and other non-Western cultures.[2]

The true, indispensable method of the history and phenomenology of religion is "creative hermeneutics. As was seen in Eliade's attacks on reductionism and in his distinguishing historical explanation from the interpretation of meaning, Eliade insists that the most important, antireductionistic, hermeneutical work must be done by the history of religion. Creative hermeneutics "will finally be recognized as the royal road of the history of religions." What is needed is a "total hermeneutics." Historians of religion have been "timid" at the very moment when the history of religions should be exemplary in the interpretation of the deep mythic symbolic meaning of "the other." Only the historian of religions can do this hermeneutical work "for only he is prepared to understand and appreciate the complexity of his documents." The road to creative synthesis leads through such hermeneutical work.[3]

In "Crisis and Renewal in the History of Religions" and in several other works, Eliade focuses on the modern crisis, provincialism, and need for renewal in his discipline. There is a connection between this disciplinary crisis and the crisis of the West and the contemporary world. Because historians of religion have been timid and have often accepted or not challenged the assumptions, paradigms, perspectives, and explanations of the modern, "scientific," historicistic, reductionistic approaches to myth and religion, they have abdicated their primary indispensable role. They have not provided irreducibly religious interpretations, have shied away from bold interpretations and creative syntheses, and have not played their proper role of transforming and enlarging consciousness and stimulating cultural renewal.

The primary justification Eliade gives for his claim that the history of religions is best equipped—or even only equipped—for this hermeneutical work of interpreting the meaning of "the other" is, not unexpectedly, the following: the hidden, camouflaged, and "foreign" other is a mythic, symbolic, spiritual creation and can only be understood from an irreducibly religious perspective. In trying to understand the spiritualities of Asia and the archaic world, Westerners must engage in a genuine and fruitful dialogue that "cannot be limited to empirical and utilitarian language. A true dialogue must deal with the central values in the cultures of the participants. Now, to understand these values rightly, it is necessary to know their religious sources. For, as we know, non-European cultures, both oriental and primitive, are still nourished by a rich religious soil. This is why we believe that the

History of Religions is destined to play an important role in contemporary cultural life." At this historical moment, how are we "to assimilate *culturally* the spiritual universes that Africa, Oceania, Southeast Asia open to us? All these spiritual universes have a religious origin and structure. If one does not approach them in the perspective of the History of Religions, they will disappear as spiritual universes." They "will not be grasped as spiritual creations; they will not enrich Western and world culture."[4]

This hermeneutical work is not some static, one-way interpretation of mythic symbolic structures and meanings of others. Modern human beings, their cultures, and the interpreters themselves will be profoundly changed by creative hermeneutics. A creative hermeneutics is "among the living sources of a culture. For, in short, every culture is constituted by a series of interpretations and revalorizations of its 'myths' or its specific ideologies. It is not only the creators *stricto sensu* who reassess the primordial visions and who reinterpret the fundamental ideas of a culture; it is also the 'hermeneuts.'" Hermeneutics leads to the creation of new cultural values. A "creative hermeneutics unveils significations that one did not grasp before, or puts them in relief with such vigor that after having assimilated this new interpretation the consciousness is no longer the same." "In the end, the creative hermeneutics *changes* man; it is more than instruction, it is also a spiritual technique susceptible of modifying the quality of existence itself. This is true above all for the historico-religious hermeneutics."[5] In this hermeneutical work of attempting to understand the existential situations expressed in the mythic religious documents of the other, "the historian of religions will inevitably attain to a deeper knowledge of man. It is on the basis of such a knowledge that a new humanism, on a world-wide scale, could develop."[6]

This hermeneutical work of cultural renewal will be divided into two interrelated parts of the same overall creative hermeneutics. First, creative hermeneutics will allow modern human beings to uncover and understand mythic and symbolic structures that are already "buried" in their long "forgotten" spiritual history and in the unconscious of contemporary secular persons. Second, creative hermeneutics will allow moderns to engage in the confrontation, encounter, and dialogue with the mythic, religious, nonWestern "other."

Rediscovering Symbolic and Mythic Structures

This entire book has focused on Eliade's many attempts to identify, unconceal, and interpret the nature, meaning, and significance of mythic and other religious phenomena. This section will only add some of his hermeneutical claims that modern, secular human beings have "forgotten" or are incapable of recognizing mythic symbolic structures that are already "there" in their spiritual histories and present unconscious. Moderns are a result of such past spiritual histories—a human cultural history of transhistorical essential mythic and symbolic structures for dealing with "boundary situations" and the deepest existential crises—and of the functioning of the mythic and symbolic structures of their unconscious. But imprisoned in the limited historical and temporal horizon of the modern mode of being, they are not aware of this. Through a creative hermeneutics, modern consciousness can be stimulated to overcome its "amnesia," recognize what has been forgotten but remains at the foundation of constituted consciousness and being, and provide the means for cultural renewal and a deeper understanding of true human nature and the nature of reality.[7]

Eliade maintains that "given the nature of the documents with which he works, the historian of religions is aware that his exegesis can eventually stimulate, through a curious process of anamnesis the creative faculties of all those who passionately wish to know what the human spirit is capable of."[8] In chapter 3, we saw Matei Calinescu's distinction of the more sceptical and agnostic "unknowable" from Eliade's "unrecognizable" as a variant of the Platonic anamnesis, in which knowledge, in principle, is accessible to those who can recognize or "remember" it. In his analysis of Eliade's "Nineteen Roses," Calinescu states that the central question of hermeneutics is linked with the broad question of memory as a way to mythical truth. He claims that in "Nineteen Roses" Eliade comes closest to presenting in narrative terms a program and methodology for reading the signs and symbolic images that communicate the sense of transcendence and can enlarge our modern consciousness. "The program can be described in one world—anamnesis. Anamnesis, literally recollection or remembering (we recall that Plato used it to denote the soul's *reminiscence* of the world of Ideas), is defined by one of the characters as 'a mode of giving meaning to the events of one's life.'" After describing Eliade's literary techniques of anamnesis, such as attempts "to translate the dialectic of mythical unrecognizability into concrete, situational symmetries and oppositions," and the narrative unfolding of anamnesis in accord with the essential structures of initiation, Calinescu concludes that Eliade's fantastic of interpretation is a hermeneutic of trust and optimism. "Eliade's fantastic of interpretation persuades the reader to look at images, symbols, metaphors, stories, or inventions as possible bearers of epiphanies or remembrances. By means of these devices the imagination breaks out of the amnesia in which modernity has trapped it to recall and revive lost worlds of meaning. The larger message of Eliade's fantastic prose is, in brief, that interpretation remains our best hope for an anamnesis of mythical truth."[9]

In his study of "Symbolism of the 'Centre,'" Eliade discusses how the history of religions could lead to a modern awakening, a renewal of consciousness, of archaic and other essential symbolic structures, whether still living or fossilized in religious traditions. What is needed is a more spiritual hermeneutical technique. "One could equally call this a new *maieutics*. Just as Socrates, according to the *Theaetetus* (149 a, 161 e), acted on the mind obstetrically, bringing to birth thoughts it did not know it contained, so the history of religions could bring forth a new man, more authentic and more complete: for, through the study of the religious traditions, modern man would not only rediscover a kind of archaic behaviour, he would also become conscious of the spiritual riches implied in such behaviour."[10]

Eliade continues: "This maieutics effected with the aid of religious symbolism would also help to rescue modern man from his cultural provincialism and, above all, from his historical and existentialist relativism." Nonhistorical symbolic structures already exist in modern human beings; "it is only necessary to reactivate them and bring them to the level of consciousness. By regaining awareness of his own anthropocosmic symbolism—which is only one variety of the archaic symbolism—modern man will obtain a new existential dimension, totally unknown to present-day existentialism and historicism: this is an authentic and major mode of being, which defends man from nihilism and historical relativism without thereby taking him out of history. For history itself will one day be able to find its true meaning: that of the epiphany of a glorious and absolute human condition."[11]

In the controversial concluding section to his study of "mythologies of memory and forgetting," Eliade focuses on anamnesis and the modern passion for historiography. He uses his interpretation of traditional mythic treatments of memory and forgetting to disclose the deeper meaning and significance of this modern secular phenomenon. Eliade is concerned not with investigations into the meaning of history but rather with historiography itself: "the *endeavor to preserve the memory* of contemporary events and the desire to know the past of humanity as accurately as possible." From the nineteenth century on, historiography has played such a prominent role that it "seems as if Western culture were making a prodigious effort of historiographic *anamnesis.*" With such a widening of the historical horizon, the modern "goal is no less than to revive the *entire past of humanity.*"[12]

Eliade finds much that is encouraging in this modern emphasis on historiography, not only in undermining Western cultural provincialism, but also "through this historiographic *anamnesis* man enters deep into himself. If we succeed in understanding a contemporary Australian, or his homologue, a paleolithic hunter, we have succeeded in 'awakening' in the depths of our being the existential situation and the resultant behavior of a prehistoric humanity." Such a historiographic anamnesis "finds expression in the discovery of our solidarity with these vanished or peripheral peoples" and in a genuine recovery of the past. This historiographic anamnesis, opening us to other perspectives, can be viewed as a way that moderns, unconsciously, defend themselves against the pressure of contemporary history, but "in the case of modern man there is something more. His historiographic horizon being as wide as it has become, he is able, through *anamnesis,* to discover cultures that, though they 'sabotaged History,' were prodigiously creative."[13]

This historiographical anamnesis of the modern Western world is only beginning. Though on a secular plane, without invoking religious myths or practices, this historiographic anamnesis continues a profound religious evaluation of memory and forgetting. There is this common element: "the importance of precise and total recollection of the past. In the traditional societies it is recollection of *mythical events;* in the modern West it is recollection of *all that took place in historical Time.* The difference is too obvious to require definition. But both types of *anamnesis* project man out of his 'historical moment.' And true historiographic *anamnesis* opens, too, on a primordial Time, the Time in which men established their cultural behavior patterns, even though believing that they were revealed to them by Supernatural Beings."[14]

This interpretation of Eliade's creative hermeneutics, as consisting of such a rediscovery of mythic and symbolic sacred structures that then serve as the basis for cultural renewal, is both instructive but also potentially misleading. There is certainly the sense in Eliade's scholarly writings that the sacred is present, but buried and unrecognized, in our spiritual history and in our unconscious. Hermeneutics allows us to overcome our amnesia. The history of religions can stimulate our imagination, enlarge our consciousness, and allow us to recall and recognize the camouflaged sacred. The unconcealed sacred can then serve as the indispensable basis for modern Western and global renewal. In Eliade's theory of myth and religion, in his hermeneutical framework for interpreting mythic religious structures and meanings, and in his understanding of the specific orientation of *homo religiosus,* there is the sense that scholarly understanding, as well as spiritual growth, consists in remembering and recognizing what is already there but has been forgotten. Trapped in the conditionings of the profane, human beings forget the mythic sacred essence that precedes their temporal historical existence. Modern persons have lost awareness of nontemporal nonhistorical structures that are permanent essential structures of consciousness. Although the sacred and its universal mythic and symbolic structures constitute the human condition as such, modern Western cultures have forgotten this and seek, unsuccessfully, to resolve their deep existential and historical crises within the nonmythic nonsacred horizon of historical temporality.

The reason such an interpretation can be misleading is that it may convey a strong, philosophically unacceptable sense of passivity on the part of constituting subjects. In his formulations of the dialectic of the sacred and in his theory of symbolism and myth, Eliade contributes to this unacceptable impression that sacred signs, images, symbols, and myths are just "there," waiting to be unconcealed, uncamouflaged, accurately remembered. As a nonhistorical atemporal "given," the sacred needs to be recognized, not created and constituted, by us. The sacred "shows itself." Modern human beings have forgotten this, and, misled by its camouflage in the profane, fail to recognize the sacred present in their unconscious and in contemporary phenomena.

Nevertheless, as was seen, a more adequate interpretation of the rediscovery of mythic and symbolic structures, including an analysis of techniques and methods of anamnesis, emphasizes the sacred not as some passive given but as *a dynamic constituted given.* There is also considerable evidence for this interpretation in Eliade's writings. For example, after stating that it is too soon to evaluate the contributions of structuralist approaches to the study of religion, especially to understanding the manifestation of religious creativity appearing in the flow of time and history, Eliade concludes *Australian Religions* with the following: "And this is of a paramount importance; for the ultimate goal of the historian of religions is not to point out that there exist a certain number of types or patterns of religious behavior, with their specific symbologies and theologies, but rather to *understand their meanings.* And such meanings are not *given* once and for all, are not 'petrified' in the irrespective religious patterns, but rather are 'open,' in the sense that they change, grow, and enrich themselves in a creative way in the process of history (even if 'history' is not apprehended in the Judeo-Christian or modern Western sense). Ultimately, the historian of religions cannot renounce hermeneutics."[15]

Here we have the emphasis found throughout Eliade's writings on the imagination and creativity of human beings who dynamically unconceal hidden symbolic and mythic structures and constitute sacred meanings and significances. The sacred may "show itself," but *homo religiosus* is not some passive receptor. The dialectic of the sacred is a dynamic complex process of transfiguration and transformation. Mythic and symbolic structures are "given," but as unfinished and "open"; given to us in such ways that require our active participation as constituting subjects. The given structures are creatively revalorized and reconstituted by concretely living human beings. What is remembered and recognized of the symbolic, mythic, sacred givenness is at least partially determined by specific historical and cultural conditions, and what is constituted as sacred meaning is at least partially determined by immediate, concrete, existential concerns. Therefore, in the general method for rediscovering mythic and symbolic structures, even in the specific emphasis on a sacred that has been forgotten and the indispensability of techniques of anamnesis, one need not endorse some passive remembrance of given, unchanging, sacred essences. Instead, anamnesis and recognition may be interpreted as part of a dynamic process of unconcealing and reconstituting sacred structures and meanings.

Of course, such an interpretation by itself does not clarify complex philosophical issues or justify bold epistemological and metaphysical claims. Philosophers, for example, continually reinterpret and debate what Plato may have intended by "anamnesis" and how this relates to his theory of reality. What precisely is meant by "recollection" of Forms or Ideas? What is the metaphysical status of the reality that is remembered? What is the relation between the forgotten ultimate reality and the world of appearances? By anamnesis, is Plato endorsing some bold metaphysical doctrine—perhaps even involving a belief in reincarnation—or is he making a more modest epistemological claim?

In short, in his assertions about hidden nontemporal, nonhistorical, mythic and symbolic structures and the need for modern persons to remember the camouflaged forgotten sacred, Eliade often makes bold philosophical judgments and highly normative claims about reality. But he does not provide the clarification, analysis, and arguments to justify his philosophical position. Once again, one possible judgment is that such writings are hopelessly uncritical; the most generous judgment is that such writings, going beyond the disciplinary boundaries of the history of religions, the social sciences, and the phenomenology of religion, may serve as a catalyst for new, more comprehensive, more creative, philosophical reflection.

Encounter, Confrontation, and Dialogue

One of Mircea Eliade's most daring attempts at creative hermeneutics is his formulation of imagined encounters between modern Western and traditional nonWestern cultures. Such encounters are indispensable for the creative renewal of modern culture. Eliade contends that "the prime phenomenon of the twentieth century" has been "the discovery of non-European man and his spiritual universe." Today "we are beginning to be aware of the nobility and spiritual autonomy of those civilizations. The dialogue with them seems to me more important for the future of European spirituality than is the spiritual revival which the radical emancipation of the proletariat could bring."[16] Eliade is not interested in establishing a dialogue with modern Western thinkers. "Personally, I think that these [modern Western] cultural horizons are provincial. The crises and problematical issues of a Freud, Nietzsche, Marx, etc., have been left behind or resolved. As for me, I'm trying to *open* windows onto other worlds for Westerners—even if some of these worlds foundered tens of thousands of years ago. My dialogue has other inter-locutors than those of Freud or James Joyce: I'm trying to understand a Paleolithic hunter, a yogi or a shaman, a peasant from Indonesia, an African, etc., and to communicate with each one."[17]

In the 1930s Eliade felt the urgency of understanding nonWestern spirituality not only because of twentieth-century historical develop-ments, but also because it seemed to him "that we Romanians could fulfill a definite role in the coming dialogue between the two or three worlds: the West, Asia, and cultures of the archaic folk type." Reversing the usual criticism of peasants as "provincial," Eliade claims that it "was precisely the peasant roots of a good part of our Romanian culture that compelled us to transcend nationalism and cultural provin-cialism and to aim for 'universalism.' The common elements of Indian, Balkan, and Mediterranean folk culture proved to me that it is *here* that organic universalism exists, that it is the result of a common history (the history of peasant cultures) and not an abstract construct. We, the people of Eastern Europe, would be able to serve as a bridge between the West and Asia."[18]

In more general terms, Eliade frequently maintains that the phenom-enology and history of religions are essential for the imminent encounter and dialogue between the modern West and traditional nonWestern cultures. In 1944 while still in Lisbon, Eliade observed that the whole world was being transformed, India would soon gain independence, and Asia was reentering history. But for him such events had much more than political significance.

> Soon there would become possible a new confrontation—on a footing of equality—between Oriental and Occidental spirituality. But the dialogue was possible only if the *true* Oriental spirituality—that is, its religious matrix—was correctly known and understood in the Occident. The phenomenology and history of religions, as I practiced it, seemed to me the most suitable preparation for this imminent dialogue. On the other hand, the archaic world—that of the 'primitives' whom anthropologists had studied for a century—could not remain very long under its colonial guise. But for Occidentals, the understanding of archaic spirituality was even more difficult, because it presupposed a minimum comprehension of mythical thought.[19]

Eliade's "encounters"—often described as "confrontations"—and "dialogues" between the modern West and the traditional Asian and archaic nonWest are, for the most part, not genuine interactive encounters and dialogues. The modern West usually serves as little more than a foil for raising valuable nonWestern critiques and alternatives. Occasionally Eliade indicates how the modern West might respond, but he usually has little time or patience formulating Western condemnations of premoderns as "primitive," backwards, subjective, irrational, nonhistorical, and unprepared for the challenges of the contemporary world. He is not concerned with addressing contemporary crises in the nonWestern world and the typical solutions the West proposes to resolve these crises. Instead he often formulates the encounter, confrontation, and dialogue around existential, historical, and cultural crises in the modern West. The encounter is intended primarily to give voice to archaic and nonWestern perspectives, to critique and expose the limitations of modern perspectives, and to suggest possibilities for Western renewal if moderns listen and learn from the nonWestern, mythic, religious "others." This hermeneutical encounter can be seen in two of Eliade's illustrations: modern anxiety and the modern response to "the terror of history."

The third and final part of *Myths, Dreams and Mysteries* is entitled "The Encounter: A Test-Case" and consists of one chapter: "Religious Symbolism and the Modern Man's Anxiety."[20] Eliade's interprets the nature, meaning, and significance of the extreme anxiety defining much of modern secular life as seen from "external," archaic and Indian, mythic and religious perspectives. He explores how these nonWestern cultures, with their basic religious structure, would understand and judge our modern Western crisis. In this encounter—which is almost entirely a one-way confrontation—the archaic and the Indian are not surprised by modern anxiety. They too analyze awareness of temporal and historical existence as generating anguish and anxiety as one confronts death and nothingness. What astonishes them is that modern persons affirm and remain at this experiential stage of temporality, historicity, and resultant anxiety rather than viewing it in relation to the symbolisms of initiation and as an indispensable rite of passage to another mode of being. In light of the mythic archaic perspective, this anxiety gains meaning and value not as an end but rather as a first transitional stage of initiation.[21] The anguish of death is the anguish of initiation: the dangerous terrifying experiences of the initiatory ordeal. But the agonizing experiences of initiatory death are necessary for a resurrection and for attaining a new mode of being. "One dies to one mode of being in order to be able to attain to another. Death constitutes an abrupt change of ontological level, and at the same time a rite of passage, just as birth does, or initiation,"[22]

In a more developed "encounter," Eliade presents the metaphysical and ontological Indian perspective with regard to the modern emphasis on temporality and historicity and the "predicament" of conditioned human existence as part of the discovery of the dialectic of Mâyâ or cosmic illusion. Judged by the scale of absolute Being, this world of limited, conditioned, temporal, historical existence is "illusory" in the sense of lacking ultimate ontological reality. In its preoccupation with Being, Indian philosophy judged History, created by becoming, as a form of Non-being. Indian metaphysics and spiritual techniques include highly refined analyses of historicity; of what Western philosophy now calls "being in the world" and "being in situation." Long before Heidegger, Indian thought identified in temporality the "fated" dimension of all human existence. In analyzing human existence as "in bondage" to illusion, Indians meant that "every existence necessarily constitutes itself as a rupture, a break-away from the Absolute." In analyzing existence as suffering, Indians meant that "the temporality of all human existence necessarily engenders anxiety and pain."[23]

What the Indian philosopher finds perplexing are the consequences certain modern philosophers draw from the discovery of historicity and the specific human mode of being in the world. While Indians try to free themselves from the illusions of the dialectic of Mâyâ, these Westerners "seem to be content with the discovery, and to put up with a nihilistic and pessimistic vision of the world." For the Indian, there is no meaning, value, and significance to this discovery of cosmic illusion unless it is followed by a quest for absolute Being. Our modern anxiety is understandable as an awareness of what we are as mortal, temporal, historical, dying beings. "The Indian, then, would agree with us inasmuch as he admits that anguish in face of the Nothingness of our existence is homologous with the anguish of facing Death—but he would immediately add, this Death that fills you with such anxiety is only the death of your illusions and your ignorance: it will be followed by a rebirth, by the realisation of your real identity, your true mode of being: that of unconditioned and free being." The Indian would tell us that "it is the consciousness of your own historicity that makes you anxious, and no wonder: for one has to die to History before one can discover and live true Being."[24]

When we look at contemporary society and the anxiety of modern persons from the standpoint of archaic cultures or Indian spirituality, "anxiety appears under the symbolism of Death. This means that, seen and evaluated by the *others,* by the non-Europeans, our anxiety reveals the same signification as we Europeans had already found in it: the imminence of Death. But agreement between our own view of it and that of the *others* goes no further. For, to the non-European, Death is neither definitive nor absurd; on the contrary, the anxiety aroused by the imminence of death is already a promise of resurrection, reveals the presentment of re-birth into another mode of being, and this is a mode which transcends Death." For both archaic and Indian, *"this anxiety is not a state in which one can remain;* its indispensability is that of an initiatory experience, of a rite of passage." Only in modern culture do we stop in the middle of the rite of passage without resolving the crisis generating our experience of anxiety.[25]

Eliade's second illustration of "the terror of history" is a common theme in his scholarly works, journals, and literary creations.[26] He often reflects on this theme in a very personal manner. He believed that in this century smaller nations would not be able to shape their destinies, so "the chief problem was: how could we survive, ethnically and spiritually, in the historical cataclysm that was coming?" He put all his hope "in the skill with which the Romanian people, in the past, had succeeded in withstanding the 'terror of history.'"[27] In reacting to invasions and historical catastrophes, Romanians and other eastern Europeans experienced "the terror of history": the awakening of consciousness to the fact that despite all of their best efforts, they are "condemned by history" because of their historical situation. Situated at the crossroads of invasions, bordered by more powerful aggressive neighbors, there is no effective military or political defense for the less powerful peoples against the terror of history. The only response to despair and nihilism is "a religious interpretation of the terror of history" in which historical tragic events are transfigured by exemplary, transhistorical, mythic and symbolic structures and meanings.[28]

We have considered "the terror of history" under such topics as Eliade's interpretation of cosmic Christianity (chapter 4), his personal and scholarly antihistorical attitudes (chapter 8), and his normative antihistorical judgments (chapter 9). When Eliade interprets the terror of history in terms of an "archaic ontology," the symbolic and mythic aspects of traditional nonhistorical religions, and the perspective of *homo religiosus,* his analysis falls most clearly within his conception of the history and phenomenology of religion. At the other extreme, when Eliade uses the terror of history to make sweeping judgments about our universal mode of being in the world, the human condition and reality as such, and why modern human beings cannot defend themselves against the terror of history, he has moved to a highly normative, onto-logical, and metaphysical level. Here we shall refer only briefly to the encounter, confrontation, and dialogue of traditional nonWestern and modern Western cultures around this theme of the terror of history.

In *The Myth of the Eternal Return*, Eliade formulates the antihistorical archaic ontology and analyzes what this ontological conception reveals about traditional persons, such as their fear of being overwhelmed by meaningless profane time and history. In the last chapter, "The Terror of History," Eliade formulates his encounter and "conflict" between the archaic, antihistorical, mythic, religious conception and the modern post-Hegelian conception which seeks to be historical. More specifically, Eliade restricts this confrontation to one aspect of "the problem": "the solutions offered by the historicistic view to enable modern man to tolerate the increasingly powerful pressure of contemporary history." "How can the 'terror of history' be tolerated from the viewpoint of historicism?"[29]

After discussing "the difficulties of historicism" and how the "terror of history becomes more and more intolerable from the viewpoints afforded by the various historicistic philosophies," Eliade presents some of the ways that traditional antihistorical religions have been able to endure and give value to the sufferings and tragedies of historical existence. Eliade briefly offers a modern critique of the archaic anti-historical, mythic orientation. "In the last analysis, modern man, who accepts history or claims to accept it, can reproach archaic man, imprisoned within the mythical horizon of archetypes and repetition, with his creative impotence, or, what amounts to the same thing, his inability to accept the risks entailed by every creative act." The modern person can be creative only as a historical being; "everything is denied him except the freedom to make history by making himself."[30] Eliade then presents countercriticisms and defenses by the traditional archaic: it is not clear that moderns, without defenses against the terror of history, can freely and creatively make history; archaic persons, with their participation in the repetition of the cosmogony and other transhistorical exemplary acts, have the right to consider themselves more creative than modern persons who restrict their concept of creativity to the historical dimension of existence; and so forth.[31]

At this point, Eliade returns to "our problem" and reaches the following conclusion: "Whatever be the truth in respect to the freedom and the creative virtualities of historical man, it is certain that none of the historicistic philosophies is able to defend him from the terror of history." Here we find the antihistorical normative judgments presented in chapter 9. Human beings, who completely make themselves through history and who reject transhistorical, mythic, sacred models or who reject a freedom grounded in the Judaeo-Christian "category of faith," cannot defend themselves against the terror of history and cannot overcome their nihilism and despair.[32] Under "Normative Antihistorical Judgments," I emphasized that such judgments about the terror of history involve an ontological stance and philosophical claims that go far beyond the usual perspectival boundaries of the history and phenomenology of religion. Eliade has gone beyond presenting such interpretations and judgments as only from an archaic perspective or as only from a general, antihistorical, mythic perspective. He is making sweeping, unqualified, universal, antihistorical judgments about the contemporary world, human nature, and reality in terms of which the modern historicistic philosophies of Hegel, Marx, Dilthey, and others cannot and will never be able to defend us from the terror of history.

In terms of his traditional-modern "encounter," it is remarkable how quickly, and perhaps indistinguishably, Eliade moved from presenting archaic views on the terror of history to making these sweeping normative judgments about the human mode of being, the human condition, history, the contemporary world, and reality. Eliade not only interprets and presents the archaic antihistorical conception, with its rejection of modern attempts to cope with the terror of history, but he also endorses it. And he endorses it not as a specific archaic or traditional approach to enduring and overcoming the terror of history, but rather as revealing essential truths about the human condition, historical existence, and reality as such.

In formulating his creative hermeneutics through confrontation and dialogue around the terror of history, Eliade is not advocating that we simply return to some archaic or premodern conception. There is a sense of "return" as a rediscovery of hidden and forgotten mythic and symbolic structures and meanings. But for Eliade the renewal of modern human beings will involve unexpected "breakthroughs" and new spiritual creations. Through the creative hermeneutical encounter with the archaic and nonWestern other, focusing on the terror of history and other existential concerns, modern culture will be renewed by rejecting major features of historical existence and by incorporating, in new creative ways, essential mythic and religious conceptions that disclose aspects of the universal human spirit.

Sometimes Eliade suggests that even the "negative" or hopeless experience of modern historical attempts to cope with the terror of history may be part of a process of cultural and spiritual renewal. In modern life, the sacred is most disguised and hidden. Even the most historical and temporal secular phenomena may reveal sacred structures and meanings. Through the encounter, confrontation, and dialogue with the traditional mythic and religious other, modern consciousness may be stimulated and enlarged so that it becomes aware of the sacred buried in the unconscious, hidden in our spiritual history, and camouflaged in seemingly secular experiences such as historical attempts to solve the terror of history. Even when Eliade grants that the modern process of desacralization is irreversible and that our technical progress and political forms render a return to the terror of history inevitable, he maintains that "there is no doubt that new religious creations of considerable importance will be born of this very terror." The key is interpreting the terror in terms of initiation which Eliade discovered was the only way of defending himself against the terror of history. "I mean that if we succeed in experiencing, taking upon ourselves, or imposing a value on the terror, the despair, the depression, the apparent absence of meaning in history, as so many initiatory trials—then all these crises and tortures will take on a meaning, will acquire a value, and the despair of the universe-as-concentration-camp will be spared us. We will find a *way out.* In that way we will transcend history in the most authentic fashion (taking upon ourselves, therefore, all the obligations of the historical moment)."[33]

THE POLITICAL AND THE SPIRITUAL

Mircea Eliade sometimes formulates this encounter between traditional and modern cultures as the confrontation between a spiritual orientation and a secular, historical, nonmythic, political mode of being in the world. As was seen, in his assumption of the irreducibility of the sacred and the autonomy of the religious plane of reality, Eliade expresses hostility toward "the political," or, better yet, toward a nonreligious political that does not acknowledge the primacy of the spiritual. In upholding the primacy of mythic, symbolic structures and meanings, Eliade deemphasizes the significance of the political and has little use for a modern political that is not grounded in spiritual reality.

In his analysis of myth, reality, and the contemporary world, Eliade often lumps together and uses interchangeably such terms as political, economic, historical, temporal, materialist, historicist, positivist, and other aspects of the modern mode of being. Therefore, the kinds of criticisms we have seen directed at modern historical existence apply to modern political existence. Secular persons, who define themselves as political beings, will be unable to cope with the terror and crises of contemporary political life without recourse to exemplary, transhistorical, mythic, sacred models. Much of what we have already seen in our analysis of Eliade's interpretations of sacred-profane, transhistorical-historical relations applies to his analysis of spiritual-political relations.

This section will focus briefly on the recent controversies involving the political and the spiritual.[34] Much of the attention around Eliade in recent years has had less to do with interest in his scholarly studies of myth and religion and more to do with the charges and countercharges about his political life and views. Following the earlier, more publicized revelations about the Nazi sympathies and involvement of Martin Heidegger and more recent disclosures about Paul de Man and others, the controversy around Eliade has tended to focus on his involvement in fascist Romania.

Eliade's defenders usually portray him as an extremely nonpolitical person whose scholarship, with its insistence on "the primacy of the spiritual," is nonpolitical and even antipolitical. Critics, of course, see things very differently. They typically charge that Eliade endorsed a xenophobic and messianic nationalism, identified with Romanian fascism, and provided intellectual ammunition for the anti-Semitic and fascistic Legion of the Archangel Michael and the Iron Guard.[35] It is not my intention to address such controversies as they relate to Eliade's personal life. It is a legitimate area of scholarly inquiry for others to debate such topics as whether Eliade personally embraced a conservative religious position that was integrally linked with a fascist political orientation; whether he identified with a highly nationalistic Romanianism that displayed anti-Semitic and fascistic tendencies; or whether his autobiographical writings reveal embarrassing silences, evasions, and cover-ups about his reactionary political-religious views.

For this general study of Eliade's theories of myth and religion, the more significant focus of such spiritual-political controversies is on how Eliade's political (or nonpolitical) involvement and views is (or is not) an integral part of his scholarly productivity. Eliade's importance for the study of myth and religion will be determined by scholarly assessments of his writings. Such a scholarly focus addresses such questions as the extent to which Eliade's political orientation shaped his methodology, selectivity and privileging of specific data, categories of interpretation, assumptions, and conclusions. Without assessing their claims, we shall briefly cite two of Eliade's critics, Adriana Berger and Russell McCutcheon, who raise important scholarly questions.

The Romanian Adriana Berger, once Eliade's assistant and author of sympathetic studies on Eliade, has emerged as his most determined critic. Her most recent attack, "Mircea Eliade: Romanian Fascism and the History of Religions in the United States," begins with the following charges:

> [T]he revelation that the writer and world-renowned historian of religion Mircea Eliade was a supporter of Nazism and an ideologue of Romanian fascism is painful and disturbing. It is shocking to discover that the "father of the history of religions" in the United States wrote viciously anti-Semitic propaganda articles in war-torn Romania and furthered theories of the racial and paganized Christian origins of the Romanian people, that he was an acknowledged member of the Romanian Fascist Movement and was reported by British intelligence (MI 5, Naval Intelligence Admiralty, Foreign Office, etc.) to be working for the Nazis; that he served as the press and propaganda attaché of the pro-Nazi Romanian governments in Portugal from 1941 to 1945.... Further, Eliade's intellectual ideology clearly reflected his politics. His later, widely accepted theories of the nature of religious "history" containing the essential

content of his thought, are but camouflaged restatements of his earlier
theories, which originated in the era of Romanian fascism.[36]

It is this latter scholarly issue that is most significant for our study: Are
Eliade's theories of myth and religion, his insistence on the primacy of
the spiritual, and his critique of modernity "camouflaged restatements"
of earlier theories reflecting his political views and activities?

Russell McCutcheon charges that Eliade was far from the apolitical
scholar portrayed by Eliade and his defenders. He was deeply involved
in Romanian political issues from youth and drawn toward the philosophical and political circle of Ionescu and the Legion and Iron Guard.
His approach to contemporary history and politics involves legitimizing
a particular way of understanding through an appeal to some golden
past; this reveals that his favoring the category of the "archaic" is really
"a *codeword* for his conservative world-view." McCutcheon delineates
many ways that "Eliade's fascist sympathies seem to saturate his later
texts" and how Eliade's political conservatism and conservative philosophical idealism have defined much of the discipline of the history of
religions. In this respect, "such ideological strategies as essentialization,
universalization, and dehistoricization played a primary role in both his
pro-Romanian writings and his later scholarly work on religion."[37]

Probably the strongest attack on Berger's interpretation, in
particular, and on critics of Eliade's political approach, in general, is
presented by Bryan Rennie.[38] Relying heavily on Ricketts for his
knowledge of Eliade's political history, Rennie attacks the
interpretations of Strenski, Berger, Volovici, and Dubuisson. He not
only defends Eliade against misunderstandings and misinterpretations
of critics, but he also accuses critics of unworthy personal motives and
hidden agendas. While conceding that there is more work to be done in
the area of Eliade's political involvement, Rennie arrives at the
following conclusion. "Yet, in conclusion, it has to be said that there is
to date no evidence of actual membership, of active services rendered,
or of any real involvement with fascist or totalitarian movements or
ideals. Nor is there any evidence of continued support for nationalist
separatist ideals after their inherently violent nature was revealed, nor
of the imprint of such ideals in Eliade's scholarship. On the other hand,

there is clear evidence that those scholars who have published their suspicions of Eliade have pursued their own agendas with little regard for the integrity of their textual sources."[39]

It was not so long ago that attempts by Berger, McCutcheon, and others at analyzing and assessing a scholar's works in terms of his or her life and personal views on the political and the spiritual would have been seen to violate generally accepted standards of rationality and objectivity. Focusing on a scholar's life and values might be of anecdotal and biographical interest and might contribute to a history of ideas, but it was irrelevant or even fallacious when analyzing the nature and truth claims of that scholar's theories. It was completely irrelevant to the truth or falsity of David Hume's ethical theory whether Hume himself was a moral or immoral human being. To confuse Hume's theory with Hume the person was to commit an *ad hominen* fallacy. Therefore, Eliade's theories of myth and religion, with his assumption of the irreducibility and primacy of the spiritual, should be analyzed and assessed independent of his personal political or nonpolitical orientation.

One problem with this sharp bifurcation is that Ricketts, Olson, Cave, and some other defenders have argued that Eliade's personal life and literary and scholarly contributions are all of one piece; that one cannot understand his scholarship without understanding his personal life, fears, ambitions, and commitments. Therefore, they have opened the gates and cannot object, in principle, when others focus on political aspects of Eliade's life to shed light on political dimensions of his scholarship about the reality of the spiritual.

Although I disagree with the sharp separation of the personal from the scholarly, it is important to keep in mind that uncovering political and other personal information does not automatically determine the nature and worth of scholarly contributions. One could be a fascist, an anti-Semite, a racist, a sexist, a defender of economic exploitation, and a supporter of dictatorship and still compose significant music, write impressive novels, be at the forefront of scientific theorizing, or provide insightful analysis of shamanism or peasant myths and rituals. This does not mean that one's personal values are irrelevant to the origin, nature, and significance of one's aesthetic and scholarly works; only that any real connections have to be established through careful documentation and argumentation.

Critics and defenders focusing on the personal and the scholarly, whether interpreting this as religious political or as nonpolitical spiritual, have to keep in mind two, often opposed considerations. On the one hand, situating specific texts within their larger historical, cultural, political, and scholarly contexts provides greater understanding. Various philosophers of science, Derrida, Foucault, Rorty, feminists, and postmodernists have shown that religious and political factors are very relevant in understanding why texts and theories are constructed in certain ways and why some gain hegemony. Situating Eliade's scholarly productions within contexts of his personal values and larger economic, political, religious, and cultural structures of his society will help us to understand not only the origin, nature, meaning, and significance of his writings, but also why his textual omissions and silences may be fraught with meaning. And if every reading of a text is to some extent a reinterpretation, then an essential part of our scholarly work is to gain awareness both of political and religious contexts within which Eliade constructed his texts and of our own specific contexts through which we filter, interpret, evaluate, appropriate, or dismiss Eliade's scholarly contributions.

On the other hand, there is a danger to this approach of understanding Eliade's scholarship through his personal political and religious attitudes and involvements and the larger political, religious, and cultural contexts. Earlier this century many philosophers wrote of "the genetic fallacy." Philosophical phenomenologists broadened this antireductionist analysis by claiming that uncovering origins and psychological, historical, and other causal factors and conditionings was not tantamount to interpreting the meaning of phenomena; that after a scholar had explained such phenomena in terms of causal factors and conditionings, there remained the task of deciphering structures and interpreting meaning and significance. Thus, to claim that one has comprehended the full intentionality, meaning, and significance of Eliade's scholarly contributions on myth and religion by uncovering fascistic and other political and religious factors that may have shaped his life and even his scholarly works is to be guilty of "psychologism," "historicism," and other forms of reductionism. This, I would submit, does not negate the earlier claim that awareness of Eliade's personal, political, and religious contexts may be invaluable in helping to illuminate the nature, meaning, and significance of his scholarship.

THE RENEWAL OF PHILOSOPHY

Eliade contends that an understanding of myth and religion will not only allow us to understand traditional religious phenomena, the archaic, Asian, and other nonWestern orientations. It will also allow us to understand better the nature of the unconscious, the imagination, dreams, fantasies, ideologies, aesthetic creativity, and other seemingly secular aspects of the contemporary life. It will also allow us to establish a creative encounter and dialogue with the mythic religious "other"; confront our own limited, self-deceptive, self-defeating, and dangerous cultural provincialism; and participate in a desperately needed Western and global cultural renewal.

When reviewing sweeping generalizations and negative judgments about the modern mode of being in the world, seen throughout this book and especially in this chapter, it is tempting to classify Eliade as antimodern premodernist. Most critics and some supporters have interpreted his scholarly approach as privileging an archaic ontology and endorsing a premodern, antihistorical, mythic, symbolic, cosmic, religious mode of being as more in touch with reality.

However, it is also possible to interpret Eliade's negative judgments about modernity as sharing many characteristics with antimodern postmodernist approaches. "Postmodernism" is a very fashionable term among many contemporary philosophers, literary theorists, and other scholars, although the term tends to be very vague. Postmodernists themselves write articles and teach courses exploring the question: what is postmodernism? Postmodernism encompasses all kinds of fragmented, contradictory positions. It tends to resist any clear definition or coherent formulation because it often upholds the inviolability of differences and sees attempts at coherence as oppressive forms of intellectual and cultural hegemony.[40]

Nevertheless, the following typical assertions of much of postmodernism seem to characterize Eliade's approach to myth and religion. We must resist the tyranny and domination of the modernist idols of science, rationalism, and "objectivity." The Enlightenment gave us narrow, oppressive, hierarchical, reductionist projects of rationalistic and scientific hegemony. But rational scientific discourse is only one of many possible ways that human beings construct their "stories" about reality. The scientific narrative does not have exclusive privileged access to truth. The mythic narrative, as another autonomous way of constructing a story about truth, history, the human condition, and reality, should not be reduced to scientific, rational, historical, and other nonmythic discourses. The mythic must be respected as one of many legitimate expressions of a multiplicity of irreducible, incommensurable stories about truth and reality. None of the particular stories mirrors or exhausts all of reality. Each of the stories has its own nature, structure, function, and significance; makes different claims about truth and reality; fulfills different emotional, imaginative, conceptual, aesthetic needs for different people; and functions differently in different historical and cultural contexts.[41]

Although Eliade sometimes sounds like this postmodernism when arguing against modern forms of reductionism, in many fundamental respects he clearly rejects such a postmodernist orientation. For example, Eliade insists on the need to respect "separate planes of reference," but he often violates this principle. Especially in his ontological moves and normative judgments, he reduces modern secular phenomena to religious interpretations and explanations. He claims that we can only understand much of modern secular behavior in terms of a mythic religious plane of reference. In addition, Eliade, in his critique of modernity, is not simply insisting on a separate, mythic, sacred space so that he can tell an alternative story. He is not embracing some postmodernist relativism by endorsing the legitimacy of a plurality of irreducibly autonomous stories about reality. He makes highly normative, universal, absolute judgments about human nature, the human condition, and ultimate reality. Eliade may submit that "the scale creates the phenomenon," but he does not believe that all "scales" are equally legitimate. He judges the scales of modernity as inauthentic, provincial, incapable of solving their own existential and historical crises, and denying human and cosmic reality. He privileges a mythic religious scale as providing access to the deepest structures and meanings of the human condition as such and reality as such. Therefore, from the above typical postmodernist perspective, Eliade would be criticized for formulating another universalizing, totalizing, essentializing, hegemonic project.

Here and previously we have noted Eliade's normative judgments that clearly involve ontological and metaphysical claims functioning on a *philosophical* "plane of reference." In this regard, we have observed Eliade's philosophical assertions seen in normative judgments about *homo religiosus* as constitutive of essential human nature; the meaninglessness and unreality of the modern mode of being; the sacred, transcendent, symbolic and mythic structure of reality. On the basis of primordial, nonhistorical, mythic and religious structures and meanings, Eliade makes bold philosophical claims about time and history, the true human mode of being, and ultimate reality. The deep universal structure of the symbolic expressions of celestial flight and ascension, as found in experiences of ecstasy, is disclosed in shamanism and in numerous other mythic and religious phenomena, but also in dreams and fantasies of modern persons. This structure reveals an essential meaning of ontological transcendence and freedom; an ontological abolition of the human condition. For Eliade this reveals a primordial, nonhistorical, universal dimension of the human condition that is coexistence with human nature.

Another example of philosophical assumptions and judgments is seen in Eliade's claim that "modern man, radically secularized, believes himself or styles himself atheist, areligious, or, at least, indifferent. But he is wrong. He has not yet succeeded in abolishing the *homo religiosus* that is in him: he has only done away with (if he ever was) the *christianus*. That means that he is left with being 'pagan,' without knowing it. It also means something else: an areligious society does not yet exist (personally, I believe that it *cannot exist,* and that if it were achieved, it would perish after a few generations from boredom, from neurasthenia, or by a collective suicide . . .)."[42]

We noted Eliade's bold metaphysical claim that any human being "whatever else he may be free of, is forever the prisoner of his own archetypal intuitions, formed at the moment when he first perceived his position in the cosmos." Eliade continues that the "longing for Paradise can be traced even in the most banal actions of the modern man. Man's concept of the *absolute* can never be completely uprooted: it can only be debased. And primitive spirituality lives on in its own way not in action, not as a thing man can effectively accomplish, but as a *nostalgia* which creates things that become values in themselves: art, the sciences, social theory, and all the other things to which men will give the whole of themselves."[43]

Similarly, in chapter 4 under "Nature and Cosmos," we noted Eliade's philosophical claim that "certain primordial revelations can never disappear." As long as we are part of the cosmic rhythm, "I don't think man can be changed." Eliade grants that we are conditioned by economic and social structures, and our specific religious expressions are conditioned. "But, nevertheless, we still assume that human condition here—here in this cosmos, whose rhythms and cycles are ineluctably given. So we assume our human condition on the basis of that fundamental experiential condition. And that 'basic' human being—it is permissible to call him 'religious,' whatever appearances may seem to say, because we are talking about the meaning of life."[44]

Obviously, philosophers and other scholars may question why a human being's becoming aware of her or his own mode of being in the world necessarily constitutes a religious experience; why a person who affirms a secular mode of being can never abolish his or her permanent religious nature; or why a concern "about the meaning of life" automatically makes a position "religious," even if the concern is expressed in nonreligious terms. As we have tried to show, Eliade can make such philosophical claims only because of his assumptions and normative judgments about the religious and mythic nature of the human condition, human nature, and ultimate reality.

In some of his writing, Eliade not only makes such philosophical assertions but he also submits that the history and phenomenology of religion themselves have great philosophical significance: They will provide the indispensable means for new, creative, philosophical reflection; as key to the renewal of Western culture, they will provide the means for the renewal of Western philosophy; and they will contribute to the formulation of new philosophical anthropologies.

In 1976, Eliade observes that his entries in his "secret journal," full of philosophical reflections, may reveal his own yearning for a scholarly work. "The fervor with which I rework to better develop reflections inspired by the camouflaging of the sacred in the profane must have a deeper meaning, and I'm just beginning to have an inkling of it. This dialectic of camouflaging is infinitely more vast and goes much farther than all that I've been able to say about it up until now. The 'mystery of the mask' is fundamental to an entire metaphysics, for it is the very mystery of the human condition. If it obsesses me so much, it is probably because I don't decide to go into it in more depth, to make a systematic presentation of it, to study it from its own unique perspective, that of philosophical meditation."[45]

In his "foreword" to *The Myth of the Eternal Return,* Eliade indicates that he will examine a certain archaic "metaphysical 'valorization' of human existence." He goes on to reaffirm his "old conviction that Western philosophy is dangerously close to 'provincializing' itself" by isolating itself from its own tradition, ignoring the problems and solutions of archaic and Oriental thought, and refusing to recognize any "situations" except those of modern historical human existence. "We hold that philosophical anthropology would have something to learn from the valorization that pre-Socratic man (in other words, traditional man) accorded to his situation in the universe. Better yet: that the cardinal problems of metaphysics could be renewed through a knowledge of archaic ontology." Such renewal can come from learning about "certain spiritual positions that, although they have been transcended in various regions of the globe, are instructive for our knowledge of man and for man's history itself."[46]

Once again, it is important to caution that Eliade is not advocating that Western philosophy "return" to pre-Socratic archaic ontologies so that contemporary philosophers can reestablish premodern philosophies. Even if some of his imaginary "nostalgias" seem to suggest that, Eliade rejects such an impossible task. Rather he advocates that philosophers "return" to the archaic other—including the archaic as part of our spiritual history and the archaic within us—in order to revalorize and reconstitute transhistorical mythic and symbolic structures and archaic primordial metaphysical insights into the human condition as part of new philosophical reflections and creativity.

In "History of Religions and a New Humanism," Eliade claims: "More than any other humanistic discipline (i.e., psychology, anthropology, sociology, etc.), history of religions can open the way to a philosophical anthropology." This is because "the sacred is a universal dimension" and the beginnings of culture are rooted in religion. In addition, even modern, radically secularized, cultural creations and values cannot be understood without knowing "their original religious matrix." "Thus, the historian of religions is in a position to grasp the permanence of what has been called man's specific existential situation of 'being in the world' for the experience of the sacred is its correlate. In fact, man's becoming aware of his own mode of being and assuming his *presence* in the world together constitute a 'religious' experience."[47]

In "Crisis and Renewal in History of Religions," Eliade maintains that the history of religions must play a unique indispensable role in opening new perspectives for Western philosophy. After repeating his judgment that Western philosophy cannot continue to restrict itself to its own tradition without the risk of becoming provincial, Eliade reaffirms that "the history of religions is able to investigate and elucidate a considerable number of 'significant situations' and modalities of existing in the world that are otherwise inaccessible." Historians of religions cannot simply present such inaccessible documents to philosophers who are incapable of interpreting their deeper meaning and significance. "The hermeneutical work ought to be done by the historian of religions himself, for only he is prepared to understand and appreciate the semantic complexity of his documents." Historians of religion, wanting to bring out the philosophical significance of their documents, must not present them in the language and according to the models of contemporary philosophers. Instead, one expects that the historian of religions "will decipher and elucidate enigmatic behavior and situations, in brief, that he will advance the understanding of man by recovering, and reestablishing meanings that have been forgotten, discredited, or abolished. The originality and importance of such contributions reside precisely in the fact that they explore and illuminate spiritual universes that are submerged or that are accessible only with great difficulty. It would be not only illegitimate but ineffectual to disguise archaic and exotic symbols, myths, and ideas in a form already familiar to contemporary philosophers."

Such "a historico-religious creative hermeneutics would be able to stimulate, nourish, and renew philosophical thought. From a certain point of view, one could say that a new *Phenomenology of the Mind* awaits elaboration by taking account of all that the history of religions is capable of revealing to us. There would be important books to write on modes of existence in the world or on the problems of time, death, and dream, based on documents that the historian of religions has at his disposal."[48]

It should be evident that Eliade endorses a view of cultural and philosophical creativity and renewal in which our encounter with essential symbolic and mythic structures is a catalyst allowing us to burst open our self-imposed cultural boundaries and experience new ways of knowing, relating, and being. In the last chapter of *Structure and Creativity in Religion,* I examined the philosophical assumptions, normative judgments, metaphysical claims, and directions for new philosophical anthropologies revealed in Eliade's approach.

On the level of greatest generality, Eliade's ontological moves and normative judgments—such as those about the human mode of being generally, the human condition as such, and reality as such—involve philosophical reflection on the level of analysis of metaphysics and philosophical anthropology. They involve a normative philosophical "leap" beyond the normal disciplinary boundaries of the history of religions. Eliade's philosophical reflections and judgments are dependent on the special ontological status of essential, nonhistorical, universal symbolisms, as they are revalorized and reactualized through mythic narratives and other religious phenomena. These symbolisms and their mythic and other symbolic expressions disclose the deepest structures and meanings of our mode of being in the world. They serve as ciphers of reality, expressing the enigmas and ambiguities of being and the inexhaustible possibilities for philosophical reflection.

Eliade would maintain that his ontological moves, normative judgments, and philosophical claims are not subjective and arbitrary since they are informed by and consistent with the basic intentionality of the essential symbolic structures, as expressed in mythic and other phenomena of the sacred. Philosophical reflection must continually return to its ontological foundation. This is necessary not only to enrich and renew consciousness, but also to check that philosophical analysis, on levels of greatest generality, has not distorted the basic intentionality of the sacred that constitutes its philosophical foundation.

In suggesting how Eliade might verify such ontological moves and philosophical judgments, one may consider a notion of a "wager" from the philosophical hermeneutics of Paul Ricoeur.[49] On the level of philosophical analysis, Eliade is claiming the following. On the basis of the assumption of an irreducibly religious perspective, especially by reflecting on the fundamental symbolic and mythic structures of the sacred, I can frame general existential concepts. My belief is that these fundamental symbolic and mythic structures disclose the deepest structures of the human mode of being and fulfill their deepest function when they reveal essential structures of the sacred. The essential symbols and their mythic expressions, when understood as particular revalorizations of coherent, transhistorical, universal symbolisms, reveal the deepest structures of "the universal"; they "open out" to the most general structures of reality.

> Now let us "wager" that such ontological concepts, formulated from the religious perspective, will reveal the nature of the human being and of reality better than the existential concepts framed in terms of some nonreligious perspective. We shall *verify* such a wager by showing that the primary symbolic structures of religious experience have the power to illuminate the fundamental structures of the human consciousness and mode of being *generally,* of the human condition *as such.* Indeed, such a level of ontological analysis will reveal that only by experiencing the symbolic structures of the sacred, only by renewing ourselves through new revalorizations of religious symbolisms, can modern Western human beings overcome their "terror of history" and their existential anxiety and live a truly meaningful human existence.[50]

Eliade's philosophical reflections involve normative judgments about the impoverishment and provincialism of our modern perspective and about the desperate need for creative "openings." These creative "breakthroughs" will allow us to "burst open" our limiting conditionings and open us to new universes of significant meaning. The modern "self" must establish a dynamic relation with the traditional, mythic, archaic and nonWestern "other." It must also establish a dynamic relation with its own "other" through the rediscovery of the forgotten "other" in our own spiritual history and in our modern unconscious. Such self-other relations will enable us to burst open our limiting structures and conditionings, allowing us to recognize new creative possibilities and to construct new philosophical anthropologies.

I shall conclude by submitting that Mircea Eliade's philosophical reflections, ontological moves, and normative judgments, as bold as they are—with sweeping generalizations, essentializing claims, and universal philosophical judgments—are in certain basic respects too narrow and too limited! We have recently quoted Eliade's claim that a creative hermeneutics of the history of religions could stimulate and renew philosophical thought leading to the creation of a new "Phenomenology of the Mind." We may use Hegel's general structural analysis in *The Phenomenology of Mind* to illustrate why Eliade's philosophical formulations must be enlarged.

Eliade is correct that empathizing with and relating to other concepts of self (other perspectives of human nature, etc.), created by other cultures and even in other historical periods, may serve as a catalyst to our own creative process of self-constitution and self-development. My relational view of the self is not unrelated to Hegel's general structural analysis of the dialectical process of self-development and self-alienation.[51] To become a more sensitive, conscious, and ethical self, Hegel tells us that the self, while maintaining its autonomy as subject, must "objectify" and "externalize" itself in relating to that which is "other." Self-alienation may result either when the self defines itself internally and refuses to externalize itself and relate authentically to the external other; or when the self objectifies itself and then gives up its capacity as an autonomous subject, thus allowing itself to be defined as immanent, nontranscending other. Through this dynamic process of self-externalization, the relation to the other provides the necessary basis for the dialectical movement of self-transcendence; for the reconstitution of the new, more conscious, more fulfilled self.

Today "the other" must be broadened beyond any modern, Western self-claims to ahistoric, universal objectivity to include other concepts of self with their different worlds of meaning. Such a creative, non-oppressive relation to the other is a necessary condition for our own dynamic process of self-constitution, freedom, and development. As Eliade states, for those of us in the modern, technological, indus-trialized West, complex nonoppressive encounters with other concepts of self can reveal new worlds of meaning: different ways to free our imaginations and be more in touch with our emotions; to experience nature and the cosmos; to relate to death, time, and history; to under-stand myths and symbols often already influencing us; in short, different ways of understanding and creating and recreating our own selves and our relations to others. Eliade is correct that the modern West has suppressed, repressed, and silenced many voices of "the other" and that it is imperative that we establish a dialogue and learn from the "messages" of these others.

Nevertheless, Eliade's approach needs to be enlarged for at least three reasons: he dismisses or devalues achievements of modernity; he excludes the voices of many "others" suppressed by the modern West; and he does not address how "others" have been and still are sup-pressed in traditional religious cultures. For example, the class and gender voices of the majority have been suppressed in *both* traditional and modern cultures.

In his specific religious and mythic assumptions, ontological moves, and normative judgments and in his reaction against a secular mode of being, Eliade has devalued or dismissed too much that is valuable in the modern constructed "self" and in the diverse experiences of "the other." In his tendency to romanticize and idealize much of the premodern mythic— in contrast to sweeping condemnations and dismissals of the modern—Eliade focuses on what is negative while ignoring what is positive about modernity; and he focuses on what is positive while ignoring what is negative about premodern cultures. For example, as someone who is quite sympathetic to many of Eliade's condemnations,

I do not believe that science or rationality is inherently oppressive, exploitative, and dehumanizing. It is the social and historical forms that modern science and rationality have taken that allow us to understand their development as forces of domination: their definition and reformulation in terms of narrow models of instrumental reason; their institutionalization and commodification as instruments of dominant power relations; and so forth. What is needed is not to devalue or dismiss nonreligious science and rationality as illegitimate profane reductionism, but instead to demystify their ideological legitimations and to disclose and reconstitute their nonoppressive potential for self-realization, human development, and greater freedom and liberation.

Similarly, Eliade too easily dismisses modern secular democracy and minimizes the dangers of antidemocratic theocracies. I agree with many of his criticisms of self-alienation and meaninglessness under modern forms of democracy. But a more complex, dialectical analysis would reveal that modern forms of democracy not only display negative features but in other respects represent historical advances. I would suggest that the problem with modern forms of democracy, with their formal rights and freedoms, is that they aren't democratic enough! Because of economic, political, and historical reasons, they don't include, and intentionally exclude, substantive economic and political democracy. A self that has formal freedoms, but has little power and lives under conditions of extreme necessity, is not very free. What is most defective in modern forms of democracy is not the superiority of premodern, hierarchical, anti-democratic, mythic and religious, economic, social, and political structures, but rather the fact that they do not address the real substantial issues of democratic empowerment.

To provide one other illustration, I agree with Eliade in his criticism of the impoverishment and dehumanization of the modern "individual." He is correct in demystifying modern secular ideologies about some exalted abstract individualism. But once again, Eliade, in his dismissal of the modern, too easily rejects what may reflect historical and social advances. I would suggest that much of what is lacking in modern individualism is evident in the dichotomy of the individual versus society (versus other individuals, versus nature.) What is needed is for new philosophical anthropologies to incorporate what is valuable in the modern conception of the autonomous individual self, while rejecting what is negative in modern relations that constitute the alienated individual self—alienated from nature, from any meaningful sense of community, and from much of one's own humanity. What is needed is not a simple rejection of the modern individual, but to reconstitute and enlarge our conception of what is authentically human in terms of the social individual: the individual who expresses the particular way one relates to the universal and who establishes harmonious organic relations with social reality, nature, and the cosmos.

Eliade is also too narrow in his formulation of "the other." This may seem strange since he has so broadened "the other" to include the mythic, religious, archaic and nonWestern other and the mythic religious other in Western spiritual history and buried in the modern unconscious. But this process of self-constitution, dependent on providing culturally diverse contexts for creative encounters with worlds of meaning of the other, must be broadened. It must include others rarely addressed by Eliade, at least not in their defining economic, historical, and social forms: the disempowered and dispossessed, the oppressed and exploited, those on the "periphery," workers, women, gays and lesbians, peoples of color, and so forth. And this applies not only to the West. The constructions of "archaic," Hindu, Buddhist, and other nonWestern texts were not free from class, caste, gender, race, and other relations of power. This is why it is important that many contemporary scholars in India, for example, are focusing on culturally-defined self-identities of "subalterns," women, peasants, tribals, and "dalits" ("the oppressed ones" or "downtrodden" Untouchables).

By establishing creative encounters with "the other," including cultural creations and concepts of self usually excluded or unrecognized by dominant modern and premodern traditions—Western, archaic, and Eastern—we create the possibility for increasing our sensitivity and awareness, overcoming some of our provincialism, "bursting open" our historically and culturally-imposed limitations on what is valuable, significant, and even possible, and reconstituting new philosophical views of self and reality. In this regard, many of us have learned much from Mircea Eliade's writings on myth and religion while we have also been highly selective, rejecting or reformulating some of his assumptions, methodological principles, interpretations, and judgments.

NOTES

1. *No Souvenirs,* pp. 69-70. See also *Myths, Dreams and Mysteries,* pp. 7-12.

2. *Mephistopheles and the Androgyne,* pp. 9-15. In *Journal 3,* Eliade states: "I am also convinced that under the pressure of history we will be forced to familiarize ourselves with the different expressions of extra-European creative genius, such as are found in Asia, Africa, and Oceania. As I've repeated over and over for thirty years, only the history of religions furnishes the discipline that can bring to light the meaning not only of traditional, but also of 'primitive' and Oriental civilizations. In a word, this is a discipline—such at least as I envision and practice it—that will contribute decisively to 'globalizing' culture" (p. 226).

3. "Crisis and Renewal in the History of Religions," pp. 5, 6, 9.

4. "History of Religions and a New Humanism," p. 2 and "Crisis and Renewal in the History of Religions," p. 16. As previously noted, both of these articles are reproduced in *Quest.* Eliade claims that "an encounter with the 'totally other,' whether conscious or unconscious, gives rise to an experience of a religious nature." It is "possible that the attraction of the unconscious and its activities, the interest in myths and symbols, the fascination of the exotic, the primitive, the archaic, and encounters with the 'others,' with all the ambivalent feelings they imply—that all this may one day appear as a new type of religious experience" *(Mephistopheles and the Androgyne,* pp. 11-12).

5. "Crisis and Renewal," pp. 7-8.

6. "History of Religions and a New Humanism," p. 3. In *No Souvenirs,* Eliade maintains: "To the degree that you *understand* a religious fact (myth, ritual, symbol, divine figure, etc.), you *change,* you are modified—and this change is the equivalent of a step forward in the process of self-liberation" (p. 310). See also *No Souvenirs,* p. 233.

7. Since this topic of rediscovering and recognizing mythic and symbolic structures and meanings is so broad and has been considered in many previous chapters, I shall focus on only a few of Eliade's writings where he discusses this in terms of techniques and methods of "anamnesis."

8. *Journal 3,* p. 262. See also *Journal 4,* p. 54.

9. Matei Calinescu, "Introduction: The Fantastic and Its Interpretation in Mircea Eliade's Later Novellas," in *Youth Without Youth and Other Novellas,* ed. Matei Calinescu and trans. Mac Linscott Ricketts (Columbus, Ohio: Ohio State University Press, 1988), pp. xxx-xxxvii.

10. *Images and Symbols,* p. 35.

11. Ibid., pp. 35-36. Obviously, this quotation and many previous citations contain ontological moves and personal judgments, often on a highly normative philosophical level. For the most part, Eliade is making sweeping criticisms and offering dramatic proposals but is not concerned with providing the careful philosophical analysis to justify his position. Focusing on this quotation, much of contemporary philosophy, especially in its non-Eliadean antifoundationalism, would agree with Eliade about the problem of historical and existential relativism. But for those philosophers for whom such relativism is a serious problem, Eliade's claim that the reactivation and recollection of nonhistorical mythic and symbolic structures is the way to overcome relativism and nihilism will hardly seem like an adequate philosophical response. The most generous response may be that Eliade—even when he is making such philosophical claims and judgments without providing rigorous philosophical analysis—is suggesting directions for more developed philosophical reflection.

12. *Myth and Reality*, pp. 134-36. In *Myths, Dreams and Mysteries* (pp. 233-35), Eliade interprets this "modern passion for historiography" as part of the modern awareness and anxiety in confronting history and one's historicity and as revealing, from a traditional religious perspective, an archaic symbolism of death.

13. *Myth and Reality*, pp. 136-37.

14. Ibid., p. 138.

15. *Australian Religions*, p. 200.

16. *Journal 1*, p. 163.

17. *No Souvenirs*, p. 179.

18. *Autobiography 1*, p. 204. Of course, with the rise of "Romanianism" and Romanian fascism at this time, one may question to what extent Romanian culture did in fact "transcend nationalism and cultural provincialism."

19. *Autobiography 2*, p. 107. See also *Journal 4*, p. 10-11. This claim for the key, essential, unique, indispensable role of the history of religions for Western and global cultural renewal was seen in "Crisis and Renewal in History of Religions" and other works by Eliade cited above.

20. *Myths, Dreams and Mysteries*, pp. 231-45.

21. See Eliade's interpretation of the initiatory significance of suffering, the symbolism of initiatory death, and other aspects of the myths, rituals, and symbolism of initiation in "Mysteries and Spiritual Regeneration," in *Myths, Dreams and Mysteries*, pp. 190-228, and the detailed treatments in *Rites and Symbols of Initiation, Shamanism*, and other scholarly works.

22. *Myths, Dreams and Mysteries*, pp. 236-38.

23. Ibid., pp. 238-39.

24. Ibid., pp. 239-41. Once again, such metaphysical and ontological formulations by Eliade, while they may serve to stimulate philosophical reflection, do not by themselves constitute adequate philosophical positions. It is not

the case that modern philosophers arbitrarily reject the archaic and Indian metaphysical and ontological absolutes and ignorantly, or even happily, embrace relativism, historicism, anxiety, and suffering. They present arguments and analysis. Obviously, any Western philosophical position, renewed through its encounters with archaic and other nonWestern perspectives, must meet rigorous criteria for philosophical adequacy.

25. *Myths, Dreams and Mysteries,* pp. 242-43. Eliade states that by seeing ourselves from the archaic and Indian perspectives, we were able "to rediscover the initiatory meanings and the spiritual values of anxiety, meanings and values well known to certain European mystical and metaphysical traditions. But this is as much as to say that a dialogue with the *true* Asiatic, African or Oceanian world helps us to rediscover spiritual positions that one is justified in regarding as universally valid" (p. 244).

26. The most developed formulation is the chapter entitled "The Terror of History" in *The Myth of the Eternal Return,* pp. 139-62.

27. *Autobiography 2,* p. 81. Eliade observes the he had been convinced "that in History we Romanians are a luckless people." He was sure that the only Romanian creations that would survive from the twenty years that "History" had allowed for national unity and political independence (1918-1938) "were those of a spiritual order" (p. 82).

28. *Zalmoxis,* pp. 254-55. Eliade submits: "The essential element lies in *the capacity to annul the apparently irremediable consequences of a tragic event by charging them with previously unsuspected [transhistorical, religious] values"* (p. 255). In Eliade's study of the popular Romanian ballad, the "Mioritza" (*Zalmoxis,* pp. 226-56), the last section is entitled "The 'Terror of History' and the Shepherd's Response" (pp. 253-56).

29. *Eternal Return,* pp. 141-42, 147-50.

30. Ibid., pp. 147-56.

31. Ibid., pp. 156-59.

32. Ibid., pp. 159-62.

33. *Journal 3,* pp. 129-30; *No Souvenirs,* p. 86. In *Journal 1,* Eliade contends: "To the extent the man of modern societies rediscovers himself in archaic anthropocosmic symbolism, he acquires a new existential dimension. Thus he regains a major and authentic mode of being which defends him from historicistic nihilism, without removing him from 'History.' It is even possible that History might reveal its true meaning: as the epiphany of a 'glorious' human condition" (p. 108).

34. Much of what follows appears in the section "Eliade's Scholarship as Political/Non-political," in Allen, "Recent Defenders of Eliade," pp. 342-46.

35. See Adriana Berger's publications: "Fascism and Religion in Romania," *Annals of Scholarship* 6 (1989): 455-65; "Anti-Judaism and Anti-Historicism in Eliade's Writings," *HADOAR—The Jewish Histadrut of America*

6 (1991): 14-17; "Mircea Eliade's Vision for a New Humanism," *Society* (July/August 1993): 84-87; and "Mircea Eliade: Romanian Fascism and the History of Religions in the United States," in *Tainted Greatness: Antisemitism and Cultural Heroes,* ed. Nancy Harrowitz (Philadelphia: Temple University Press, 1994), pp. 51-74; Seymour Cain, "Mircea Eliade, the Iron Guard, and Romanian Anti-Semitism," *Midstream* 25 (1989): 27-31; Daniel Dubuisson, "Metaphysique et politique: l'ontologie antisémite de Mircea Eliade," *Faut-il Avoir Peur de la Democratie?* 26 (autumn 1992/winter 1993): 103-18, and Daniel Dubuisson, *Mythologies du XXe Siècle: Dumézil, Lévi-Strauss, Eliade* (Lille: Presses Universitaires de Lille, 1993); Norman Manea, "Happy Guilt: Mircea Eliade, Fascism, and the Unhappy Fate of Romania," *The New Republic* (August 5, 1991): 27-36; Russell T. McCutcheon, "The Myth of the Apolitical Scholar: The Life and Works of Mircea Eliade," *Queen's Quarterly* 100 (1993): 642-63; Bryan S. Rennie, "The Diplomatic Career of Mircea Eliade: A Response to Adriana Berger," *Religion* 22 (1992): 375-92, and Rennie, *Reconstructing Eliade,* pp. 143-77; Strenski, *Four Theories of Myth,* pp. 76-79, 88-103; Leon Volovici, *Nationalist Ideology and Antisemitism: The Case of Romanian Intellectuals in the 30s* (New York: Pergamon Press, 1991).

36. Berger, "Mircea Eliade: Romanian Fascism and the History of Religions in the United States," pp. 51-52. Similarly, in her critical review of Cave's book in *Society,* Berger argues that Eliade's specific spiritual vision of the new humanism can only be grasped fully as based on his influential ideological stance and political involvement in Romanian fascism.

37. McCutcheon, "The Myth of the Apolitical Scholar," pp. 657, 658-59, 661-62. As with Berger, some of McCutcheon's charges need much more evidence and argumentation. Nevertheless, he raises troubling charges and incriminating evidence, not only about Eliade's life and especially about his scholarship, but also about Eliade's politically and religiously conservative influence on the contemporary study of religion.

38. Rennie, *Reconstructing Eliade,* pp. 143-77. Most of Rennie's treatment of Berger consists of criticisms of her interpretation of the British Foreign Office documents in her article in *Annals of Scholarship.* See *Reconstructing Eliade,* pp. 152-58, which repeats attacks made in Rennie's "The Diplomatic Career of Mircea Eliade."

39. Rennie, *Reconstructing Eliade,* p, 177. Rennie has made a valuable contribution to the political-spiritual debate by offering such a strong defense of Eliade, but he employs a double standard. On the one hand, he is too apologetic and uncritical in defending Eliade. One cannot always defend Eliade by claiming that his political formulations refer only to attitudes and beliefs of religious believers, of *homo religiosus,* and do not reflect his own position. Rennie is too uncritical in overlooking potentially damaging passages, in asserting Eliade's innocence, and in providing alternative pro-Eliade readings

of the material. On the other hand, while many critics deserve to be criticized, Rennie is too suspicious of motives and hidden agendas and too easily dismisses all of the objections and interpretations raised by critics.

40. Although I appreciate the valuable insights and legitimate critiques of modernity found in many postmodernist writers, I tend to be critical of much of postmodernism for what often seem to be facile dismissals of modernity with assertions that are vague, uncritically eclectic, and lack rigorous analysis. I prefer to incorporate certain postmodernist insights—as well as premodernist insights—to reformulate in radically new ways certain modernist projects.

41. Taking this to an extreme relativism, as some postmodernists do, postmodernism may be open to the following typical criticisms offered by Michael Albert in "Science, Post Modernism, and the Left," *Z Magazine* 9 (July/August 1996): "If one says there are no truths and there are only stories, then there is no reason to strive for objectivity, no reason to bother with facts, no reason to be logically consistent, no reason not to make up any old thing just because we like the way it sounds or favor its implications. More, the only sanction for any claim would be the linguistic or emotive quality of the supporting rhetoric, or the stature of its proponents, or whether we like the implications . . ." (p. 67).

42. *No Souvenirs,* pp. 164-65.

43. *Patterns,* pp. 433-34.

44. *Ordeal by Labyrinth,* pp. 116-17. Concerning this basic "human condition," Eliade asserts that "the best expression and the most accurate definition of the human condition is as a series of initiation trials or ordeals—which is to say, of deaths and resurrections" (p. 89). He submits that the symbolism of the labyrinth "is the model of all existence, which passes through many ordeals in order to journey toward its own center . . ." (p. 185).

45. *Journal 3,* p. 221. Eliade concludes: "It is thus possible that these reflections, because of their intimate character, only amplify better, although indirectly, my remorse in betraying my vocation as a philosopher . . ."

46. *Eternal Return,* pp. ix-xi. Heidegger and some other contemporary philosophers have attempted to return to the pre-Socratic for philosophical renewal. See Lawrence J. Hatab, *Myth and Philosophy: A Contest of Truths* (La Salle, Illinois: Open Court, 1990) for an attempt to return to Greek myth and philosophy. Strongly influenced by Nietzsche and Heidegger, Hatab examines the rejection of myth by Greek philosophy, argues for a pluralistic notion of truth with myth as a legitimate form of understanding and unconcealment of existential meaning, maintains that philosophy itself retains certain mythic features, and proposes that philosophy can be renewed by reexamining its hostility toward myth. I might add that Hatab defines "myth" in much more narrow terms than does Eliade.

47. *Quest,* p. 9.

48. Ibid., pp. 63-64.

49. See Ricoeur, *The Symbolism of Evil,* pp. 355-57; Allen, *Structure and Creativity in Religion,* pp. 236-43.

50. Allen, *Structure and Creativity in Religion,* pp. 242-43.

51. This analysis is developed in Douglas Allen, "Social Constructions of Self: Some Asian, Marxist, and Feminist Critiques of Dominant Western Views of Self," in *Culture and Self: Philosophical and Religious Perspectives, East and West,* ed. Douglas Allen (Boulder, Colo.: Westview Press, 1997), pp. 3-26.

Bibliography

Many of Eliade's publications reappear, in identical or slightly revised form, in later works. Journal articles are often reprinted as chapters in Eliade's books. One of the goals of *Mircea Eliade: An Annotated Bibliography* by Douglas Allen and Dennis Doeing was to provide extensive cross-references so that readers could avoid the frustration of searching for some publication only to find that they had already read it in a different language or as a chapter in a book. I have listed articles by Eliade used in writing this book. Sometimes I have added information about major publications in which articles are reprinted. If I used the later publications, such as books by Eliade, I have not listed the original articles.

PRIMARY SOURCES

Books

Eliade, Mircea. *Australian Religions: An Introduction.* Ithaca: Cornell University Press, 1973.

———. *Autobiography, Volume I: 1907-1937, Journey East, Journey West.* Translated by Mac Linscott Ricketts. San Francisco: Harper & Row, 1981.

———. *Autobiography, Volume II: 1937-1960, Exile's Odyssey.* Translated by Mac Linscott Ricketts. Chicago: University of Chicago Press, 1988.

———. *Bengal Nights.* Translated by Catherine Spencer (from the 1950 French translation of *Maitreyi* entitled *La nuit bengali*). Chicago: University of Chicago Press, 1994.

———. *Comentarii la legenda Meșterului Manole* ("Commentaries on the Legend of Master Manole"). Bucharest: Publicom, 1943.

———. *Cosmos and History: The Myth of the Eternal Return.* Translated by Willard R. Trask. New York: Harper & Row, Torchbooks, 1959.

———. *The Forbidden Forest.* Translated by Mac Linscott Ricketts and Mary Park Stevenson. Notre Dame: University of Notre Dame Press, 1978.

———. *From Primitives to Zen: A Thematic Sourcebook of the History of Religions.* New York: Harper and Row, 1967. (A paperback edition was published in 1977 as *From Primitives to Zen* and later as *Essential Sacred Writings From Around the World.*)

———. *The Forge and the Crucible.* Translated by Stephen Corrin. New York: Harper & Brothers, 1962.

———. *Fragmentarium* ("Essays"). Bucharest: Vremea, 1939.

———. *A History of Religious Ideas.* Vol. 1: *From the Stone Age to the Eleusinian Mysteries.* Translated by Willard R. Trask. Chicago: University of Chicago Press, 1978.

———. *A History of Religious Ideas.* Vol. 2: *From Gautama Buddha to the Triumph of Christianity.* Translated by Willard R. Trask. Chicago: University of Chicago Press, 1982.

———. *A History of Religious Ideas.* Vol. 3: *From Muhammad to the Age of Reforms.* Translated by Alf Hiltebeitel and Diane Apostolos-Cappadona. Chicago: University of Chicago Press, 1985.

———. *Images and Symbols: Studies in Religious Symbolism.* Translated by Philip Mairet. New York: Sheed and Ward, 1961.

———. *Journal I, 1945-1955.* Translated by Mac Linscott Ricketts. Chicago: University of Chicago Press, 1990.

———. *Journal II, 1957-1969.* See Eliade, *No Souvenirs.*

———. *Journal III, 1970-1978.* Translated by Teresa Lavender Fagan. Chicago: University of Chicago Press, 1989.

———. *Journal IV, 1979-1985.* Translated by Mac Linscott Ricketts. Chicago: University of Chicago Press, 1990.

———. *Mademoiselle Christina.* Paris: L'Herne, 1978.

———. *Maitreyi.* Bucharest: Cultura Nationala, 1933.

———. *Mephistopheles and the Androgyne: Studies in Religious Myth and Symbol.* Translated by J. M. Cohen. New York: Sheed and Ward, 1965. This book was also published under the title *The Two and the One.*

———. *Mitul Reintegrării* ("The Myth of Reintegration"). Bucharest: Vremea, 1942.

———. *Myth and Reality.* Translated by Willard R. Trask. New York: Harper & Row, 1963.

———. *The Myth of the Eternal Return.* Translated by Willard R. Trask. New York: Pantheon Books, 1954.

———. *Myths, Dreams and Mysteries.* Translated by Philip Mairet. New York: Harper & Row, Torchbooks, 1967.

———. *No Souvenirs: Journal, 1957-1969.* Translated by Fred H. Johnson, Jr. New York: Harper & Row, 1977. Also published as Mircea Eliade, *Journal II, 1957-1969.* Translated by Fred H. Johnson, Jr. Chicago: University of Chicago Press, 1989.

———. *Occultism, Witchcraft, and Cultural Fashions: Essays in Comparative Religions.* Chicago: University of Chicago Press, 1976.

———. *The Old Man and the Bureaucrats.* Translated by Mary Park Stevenson. Chicago: University of Chicago Press, 1988.

———. *Ordeal by Labyrinth: Conversations with Claude-Henri Rocquet.* Translated by Derek Coltman. Chicago: University of Chicago Press, 1982.

———. *Patterns in Comparative Religion.* Translated by Rosemary Sheed. New York: World Publishing Co., Meridian Books, 1963.

———. *The Quest: History and Meaning in Religion.* Chicago: University of Chicago Press, 1969.

———. *Rites and Symbols of Initiation: The Mysteries of Birth and Rebirth.* Translated by Willard R. Trask. New York: Harper Torchbooks, 1965. Reprinted from *Birth and Rebirth: The Religious Meaning of Initiation in Human Culture.* Translated by Willard R. Trask. New York: Harper and Brothers, 1958.

———. *Şarpele* ("The Snake"). Bucharest: Naţională Ciornei, 1937.

———. *Shamanism: Archaic Techniques of Ecstasy.* Translated by Willard R. Trask. New York: Pantheon Books, 1964.

———. *Symbolism, the Sacred, and the Arts.* Edited by Diane Apostolos-Cappadona. New York: Crossroad, 1986.

———. *Two Tales of the Occult.* Translated by William Ames Coates. New York: Herder and Herder, 1970. Republished as *Two Strange Tales.*

Boston: Shambala, 1986. Includes Eliade's "Nights at Serampore" and
"The Secret of Dr. Honigberger."

————. *Traité d'histoire des religions.* Paris: Payot, 1949. Translated as
Patterns in Comparative Religion.

————. *Yoga: Immortality and Freedom.* Translated by Willard R. Trask. New
York: Pantheon Books, 1958.

————. *Youth Without Youth and Other Novellas.* Edited by Matei Calinescu
and translated by Mac Linscott Ricketts. Columbus, Ohio: Ohio State
University Press, 1988. Includes Eliade's "The Cape," "Youth Without
Youth," and "Nineteen Roses."

————. *Zalmoxis, The Vanishing God: Comparative Studies in the Religions
and Folklore of Dacia and Eastern Europe.* Translated by Willard R.
Trask. Chicago: University of Chicago Press, 1972.

————, editor in chief. *The Encyclopedia of Religion.* 16 vols. New York:
Macmillan, 1987.

———— and Ioan P. Couliano [Culianu]. *The Eliade Guide to World Religions.*
San Francisco: HarperCollins Publishers, 1991.

———— and Mihai Niculescu. *Fantastic Tales.* Translated and edited by Eric
Tappe. London and Boston: Forest Books, 1990. First published by
Dillons, London, 1969. Includes Eliade's "Twelve Thousand Head of
Cattle" and "A Great Man."

Articles

Eliade, Mircea. "Afterword." In Nae Ionescu, *Roza vânturilor.* Bucharest: Ed.
Cultura Nationala, 1937.

————. "Archaic Myth and Historical Man." *McCormick Quarterly* 18 (1965):
23-36.

————. "Bucureşti, 1937," in *Fiinţa Românească* 5 (1967): 47-66.

————. "The Cape." In *Youth Without Youth and Other Novellas,* edited by
Matei Calinescu and translated by Mac Linscott Ricketts, 3-47. Columbus,
Ohio: Ohio State University Press, 1988.

————. "Comparative Religion: Its Past and Future." In *Knowledge and the
Future of Man,* edited by Walter J. Ong, S.J., 245-54. New York: Holt,
Rinehart and Winston, 1968.

————. "Cosmical Homology and Yoga." *Journal of the Indian Society of Oriental Art* 5 (1937): 188-203.

————. "Cosmogonic Myth and 'Sacred History,'" *Religious Studies* 2 (1967): 171-83. Reprinted in Eliade, *The Quest: History and Meaning in Religion.*

————. "Crisis and Renewal in History of Religions." *History of Religions* 5 (1965): 1-17. Reprinted as "Crisis and Renewal" in Eliade, *The Quest: History and Meaning in Religion.*

————. "Cultural Fashions and History of Religions." In *Occultism, Witchcraft, and Cultural Fashions: Essays in Comparative Religions*, 1-17. Chicago: University of Chicago Press, 1976. Reprinted from *The History of Religions: Essays on the Problem of Understanding*, edited by Joseph M. Kitagawa, 21-38. Chicago: University of Chicago Press, 1967.

————. "The Dragon and the Shaman: Notes on a South American Mythology." In *Man and His Salvation: Studies in Memory of S. G. F. Brandon*, edited by E. J. Sharpe and J. R. Hinnells, 99-105. Manchester: Manchester University Press, 1973.

————. "Foreword." In Douglas Allen, *Structure and Creativity in Religion.* The Hague: Mouton Publishers, 1978.

————. "Fragment autobiographic." *Caete de Dor* 7 (1953): 1-13.

————. "Fragmente de Jurnal." *Caete de Dor* 8 (1954): 16-29.

————. "Historical Events and Structural Meaning in Tension." *Criterion* 6, no. 1 (1967): 29-31.

————. "History of Religions and a New Humanism." *History of Religions* 1 (1961): 1-8. This appears as "A New Humanism" in Eliade, *The Quest : History and Meaning in Religion.*

————. "History of Religions and 'Popular' Cultures." *History of Religions* 20 (1980): 1-26.

————. "Homo Faber and Homo Religiosus." In *The History of Religions: Retrospect and Prospect*, edited by Joseph M. Kitagawa, 1-12. New York: Macmillan, 1985.

————. "Itinerariu spiritual" ("Spiritual Itinerary"). *Cuvântul* 3, nos. 857, 860, 862, 867, 874, 885, 889, 903, 911, 915, 924, 928 (Sept.-Nov. 1927).

————. "Literary Imagination and Religious Structure." *Criterion* 17, no. 2 (1978): 30-34.

———. "Littérature orale." In *Histoire des littératures. Vol. 1: Littératures anciennes orientales et orales,* edited by R. Queneau, 3-26. Paris: Gallimard, 1956.

———. "Les livres populaires dans la littérature roumaine." *Zalmoxis* 2 (1939): 63-78.

———. "Masks: Mythical and Ritual Origins." In *Encyclopedia of World Art.* Vol. 9, col. 524. London and New York: McGraw-Hill, 1964. Reprinted in Eliade, *Symbolism, the Sacred, and the Arts,* edited by Diane Apostolos-Cappadona, 64-71. New York: Crossroad, 1986.

———. "Methodological Remarks on the Study of Religious Symbolism." In *The History of Religions: Essays in Methodology,* edited by Mircea Eliade and Joseph M. Kitagawa, 86-107. Chicago: University of Chicago Press, 1959. Reprinted as "Observations on Religious Symbolism," in Eliade, *Mephistopheles and the Androgyne: Studies in Religious Myth and Symbol.*

———. "Mircea Eliade" (interview of Eliade by Delia O'Hara). *Chicago* 35, no. 6 (June 1986): 147-51, 177-80.

———. "The Myth of Alchemy" *Parabola* 3, no. 3 (1978): 7-23.

———. "Mythologie et histoire des religions." *Diogène* 9 (1955): 99-116.

———. "Myths-and-Symbols Tracer Has a View to Conjure With" (interview of Eliade by Leslie Maitland). *New York Times* (February 4, 1979): 44.

———. "Nineteen Roses." In *Youth Without Youth and Other Novellas,* edited by Matei Calinescu and translated by Mac Linscott Ricketts, 153-285. Columbus, Ohio: Ohio State University Press, 1988.

———. "Notes for a Dialogue." In *The Theology of Altizer: Critique and Response,* edited by J. B. Cobb, 234-41. Philadelphia: Westminster Press, 1970.

———. "Notes on the Symbolism of the Arrow." In *Religion in Antiquity: Essays in Memory of Erwin Ramsdell Goodenough,* edited by Jacob Neusner, 463-75. Leiden: E. J. Brill, 1968.

———. "On Understanding Primitive Religions." In *Glaube, Geist, Geschichte: Festschrift für Ernst Benz,* edited by Gerhard Müller and Winfried Zeller, 498-505. Leiden: E. J. Brill, 1967.

———. "Preface." In Thomas N. Munson, *Reflective Theology: Philosophical Orientations in Religion.* New Haven: Yale University Press, 1968.

————. "Profanii." *Vremea* (December 11, 1936), reprinted in Mircea Eliade, *Fragmentarium.* Bucharest: Vremea, 1939, pp. 86-89;

————. "The Quest for the 'Origins' of Religion." *History of Religions* 4 (1964): 154-69. This appears in Eliade, *The Quest: History and Meaning in Religion.*

————. "Recent Works on Shamanism: A Review Article." *History of Religions* 1, no. 1 (1961): 152-86.

————. "Religia în viața spiritulu." *Est-Vest* 1, no. 1 (January 1927): 28.

————. "The Sacred and the Modern Artist," *Criterion* 4, no. 2 (1965): 22-24.

————. "The Sacred in the Secular World." *Cultural Hermeneutics* 1 (1973): 101-13. The title of this journal was changed to *Philosophy and Social Criticism* in 1978.

————. "Sacred Tradition and Modern Man: A Conversation with Mircea Eliade." *Parabola* 1, no. 3 (1976): 74-80.

————. "Structures and Changes in the History of Religions." Translated by Kathryn K. Atwater. In *City Invincible,* edited by Carl H. Kraeling and Robert M. Adams, 351-66. Chicago: University of Chicago Press, 1960.

————. "Survivals and Camouflages of Myths." *Diogenes* 41 (1963): 1-25. Reprinted in Eliade, *Myth and Reality.*

————. "Le symbolisme des ténèbres dans les religions archaïques." In *Polarités du symbole,* Études Carmélitaines 39 (1960): 15-28. Translated as "The Symbolism of Shadows in Archaic Religions" in Eliade, *Symbolism, the Sacred, and the Arts,* edited by Diane Apostolos-Cappadona, 3-16. New York: Crossroad, 1986.

————. "The Yearning for Paradise in Primitive Tradition." *Daedalus* 88 (1959): 255-67. Reprinted as "Nostalgia for Paradise in the Primitive Traditions," in *Myths, Dreams and Mysteries.*

———— and Lawrence E. Sullivan. "Hierophany." In *The Encyclopedia of Religion,* vol. 6, 313-17. New York: Macmillan, 1987.

SECONDARY SOURCES

Books

Allen, Douglas. *Mircea Eliade et le phénomène religieux.* Paris: Payot, 1982.

————. *Structure and Creativity in Religion: Hermeneutics in Mircea Eliade's Phenomenology and New Directions.* The Hague: Mouton Publishers, 1978.

————, ed. *Culture and Self: Philosophical and Religious Perspectives, East and West.* Boulder, Colo.: Westview Press, 1997.

———— and Dennis Doeing. *Mircea Eliade: An Annotated Bibliography.* New York: Garland, 1980.

Altizer, Thomas J. J. *Mircea Eliade and the Dialectic of the Sacred.* Philadelphia: Westminster Press, 1963.

Baird, Robert D. *Category Formation and the History of Religions.* The Hague: Mouton, 1971.

Barbosa da Silva, Antonio. *The Phenomenology of Religion as a Philosophical Problem.* Uppsala: CWK Gleerup, 1982.

Bonevac, Daniel. *Reduction in the Abstract Sciences.* Cambridge: Hackett, 1982.

Caillois, Roger. *Man and the Sacred.* Translated by Meyer Barash. Glencoe, Ill.: Free Press, 1959.

Cave, David. *Mircea Eliade's Vision for a New Humanism.* New York: Oxford University Press, 1993.

Dawson, Lorne. *Reason, Freedom and Religion: Closing the Gap Between the Humanistic and the Scientific Study of Religion.* New York: Peter Lang, 1988.

Descartes, René. *Discourse on Method.* New York: Library of Liberal Arts, 1956.

Devi, Maitreyi. *It Does Not Die: A Romance.* Translated from the 1974 Bengali *Na Hanyate.* Calcutta: Writers Workshop, P. Lal, 1976 and Connecticut: Inter-Culture Associates, 1976. A more recent edition is Maitreyi Devi, *It Does Not Die: A Romance.* Chicago: University of Chicago Press, 1994..

Dubuisson, Daniel. *Mythologies du XXe Siècle: Dumézil, Lévi-Strauss, Eliade.* Lille: Presses Universitaires de Lille, 1993.

Dudley III, Guilford. *Religion on Trial: Mircea Eliade and His Critics.* Philadelphia: Temple University Press, 1977.

Duerr, Hans Peter, ed. *Die Mitte der Welt.* Frankfurt: Suhrkamp, 1984.

Freud, Sigmund. *The Future of an Illusion.* Translated by W. D. Robson-Scott. New York: Liveright Co., 1961.

Girardot, Norman J. and Mac Linscott Ricketts, eds. *Imagination and Meaning: The Scholarly and Literary Works of Mircea Eliade.* New York: Seabury Press, 1982.

Handy, E. S. C. *Polynesian Religion.* Honolulu: Bernice P. Bishop Museum Bulletin 34, 1927.

Hatab, Lawrence J. *Myth and Philosophy: A Contest of Truth.* La Salle, Ill.: Open Court, 1990.

Hegel, G. W. F. *The Phenomenology of Mind.* Translated by J. B. Baillie. New York: Harper and Row, 1967.

Heidegger, Martin. *Being and Time.* Translated by John Macquarrie and Edward Robinson. New York: Harper, 1962.

Hempel, Carl. *Philosophy of Natural Science.* Englewood Cliffs, N.J.: Prentice-Hall, Inc., 1966.

Idinopulos, Thomas A. and Edward A. Yonan, eds. *Religion and Reductionism: Essays on Eliade, Segal, and the Challenge of the Social Sciences for the Study of Religion.* Leiden: E. J. Brill, 1994.

Ionescu, Nae. *Roza vânturilor.* Bucharest: Ed. Cultura Nationala, 1937.

Kirk, G. S. *Myth: Its Meaning and Function.* Cambridge: Cambridge University Press, 1970.

Kitagawa, Joseph M., ed. *The History of Religions: Essays on the Problem of Understanding.* Chicago: University of Chicago Press, 1967.

———— and Charles H. Long, eds. *Myths and Symbols: Studies in Honor of Mircea Eliade.* Chicago: University of Chicago Press, 1969.

Kraemer, Hendrik. *The Christian Message in a Non-Christian World.* London: James Clarke & Co., 1956.

————. *Religion and the Christian Faith.* Philadelphia: Westminster Press, 1956.

Kristensen, W. Brede. *The Meaning of Religion.* Translated by John B. Carman. The Hague: Martinus Nijhoff, 1960.

Levinas, Emmanuel. *Otherwise Than Being or Beyond Essence.* Translated by Alphonso Lingis. The Hague: Martinus Nijhoff, 1981.

————. *Totality and Infinity.* Translated by Alphonso Lingis. Pittsburgh: Duquesne University Press, 1969.

Long, Charles H. *Alpha: The Myths of Creation.* New York: George Braziller, 1963.

Marino, Adrian. *L'Herméneutique de Mircea Eliade.* Translated by Jean Gouillard. Paris: Gallimard, 1981.

Merleau-Ponty, Maurice. *Signs.* Translated by Richard C. McCleary. Evanston: Northwestern University Press, 1964.

Mill, John Stuart. *Collected Works of John Stuart Mill.* Edited by J. M. Robson. Vol. 21. Toronto: University of Toronto Press, 1984.

———. *The Philosophy of John Stuart Mill.* Edited by Marshall Cohen. New York: Random House, 1961.

Nagel, Ernest. *The Structure of Science.* New York: Harcourt, Brace and World, 1961.

Okin, Susan Moller. *Justice, Gender, and the Family.* New York: Basic Books, 1989.

Olson, Carl. *The Theology and Philosophy of Eliade: A Search for the Centre.* New York: St. Martin's Press, 1992.

Otto, Rudolf. *The Idea of the Holy.* Translated by John W. Harvey. New York: Oxford University Press, A Galaxy Book, 1958.

Pals, Daniel L. *Seven Theories of Religion.* New York: Oxford University Press, 1996.

Peacocke, Arthur, ed. *Reductionism in Academic Disciplines.* Worcester, England: Billing & Sons Ltd., 1985.

Penner, Hans H. *Impasse and Resolution.* New York: Peter Lang, 1989.

Pettazzoni, Raffaele. *Essays on the History of Religions.* Translated by H. J. Rose. Leiden: E. J. Brill, 1954.

Plato. *The Collected Dialogues of Plato.* Edited by Edith Hamilton and Huntington Cairns. New York: Pantheon Books, Bollingen Series LXXI, 1963.

———. *The Republic of Plato.* Translated by Francis MacDonald Cornford. New York and London: Oxford University Press, 1945.

Preus, J. Samuel. *Explaining Religion.* New Haven: Yale University Press, 1987.

Rennie, Bryan S. *Reconstructing Eliade: Making Sense of Religion.* Albany: State University of New York Press, 1996.

Ricketts, Mac Linscott. *Mircea Eliade: The Romanian Roots, 1907-1945.* 2 vols. Boulder, Colo.: East European Monographs, No. 248, 1988.

Ricoeur, Paul. *The Symbolism of Evil.* Translated by Emerson Buchanan. New York: Harper & Row, 1967.

Said, Edward W. *Orientalism.* New York: Vintage Books, 1979.

Saliba, John A. *"Homo Religiosus" in Mircea Eliade: An Anthropological Evaluation.* Leiden: Brill, 1976.

Sartre, Jean-Paul. *Being and Nothingness: An Essay in Phenomenological Ontology.* Translated by Hazel E. Barnes. New York: Philosophical Library, 1956.

———. *Existentialism.* Translated by Bernard Frechtman. New York: The Philosophical Library, 1947.

Schärer, Hans. *Ngaju Religion: The Conception of God among a South Borneo People.* Translated by Rodney Needham. The Hague: M. Nijhoff, 1963.

Segal, Robert A. *Explaining and Interpreting Religion: Essays on the Issue.* New York: Peter Lang, 1992.

———. *Religion and the Social Sciences: Essays on the Confrontation.* Atlanta: Scholars Press, 1989.

Smith, John E. *Reason and God.* New Haven: Yale University Press, 1967.

Smith, Jonathan Z. *Map Is Not Territory.* Leiden: E. J. Brill, 1978.

Smith, Wilfred Cantwell, *Faith and Belief.* Princeton: Princeton University Press, 1979.

———. *The Faith of Other Men.* New York: Mentor Books, 1963.

———. *The Meaning and End of Religion.* New York: Macmillan, 1963.

Strasser, Stephen. *The Soul in Metaphysical and Empirical Psychology.* Pittsburgh: Duquesne University Press, 1962.

Strehlow, T. G. H. *Aranda Traditions.* Melbourne: Melbourne University Press, 1947.

Strenski, Ivan. *Four Theories of Myth in Twentieth-Century History: Cassirer, Eliade, Lévi-Strauss and Malinowski.* Iowa City: University of Iowa Press, 1987.

Tacou, Constantin, ed. *Mircea Eliade.* Cahiers de l'Herne, no. 33. Paris: Editions de l'Herne, 1978.

Volovici, Leon. *Nationalist Ideology and Antisemitism: The Case of Romanian Intellectuals in the 30s.* New York: Pergamon Press, 1991.

Wach, Joachim. *The Comparative Study of Religions.* Edited by Joseph M. Kitagawa. New York: Columbia University Press, 1961.

Webster's Ninth New Collegiate Dictionary. Springfield, Mass.: Merriam-Webster, 1987.

Webster's Third New International Dictionary of the English Language. Springfield, Mass.: Merriam-Webster, 1959.

Zimmer, Heinrich. *Myths and Symbols in Indian Art and Civilization.* Edited by Joseph Campbell. New York: Harper Torchbooks, 1962.

Articles

Albert, Michael. "Science, Post Modernism, and the Left." *Z Magazine* 9 (July/August 1996): 64-69.

Allen, Douglas. "Eliade and History." *Journal of Religion* 68 (1988): 545-65.

———. "Phenomenology of Religion." In *The Encyclopedia of Religion,* vol. 11, 272-85. New York: Macmillan, 1987.

———. "Recent Defenders of Eliade: A Critical Evaluation." *Religion* 24 (1994): 333-51.

———. "Religious-Political Conflict in Sri Lanka: Philosophical Considerations." In *Religion and Political Conflict in South Asia: India Pakistan, and Sri Lanka,* edited by Douglas Allen, 181-203. Westport, Conn.: Greenwood Publishers, 1992; New Delhi: Oxford University Press, 1993.

———. Review of *Four Theories of Myth in Twentieth-Century History* by Ivan Strenski. *Journal of the American Academy of Religion* 59 (Winter 1991): 874-77.

———. Review of *Mircea Eliade: The Romanian Roots, 1907-1945* by Mac Linscott Ricketts. *Journal of the American Academy of Religion* 60 (Spring 1992): 174-77

———. "Social Constructions of Self: Some Asian, Marxist, and Feminist Critiques of Dominant Western Views of Self." In *Culture and Self: Philosophical and Religious Perspectives, East and West,* edited by Douglas Allen, 3-26. Boulder, Colo.: Westview Press, 1997.

Alles, Gregory D. *"Homo Religiosus."* In *The Encyclopedia of Religion,* vol. 6, 442-45. New York: Macmillan, 1987.

Altizer, Thomas J. J. "Mircea Eliade and the Death of God." *Cross Currents* 29, no. 3 (1979): 257-68.

———. "Mircea Eliade and the Recovery of the Sacred." *The Christian Scholar* 45, no. 4 (1962): 267-89.

Bascom, William. "The Forms of Folklore: Prose Narratives." In *Sacred Narrative: Readings in the Theory of Myth,* edited by Alan Dundes, 5-29. Berkeley: University of California Press, 1984.

Berger, Adriana. "Anti-Judaism and Anti-Historicism in Eliade's Writings." *HADOAR—The Jewish Histadrut of America* 6 (1991): 14-17.

———. "Cultural Hermeneutics: The Concept of Imagination in the Phenomenological Approaches of Henry Corbin and Mircea Eliade." *Journal of Religion* 66 (April 1986): 141-56.

———. "Fascism and Religion in Romania." *Annals of Scholarship* 6 (1989): 455-65.

———. "Mircea Eliade: Romanian Fascism and the History of Religions in the United States." In *Tainted Greatness: Antisemitism and Cultural Heroes,* edited by Nancy Harrowitz, 51-74. Philadelphia: Temple University Press, 1994.

———. "Mircea Eliade's Vision for a New Humanism." *Society* (July/August 1993): 84-87.

Breu, Giovanna. "Teacher: Shamans? Hippies? They're All Creative to the World's Leading Historian of Religions." *People Weekly* 9, no. 12 (March 27, 1978): 43, 49.

Brown, R. F. "Eliade on Archaic Religions: Some Old and New Criticisms." *Sciences Religieuses* 10, no. 4 (1981): 429-49.

Cain, Seymour. "Mircea Eliade." In *International Encyclopaedia of the Social Sciences Biographical Supplement,* vol. 18, 166-72. New York: Macmillan, Free Press, 1979.

———. "Mircea Eliade: Attitudes Toward History." *Religious Studies Review* 6 (January 1980): 13-16.

———. "Mircea Eliade, the Iron Guard, and Romanian Anti-Semitism." *Midstream* 25 (November 1989): 27-31.

Calinescu, Matei. "Creation as Duty." *Journal of Religion* 65 (April 1985): 250-57.

———. "Imagination and Meaning: Aesthetic Attitudes and Ideas in Mircea Eliade's Thought." *Journal of Religion* 57 (Jan. 1977): 1-15.

———. "Introduction: The Fantastic and Its Interpretation in Mircea Eliade's Later Novellas." In Eliade, *Youth Without Youth and Other Novellas,* edited by Matei Calinescu and translated by Mac Linscott Ricketts, xiii-xxxix. Columbus, Ohio: Ohio State University Press, 1988.

Carrasco, David. "Prologue: Promise and the Labyrinth." In *Waiting for the Dawn: Mircea Eliade in Perspective,* edited by David Carrasco and Jane Marie Law, xv-xx. Boulder, Colo.: University Of Colorado Press, 1991.

Christ, Carol. "Mircea Eliade and the Feminist Paradigm Shift." *Journal of Feminist Studies* 7 (1991): 75-94.

Culianu, Ioan P. "Mircea Eliade at the Crossroads of Anthropology." *Neue Zeitschrift für systematische Theologie und Religionsphilosophie* 27, no. 2 (1985): 123-31.

Dawson, Lorne. "Human Reflexivity and the Nonreductive Explanation of Religious Action." In *Religion and Reductionism: Essays on Eliade, Segal, and the Challenge of the Social Sciences for the Study of Religion,* edited by Thomas A. Idinopulos and Edward A. Yonan, 143-61. Leiden: E. J. Brill, 1994.

Dubuisson, Daniel. "Metaphysique et politique: l'ontologie antisémite de Mircea Eliade." *Faut-il Avoir Peur de la Democratie?* 26 (autumn 1992/winter 1993): 103-18.

Edwards, Tony. "Religion, Explanation, and the Askesis of Inquiry." In *Religion and Reductionism: Essays on Eliade, Segal, and the Challenge of the Social Sciences for the Study of Religion,* edited by Thomas A. Idinopulos and Edward A. Yonan, 162-82. Leiden: E. J. Brill, 1994.

Elzey, Wayne. "Mircea Eliade and the Battle Against Reductionism." In *Religion and Reductionism: Essays on Eliade, Segal, and the Challenge of the Social Sciences for the Study of Religion,* edited by Thomas A. Idinopulos and Edward A. Yonan, 82-94. Leiden: E. J. Brill, 1994.

Fenton, John Y. "Reductionism in the Study of Religions." *Soundings* 53 (1970): 61-76.

Feyerabend, Paul. "Explanation, Reduction, and Empiricism." *Minnesota Studies in the Philosophy of Science,* vol. 3, edited by Herbert Feigl and Grover Maxwell, 28-97. Minneapolis: University of Minnesota Press, 1962.

Frye, Northrop. "World Enough Without Time." *The Hudson Review* 12 (1959): 423-31.

Hamilton, Kenneth. "*Homo Religiosus* and Historical Faith." *Journal of Bible and Religion* 33, no. 3 (1965): 213-22.

Heisig, James W. "Symbolism." In *The Encyclopedia of Religion,* vol. 14, 198-208. New York: Macmillan, 1987.

Honko, Lauri. "The Problem of Defining Myth." In *Sacred Narrative: Readings in the Theory of Myth,* edited by Alan Dundes, 41-52. Berkeley: University of California Press, 1984.

Hudson, Wilson M. "Eliade's Contribution to the Study of Myth." In *Tire Shrinker to Dragster,* edited by Wilson M. Hudson, 219-41. Austin: The Encino Press, 1968.

Idinopulos, Thomas A. "Must Professors of Religion be Religious? Comments on Eliade's Method of Inquiry and Segal's Defense of Reductionism." In *Religion and Reductionism: Essays on Eliade, Segal, and the Challenge of the Social Sciences for the Study of Religion,* edited by Thomas A. Idinopulos and Edward A. Yonan, 65-81. Leiden: E. J. Brill, 1994.

Ierunca, Virgil. "The Literary Work of Mircea Eliade." In *Myths and Symbols: Studies in Honor of Mircea Eliade,* edited by Joseph M. Kitagawa and Charles H. Long, 343-63. Chicago: University of Chicago Press, 1969.

Kirk, G. S. "On Defining Myth." In *Sacred Narrative: Readings in the Theory of Myth,* edited by Alan Dundes, 53-61. Berkeley: University of California Press, 1984.

Leach, Edmund "Sermons by a Man on a Ladder." *New York Review of Books* 7, no. 6 (October 20, 1966): 28-31.

Long, Charles H. "The Meaning of Religion in the Contemporary Study of Religions." *Criterion* 2 (1963): 23-26.

Luyster, Robert. "The Study of Myth: Two Approaches." *Journal of Bible and Religion* 34 (1966): 235-43.

Manea, Norman. "Happy Guilt: Mircea Eliade, Fascism, and the Unhappy Fate of Romania." *The New Republic* (August 5, 1991): 27-36.

Marx, Karl. "Contribution to the Critique of Hegel's *Philosophy of Right:* Introduction." In *The Marx-Engels Reader,* edited by Robert C. Tucker, 11-23. New York: W. W. Norton & Co., 1972.

―――. "Theses on Feuerbach." In *The Marx-Engels Reader,* edited by Robert C. Tucker, 107-109. New York: W. W. Norton & Co., 1972.

McCutcheon, Russell T. "The Myth of the Apolitical Scholar: The Life and Works of Mircea Eliade." *Queen's Quarterly* 100 (1993): 642-63.

Mill, John Stuart. "Nature" from *Three Essays on Religion.* In *The Philosophy of John Stuart Mill,* edited by Marshall Cohen. New York: Random House, 1961.

————. "The Subjection of Women." In *Collected Works of John Stuart Mill,* edited by J. M. Robson. Vol. 21. Toronto: University of Toronto Press, 1984.

Mills, C. Wright. "Situated Actions and Vocabularies of Motive." *American Sociologist Review* 5 (1940): 904-13.

Obeyesekere, Gananath. "Duṭṭhagāmaṇī and the Buddhist Conscience." In *Religion and Political Conflict in South Asia: India Pakistan, and Sri Lanka,* edited by Douglas Allen, 135-60. Westport, Conn.: Greenwood Publishers, 1992; New Delhi: Oxford University Press, 1993.

Oxtoby, Willard G. *"Religionswissenschaft* Revisited." In *Religions in Antiquity: Essays in Memory of Erwin Ramsdell Goodenough,* edited by Jacob Neusner, 560-608. Leiden: E. J. Brill, 1968.

Paden, William E. "Before 'The Sacred' Became Theological: Rereading the Durkheimian Legacy." In *Religion and Reductionism: Essays on Eliade, Segal, and the Challenge of the Social Sciences for the Study of Religion,* edited by Thomas A. Idinopulos and Edward A. Yonan, 198-210. Leiden: E. J. Brill, 1994.

Pals, Daniel L. "Explaining, Endorsing, and Reducing Religion." In *Religion and Reductionism: Essays on Eliade, Segal, and the Challenge of the Social Sciences for the Study of Religion,* edited by Thomas A. Idinopulos and Edward A. Yonan, 183-197. Leiden: E. J. Brill, 1994.

————. "Is Religion a *Sui Generis* Phenomenon?" *Journal of the American Academy of Religion* 55, no. 2 (Summer 1987): 259-82.

————. "Reductionism and Belief: An Appraisal of Recent Attacks on the Doctrine of Irreducible Religion." *Journal of Religion* 66, no. 1 (January 1986): 18-36.

Penner, Hans H. and Edward A. Yonan. "Is a Science of Religion Possible?" *Journal of Religion* 52, no. 2 (April 1972): 107-33.

Pettazzoni, Raffaele. "The Supreme Being: Phenomenological Structure and Historical Development." In *The History of Religion: Essays in Methodology,* edited by Mircea Eliade and Joseph M. Kitagawa, 59-66. Chicago: University of Chicago Press, 1959.

Progoff, Ira. "Culture and Being: Mircea Eliade's Studies in Religion." *International Journal of Parapsychology* 2 (1960): 47-60.

————. "The Man Who Transforms Consciousness." In *Eranos-Jahrbuch 1966,* Band 35 (1967): 99-144.

Rasmussen, David. "Mircea Eliade: Structural Hermeneutics and Philosophy." *Philosophy Today* 12 (1968): 138-46.

Rennie, Bryan S. "The Diplomatic Career of Mircea Eliade: A Response to Adriana Berger." *Religion* 22 (October 1992): 375-92.

Reno, Stephen J. "Eliade's Progressional View of Hierophanies." *Religious Studies* 8 (1972): 153-60.

Ricketts, Mac Linscott. "Eliade and Altizer: Very Different Outlooks." *Christian Advocate* (Oct. 1967): 11-12.

———. "In Defense of Eliade: Bridging the Gap between Anthropology and the History of Religions." *Religion* 1, no. 3 (1973): 13-34.

———. "Mircea Eliade and the Death of God." *Religion in Life* (Spring 1967): 40-52.

———. "The Nature and Extent of Eliade's 'Jungianism.'" *Union Seminary Quarterly Review* 25 (Winter 1970): 211-34.

Ryba, Thomas. "Are Religious Theories Susceptible to Reduction?" In *Religion and Reductionism: Essays on Eliade, Segal, and the Challenge of the Social Sciences for the Study of Religion,* edited by Thomas A. Idinopulos and Edward A. Yonan, 15-42. Leiden: E. J. Brill, 1994.

Saiving, Valerie. "Androcentism in Religious Studies." *Journal of Religion* 56 (1976): 177-97.

Sarkar, Sahotra. "Models of Reduction and Categories of Reductionism." *Synthese* 91, no. 3 (June 1992): 167-94.

Schimmel, Annamarie. "Summary of the Discussion." *Numen* 7, no. 2-3 (1960): 235-39.

"Scientist of Symbols." *Time* 87, no. 6 (February 11, 1966): 68, 70.

Segal, Robert A. "Are Historians of Religions Necessarily Believers?" *Religious Traditions* 10 (July 1983): 71-76. Reprinted in Segal, *Religion and the Social Sciences: Essays on the Confrontation.*

———. "Eliade's Theory of Millenarianism." *Religious Studies* 14 (1978): 159-73. Reprinted in Segal, *Religion and the Social Sciences: Essays on the Confrontation.*

———. "How Historical Is the History of Religions?" *Method and Theory in the Study of Religion* 1 (Spring 1989): 2-19. Reprinted in Segal, *Explaining and Interpreting Religion.*

———. "Reductionism in the Study of Religion." In *Religion and Reductionism: Essays on Eliade, Segal, and the Challenge of the Social*

Sciences for the Study of Religion, edited by Thomas A. Idinopulos and Edward A. Yonan, 4-14. Leiden: E. J. Brill, 1994. Revision of Segal, "In Defense of Reductionism." *Journal of the American Academy of Religion* 51 (March 1983): 97-124.

―――― and Donald Wiebe. "Axioms and Dogmas in the Study of Religion." *Journal of the American Academy of Religion* 57 (Fall 1989): 591-605. Reprinted in Segal, *Explaining and Interpreting Religion.*

Sharma, Arvind. "What Is Reductionism?" In *Religion and Reductionism: Essays on Eliade, Segal, and the Challenge of the Social Sciences for the Study of Religion,* edited by Thomas A. Idinopulos and Edward A. Yonan, 127-42. Leiden: E. J. Brill, 1994.

Shaw, Rosalind. "Feminist Anthropology and the Gendering of Religious Studies." In *Religion and Gender,* edited by Ursula King, 65-76. Oxford: Blackwell, 1995.

Smart, Ninian. "Beyond Eliade: The Future of Theory in Religion." *Numen* 25 (1978): 171-83.

Smith, John E. "The Structure of Religion." *Religious Studies* 1, no 1 (1965): 63-73.

Smith, Wilfred Cantwell. "Comparative Religion: Whither—and Why?" In *The History of Religions: Essays in Methodology,* edited by Mircea Eliade and Joseph M. Kitagawa, 31-58. Chicago: University of Chicago Press, 1959.

Strehlow, T. G. H. "Personal Monototemism in a Polytotemic Community." In *Festschrift für Ad. E. Jensen,* Vol. 2, edited by Eike Haberland, 723-54. Munich: K. Renner, 1964.

Strenski, Ivan. "Mircea Eliade: Some Theoretical Problems." In *The Theory of Myth: Six Studies,* edited by Adrian Cunningham, 40-78. London: Sheed and Ward, 1973.

―――― . "Reduction without Tears." In *Religion and Reductionism: Essays on Eliade, Segal, and the Challenge of the Social Sciences for the Study of Religion,* edited by Thomas A. Idinopulos and Edward A. Yonan, 95-107. Leiden: E. J. Brill, 1994.

Tillich, Paul. "The Meaning and Justification of Religious Symbols." In *Religious Experience and Truth,* edited by Sidney Hook. New York: New York University Press, 1961.

―――― . "The Religious Symbol." In *Religious Experience and Truth,* edited by Sidney Hook. New York: New York University Press, 1961.

————. "Theology and Symbolism." In *Religious Symbolism,* edited by F. Ernest Johnson. New York: Harper & Brothers, 1955.

Welbon, G. Richard. "Some Remarks on the Work of Mircea Eliade." *Acta Philosophica et Theologica* 2 (1964): 465-92.

Wiebe, Donald. "Beyond the Sceptic and the Devotee: Reductionism in the Scientific Study of Religion." In *Religion and Reductionism: Essays on Eliade, Segal, and the Challenge of the Social Sciences for the Study of Religion,* edited by Thomas A. Idinopulos and Edward A. Yonan, 108-16. Leiden: E. J. Brill, 1994.

————. "Postscript: On Method. Metaphysics and Reductionism." In *Religion and Reductionism: Essays on Eliade, Segal, and the Challenge of the Social Sciences for the Study of Religion,* edited by Thomas A. Idinopulos and Edward A. Yonan, 117-26. Leiden: E. J. Brill, 1994.

————. "Theory in the Study of Religion." *Religion* 13 (1983): 283-309.

Yonan, Edward A. "Clarifying the Strengths and Limits of Reductionism in the Discipline of Religion." In *Religion and Reductionism: Essays on Eliade, Segal, and the Challenge of the Social Sciences for the Study of Religion,* edited by Thomas A. Idinopulos and Edward A. Yonan, 43-48. Leiden: E. J. Brill, 1994.

Index